William Holman Hunt

PAINTER, PAINTING, PAINT

MANCHESTER
1824

Manchester University Press

William Holman Hunt

PAINTER, PAINTING, PAINT

Carol Jacobi

MANCHESTER UNIVERSITY PRESS
Manchester and New York
distributed exclusively in the USA by Palgrave

Published by Manchester University Press
Oxford Road, Manchester M13 9NR, UK
and Room 400, 175 Fifth Avenue, New York, NY 10010, USA
www.manchesteruniversitypress.co.uk

Distributed exclusively in the USA by
Palgrave, 175 Fifth Avenue, New York,
NY 10010, USA

Distributed exclusively in Canada by
UBC Press, University of British Columbia, 2029 West Mall,
Vancouver, BC, Canada V6T 1Z2

British Library Cataloguing-in-Publication Data
A catalogue record for this book is available from the British Library

Library of Congress Cataloging-in-Publication Data applied for

ISBN 0 7190 7288 3 *hardback*
EAN 978 0 7190 7288 8

First published 2006

15 14 13 12 11 10 09 08 10 9 8 7 6 5 4 3

Typeset in 10/12pt Minion
by Graphicraft Ltd., Hong Kong
Printed in Great Britain
by Alden Hendi, Oxfordshire

To Max, for reminding me who I am

Contents

Plates and figures

Dimensions are in centimetres, colour plates appear between pages 144 and 145

Plates

Figures

Acknowledgements

Thanks to all those who provided moral and practical support in the making of this book, Max Jacobi, Deann and Peter Richmond, Stephen Jacobi, Judith Walker, Rachel Barker, Helen Draper, Robin Stummer, Graham Lovatt and Martin Guy especially. Thanks to Paul Shakeshaft, to Will Vaughan and to Lynda Nead for her guidance, to Elizabeth Prettejohn, Alison Smith and George Landow for their encouragement and to the team at Manchester University Press. I am also very grateful for the generosity of the Paul Mellon Centre for British Art, the British Academy and the Westminster School Zilkha Fund. Acknowledgement finally to Robert Raphael, the sweetest impediment.

Note on the text

Hunt's letters to Tupper and his letters and journals in the Bodleian and John Rylands Libraries are quoted as they appear in manuscript form. I consider the numerous errors, deletions, underlinings and idiosyncrasies of spelling and punctuation to be of interest, and have not corrected them. Words or phrases that have been inserted between the lines are enclosed between two slashes.

References to William Holman Hunt's two-volume memoir, *Pre-Raphaelitism and the Pre-Raphaelite Brotherhood* (London: Macmillan and Co., 1905–6) are cited by volume and page number in brackets within the text.

Introduction

William Holman Hunt's rectangles of exotic moral theatre, with their coruscatingly vivid surfaces, are familiar fixtures in the galleries of English post-industrial cities and of the 'New World'; they are stalwarts of the gallery shop and sit uncomfortably among the more graceful images decorating books on the Pre-Raphaelite Brotherhood. It is this lack of comfort, and its reflection in critical writing which is, in my opinion, the most intriguing aspect of Hunt, a symptom of the test he poses the art historian and his or her methods.

In his 1970 history of Pre-Raphaelitism, Tim Hilton said of Hunt: 'We should not ignore, as one is apt to do when discussing meanings, influences, historical parallels, the devastatingly obvious fact about him. His paintings are not good-looking.'[1] This investigation has been prompted by a curiosity about the silence over this 'devastatingly obvious fact' and by the diffidence exhibited by art history towards Hunt in general. Despite the persistent profile of Pre-Raphaelite art, and Hunt's primary role in and beyond the movement, it is thirty years since any monograph appeared. The only overview of his work remains his own autobiography. This oddity is, I believe, itself significant, and a measure of the challenge that his paintings represent to our discipline.

As Hilton has noted, writers are often curiously reserved about the striking appearance of Hunt's pictures, tending to privilege literary aspects of his work. Analysis of symbolism and iconography is accompanied by a preoccupation with the artist's life. This approach is fuelled by Hunt's own writings, especially the memoir, *Pre-Raphaelitism and the Pre-Raphaelite Brotherhood* (1905–6). Of the six publications devoted exclusively to him since his death, three are biographies[2] and two of the most recent essays, by Julie Codell and Herbert Sussman, focus on the artist's persona.[3] Of serious critical works, George Landow's *William Holman Hunt and Typological Symbolism* (1979) concentrates on symbolic readings, and Jeremy Maas's *Holman Hunt and the Light of the World* (1984) combines art history with biography.[4] Even texts that are conceived as a commentary on an exhibition of the paintings themselves stress iconography and life story. Mary Bennett's invaluable catalogue for the 1969 Walker Art Gallery exhibition, *William Holman Hunt*,[5] discusses paintings, drawings and prints in the context of the history of their production, and Hunt's writings are used to elucidate their subject matter. Judith Bronkhurst's catalogue entries for the 1984, Tate Gallery exhibition, *The Pre-Raphaelites*[6] and her recently completed catalogue raisonné also concentrate on subject matter and iconography.[7]

The cluttered, narrative format of Hunt's work encourages this approach, inviting the observer to 'read' the painting and to see it as image rather than object. This is enhanced by his extremely illusionistic style, a process of painting which has been conscientiously chosen to deny itself. The effect is exacerbated by viewing the works as reproductions. We do not see the art object and only the image survives, diminished and altered according to the quality of photography and printing. The position of reproductions within literary text also tends to produce 'readings'. Aspects which relate to literary concerns, which can be thought of and expressed in a literary way, are emphasised. An extreme and early example of this can be found in *The Life and Work of William Holman Hunt* (1893) by Archdeacon Farrar and Alice Meynell, where black and white engravings of Hunt's works and a version of his life story are submitted to exegesis as though they were religious tracts or sermons.[8]

Farrar's treatment is characteristic of commentaries on Hunt in that it relies heavily on the artist's own writings. Hunt's copious literary output encourages and directs readings of the images and can appear to provide short cuts to interpretation. More interestingly, appraisals of the paintings are often accompanied, or even superseded, by appraisals of the painter, a tendency again encouraged by Hunt's writings about himself. Farrar valorises *The Scapegoat* (1854–55, Lady Lever Art Gallery, plate 1), for example, by stressing the 'perils of death by malaria, perils of wild beasts, perils of wandering robbers, perils of venomous insects, of murder and semi-starvation' claimed to have been undergone by the artist while painting it at the Dead Sea.[9] Press responses to exhibitions of the work in Tate Britain in 1984 and 2004 exhibit the same preoccupation. The catalogue entries refrain from repeating the legend of deprivations in the wilderness, but itemise Hunt's journeys in detail.[10]

Constructive and serious evaluations of Hunt's work exhibit a conspicuous restriction of focus to literary and biographical aspects. Farrar, Landow, Bronkhurst and Staley offer detailed accounts of the symbolism of *The Scapegoat*, but none of them address its extraordinary colour. These paintings are, however, objects, possessing aesthetic and physical characteristics proceeding from particular choices and negotiations with paint. They are weighty, rigid, yet fragile constructions. Moreover, Hunt's own writings display an interest in technique and materials unusual for the time, in particular his long 1880 lecture to the Society of Arts.[11] An exploration of his attitude to style and art-making can contribute to a new understanding of the image which embraces form as well as content.

Materialism and mysticism

If we start with the few observations which do address stylistic appearance, we find them to be, as I have said, negative, and to exhibit a striking continuity across the centuries. The accusation against the young Pre-Raphaelites of 'a strange disorder of the mind or the eyes', which produced 'ugliness and conceit',[12] haunts nineteenth-century commentaries on Hunt. John Ruskin says of *The Scapegoat*: 'This picture, regarded merely as a landscape, or as a composition, is a total failure.'[13] Reviewers find *The Shadow of Death* (1869–73, Manchester Art Gallery, plate 2) garish,[14] 'crude' and 'sharp and severe'.[15] The trend continues into the twenty-first century. In the 1940s, Robin Ironside finds this painting 'difficult to contemplate without real discomfiture', like having his eyes pinned open.[16] During the 1960s, Hunt's style is seen as comparable with 'crazy Surrealism'.[17] Hilton indicts *The Scapegoat* as a 'pink monument to folly'[18] and reproduces it (in colour), at the point in the text where he makes a general criticism about the 'distastefulness' of Hunt's paint.[19] Christopher Wood's 1980s text on the movement also finds Hunt's execution as 'harsh and unattractive',[20] Elizabeth Prettejohn's twenty-first century survey focuses to an unprecedented degree on technique, but still singles out Hunt's style as 'mesmeric', 'rigid' and 'machine-like', especially in the case of the later works.[21] Recent reviews share this language.[22]

This apprehension of aesthetic disturbance is almost always linked to a sense of dislocation between Hunt's verisimilitude and his subject matter. His contemporaries persistently constructed the relationship between style and the poetic or spiritual content as unsatisfactory. The *Illustrated London News* criticises the function of material facts in the depiction of the 'principle truth', or concept, of *The Shadow*: 'High art is . . . free as poetry . . . it is not merely a record of external appearances.'[23] The *Saturday Review* is more tolerant of what it sees as an 'attempt . . . to elevate materialism to mysticism',[24] but a 'layman' in the *Spectator* declares: 'Has not his realism betrayed him?'[25] The *Illustrated London News* also considers Hunt's 'transposition of the real and imaginary elements' in *The Triumph of the Innocents* (1876–87, Walker Art Gallery, plate 3) to be 'grotesque'.[26]

Hilton continues this pattern when he makes a stark comparison between *The Scapegoat*'s sacred meaning and the actual 'unfortunate beast', 'saline marsh' and 'turgid currents' depicted.[27] He asserts that, 'Hunt, intent on being the great moral painter, came to deny himself the ravishments of paint.'[28] Landow notes that the realism of the 'suffering goat' detracts from its sacrificial identity[29] and Wood sees

Hunt's exactitude as generally more suited to non-religious, descriptive painting.[30] Prettejohn concurs: 'the hard execution . . . asserts the material "reality" of the spiritual content too aggressively'.[31] In short, it can be said that when critics do not neglect the aesthetic aspects of Hunt's work, they find themselves confronted by an uncomfortable inconsistency between style and subject matter. It is the sense of disruption between form and content, realism and spirituality, that I wish to interrogate.

In 'Hunt, Ruskin, and "The Scapegoat"' (1968), Herbert Sussman notes this failure of nineteenth-century reviewers to reconcile Hunt's realism and his symbolism.[32] He draws attention to a general tendency to make 'droll' contrasts between the earnestly spiritual images and their prosaic actuality, citing the alternative identity of the robe of Christ in *The Light of the World* (1852–53, Keble College, plate 4), a damask tablecloth belonging to the artist's mother.[33] On the other hand, he seeks to reconcile Hunt's mimetic style with his spiritual subjects by outlining the artist's concept, shared with Ruskin, of a sacramental universe where natural objects possess symbolic value,[34] and by explaining Hunt's use of the 'naturalistic symbol' (exhaustively analysed by Landow in *Typological Symbolism*). Sussman asserts that a work such as *The Scapegoat* represents a literal visualisation of biblical text and blames critical hostility on a failure to accept Hunt's application of the principle of typology to unfamiliar motifs. Sussman maintains that Hunt's system achieves a reconciliation of 'two artistic categories – precision of natural detail, religious symbolism and Protestant faith', which held 'no contradiction' for the artist himself.[35] I concur with his assertion that 'naturalistic symbolism' is a central issue of Hunt's work, but do not accept that the idea produced no contradictions for the artist, or that critical dissatisfaction is entirely due to misreading. Sussman's explanation that the picture is 'too difficult to interpret'[36] does not necessarily account for the apparent aesthetic failure of *The Scapegoat*,[37] or other paintings. Nor does the rationale of the 'natural symbol' quite diffuse the absurdity of a Christ in a tablecloth.

Hunt's style of painting is clearly problematic, but just as clearly, it is of immense importance. His output was severely curtailed by fastidious execution and his labours were carefully publicised.[38] The legend of Hunt's 'studious search for truth' becomes a cliché well before his death.[39]

Farrar, like Sussman, also offers us a reconciliation between the verisimilitude of *The Scapegoat* and a profound meaning, but displaces it from the paint to the painter: 'Assuredly Mr Hunt would never have faced, as he did, many perils . . . to paint a miserable goat upon a desolate shore, if he had not desired to fill the minds of those who gazed upon this picture with some at least of the deep thoughts – thoughts the deepest which occupy the mind of man.'[40] *The Shadow* requires similar defence. The individual features of the painting are listed in great detail and he continues: 'The accessories, however, are only the merest framework of the central thought.'[41] The *Illustrated London News* is less sure:

> He spent three years over the present work in voluntary exile in Jerusalem, Bethlehem and Nazareth – and for what? Simply to ascertain as far as possible . . . the probable details of a carpenters shop about the date of our Saviour's life; the aspect of an effect of sunset within the same; the garments and trinkets worn by a Jewish woman of the same period; and (of necessity still more inferentially) the constituent objects of the Wise Men's offerings. For Mr Hunt the mission of the painter is to search the world through in the scientific spirit of the geologist or comparative anatomist in order to present a fact of momentous importance with the utmost attainable veracity.[42]

For this reviewer, the mere search for clues, 'fragments of the dry bones of the past', although 'conscientious', fails to present 'a nobly imaginative thought'. What both the positive and the negative reviews have in common, however, is that they note the unusual industry of the artist in pursuing accuracy and layer a verbal map of the items contained within the painting alongside an explanation of their significance. Two types of evaluation, description and interpretation, are juxtaposed without being integrated. Neither account directly relates representational fidelity to meaning.

Wood also stresses Hunt's 'herculean labours'[43] in the pursuit of accuracy and identifies the symbolic roles of the motifs in *The Hireling Shepherd* (1851–52, Manchester Art Gallery, plate 5) without relating them to its 'surrealistic clarity of detail'. His sense of dislocation between mimesis and message is expressed when he describes the work as 'another elaborate moral fable, *but also* a brilliant piece of painting' (emphasis added).[44] Similarly, Hilton remarks that 'the import' of *The Scapegoat*, 'a dead letter', is 'buried in simple wonder at the painting's capacity for mimesis'.[45] The point is that in all these cases, when a connection between style and content cannot be found in the art itself, it is elided by a shift of focus towards the artist. Farrar finds spirituality in Hunt's mimetic endeavours by presenting the 'strenuous' labour involved as a measure of the artist's bravery, piety and 'deep thoughts'. Recent writers have surveyed the ways in which the tales of Hunt's laborious exactitude contribute to a heroic, 'vigorous, manly and English'[46] persona, that aspires to a prophet-like status.[47] Sussman sees the thorough, controlled, encyclopaedic quality of Hunt's style as, itself, an expression of the artist's morality and masculinity.[48]

On other occasions, Hunt's style is related to the artist's character in less flattering terms of fanatical madness rather than heroic piety. Nineteenth-century, twentieth- and twenty-first-century reviews present his elaborations as a product of religious and artistic obsession. *The Finding of the Saviour in the Temple* (1854–60, Birmingham Museum and Art Gallery, plate 6) is greeted in 1860 as 'too wild, and weird, and painful, too Pre-Raphaelite'.[49] Hunt is an 'apostle of Pre-Raphaelitism'.[50] In 1873, he still exhibits an 'unfaltering faith in the creed of Pre-Raphaelitism',[51] and in 1891, a 'theorist's fanaticism'.[52] Diana Holman-Hunt records that her grandfather's friends nicknamed him 'the Mad'.[53] Hilton, too, portrays Hunt as a 'madman', 'whose beliefs have become obsessive'.[54] In a strange leap of fantasy, he goes so far as to imagine him eating the unfortunate model for *The Scapegoat* after it has died. Thirty-five years later, Waldermar Januszczak's *Sunday Times* review of the same work has Hunt torturing a whole series of them. For him Hunt is 'an unusually angry and unusually righteous fanatic', 'a buffoon, a creepy and at best half-sane odd-ball who boasted the full set of Victorian inadequacies: sexual, behavioural, religious, political and mental . . . disapproving of the world to the point of mania, and beyond'.[55] Such vivid personifications are shared by academic commentaries. They also describe Hunt's practice as fanatical, a result of religious obsession, eccentric and egocentric.[56] Marcia Pointon and Codell detect symptoms of a masochistic pathology.[57] Albert Boime's recent meticulous unravelling of *The Scapegoat*'s theology sees an 'attempt to exorcise his own tormenting demons', religious and sexual.[58] Artists and art are connected through a conspicuously repetitive use of a vocabulary of sickness and death as well as insanity. Prettejohn's apprehension of 'petrification'[59] recalls the *Illustrated London News*'s 'dry bones of the past'.[60] Wood finds Hunt's life *and* imagery 'morbid and gloomy'.[61] Januszczak experiences a 'purple and yellow migraine throb', and says, 'when he looked at something with those mad religious eyes of his, it certainly stayed looked at. His eyes were an instrument of torture.'[62]

Hunt's output is considered, at best, pious and earnest and, at worst, incomprehensible, ugly, moribund and even insane. This pattern of reception would seem, perhaps, to justify Hunt's neglect and hinder critical reassessment, but there is a venerable tradition of understanding negative responses as revelations of the radical, pointers to the particular power of a work. These reactions should not be dismissed as merely reflecting ignorance of subject matter, as claimed by Sussman. They respond to a quality within the paintings themselves. Inconvenient though it may be for the hagiographer, it is clearly a singular and powerful effect. To evade it is to limit Hunt's works to a minority taste. To embrace it is to discover a genuine discord, a tragic drama which does indeed proceed from links between the persona of the painter, issues of religion, insanity and death, and a laborious painting practice.

Evidence and belief

This book will investigate both iconography and style. The singularity of the former extends well beyond a Christ in a tablecloth. The year 1851 found Hunt on the one hand, borrowing legitimacy from Shakespeare and on the other, clearly preoccupied with rape, choosing scenes from *Two Gentleman of Verona, Valentine Rescuing Sylvia from Proteus* (1850–51, Birmingham Museum and Art Gallery, plate 7) and *Measure for Measure, Claudio and Isabella* (1850–53, Tate Britain). Two years later, the Academy exhibition of *The Awakening Conscience* (1853–54, Tate Britain, figure 5.2), his modern-life prostitute accessorised with shawl, cat and client, accompanied by *The Light of the World*, pre-dated by a decade the appearance of Manet's *Olympia* (1863, Musée d'Orsay) and *Christ Scourged* (1865, The Art Institute of Chicago) at the Salon of 1865. A thorough re-examination of these youthful works is for another day. Here I wish to focus on the key religious paintings, particularly *The Scapegoat, The Shadow of Death* and *The Triumph of the Innocents*. The two latter, executed in middle age, fall within what is often dismissed as 'an unproductive late career',[63] yet they present us with imagery of unprecedented strangeness. A Virgin recoils from the crucifixion as she always has, but a shadow crucifixion; and, vainly bedecked in cheap jewels, she presents only her shapely back. The Innocents too are removed from their conventional tableau and presented as a spectacle of ecstasy and inviolate flesh. These two works alone absorbed the artist for over eighteen years, dominating his letters and diaries. They richly reward investigation.

The system of religious belief presented in Hunt's iconography is odd and not easily read, even by his contemporaries. Landow cites a range of popular artistic, literary and exegetic sources for his work, but he joins Sussman in noting the dependence of Victorian readings on textual glosses on the frames, or on exhibition notes, and the confusion that arose when these were not available.[64] Although Sussman describes Hunt's creed as Protestant and Landow identifies a more complex combination of 'evangelical and Broad Church Protestantism',[65] I agree with Boime when he suggests that Hunt's iconography represents a very particular, personal mythology. This conclusion is born out by a close analysis of his writings. I shall propose that the fanaticism ascribed to Hunt's artistic endeavour relates to an intensely debated and *doubted* private version of Christianity, which attempts to resolve and control fearful dislocations between religious conviction and experience. In particular, a fantasised prophetic self-image attempts to answer fears about belief and mortality, but prompts anxieties about delusion and insanity, especially after a brush with death. We shall see that Hunt's own constructions of self exhibit an ambivalence which foreshadows and produces that put forward by his critics.

I shall suggest that the 'combining [of] scientific detachment and intense emotion'[66] in Hunt's work, represents the anxious desire for material 'proof' of the religious fantasies he depicts, within a broader context of personal insecurity and failures of faith, familiar in the modern text. The process of the painting's production is concealed in order to preserve its status as an unmediated representation of a 'found', naturally sacred reality. Hunt's published writings steadfastly elide differences between object and image. Art is the 'chosen task of the Gods – the directing of inert matter to a spiritual end'.[67] His alliance with science and profound antagonism towards the aesthetic movement (2, 364–5) reflects his investment in the pre-modern conviction that art might be a reflection of something outside itself, a contender with the actual on its own terms.

The literal mimesis which many critics find irreconcilable to the sacred is, for Hunt, essential evidence of it. Their sense of dislocation constitutes an awareness of the incomplete realisation of this aim. An insistence that all material phenomena 'naturally' manifest a personal spiritual code throws up particular anxieties about differences between subjective interpretation and objective evidence, between what is made and what is found. On the one hand, material phenomena tend to subvert the hopeful beliefs for which they are supposed to stand as evidence, just as their depiction does for observers such as Hilton. This is particularly the case when the images deal with death. On the other hand, the inherently constructed nature of the art object tends to subvert the claim that it represents something objective and universal. The image becomes a fabrication, an eccentric fantasy.

Hunt's private writings about painting and self echo the critics' vocabulary of madness and mortality. They are far from complacent or obtuse, expressing profound problems with both the conception and the practical representation of a sacred naturalism. I shall show that biographical texts exhibit a keen and timely awareness both of the tension between objective evidence and subjective belief and of the subjective input of the artist implied by processes of manufacture. They reluctantly exhibit a modern, relativist sensibility. Hunt's style and practice are orientated towards a strenuous, but imperfect, suppression of this in an effort to cling to artistic authority and non-relativist religious certainty. His extensive research into technique is a means of controlling and disguising the material nature of the object, but also represents a paradoxical awareness and advertisement of its constructed identity.

The Scapegoat, *The Shadow of Death* and *The Triumph of the Innocents*, produced under similar circumstances during the central thirty years of Hunt's career, dramatise an increasingly complex struggle with these issues. His two journals (written during 1854–55 and in 1872), deal with the execution of the first two, and Hunt's letters are particularly informative about all three. These texts provide important insights into the relationship between difficulties with belief and problems of practical representation. *The Shadow* and *The Triumph* are of particular interest because they coincide with a simultaneous acceleration of anxieties about faith and mortality and about painting materials and technique.

Art historical problems

One of the most interesting aspects of this project has been meeting the challenges to existing art history practice posed by Hunt and his legacy. In his own lifetime, his work sold for unprecedented amounts due to the enthusiasm of the mass audience exploited by Ernest Gambart's practice of exhibiting and touring single narrative paintings. Millions paid individually to view the work, lit in solitary splendour in a darkened room, encouraged by publicity provided by printed media and accompanied by merchandising in the form of engravings and explanatory pamphlets, a practice somewhere between the exhibition of a relic and a blockbuster film. This popular following persists, as Hunt's gallery success indicates. Hunt' s personal profile was high at the end of the nineteenth century, spawning pocket monographs featuring accounts of his adventurous career and a special edition of the *Art Journal* (a prototype *Hello*, including images of his home). This too has continued with Diana Holman-Hunt's lively *My Grandfather, His Wives and Loves* and Anne Clark Amor's *William Holman Hunt: The True Pre-Raphaelite*. The 1960s, which saw a resurgence of figurative art in the Pop movement, found some interest in the stories of prototype hippy lifestyles in the Pre-Raphaelite's memoirs and letters, and the paintings became popular for quite the opposite reason in the 1980s' fad for back-to-basics Victorian values of Thatcher's Britain.

One peculiarity of Hunt's career is the imbalance between a relatively small output of major paintings and the wealth of material orientated towards directing and augmenting viewings of them. The publicity and memoirs effectively slide a literary veil between the viewer and the work. The paradox of art history is that it too turns image into a text which becomes a veil through which the work is viewed. This process has represented, in Hunt's case, and in the case of many Victorian artists, a displacement of viewing by reading. It constitutes, in particular, a strategy of detachment, a distancing of the object which complements the distaste expressed by many critics. As the twentieth century rewrote the nineteenth, Hunt became an increasingly marginal figure. While his apparent stylistic conservatism excluded him from the narrative of modernism as conceived by Fry, Barr, Greenberg et al. (still dramatised in most canonical accounts and collections – Manet in the National Gallery, Hunt in Tate Britain), an image of ideological conservatism was reinforced by the narrative of the cultural historians, who saw his images as evidence of a range of Victorian ideological positions, sexual, economic, racial and imperial.

Opposing idealist and materialist critical tendencies unite in excluding consideration of Hunt's style and constructing a partial persona which lacks the qualities of painterly activity and general radicalism valued in our culture. Theory and pluralism do not have to be agents of detachment and fragmentation, however. A detailed examination and deconstruction of these myths paradoxically presents Hunt in both a more complex and more positive relation to his times. A reconnection of the literary aspects of the works with their physical properties will reveal a surprisingly radical artist, engaged in an intricate struggle with the central questions of nineteenth-century materialism and modernity. In order to bypass entrenched patterns of commentary, I have adopted a heterogeneous method, neither materialist nor idealist.

The fact that Hunt's work is frequently valorised or detracted through assessments of his personality points to a close relationship between image and self-image. The memoir is an important primary resource, but autobiographical material must be questioned, particularly in the case of publicity-smart Victorian art. Recent scholarship has unmasked this unreliability and in some cases analysed it.[68] Such analysis has focused on identifying cultural themes, such as, in the case of Hunt, Victorian tropes of masculinity or Englishness. Although these throw light on pictorial work too, we are still left with the basic problem of whether to treat an artist's direct statements about his/her pictures as 'true' or not. This has, up to know, been settled in an ad hoc way according to whether a statement fits prevailing fashion, argument and/or other evidence. The first four chapters of this book propose and experiment with another approach to artists' writings. The fictionality of autobiographical output is embraced, analysed and brought into a different and more constructive relation with the painted works, bringing them back into focus.

The autobiography attempts to promote a sense of realism and honesty which is at odds with its dogmatic presentation of a particular philosophy and self-image. It exhibits 'two voices', an ambiguous persona and a dislocated structure. This ambivalence revolves around a marked awareness of, and discomfort about, the process of literary fabrication, and a consequent insecurity about the integrity of its protagonist. These issues of authority and integrity are also manifested in the iconography of the paintings and in unpublished material written during their production.

Like many Victorian artists, Hunt's apparently anachronistic, religious subjects have inhibited serious consideration of his career, especially later works. Christian subject matter can, however, be returned to centre stage and re-examined in the light of the themes of materialism, and relativism and alienation which characterise nineteenth-century art and literature as a whole. Hunt's letters and journals reveal that a construction of prophetic empowerment and immortality, related to the public, heroic role recently examined by Sussman and Codell, alternates with a private self-image which exhibits the mortality and delusion of the madman, the savage or the child. This ambiguous self-image informs contradictions in the memoir and the iconography of the paintings, particularly their depiction of violent and 'primitive' subjects as sacred and hopeful. Existing research can be developed and put into the context of the artist's search for a secure self-definition, demonstrating a profound relationship between visual image and textual self-image.

Having proposed new readings and relations in written and visual texts, the book confronts the second and more urgent issue raised by Hunt's output and Victorian painting in general: how to replace the work of art itself at the centre of consideration and how to relate the formal and physical aspects of it to autobiography and iconography. In attempting to re-engage with the visual impact of the works, it has been important to become familiar with the art objects themselves and re-evaluate their physical and stylistic qualities. Long-standing orthodoxies about Pre-Raphaelite technique are questioned. The mimetic process is subjected to precise examination and interrogated through analysis of information about painting practice drawn from conservation records,[69] contemporary writings on technique and viewing. This reassessment suggests a new relation to the themes and debates of the period that have since been labelled as 'modernism', and is intended to complement and contribute to the debates about modernism which are beginning to be broached in other areas of nineteenth-century scholarship.[70]

The issue of so called 'realism' can be further clarified by analysing the process of meaning-making in the mimetic image, building on the semiotic work of Charles Pierce and others. Hunt's anxious awareness of the fabricated nature of the image accompanies efforts to disguise it through elaborating the conceptual and the mimetic aspects of the painting in two separate stages: design and mimesis. This split technique fragments the image in several ways and explains the sense of aesthetic morbidity and eccentricity attributed to his work. Each element of the painting has a double role, as both symbol and icon, which tends to produce dislocation rather than resolution.

My final chapter brings the material in the preceding chapters to bear on the Victorian medico-moral issues, and links these to modernist themes of corporeal mutilation and fragmentation explored by Linda Nochlin.[71] It demonstrates an attempt to reconcile the material aspects of the work of art, as well as its mimetic appearance, with symbolic content. The deterioration of works of art and the body of the artist are countered by an interest in conservation and themes of fitness in the published writings. The private writings, however, express an awareness of the imperfections of materials and the constructive process which is voiced through a vocabulary of incompleteness, madness, sickness and mutilation that again reprise the artist's private persona and the underlying contradictions within his iconography.

These analyses of specific procedures of manufacture demonstrate the practical ways in which nineteenth-century paradoxes of belief and self-image could be constituted within textual constructions of the artist, and within the art object through the materials, painting and design, proposing the possibility of a seamless set of exchanges between painter, painting and paint itself. They aim to underline the general thrust of the book as a whole away from exclusive theoretical positions and towards an art history of juxtaposition. A combined methodology – an analysis of constructions of the artist, art-making and the art object – is intended to reveal the possibility of intimate and reciprocal connections between iconography and the stylistic and physical characteristics of a painting. All of these relate back to the persona of the painter via the painting process.

Tim Barringer calls for a reconsideration of Victorian art: 'the boundaries between Modernist art and its supposed others are permeable . . . [R]etrospectively constructed distinctions as "academic v. avant-garde" inevitably over-simplify a complex web of relationships'.[72] Hunt's work during the latter part of the nineteenth century cannot be dismissed as a mere dogged reworking of outdated Pre-Raphaelite ideals. Rather, it represents a confrontation between pre-modern and modern sensibilities and exhibits the doubt and fragmentation associated with this transition.

Notes

1 Hilton, T., *The Pre-Raphaelites* (London: Thames and Hudson, 1970), p 93

2 Gissing, A.C., *William Holman Hunt: A Biography* (London: Duckworth, 1936); Holman-Hunt, D., *My Grandfather, His Wives and Loves* (1969) (London: Columbus, 1987); Clark Amor, A., *William Holman Hunt: The True Pre-Raphaelite* (London: Constable, 1989)

3 Sussman, H.L., 'Artistic Manhood: The Pre-Raphaelite Brotherhood', *Victorian Masculinities* (Cambridge, Cambridge University Press, 1995), pp 111–79; Codell, J.F., 'The Artist Colonised: Holman Hunt's "Bio-history", Masculinity, Nationalism and the English School', in *Re-framing the Pre-Raphaelites: Historical and Theoretical Essays*, ed. E. Harding

(Aldershot: Scolar Press, 1996), pp 211–29; also, Marcus, L., 'Brothers in Their Anecdotage: Holman Hunt's "Pre-Raphaelitism and the Pre-Raphaelite Brotherhood"', in *The Pre-Raphaelites Re-viewed*, ed. M. Pointon (Manchester: Manchester University Press, 1989), pp 11–21 and Pointon, M., 'The Artist as Ethnographer: Holman Hunt in the Holy Land', ibid., pp 22–44

4 Landow, G.P., *William Holman Hunt and Typological Symbolism* (London: Yale University Press, 1979); Maas, J., *Holman Hunt and the Light of the World* (1984) (Cambridge: Wildwood House, 1987)

5 Bennett, M., *William Holman Hunt, An Exhibition Arranged by the Walker Art Gallery* (Liverpool: Walker Art Gallery, 1969)

6 Parris, L., ed., *The Pre-Raphaelites* (London: Allen Lane/Tate Gallery, 1984) (hereafter cited as *The Pre-Raphaelites* (Tate Gallery, 1984))

7 Bronkhurst, J.E., *William Holman Hunt: A Catalogue Raisonnée* (London: Yale University Press, forthcoming)

8 Farrar, Archdeacon F.W., and Mrs A. Meynell, *The Life and Work of William Holman Hunt* (London: Art Journal Special Edition, November 1893). Some commentators openly prefer Hunt's work in black and white, *Illustrated London News* (6 December 1891), p 275

9 Farrar and Meynell, *Hunt*, p 12

10 Staley, A., et al., *Pre-Raphaelite Vision: Truth to Nature* (London: Tate Publishing, 2004), p 114; see also *The Pre-Raphaelites* (Tate Gallery, 1984), pp 153–4

11 'The Present System of Obtaining Materials in use by Artist Painters as Compared with that of the Old Masters', *Journal of the Society of Arts*, 28 (23 April 1880), pp 485–99 (hereafter cited as 'Materials')

12 'Exhibition at the Royal Academy', *The Times* (7 May 1851), p 8

13 Ruskin, J., 'Academy Notes' (1856), in *The Works of John Ruskin*, eds E.T. Cook and A. Wedderburn (39 vols, London: George Allen, 1903–1912), 14, p 66 (hereafter cited as *Works*)

14 'The Shadow of Death', *Illustrated London News* (6 December 1873), p 543

15 'Mr Holman Hunt's "Shadow of Death"', *Saturday Review*, 26 (6 December 1873), p 728

16 Ironside, R., and J.A. Gere, *Pre-Raphaelites Painters* (London: Phaidon, 1948), p 18

17 Holman-Hunt, *My Grandfather*, p 14; also, Wood, C., *The Pre-Raphaelites* (1981) (London: Weidenfeld and Nicolson, 1994), p 81

18 Hilton, *Pre-Raphaelites*, p 110

19 Ibid., pp 92–3

20 Wood, *Pre-Raphaelites*, p 106

21 Prettejohn, E., *The Art of the Pre-Raphaelites*, London: Princeton University Press, 2000, pp 111–13

22 Januszczak, W., 'Unhinged by Hunt's Scapegoat', *Sunday Times* (12 March 2004), p 6

23 *Illustrated London News* (6 December 1873), p 543

24 *Saturday Review* (6 December 1873), p 728

25 'A Layman on Mr Holman Hunt's New Picture', *Spectator*, 46 (29 November 1873), p 1497

26 'Three Religious Pictures', *Illustrated London News* (14 March 1885), p 288
27 Hilton, *Pre-Raphaelites*, p 110
28 Ibid., p 93
29 Landow, *Typological Symbolism*, p 107
30 Wood, *Pre-Raphaelites*, p 46
31 Prettejohn, *Pre-Raphaelites*, p 113
32 Sussman, H.L., 'Hunt, Ruskin, and "The Scapegoat"', *Victorian Studies*, 12 (September 1968), p 88
33 Ibid., p 83
34 Ibid., pp 85–9
35 Ibid., p 84
36 Ibid., p 88
37 Hilton, *Pre-Raphaelites*, p 108; Ruskin, 'Academy Notes', in *Works*, 14, p 66; Hunt quotes four negative reviews, including that of Ruskin, in *Pre-Raphaelitism*, 2, 110–13
38 Pointon notes that 'the myths of production . . . were well known and . . . well rehearsed in the press at exhibition time', 'Artist as Ethnographer', p 34. Hunt also published 'Painting "The Scapegoat"', *Contemporary Review*, 52 (July 1887), pp 21–38 (August 1887), pp 206–20, and 'The Pre-Raphaelite Brotherhood: A Fight for Art', *Contemporary Review*, 49 (April 1886), pp 471–88 (May 1886), pp 737–50 (June 1886), pp 820–33; as well as overseeing F.G. Stephens's, *William Holman Hunt and His Works: A Memoir of the Artist's Life, with descriptions of his pictures* (London: Nisbet, 1860), and exhibition pamphlets
39 For example, *Illustrated London News* (14 March 1885), p 288; Farrar and Meynell, *Hunt*, p 1
40 Farrar and Meynell, *Hunt*, pp 1, 12
41 Ibid., p 18
42 *Illustrated London News* (6 December 1873), p 543
43 Wood, *Pre-Raphaelites*, p 46
44 Ibid., p 41
45 Hilton, *Pre-Raphaelites*, pp 110–11
46 Codell, 'Artist Colonised', p 211; Pointon, 'Artist as Ethnographer' pp 34–7; Sussman, 'Artistic Manhood', p 117
47 Sussman, 'Artistic Manhood', p 164; Codell, 'Artist Colonised', p 219
48 Sussman, 'Artistic Manhood', p 117, also Codell, 'Artist Colonised', p 221
49 'The Finding of the Saviour in the Temple', *Art Journal*, 22 (1860), p 182
50 'Holman Hunt's Picture of "The Finding of the Saviour in the Temple"', *Illustrated London News*, 38 (28 April 1860), p 411
51 *Saturday Review* (6 December 1873), p 727
52 'Mr Holman Hunt's New Picture' [*May Morning at Magdalen Tower*, 1888–90, Lady Lever Art Gallery, Port Sunlight], *Spectator*, 66 (23 May 1891), p 724
53 Holman-Hunt, *My Grandfather*, p 44
54 Hilton, *Pre-Raphaelites*, p 108
55 Januszczak, 'Unhinged by Hunt's Scapegoat', pp 6–7
56 Prettejohn, *Pre-Raphaelites*, pp 112–13; Hughes, R., *Nothing If Not Critical* (London: Collins Harvill, 1990), p 116; Wood, *Pre-Raphaelites*, pp 105–6

57 Codell, 'Artist Colonised', pp 216–20; Pointon, Artist as Ethnographer', p 42
58 Boime, A., 'William Holman Hunt's *The Scapegoat*: Rite of Forgiveness/Transference of Blame', *Art Bulletin*, 84, 1 (March 2002), p 105
59 Prettejohn, *Pre-Raphaelites*, p 113
60 *Illustrated London News* (6 December 1873), p 543
61 Wood, *Pre-Raphaelites*, p 41
62 Januszczak, 'Unhinged by Hunt's Scapegoat', p 6
63 Bowness, A., 'Introduction', in *The Pre-Raphaelites* (Tate Gallery, 1984), p 21; also Wood, *Pre-Raphaelites*, p 106, Prettejohn, *Pre-Raphaelites*, p 112; Hilton barely mentions Hunt's career after 1860, *Pre-Raphaelites*
64 Landow, *Typological Symbolism*, p 163; Sussman, 'Scapegoat', p 88
65 Landow, *Typological Symbolism*, pp 17, 168–9
66 Ibid., p 17
67 'Materials', p 499
68 See note 3
69 Townsend, J., J. Ridge and S. Hackney, *Pre-Raphaelite Painting Techniques*, London: Tate Gallery, 2004.
70 Barlow, P., 'Pre-Raphaelitism and Post-Raphaelitism: The Articulation of Fantasy and the Problem of Pictorial Space', in *Pre-Raphaelites Re-viewed*, pp 66–82; Smith, L., '"The Seed and the Flower": Photography and Pre-Raphaelitism', *Victorian Photography, Painting and Poetry: The Enigma of Visibility in Ruskin, Morris and the Pre-Raphaelites* (Cambridge: Cambridge University Press, 1995), pp 93–112. Prettejohn draws attention to the potential of refocusing on Pre-Raphaelite technique in the light of broader continental developments in *Pre-Raphaelites*, chapter 4
71 Nochlin, L., *The Body in Pieces: The Fragment as a Metaphor of Modernity* (London: Thames and Hudson, 1994)
72 Barringer, T., 'Rethinking Delaroche/Recovering Leighton', *Victorian Studies*, 44, 1 (2001), p 17. A repositioning of some aspects of Victorian art in relation to established narratives of Modernism and a questioning of those narratives themselves is broached in Tillyard, S., *The Impact of Modernism: The Visual Arts in Edwardian England* (London: Routledge, 1988); Corbett, D. Peters and L. Perry, *English Art 1860–1914* (Manchester: Manchester University Press, 2000); Prettejohn, *Pre-Raphaelites*; Barringer, T. and E. Prettejohn, *Frederic Leighton: Antiquity, Renaissance, Modernity* (London: Yale University Press, 1999)

1 Autobiography: experience and interpretation

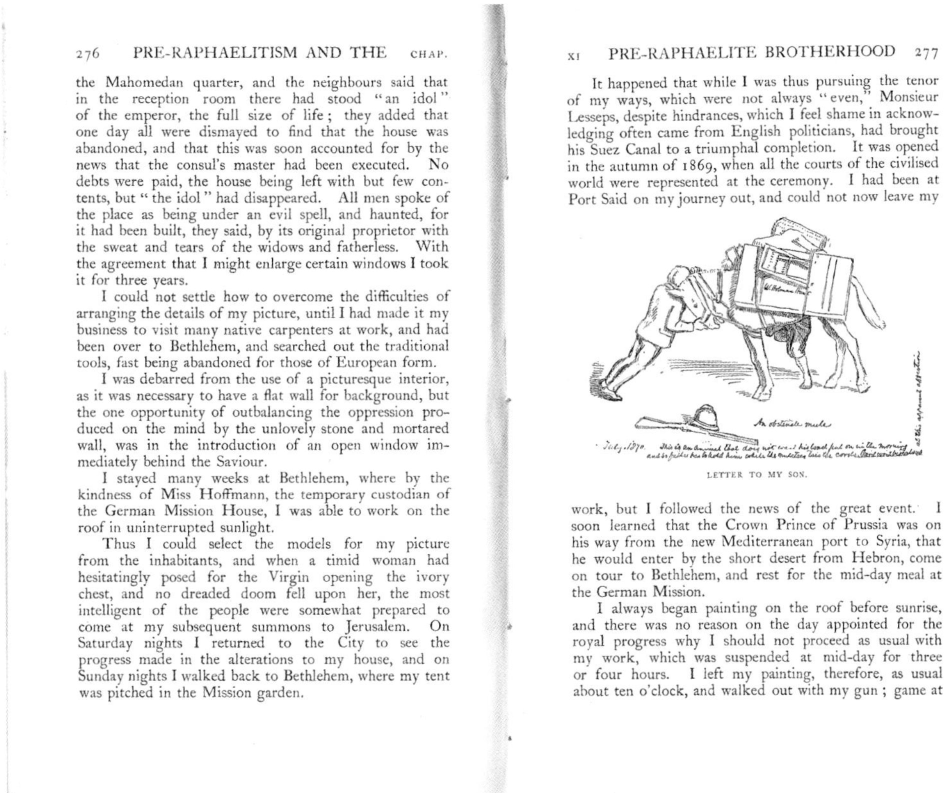

276 PRE-RAPHAELITISM AND THE CHAP.

the Mahomedan quarter, and the neighbours said that in the reception room there had stood "an idol" of the emperor, the full size of life; they added that one day all were dismayed to find that the house was abandoned, and that this was soon accounted for by the news that the consul's master had been executed. No debts were paid, the house being left with but few contents, but "the idol" had disappeared. All men spoke of the place as being under an evil spell, and haunted, for it had been built, they said, by its original proprietor with the sweat and tears of the widows and fatherless. With the agreement that I might enlarge certain windows I took it for three years.

I could not settle how to overcome the difficulties of arranging the details of my picture, until I had made it my business to visit many native carpenters at work, and had been over to Bethlehem, and searched out the traditional tools, fast being abandoned for those of European form.

I was debarred from the use of a picturesque interior, as it was necessary to have a flat wall for background, but the one opportunity of outbalancing the oppression produced on the mind by the unlovely stone and mortared wall, was in the introduction of an open window immediately behind the Saviour.

I stayed many weeks at Bethlehem, where by the kindness of Miss Hoffmann, the temporary custodian of the German Mission House, I was able to work on the roof in uninterrupted sunlight.

Thus I could select the models for my picture from the inhabitants, and when a timid woman had hesitatingly posed for the Virgin opening the ivory chest, and no dreaded doom fell upon her, the most intelligent of the people were somewhat prepared to come at my subsequent summons to Jerusalem. On Saturday nights I returned to the City to see the progress made in the alterations to my house, and on Sunday nights I walked back to Bethlehem, where my tent was pitched in the Mission garden.

XI PRE-RAPHAELITE BROTHERHOOD 277

It happened that while I was thus pursuing the tenor of my ways, which were not always "even," Monsieur Lesseps, despite hindrances, which I feel shame in acknowledging often came from English politicians, had brought his Suez Canal to a triumphal completion. It was opened in the autumn of 1869, when all the courts of the civilised world were represented at the ceremony. I had been at Port Said on my journey out, and could not now leave my

LETTER TO MY SON.

work, but I followed the news of the great event. I soon learned that the Crown Prince of Prussia was on his way from the new Mediterranean port to Syria, that he would enter by the short desert from Hebron, come on tour to Bethlehem, and rest for the mid-day meal at the German Mission.

I always began painting on the roof before sunrise, and there was no reason on the day appointed for the royal progress why I should not proceed as usual with my work, which was suspended at mid-day for three or four hours. I left my painting, therefore, as usual about ten o'clock, and walked out with my gun; game at

1.1
William Holman Hunt, *Letter to my Son*: 'This is an animal that does not want his load put on in the morning and so father has to hold him while the muleteer ties the cords. Cyril won't be jealous at this apparent affection', *Pre-Raphaelitism*, 2, 277

1

A biographical problem

Hunt's paintings are associated with a profusion of literary texts: subjects drawn from literary sources, titles, frames incorporating symbols and words, his catalogue notes, letters to newspapers, key plates and pamphlets for exhibitions, published accounts of the making of the paintings (scientific, philosophical and biographical) and private letters and diaries. Writings about Hunt's work draw heavily on these.

The two-volume *Pre-Raphaelitism and the Pre-Raphaelite Brotherhood* is the most substantial and dominant voice in this chorus of commentaries. It presents an ambitious, meticulous, rambling account of over seventy years of the artist's life and times – part anecdotal memoir, part Carlylean history – varying in tone from wry spectator to swashbuckler to sage. Clearly it is an especially important source, and it is often treated as a definitive record of Hunt, if not of the Brotherhood. As Laura Marcus says: 'written accounts tend to be employed less analytically and more evidentially in art historical practice than in contemporary literary theory'.[1]

Farrar and Meynell's *The Life and Work of William Holman Hunt*, George Williamson's *Holman Hunt* (1902), and Mary Coleridge's *Holman Hunt* (1910) are early examples of this.[2] They imitate the heroic tone of *Pre-Raphaelitism* and quote both anecdotes and interpretations of the paintings almost verbatim. Biographies, such as Gissing's *William Holman Hunt: A Biography* (1936) and Anne Clark Amor's *William Holman Hunt: The True Pre-Raphaelite* (1989), share this dependence. Gissing presents Hunt as a 'misunderstood' genius and, like Farrar, stresses perils, 'struggles' and 'public neglect and discouragement'.[3] Fifty years later, Clark Amor employs equally familiar terms, with Hunt

> reconciling himself . . . to a solitary professional existence, in which each new painting that he began was an individual struggle for perfection.
>
> No expense of time or effort, no physical danger was too great for Hunt in his pursuit of realism.[4]

These texts re-present the protagonist of the memoir: a singular model of broadly Christian Socialist values of piety, honesty, courage, hard work and social and national responsibility.

In her introduction to Clark Amor's biography, Diana Holman-Hunt provides an alternative view. She reminds the reader that Hunt's image is fabricated and flexible. She contrasts his youthful notoriety with his later elevation to national hero: 'Hunt became Holy Hunt, a favourite of the Queen, the grand old man, the only true Pre-Raphaelite.' She mourns his fall from favour between World War One and the 1950s, but also interrogates Clark Amor's positive view: 'Hunt has become Clark Amor's hero.'[5] Her own book, *My Grandfather, His Wives and Loves* (1969), employs private correspondence to puncture the piety of *Pre-Raphaelitism*.

Marcus's solution to the recurrence of such autobiographical tales in histories of this kind is to remove autobiographical writing from that discipline and treat it instead as an autonomous literary genre: 'to engage with the biographical directly, and to critically interrogate biography, autobiography and the "'lives and letters'" form';[6] 'If we examine the nature of the relationship between history, biography and art more closely, we may loosen the bond between the history of art and the lives of artists.'[7] More recent essays, such as Pointon's 'The Artist as Ethnographer: Holman Hunt and the Holy Land' (1989), Sussman's 'Artistic Manhood' (1995), and Codell's 'The Artist Colonised' (1996) have done this, offering critical interrogations of the image of the artist in the memoir and setting it within the context of Victorian themes of masculinity and nationalism. The bond between history and biography is, however, loosened only temporarily. Sussman, for example, points out that the tale of Hunt's youthful determination in the face of opposition and his 'diligent labour' resembles a perfect 'illustration' of the Smilesean ideal, but accepts is as an historical account.[8] Other accounts of the artist and the movement continue to find the memoir useful evidence, and commentaries on the paintings make substantial use of Hunt's own descriptions of their adventurous production.

In one way or another, all these writings perpetuate a long-standing preoccupation with Hunt's persona which originates in his own self-histories. It is helpful to 'loosen the bond between the history of art and the lives of artists', as Marcus says, but the insistent recurrence of this bond suggests that there is a stubborn connection between them. If this is the case, then it is important to clarify the exact nature of this connection. Is Hunt's memoir a venerable guide to art historical appraisal, or is it merely an encumbrance, pompously interrupting and misrepresenting, like Juliet's nurse, our truer relationship with the art itself?

Its role as guide is overvalued. The memoir cannot be considered as factual history and is misleading in its readings of art. It will be seen, for example, that Hunt's two most ubiquitous boasts – his fidelity to Christian belief and to natural appearance – are deeply problematic, if not contradictory. But the untrustworthy nature of the autobiography does not exclude the possibility of a relation between it and the art. An acknowledgement of its fictionality can not only allow us to bypass the dangers of considering it as art historical evidence, but also facilitate a different and more constructive relation with the painted works. If the 'life' is viewed as itself yet another 'work', as story rather than history, then autobiographical texts might be viewed alongside pictorial texts as pictorial texts are viewed alongside each other, their shared status as constructed artefact allowing us to identify shared thematic and structural patterns.

This chapter, therefore, treats the autobiography as a literary object, not to loosen the traditional bond between the history of art and the life of the artist, but to change it. It clarifies the profound untrustworthiness of the account, and discourages over-reliance on its statements, whilst also unearthing thematic and structural characteristics which can throw light on the paintings in another way. Both the content and the style of *Pre-Raphaelitism* can inform the painted works. In particular, it is shown that the memoir exhibits an acute regard for realism and a defensive awareness of the tension between objective and subjective modes of expression.

This approach delivers us from the problem of dealing with the irrecoverable origin of Hunt's works. We deal not with Hunt himself, but with an exchange between constructions of authorial and artistic *personae* in the autobiographical and the painted productions. As George Landow says in *Approaches to Victorian Autobiography*, the identification of a 'persistent level of textual organisation' can offer 'a methodology which promises to bridge various disciplines': 'Broad approaches to the subject of autobiography, which see it present in all forms of discourse, . . . make us aware of what autobiography, strictly conceived, shares with all other forms of literature and similar semiotic systems, such as painting, which may also be used for self-representation'.[9] The persona of the artist must relate to definitions of art-making and so affect the appearance of the work of art. This chapter considers this persona.

The life as history

Landow describes autobiography as embodying a confrontation between interior and exterior perspectives: 'the question of how the individual relates to what is outside himself', and identifies the Victorian age as a time when this concern was particularly problematic: 'The major writers of the Victorian age attempted to maintain their hold upon a series of polarised oppositions, refusing to choose between (and thus relinquish) either private or public, subjective or objective, feeling or fact.'[10] This tension is part of a general cultural response to nineteenth-century 'materialism'. In *Typological Symbolism*, he attributes a similar 'double awareness' or 'materialism and mysticism' to Hunt.[11] It is an apt description of the dual viewpoint which will be explored here, and the difficulties which arise when synthesis is challenged.

Pre-Raphaelitism clearly exhibits the polarity between public and private. Its title suggests that it aims to transcend autobiography, to be a historical account of an art movement. Hunt's letters indicate romantic associations with at least three women in his lifetime, two of which were marriages (to Fanny Waugh and to her younger sister

Edith), but the memoir barely alludes to them beyond the bare fact of a marriage or a death. It reports Dickens burning private papers, denying posterity 'sore revelations made by the writer only for the passing hour' (2, 252), and assumes a similar reserve: 'Respecting thus the sacredness of private life in others, I claim it for myself, however much at some points this book may seem of the nature of an autobiography' (2, 256). All personal writings still in Hunt's possession in later life were evidently censored, although it is unclear whether he or his second wife wielded the Indian ink so thoroughly. Despite this, however, the two volumes are dominated by descriptions of incidents claiming to be drawn from the author's own life. A night in a Parisian hotel (on, appropriately, Rue Jean Jacques Rousseau) produces thoughts of the city's violent past: 'I was awakened by a repetition of a not infrequent nightmare, with screams added, " 'It's death, it's death, it's death!' " and I resolved not to stay in Paris beyond a day' (1, 366). Campfires in Syria, holidays with Tennyson, insults from Rossetti are vividly recounted in the first person.

This awkwardly simultaneous role as art history and self-history is manifested by the fragmented structure of the books, set out in the strangely disconnected sub-headings on the contents pages (figure 1.2). A chronologically arranged series of autobiographical anecdotes are regularly and abruptly interrupted by extended reflections on more general issues. The narrative as a whole is bracketed by a dogmatic 'Preface' and three final chapters, all entitled 'Retrospect', which also contextualise the intervening autobiographical material with general philosophy. This odd combination expresses a fundamental problem. The authenticity of the text depends on the autobiographical, eyewitness status of its contents, but the I/eye must be expanded to a more general and authoritative viewpoint in order to endow the book with broader significance, to make it more than the personal account of an individual life.

This ambivalence is characteristic of other autobiographies of the time. The writer Edmund Gosse's memoir, *Father and Son* (1907) exhibits a similarly 'schizoid split between public and private, between the large, formal gesture and the intimate, personal actuality',[12] a tension between what Peter Abbs calls the 'scientific' and the 'rhetorical'. He, too, sees this tension as symptomatic of a transition between the Victorian and the modern sensibility: discrete intrusions of experience, valorised by an ideology of scientific objectivity, undermine prescribed schemes of belief, in particular, religious and social systems. Landow identifies two voices in the writings of John Ruskin: 'the Master of Interpretation' and 'the Master of Experience'.[13] We will find that Hunt's memoir stresses experience and disclaims any accusation of being rhetorical, but that rhetorical techniques are mobilised at instances where facts threaten the ideas and self-image

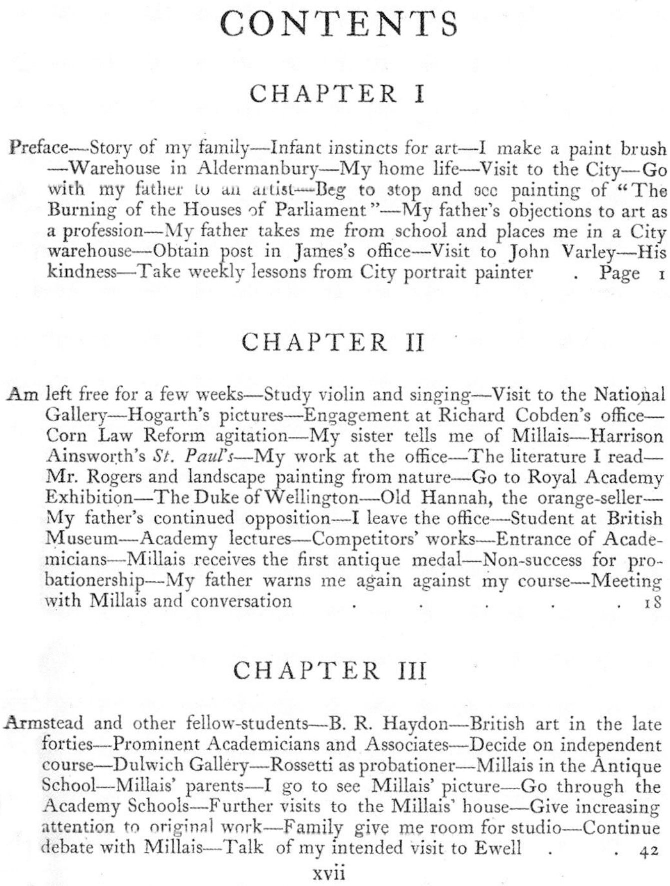

CONTENTS

CHAPTER I

CHAPTER II

CHAPTER III

xvii

1.2
William Holman Hunt, 'Contents', *Pre-Raphaelitism*, 1, xvii

that it is proposing. The hero's position in relation to an overall moral and religious scheme is dependent on a particular interpretation of the events portrayed, but the presentation of these events must also appear objective.

Hunt's writings attempt to build objective experience into a coherent and unified philosophy and self-image. Threats to this process arise in two main areas: the limitations of the artist/writer's skills of literary representation, such as a failure of memory or embroidered or distorted description, and the non-alignment of other texts which also proclaim to be true, but offer a different version of experience or belief. To some extent, any audience represents this second type of threat of an alternative reading of the facts offered. Anxiety about the relativity of the author's point of view is compounded by the nineteenth-century proliferation of printed material which provided a range of multivalent viewpoints and information, and promoted a need for consensus, and concern about its lack.[14] On the other hand, a strict dependence on verifiable facts can imply a possible loss of autonomy to them. Hunt's memoir, his history of himself, manifests difficulty with both of these issues.

In his exploration of Trollope's *An Autobiography* (1875), 'Credence and Credibility: The Concern for Honesty in Victorian Autobiography', Howard Helsinger defines two modes of defence against the suspicion of dishonesty implicit in the autobiographical medium: a historical mode, relating plain facts chronologically in the past tense, and a claim to a simple style, countering suspicion of manipulative rhetoric or similarity with fictional literature.[15] The first pages of *Pre-Raphaelitism* defend the memoir's narratorial directness in similar terms: 'I have undertaken the duties of a historian and feel myself responsible for the validity of the statements offered' (1, 1). Both authors describe themselves as ordinary labourers writing an account of the actualities of their occupations, 'the actual life of men pursuing the profession of art in England' (1, 2). Hard work is linked to realism in the sense that it implies a practical, down-to-earth 'personal experience' of the real world, in 'everyday dress', rather than 'Court attire' (1, 3).

However, both texts also seek to set their personal tale within a broader perspective, to establish for their respective personae a paradoxically *extra*ordinary, heroic status and, with it, an authoritative, transcendent voice. A contradiction arises: 'an ambivalent desire to be both common and unique, of the masses and above them'.[16] The account of Trollope's labour is, therefore, elevated to exceptional performance in terms of endeavour and the overcoming of adversity. In Hunt's case, the 'incessant difficulties barring the artist's path in modern days' (2, 489) comprise the legendary neglect of support from family, critics and art institutions and the deprivations of his travels abroad, so often accepted without question by subsequent writers.

The beginning and the end of the memoir stress the importance of these labours to the nation at large (1, xiv; 2, 493). At this time individual self-history came to play a general social role, as Phyllis Grosskurth has noted:

> In a period where the foundations of orthodox Christianity were revealing alarming cracks, religious leaders constantly urged their flocks to study the lives and works of good men as illustrations of the active virtues . . . [T]he majority, in an era in which the Carlylean Hero tended to absorb the qualities of godhead, erected the lives of great men into quasi-hagiography.[17]

The memoir's self-conscious exclusion of private affairs echoes a more general tendency for such texts to concentrate on public works and suppress personal details. It also sets its protagonist within a wider historical context by praising past heroes (including Christ) according to standards of practice and lifestyle which mirror descriptions of his own.[18] The preface asks: 'Who is truly an artist?' The reply, 'It is I' is unspoken but, nonetheless, implicit in the references to the old masters which follow. Their art gives 'a tangible and worthy image of the national body and mind', is 'a triumph of patient endeavour . . . [and they] endowed the colourless world with prismatic radiance' (1, xiii).

The memoir establishes the place of the artist within a particular construction of history and art history. That history is selected to provide a comfortable fit for Hunt's self-image, yet is able to be presented as fact: 'Had China accepted the teachings of Greek art the nation would have been incapable of laming its women' (1, xiv). 'Constable . . . tried to paint landscape green' (1, 25). The artist's own life also provides, in return, a fit to well-known prototypes. His 'infant instincts for art' (1, xvii, 5–17) imitates the convention of Vasari's *The Lives of the Artists*, the tales of wandering the countryside guilessly drawing from nature as she actually appeared (1, 24) paralleling, in particular, the young Giotto.[19] The determination to pursue painting against the will of the father recalls Michelangelo,[20] but the premature commitment to wage labour in the grim but vivid City evokes Dickens and his notorious consignment to Warren's blacking factory. The auspicious astronomical reading of his birth date by John Varley (1, 16) also recalls Michelangelo and the prolific production of drawings and designs emulates the early Leonardo.[21] By allowing the reader to manufacture connections between Hunt-the-protagonist and other great men, Hunt-the-narrator attempts to obscure his hand in the process of historical meaning-making.

Rhetoric and realism

The first chapter of *Pre-Raphaelitism* disowns an organising, authorial viewpoint, or 'theory' and underlines the factual nature of its sources:

> My evidence is not derived from outside suggestions bent to suit a pretty theory, but drawn from the records of my own memory, confirmed by the testimony left to us in the works of the active members of our circle, by documents of the time referred to, and by spontaneous admissions in the works published by the originators of the romances which I have to overturn. (1, 1)

In order to validate reminiscence as evidence, the narrator's 'memory' is presented as unusually vivid and accurate. Hunt's lecture to the Society of Arts in 1880 also begins with a claim about the speaker's accuracy of mind and experience: 'I need scarcely apologise for having to trust only to my memory of past reading for the data . . . of my lecture.'[22] Hunt presents his memory as a dependable source even when speaking of facts to a scientific audience. This boast passes into legend and both Diana Holman-Hunt and Jeremy Maas pay tribute to Hunt's powers of recall.[23] The autobiography and the address do indeed contain a wealth of vivid incident and observation; but there is so much of it that it is, in fact, impossible to accept that they are purely based on recollection. In actuality, Hunt kept diaries which recorded names, dates and events in preparation for the memoir and reread several books on technique before his presentation to the Society of Arts.[24] The claims for his powers of retention are at least partly another rhetorical device.

Pre-Raphaelitism carefully attempts to set itself apart from all fictional genres. The first pages of the preface discuss a piece of hearsay: 'Art is generally regarded as a light and irresponsible pursuit', and an eighteenth-century novel (not identified) which depicts a rosy view of an artist's easy achievement of fame and success. These two unreliable sources, gossip and fiction, are firmly identified as other to the text which is to follow (1, vii–viii). Despite this, however, the anxiety about alternative views, noted by Landow, emerges early on. Chapter 1 kicks off by dismissing other versions of the history of the movement – anecdotes, articles in newspapers and journals and other memoirs – as 'romances' or rumour, not privy to the author's objective act of witness (1, 1–2), and throughout the memoir, such accounts are acknowledged and referenced in order to be discredited. Diana Holman-Hunt records her grandmother maintaining that 'Beloved Holman so rightly disapproved of tittle-tattle',[25] and chapter 18 recalls a drawing of an imaginary gun made during a period of political unrest in the Crimea, when 'men without honest occupation are given to invent fables' (1, 512). The sketch is seized upon as genuine, the gun a secret weapon of the Russians, 'and soon we heard the old carriers of evil tidings delighting in this last news'. This is followed up with a more outrageous design, to signal the fabrication of the first, and so 'at last false Rumour saw that she was made ridiculous' (1, 513). These are the final words of the first volume, echoing the call for truth and virtue at the end of the second. Here, the narrator is particularly negative about critics and journalists and speaks on the subject at length in the final chapter, concluding:

> The writers who became mouthpieces of the cabal that sought to ruin Pre-Raphaelitism had scarcely drawn a line, and they came to their task without understanding, humility or restraint. It is devoutly to be hoped that writers determining the fate of future art will think seriously of the havoc wrought in the past. (2, 490)

These journalists are also gossips. They are thus distanced from the author by constructing their lack of 'experience' as laziness and lack of moral fibre.

This section contains a parallel attack on false, 'flaunting and meretricious' art contrasting Pre-Raphaelite truth to nature (2, 490–3). Both the literary and painted production of the author/artist are promoted as a straightforward reflection of nature. Realism, or integrity, is valorised above artifice. Practical differences between the two media are sidestepped and the description of the written style is couched in painterly terms: 'I disclaim all pretensions to those graces of style and deft mingling of exquisitely selected words into variegated tints of meaning' (1, xi). Whether or not the propagandising of the protagonist's objectivity is based on myth, it is clearly essential to the status of the text as a representation of both spiritual and empirical truth. It constructs Hunt as moral and objective, which in turn informs his painting practice. Text and writer, painting and painter become blurred and mutually reliant constructions.

Despite frequently expressed doubts about the potentially subjective nature of verbal and literary pronouncement, the extensive nature of the memoir and the abundance of Hunt's other published writings testify to an awareness of its power to undermine or support the painted work. The memoir therefore negotiates the contradictory position of exploiting literature as a potent cultural force whilst attempting to distance itself from accusations of literary manipulation. Quotations from literature head each chapter and crop up within the text as witness to the right-mindedness of the opinions in the narrative, as well as indicating the educated nature of the author. The hero is also valorised by the status of the plethora of literary figures with whom he associates, such as Ruskin, Carlyle, Dickens, Tennyson and Thackeray. Their words and actions are often 'quoted' in order to offer apparently unbiased adulation of the artist. Tennyson, for example, commends Hunt's exceptional eyesight when he identifies a distant eagle during one of their walks. Later, Hunt contrives a poetic metaphor which Tennyson admires (2, 173, 177). This technique presents both narrator and protagonist as on nodding terms with nineteenth-century, literary, high culture.

The construction of literature is, therefore, ambiguous. Hunt expresses suspicion of it, but employs sympathetic texts, including his own, to support his viewpoint. The memoir acknowledges the fanciful and fabricated nature of some texts, such as the sketch of the gun or the tales of false 'historians of Pre-Raphaelitism'. These represent an exploitation of the freedom of the literary form: 'The results of personal action may be made more conformable to human desires than they are found to do in simple nature' (1, 1). The memoir does not overtly admit that doubts about the trustworthiness of the medium might affect itself: 'My evidence is not . . . bent to suit a pretty theory'. I shall show, however, that such doubts are, nonetheless, manifested in its very elaboration of themes and devices of realism.

In his address to the Society of Arts, Hunt denies any gift for 'oratory' and again claims to be offering a descriptive, scientific survey, substantiated with 'data' in the form of samples and the results of experiments.[26] This role of teacher/historian, or 'sage', is echoed in the memoir's description of earlier artists passing on their learning by practical example, 'tangible knowledge – instead of mere verbal wonders' (1, ix). *Pre-Raphaelitism* is distinguished by an abundance of vivid observations. These are intended to perform a function similar to the visual aids in the address; they, too, are presented as 'tangible knowledge', or 'data'.

Jean-Jacques Rousseau's *Confessions* (1782) reinforces credibility by claiming that he is objectively surveying his life and will include even trivial details.[27] Hunt's memoir also claims to be an inventory of hard-won 'experience' (1, 2). Events are recounted in apparently encyclopaedic detail and the narrator feels the need to excuse silences about private matters, as we have seen. This apology draws attention to the Victorian distrust of unmediated, auto-biographical displays of self which are not orientated towards more general public improvement.[28] A paradox arises: the agenda of objectivity can undermine authority if taken too far.

A sense that the author is not subjectively selecting incidents is promoted by a chronological narrative structure, a pseudo-scientific logic of development.[29] Landow observes that nineteenth-century biographies often adopt a scientific mode by emphasising causal development: 'it was at the point in history when man began to accept a determinist causation that he also began to describe human life in terms of choice and explanation'.[30] The opening chapters of *Pre-Raphaelitism* demonstrate an evolutionary 'cause and effect' model, constructing the young protagonist's equally scientific research for a philosophy of art. The process is signposted by taking the reader through a sequence of formative experiences, articulated in the sub-headings on the contents page.

In chapter 1, the hero's 'Infant instincts for art' (1, xvii) are established in the tales of taking every opportunity to draw, to view prints and to meet artists. Chapter 2 catalogues responses to the art tradition demonstrated through his reading (1, 23), his viewing of the National Gallery collection (1, 19), and his observations of nature. This is developed in chapter 3, where he discusses other London collections, Reynolds, the Royal Academy and the contemporary art scene (1, 46–53) and decides on an 'independent course' (1, xvii). The nature of this is refined in the succeeding pages in the context of further research, more excursions into the countryside, reading Ruskin's *Modern Painters*, debates with Millais and Rossetti over the status of nature with regard to art, and a survey of European art (1, 185–93).

These diverse influences are united in their status as evidence. The formulation of Hunt's artistic philosophy and his identity as an artist follow an experimental pattern. General conclusions are derived from the inquisitive scrutiny of ideas and phenomena of all kinds. The culmination of youthful explorations is presented, in chapter 4, in the form of the discussions with Millais (1, 81–91). This covers ten pages and flits through a jumbled variety of references to nature, art and literature which imitates the heterogeneous texture of the artist's broader investigations. It is also informed by the preceding parts of the chapter, which begins with a description of the landscape of Ewell (1, 68–71), followed by the reading of *Modern Painters* (1, 73). Both are echoed at the conclusion of the discussion with Millais where Hunt famously determines to 'paint an out-of-doors picture . . . direct on the canvas itself, with every detail I can see, and with the sunlight brightness of the day itself' (1, 91). As a teenager, the hero is 'searching for a perfect guide. Though I looked upon artists with boundless wonder . . . I could see no one who stirred my complete sympathy' (1, 48). He admires parts, but their 'conventionality' compares poorly with his own perceptions of 'sensual' life. He never does find a single master, but continues to rely upon his own varied observations. The structure of the memoir thus mimics both the deductive, encyclopaedic development of the protagonist's beliefs and his style of painting, responding to 'every detail'.

In the text, detail is included in apparently natural, or 'direct', literary forms, dramatic narrative, lists and vivid eyewitness descriptions. This parallels the style of the painting, as Pointon has noted:

> Like his 1905 book . . . , Hunt's paintings were composited productions, carefully organised to deliver the effect of authenticity. The most obvious way in which this could be achieved was, of course, by the introduction of a vast array of ethnographic detail such as typifies *The Finding of the Saviour in the Temple*.[31]

Pointon's discussion takes place within the context of a 'colonisation' of abroad, and concentrates on Hunt's experiences in the Holy Land, but a similar ethnographic approach is manifested throughout the memoir. Events are portrayed in discrete cameos within the chronological flow. The composite structure is, again, articulated by the lists of episodes below each chapter heading on the contents pages. This can be construed as an attempt to colonise history; constructing an image of the artist and a firm territory within history for the eyes of posterity, the perceived authenticity of this self-portrait being paramount in the light of Hunt's reputation as a painter of natural and spiritual truth.

Pointon observes that the books are studded with proper nouns; names of real people and places lend a sense of factual certainty. This is no less true of the passages concerning Hunt's time in England. When describing the making of *Valentine Rescuing Sylvia from*

Proteus (1850–51, Birmingham Museum and Art Gallery, plate 7), he carefully lists his models:

> I was fortunate enough to obtain as a model for Valentine, James Lennox Hannay, then a young barrister; and for Proteus, James Aspinal, also a barrister and journalist, who eventually went to the Colonies and made a great position in the local parliament. For Julia I had the services of a very excellent young lassie. I was at no loss for Sylvia; the beauty and grace of Miss Siddal would make her of perfect type for the Duke's daughter. (1, 237–8)

Hunt also records the source of props, 'Mr. W.P. Frith kindly lent me some armour', and the location and seasonal conditions of the background (an autumnal Knole park) (1, 236). The methodical, documentary identification of these sources stands in for the veracity of the images themselves, as do the lengthy accounts of getting Jewish models for *The Finding*, or the succession of goats for *The Scapegoat*. The appropriate character of the models, fitting their roles (the two-faced Proteus is a journalist and a barrister), also serves to diminish the gap between art and reality.

The style in which these anecdotes are written itself exploits a range of devices to enhance the impression of realism. The *Valentine* episode includes a long story about how Hunt's progress is hindered by lending money to a false friend (1, 239–46). At one point, he visits a moneylender:

> I went to the narrow windowed, misery begrimed house, up a steep staircase to the second floor, where stood a posse of shabby men. Surveying these for a few moments while I waited, I heard a door opened, and from the room behind came a short, bloated, dirty, satin waistcoated Jew of about forty. 'Wha' d'ye-want?' said he as he snatched paper after paper out of the hands of the company. (1, 244)

This tale is typical of others scattered throughout the memoir. A chronological unfolding of observations is narrated from a single point of view. This is augmented by suspense, vivid sensory detail, reported speech (including 'everyday' or colloquial language), popular stereotypes (an irresponsible aristocrat, a rude Jewish moneylender), common-sense morality and a neat conclusion, or closure (eventually the aristocratic friend is discredited and comes to an ignominious end). The young protagonist's naive perception of the false friend is modified, through experience, to coincide reassuringly with the understanding of the mature author and the reader, in the style of classic realist fiction,[32] as dependent on the style as on the subject matter, perhaps, of Dickens's *Oliver Twist*.

Hunt uses direct speech frequently, giving the friend twenty-one lines at once earlier in this story (1, 242). His first encounter with Millais' parents is also told mainly through substantial 'quotations' (1, 60–4).

This format seeks to emphasise the impartiality of the narrator, especially when what is being expressed is detrimental to others or complimentary to Hunt. However, many of the reported conversations are far too long to be convincing as something spoken or something recalled. Carlyle's tirade against *The Light of the World* spans four and a half pages (1, 355–60); several writers, including Sussman and Landow, quote these words as though Carlyle himself spoke them, but this seems unlikely.[33] Pointon demonstrates how diary accounts and conversations are edited for effect in her comparison of Hunt's journal and later published descriptions of an encounter with an Arab sheik on the way to the Dead Sea in 1854.[34] What is presented as real reminiscence in this and other parts of the books, is clearly persuasive picture-making rather than a series of verbal snapshots.

Anecdotes are also selected and arranged in a way which is obviously favourable. Pointon draws attention to the reported incident where local Arabs beg to see the back of *The Shadow* in order to see the other side of the figures (2, 306–7). This advertises the painter's feat of illusionism. In one of many similar instances, the memoir describes a conversation with the Prince of Wales where His Highness recognises the tiny figure of Mr Combe among the throng in *London Bridge on the Night of the Marriage of the Prince and Princess of Wales* (1863–66, Ashmolean Museum, Oxford) (2, 244). As the autobiography strives to create a sense of transparent realism, it betrays an elaborate, organising, authorial programme.

Evidence and anxiety

This organising process is most clearly manifested at points in the book where the 'natural' chronological structure breaks down. Interestingly, this tends to occur when contradictory discourses are being discussed, especially in the final chapters, 13–17. On these occasions, detail, or 'data', is often particularly carefully presented in its most authentic form, as actual transcripts from other texts, such as letters and reviews. However, the way these are arranged becomes especially contrived and unnatural, itself a means of rhetorical interpretation. In other words, the weave of subjective and objective, interpretation and experience, unravels.

Chapter 15 reveals this paradox in its double title, 'Retrospect' and '1897'; the one implies opinion and hindsight, the other is documentary and immediate. The chapter does not contain an orderly, narrative record of the year, but reproduces letters between Hunt and Keble College about the care of *The Light of the World* (2, 404–17), followed by a variety of accounts about the early days of the Brotherhood (2, 417–37). The latter section dwells on the claim that Dante Gabriel Rossetti was the true initiator of the movement. The prevalence of this notion is demonstrated by extracts from texts such as Ruskin's lectures given in Oxford, *The Art of England* (1884) and an article by Robert de la Sizeranne from *Revue des Deux Mondes* (1889) (reproduced in French!). The 'romantic fable' (2, 421) of Rossetti's pre-eminence is contradicted using other quotes from letters by Ruskin and extracts from the diaries of Ford Madox Brown, Rossetti and his brother, William Michael. The 'enchanting' pictures of Rossetti and his followers (2, 417) are also distanced from the verisimilitude of the art of 'Pre-Raphaelite workers' (2, 418). The display of dates and textual evidence pointedly parallels and valorises Hunt's laborious, documentary method of painting against what he considers to be the more casual, 'ephemeral' artistic and literary methods of his opponents.

Chapter 13, '1887, 1888', provides us with a vivid example of all aspects of Hunt's literary style in overdrive when dealing with issues of particular concern. It again departs from a chronological format and reprints a series of letters published in the *Pall Mall Gazette* which question the historical authenticity of a sword depicted in *Valentine* (2, 345–9). The chapter is headed by a warning from Thomas Hood: 'Evil is wrought from want of thought.' It begins as a conventional narrative, an account of a visit to an exhibition of *Valentine* and *The Scapegoat* (2, 344). A familiarly workmanlike justification for Hunt's presence there is provided: 'I went to scrutinise how the colours and varnishes had stood the test of time', and the flattering 'fact' that the 'number of visitors . . . exceeded the number recorded at any one artist's exhibition', is added.

The memoir mentions seeing the critic, Frederick Stephens, amongst 'a posse [the same word uses to describe the predatory moneylender's' clients, 1, 244] of gentlemen', for whom he 'was acting as the great exponent of P.R.B. story'. Here, the reader is being included in an authorial irony at Stephens's expense, but the text then becomes carefully objective. We are told that Hunt and Stephens were, at that time, no longer friends, that Stephens was standing in front of *Valentine* talking to the art correspondent for the *Pall Mall Gazette*, and that he was there so long that the busy Hunt had to leave without achieving his end (2, 344). Through this incident, couched as a straightforward eyewitness account, Stephens is effectively implicated as colluding with the journalist. He is also constructed as playing to the crowd, a talker, rather than a doer like Hunt. This section (unaccountably entitled 'Photogravure executed by Goupil' on the contents page), prompts the reader to conclude that Stephens is the source of the letters even though their author remains anonymous – Hunt makes great play of this want of manliness. He does not refer directly to Stephens in the next section, entitled 'The *Pall Mall Gazette* letters', but appears to allow us to make our own connection from 'evidence'.

Despite this contextualising preamble, there are signs of discomfort with the ability of the raw correspondence between Hunt and his attacker to show the artist in the desired light. Each letter is sandwiched between a few lines of comment and the last letter, though by Hunt himself and not refuted, is followed by a long non sequitur about the ground-breaking nature of the Pre-Raphaelites and the importance of this to younger artists (2, 349–53). Structure is practically lost in this almost paragraph-less, three-page declamation. The six pages of argument about a sword do not sit easily with what follows. What does connect the two is an underlying subtext of anxiety.

As we have seen, the rigorous realism of Hunt's painting relates to the perceived veracity of the memoir itself. The *Pall Mall Gazette* controversy is not satisfactory in this respect because the artist is only able to claim an approximate fidelity to history, as the sword was not of precisely the right period. He also has to admit a failure of memory, the very thing that the book relies on. In the last letter, he confesses: 'What the sword was itself I do not remember' (2, 349). He goes on to supply contradictory excuses for this: the sword he used perfectly fitted the one conceived in his mind, and short cuts were necessary in order to finish work in the less than ideal circumstances of the pioneering painter. The second theme, the innovator's struggles and lack of assistance, forms an obscure connection to the subsequent section. This features the list motif, cataloguing artists assisted by the Brotherhood's reforms. It implies criticism of the *Pall Mall Gazette* episode by bemoaning the bad press which precluded the young Pre-Raphaelites from gaining support themselves (2, 352).

In the latter passage, the narrator changes from 'I' to 'we' and talks on behalf of the group as a whole. This transition from the solitary, misunderstood campaigner ('Mr. Holman Hunt Ready for the Fray' heads the first letter) to the plurality of an established movement, reads awkwardly. The withdrawal into the safety of the collective voice reinforces Hunt's argument in the previous section, however. Accordingly, the next part (2, 354–60) quotes another publication in the *Pall Mall Gazette* of 1887, written by Hunt to commemorate Rossetti's death (1882). This long (about 2,600 words) and quite charitable address is reproduced in full, in order, Hunt says, to rebuff accusations of hostility towards Rossetti. Although chapter 15 airs disagreements with Rossetti, here, brotherhood is temporarily embraced.

The collective appellation, 'Pre-Raphaelite', buttresses the authority of Hunt as narrator at a point where it is threatened. This recalls the memoir's oddly non-autobiographical title. However, at the same time, it brings into the picture other discourses, particularly those by and about Rossetti, that challenge control of Hunt's image as leader. Hunt's references to Rossetti are, therefore, ambivalent and clearly dramatise the tension between public and private, identified by Landow. The inclusive tone of the address is compromised by a confession that it was hurriedly executed, 'scribbling some of the sentences . . . in the cab', and made as admiring as possible because of the sad occasion (2, 354). It also is followed by another apparent non sequitur, a passage which parodies the Aesthetic Movement with more pertinent quotations, this time from Gilbert and Sullivan's *Patience* (2, 364–6). The subtext, a criticism of Rossetti's association with these artists, is the unspoken link.

Hunt neutralises this new anxiety over Rossetti more overtly in the last pages of the chapter (2, 369–76), but again feels the need to refrain from direct comment. It begins with an unfeasibly long, one-and-a-half page speech about Rossetti's jealousy and unfriendliness, 'quoted' from a conversation with Millais (2, 369–70). The narrator's independence from this judgement is reinforced by an interruption from Hunt asserting that Millais is mistaken, but Millais is represented as correcting him and going on to support his claim through the opinion of a third party, Rossetti's biographer.

In conclusion, Millais is reported to speak of his own surrender to public taste and Hunt's stubborn individualism and idealism (2, 372–6). He catalogues Hunt's achievements and notes the unnecessariness that he be accepted as a Royal Academician and the unfairness that Hunt has not been accepted. The oddly contradictory logic of this argument receives a further twist in the closing sentence, where Millais' opinions are given authority by a reminder of his social status and equality with Frederick Lord Leighton, President of the Royal Academy.

Chapter 13 demonstrates two important features of the memoir: an unstable narrator/protagonist and a fragmented structure. We witness an uncomfortable oscillation between two personae, singular (embattled, outside, and above, the Brotherhood, the Academy and society) *and* integrated (inside, part of the Brotherhood and society), which parallels an uncomfortable combination of authorial intervention and evidence.

Codell asserts that the memoir is not strictly an autobiography and traces its collective agenda: 'It links three claims – Hunt as originator of the PRB; the PRB as linchpin of the English school; and the English school as culturally hegemonic in the West.'[35] The very breadth of this definition points to a tension between the personal and the general, revealed in the next sentence: 'While posturing as a rebellious outsider, Hunt claimed to have influenced most major English artists.' Codell ascribes this inside/outside dichotomy to a masochistic personality.[36] I shall deal with this in Chapter 3. My point here is that the dual voice of *Pre-Raphaelitism* also relates to the concern for realism in the text itself. The account's reliability is bound up with its singleness of purpose as autobiography – one man's eyewitness account of one man's experience – but this objective record must be interpreted in order that it might achieve a more general, social significance. The inconsistent narrator of Pre-Raphaelitism articulates what Marcus calls an autobiographical 'hybrid between self and other',[37] a failure to synthesise two voices, the one subjective and rhetorical and the other objective and scientific.

Codell maintains that the inconsistencies of Hunt's persona are disguised in the memoir, 'by eliding diverse life patterns'.[38] This 'incoherence' is, however, clearly displayed in the *form* of the writing. Chapter 13 demonstrates a strikingly idiosyncratic structure characterised by the nervous patchwork of 'objective' material linked by a highly subjective subtext. Texts by other hands – letters, lines from a popular musical, paintings by other artists, speech and hearsay – sit within the memoir like specimen butterflies pinned to a board.

These alternative discourses represent the narratorial fear of lack of consensus, noted by Landow, and flagged by Hunt in the first chapter: 'Since I have undertaken the duties of a historian and feel myself responsible for the validity of the statements offered to the world, my narrative must conflict with nearly all those who have hitherto appeared on the purpose and progress of Pre-Raphaelitism' (1, 1–2). The scientific recording of experience privileges the single viewpoint, but brings with it a fear of its relative nature, and of the threat of the viewpoints of others. The importance of this threat is evidenced in the very act of displaying these alternative accounts, and in the elaborate organisation of the exhibits into a pattern which is intended to direct our reading.

Helsinger notes that Trollope also records criticisms against himself in order to establish narratorial honesty.[39] In the context of an autobiography which privileges the narrator-hero, the mocker will ultimately be mocked. Carlyle's ventriloquised objection to *The Light of the World* is an example of this device. He is quoted as calling the picture a 'papistical fantasy' (1, 355), and goes on to assert the impossibility of depicting Christ as a 'Man toiling in the hot sun', in his true surroundings (1, 358). His words, in fact, valorise Hunt's subsequent execution of *The Finding* and *The Shadow*, of which the reader will, of course, be aware. However, Hunt makes additional attempts to guarantee interpretation. He abuses the freedom of reported speech and the philosopher's lecture becomes overextended. The effect is artificial, and paradoxically reinforces Carlyle's accusation of a failure of realism.[40]

When actual transcriptions of critical texts are used, authorial intervention becomes even more awkward, having to take place alongside the 'evidence', rather than in the reporting of it, and requiring contradictory evidence of equivalent weight, that is, more quotations. Chapters 13 and 15 are typical of the final part of the memoir, dominated almost exclusively by difficult issues such as Rossetti and modern art. These chapters are riddled with extracts from other texts. The single I/eye multiplies into a concoction of multivalent viewpoints which fragment the authorial persona. The narrator is revealed as he struggles to preserve the integrity of the protagonist. Alternative discourses literally deconstruct the narrative as the chronological structure disintegrates and is replaced by contrived juxtapositions and conspicuously subjective comments.

The events, beliefs, individuals and institutions that stand against the hero of *Pre-Raphaelitism* represent more general fears about other viewpoints which might disclose those of the author to be relative, unilateral, subjective or 'fantasy'. This concern is inherent within the ambiguity of the autobiographical form and common in nineteenth-century writings on the subject.[41] However, *Pre-Raphaelitism*'s preoccupation with criticism, and its inclusion of contradictory 'data' in such quantities, suggests a heightened vulnerability to the threat of alternative evidence of all kinds, and a particularly pressing need to re-present it in order to neutralise it and accommodate it within an overall philosophy.

A strange anecdote, cited as 'Max and the pistol' on the contents page, provides an intriguing example of an unfavourable incident which could easily have been omitted (2, 9–12). The memoir describes Hunt sending a troublesome pistol to Frederick, a German speaker, the regular firearm mender. He asks his landlord, Max, another German speaker, to deliver it, with explicit instructions to remind Frederick that it is still loaded. A few days later, Frederick is accidentally shot and killed by his assistant with Hunt's faulty gun. Had this episode been reported with reasonable succinctness it would not attract question, but its drawn-out treatment betrays a preoccupation with the threat of this 'data', or event, to the protagonist's self-construction.

The subject is again introduced casually in the midst of a narrative about the departure of Hunt's English friends from Jerusalem and their invitation to join them; 'but . . . a discovery I had made did much to decide the question for me' (2, 9). This 'discovery' is the broken gun, needed for protection outside the city. The paragraph becomes a long history of the problems with the pistol (twelve lines). Hunt then quotes his own careful instruction to Max (nine lines). The conversation also tells the reader that Frederick is depressed and morbid. Max reports Frederick's words:

> 'I stay 'ere only to die like my vrent [friend] die . . . He tocht in 'ed pooh fellaw.' [Hunt replies] 'I know, I know, Max, but mind you give him my message, and take care that no one touches the pistol but yourself, till you deliver it into his hands with the caution that it is loaded.' (2, 10)

Quotation *and* secondary quotation are used as 'evidence' of Hunt's knowing responsibility in contrast to Max's amiable vagueness. Max speaks in comical pidgin to underline this. However, in the very next sentence he is described as 'as conscientious as he was proud of his proficiency in English'. A contradiction arises from the need to support Hunt's conviction that Max is reliable enough to take the message, whilst also asserting a vagueness which could explain the resultant misunderstanding.

Hunt then recalls a previous, brief conversation with Frederick in Arabic; who 'smiled pleasantly but sadly'. This simultaneously underlines Frederick's depression, Hunt's linguistic inability to warn him about the loaded gun himself, and the good terms they shared. The death itself is reported to Hunt, second-hand, by his friend, Sim, thus further distancing authorial input. Hunt closes the subject with a reflection on the strangeness of it being his gun which killed Frederick.

The memoir claims: 'I tell such stories not in support of any theory, but because they claim record as strange personal experience' (2, 12), reprising its introductory comments (1, 1). The suspicion that Hunt's part in the tragedy might be negatively construed is, however, revealed by the carefully contrived nature of the story, the attempt to emphasise Frederick's desire to die (irrelevant if his death was an accident) and Max's odd representation as both reliable and vague. This seemingly trivial story is significant because it questions the hero's honesty and ability to communicate clearly. Moreover, it brings together false representation (the deceptive gun, the obscured message) and death, echoing the association between 'Rumour' and the sketch of an invented gun referred to above. A profound link in Hunt's work between mortality and the failure to truthfully represent will be proposed in Chapter 4.

This pattern of displaying anxiety in order to disown it is even manifested in the language of the memoir, by a strikingly frequent use of double negatives and irony. On the thorny subject of Rossetti's 'shadowy pretensions', Hunt says: 'In disproving all right to leadership for him, it must not be assumed that I fail to acknowledge the distinction which, in its degree, his genius brought to our cause' (2, 418–19). Hunt recalls his father: 'He did not repress my disposition to draw; on the contrary, when I left home for boarding school he provided me with some large drawing books and some lithographs to copy; and when visiting me there, he looked over these and could not resist making some sketches himself' (1, 12). The tangled structure of these statements reflects disquiet about their subject matter. Hunt's father is presented as hindering his artistic ambitions and associating the profession with irresponsibility, intemperance and a foreign, non-Protestant lifestyle (1, chapters 1–2). The memoir returns again and again to justifying the protagonist's patriotism and religious seriousness, as well as his central role in the Pre-Raphaelite movement in relation to Rossetti.

These threats to the integrity and moral rectitude of the author undermine the authorial voice, and the language itself becomes defensive and convoluted. Sentences run on, propagating clauses and subclauses which continually adjust meaning. This linguistic unease is even more conspicuous in letters and journals. They are littered with deletions and additions squeezed between other words. Sentences again run on and into each other, without punctuation. Sensitive issues are aired repeatedly, as they are in the memoir. Language is never clear or definitive and is constantly being 'bent' (1, 1) and 'retouched'.

Hunt's writings display a similar preoccupation with clarity and control over readings of his paintings. Constant concerns that others will misunderstand them prompt the use of quotes on the frames, long catalogue notes and the production of the memoir itself.[42] A typical comment to his friend, John Lucas Tupper, conveys anxiety about communicating to a diverse audience: 'I am extremely anxious how the world will regard it [*The Triumph*] – first that portion of it made up of artistic friends who care for Art as for their life and then for the ignorant – the professedly ignorant public.'[43] Hunt habitually keeps a picture concealed until he has made numerous alterations and the event of a viewing is always given importance in his writings.[44] *Pre-Raphaelitism* often lists the numbers who visit a particular exhibition and quotes negative and positive reviews (2, 111, 193). As an artist who painstakingly paints in such a lucid and realistic style, there is a suspicion that meaning is not completely clear or convincing.

In Chapter 7, I shall demonstrate that Hunt's paintings attempt to build likenesses of parts of the real world into a preconceived pictorial design in much the same way as his memoir attempts to build objective experience into a coherent and unified philosophy and self-image. I shall suggest that difficulties with this process arise from the fact that the mimesis of objective evidence in the paintings undermines the organising viewpoint of the design, rendering it vulnerable to different interpretations, just as 'documentary' evidence disrupts the design of the autobiography. The length and awkward structure of *Pre-Raphaelitism* are symptomatic of difficulties in achieving a textual synthesis of the scientific and the rhetorical, or experience and interpretation, and offer clues to the lengthy manufacture and awkward appearance of the paintings.

James Eli Adams's investigation of the Victorian crisis of authority, *Dandies and Desert Saints: Styles of Victorian Masculinity*, notes:

> The writer's vocation, which is centrally preoccupied with varieties of self-representation and problematics of audience, condenses with special clarity [the] pursuit of self-mastery through self-definition. But the sense of vulnerability that prompts increasingly elaborate and guarded forms of self-presentation to an imagined audience also animates a deep mistrust of such strategies in others.[45]

The accommodation of 'data' within the philosophical scheme proposed by the memoir is essential to its authenticity, and to the integrity of the narrator/protagonist. However, the text continually draws attention to the potential dishonesty and artificiality of both the visual and literary language. The first page of the preface begins with the words: 'Art is generally regarded as a light and irresponsible pursuit, entailing for its misuse no penalty to the artist or to the nation of which he is citizen' (1, vii). Chapter 1 quotes Sir Robert Walpole: '*written* history cannot possibly be true' (emphasis added) (1, 2). Two hefty volumes strive to disprove the accusation, but the final chapters dwell on the same concern and the last sentence re-expresses a basic discomfort with processes of representation and their potential to manipulate: 'The purpose of art is, in love of guileless beauty, to lead man to distinguish between that which, being clean in spirit, is productive of virtue, and that which is flaunting and meretricious and productive of ruin to the nation' (2, 493). The memoir's exhaustive emphasis on the fabricated nature of so many other texts paradoxically draws the reader's attention to the possibility that it might, itself, be a seen as a fabrication. The comic, unclear, colloquial speech, literary manipulations or downright lies that are attributed to the language of others, such as Max, Rossetti or critics, betray a general anxiety about linguistic limitations per se.

These repeated allusions to the non-transparent nature of text and language could be construed as a modern awareness of its inherent artificiality. As Landow says, however, 'Victorian can be taken to mean parent of the modern and, like most powerful parents, the age provoked a powerful reaction against itself.'[46] In order to keep the authority of the hero intact, Hunt's story of himself restricts recognition of the dishonesty of the literary form to other texts. A modernist cognisance of this paradox is, nonetheless, revealed in the style of the memoir: its awkward language, fragmented structure, the intrusion of other discourses and an overall sense of conflict and contradiction.

Marcus identifies the dogmatic philosophical thrust of *Pre-Raphaelitism* and suggests that the literary mode endows a freedom to speak in the abstract: 'Memoir writing can offer an insight into the historical, the artistic, and the individual as conceptions.'[47] This freedom is, as we have seen, problematic. It cannot be acknowledged and is at odds with the memoir's proclaimed status as objective history. A system of belief is proposed to be self-evident in documentary and remembered evidence, but this position requires an evasion of the process of *making* text: the subjective mechanisms of perception and memory and the interventions of rhetoric and interpretation. The fragmented, artificial effect of Hunt's autobiography relates to a failure to suppress anxieties about the process of representation. The instability of the narratorial voice and dislocations between content and form, evidence and meaning, 'materialism and mysticism'[48] reflect the ambiguous position of belief and identity in a context of modern, scientific relativism.

Notes

1 Marcus, 'Brothers in Their Anecdotage', p 13
2 Farrar and Meynell, *Hunt*; Williamson, G., *Holman Hunt* (London: George Bell and Sons, 1902); Coleridge, M.E., *Holman Hunt* (London: T.C. and E.C. Jack, 1910)
3 Gissing, *Hunt*, pp ix, 217–21; Farrar and Meynell, *Hunt*, p 1
4 Clark Amor, *Hunt*, p 274
5 Ibid., p 13
6 Marcus, 'Brothers in Their Anecdotage', p 12. This approach is implemented in her publication, Marcus, L., *Auto/biographical Discourses: Theory, Criticism, Practice* (Manchester: Manchester University Press, 1994)
7 Marcus, 'Brothers in Their Anecdotage', p 21
8 Sussman, 'Artistic Manhood', p 158
9 Landow, G.P., *Approaches to Victorian Autobiography*, ed. G.P. Landow (Ohio: Ohio University Press, 1979), p xliii
10 Ibid., pp viii–ix, also Marcus, *Auto/biographical Discourses*, p 15
11 Landow, *Typological Symbolism*, p 1
12 Gosse, E., *Father and Son, A Study of Two Temperaments* (1907), ed. P. Abbs (Harmondsworth, Middlesex: Penguin, 1986), pp 11–12
13 Landow, G., 'How to Read Ruskin: The Art Critic as Victorian Sage', in *John Ruskin and the Victorian Eye*, essays by S. Casteras et al. (New York: Harry N. Abrams/Phoenix Art Museum, 1993), p 56
14 Landow, *Approaches*, pp xxii–xxiii
15 Helsinger, H., 'Credence and Credibility: The Concern for Honesty in Victorian Autobiography', in ibid., pp 46–7
16 Ibid., p 48
17 Grosskurth, P., 'Where was Rousseau?', in Landow, *Approaches*, p 29
18 Codell, 'Artist Colonised', pp 213–14
19 Vasari, G., *The Lives of the Artists* (1549) (Oxford: Oxford University Press, 1991), p 17. The Romantic poet is, of course, also evoked
20 Ibid., p 416
21 Ibid., p 285
22 'Materials', p 485
23 Holman-Hunt, *My Grandfather*, p 30; Maas, *Hunt*, p 28; Maas also quotes Edward Clodd's *Memories* (1926): 'As with his work, so with his talk. Everything was related in minutest detail, pouring forth from a phenomenal memory', p 92
24 Letter to Stephens, February 28 1880, Boleian Library, Oxford (hereafter BL), MS Don. e 68, 82
25 Holman-Hunt, *My Grandfather*, p 19
26 'Materials', p 485

27 Landow, *Approaches*, pp xxvi–xxvii
28 Marcus, *Auto/biographical Discourses*, pp 21–3
29 'A Fight for Art' and 'Materials'
30 Landow, *Approaches*, p xix
31 Pointon, 'Artist as Ethnographer', p 34
32 Belsey, C., *Critical Practice* (1980) (London: Routledge, 1990), pp 76–82
33 Landow, G.P. and R.M. Landow, 'William Holman Hunt's "The Shadow of Death"', *Bulletin of the John Rylands University Library of Manchester*, 55, 1 (Autumn 1972), pp 217–18; Sussman, 'Artistic Manhood', p 159
34 Pointon, 'Artist as Ethnographer', pp 23–5
35 Codell, 'Artist Colonised', p 213
36 Ibid., pp 217–20
37 Marcus, *Auto/biographical Discourses*, p 15
38 Codell, 'Artist Colonised', p 216
39 Helsinger, 'Credence and Credibility', p 49. Hunt also cites his comic failure to recognise the old masters in the National Gallery when a child (1, 19), but this is carefully contrasted with later confident and informed criticism of those in the Louvre in 1849 (1, 185–91)
40 The memoir also diffuses Carlyle's criticism of *The Light of the World* by attributing to him an error when viewing the *Awakening Conscience*: he mistakes a reflection for moonlight (1, 355)
41 Marcus, *Auto/biographical Discourses*, pp 22–3
42 Landow, *Typological Symbolism*, p 44
43 Letter to Tupper, July 1879, *A Pre-Raphaelite Friendship, The Correspondence of William Holman Hunt and John Lucas Tupper*, eds J.H. Coombs, et al. (Ann Arbor, Mich.: University of Michigan Research Press, 1986), p 290 (hereafter cited as *Correspondence*)
44 Ibid., September 1879, p 292
45 Adams, J. Eli, *Dandies and Desert Saints: Styles of Victorian Masculinity* (London: Cornell University Press, 1995), p 13
46 Landow, 'How to Read Ruskin', p 55
47 Marcus, 'Brothers in Their Anecdotage', p 21
48 Landow, *Typological Symbolism*, p 1

2

Belief: seen and unseen landscapes

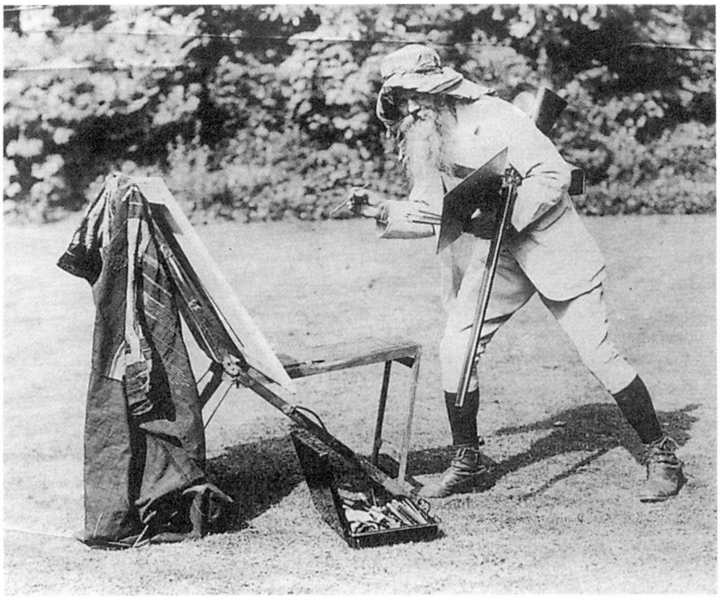

2.1
William Holman Hunt re-enacting Painting at the Dead Sea, 1894

Victorian commentators categorise Hunt as a religious painter. Williamson's summary is typical:

> Hard work, devotion to duty, intense belief in religion, devoted attachment to the person of Christ, and the consequent determination to use his art to teach others and expound scripture, are the main characteristics of this painter of Christian art, and the more ordinary methods of painting are all . . . to be subordinated to these ruling forces.[1]

Although Williamson is clearly repeating the familiar, heroic construction of the artist propagated by Hunt's own self-publicity, I believe that he is correct in seeing Hunt's faith as a profound concern, affecting both the subject matter and the 'ordinary methods' of his painting.

In the twentieth century, Hunt's religious imagery has increasingly inhibited critical appreciation of his work, rendering him an establishment figure, associated with long superseded beliefs and norms and cut off from the developments of modernism. Only Landow's *Typological Symbolism* provides serious consideration of his religious thought in later, pious pictures such as *The Triumph of the Innocents. The Light of the World* has been considered by Jeremy Maas and, more recently, Michael Wheeler has set it in the context of intricate, mid-century reassessments of Christology, particularly those of Ruskin.[2] Hunt's religious subject matter can, however, be seen as a vehicle for broader themes of materialism and relativism that were central to modern experience in the nineteenth century. A closer look at constructions of belief set out in his public and more especially his private writings reveals a faith and self-image which are deeply doubted, closely tied to issues of evidence and processes of representation. They provide insights into the tension between the subjective and the objective that is exhibited in *Pre-Raphaelitism* and cast new light on Hunt's Ruskinian 'truth to nature'.

Evidence and belief

During the nineteenth century, religious consensus was undermined by discoveries in the natural sciences and literary and historical criticism of the Bible, and by a range of increasingly individual religious attitudes. Alex Vidler calls it an 'age of revolution': 'Beneath the surface of respectable religious conformity was a turmoil of doubt and uncertainty . . . It would be truer to say that the age was one of religious seriousness rather than of faith. No considering man felt able to ignore the question of religious belief, as is easily done today.'[3] Our relatively atheistic age can overlook the very practical nature of this question, how profoundly it affected nineteenth-century perceptions of history, self, life and death. Hunt engages with all of these, and is an energetic participant in the debate. It dominates his writings throughout his life.

Evidence again plays a central role. The memoir presents Hunt's early years as a period of considered reserve on spiritual matters due to an absence of evidence and experience, 'for of spiritual powers we knew nothing and we saw no profit in relying upon a vision, however beautiful it might be' (1, 159). It demonstrates curiosity about, and general tolerance of the variety of beliefs available at the time, both Christian[4] and non-Christian (2, 279–80), and does not ally itself to any one particular dogma.[5] The creed that develops is represented as being dependent on the protagonist's own observations, 'denying all that could not be tangibly proved' (1, 160). This respect for a rational or empirical analysis of faith is central to understanding both the writings and paintings.

In his essay 'Realism and Tradition in Religious Art', William Vaughan notes that Hunt's paintings confront the fundamental problem of 'how rational enquiry could be aligned with faith'.[6] The apparent naturalism of *The Finding of the Saviour in the Temple*, for example, represents an attempt to render a religious subject in an accessible way, in keeping with the materialism of the day and Hunt's artistic principle of 'truth to nature'.[7] Hunt's mimetic style has a reciprocal relationship to content which is also very important, however: in an age of religious questioning, the reconciliation of scripture and natural, historical facts justifies faith itself.

Hunt disagrees with Rossetti's opinion that the inclusion of empirical information might undermine mystical aspects of design (1, 148–9) and his work insists on a painstaking historical and visual realism. His antidote to the spiritual insecurity arising out of contemporary religious debates is to dismiss them as ill-informed. Objective religious truth is to be found in research and experience, an energetic exploration of the historical evidence of the bible and its extant landscape. *Pre-Raphaelitism* sets out these ideas in the form of a conversation with Augustus Egg:

> My project of going to Syria had originated when I was a boy at school when lessons from the New Testament were read . . . '[A]lthough the revelations of science, and more transiently the conclusions drawn from these by theorists and commentators, had often compelled me to reconsider my earlier understanding of the story, yet the doings of the Divine Master in Syria never ceased to claim my homage. The pursuit of painting only gave my childish Palestine project distincter purpose. The gain in thoughtfully spent life is,' I said, 'the continual disturbance of obsolete convictions; at such tremulation of ideas one is tempted to shoot off to any extreme harbour of rest, and to violently denounce all others. I would guard against this danger with my respect for impartial investigation, built upon confidence that truth, whatever it be, is above

> all price, and my desire is very strong to use my powers to make more tangible Jesus Christ's history and teaching. Art has often illustrated the theme, but it has surrounded it with many enervating fables, and perverted the heroic drama with feeble interpretation.' (1, 348–9)

Hunt makes it clear that he considers the Bible to be an authentic historical text, a viable piece of evidence.

Hunt feels that scientific discoveries should also 'be used to convey messages of hope to fresh broods of men' (1, 148–9). The term 'hope' conflates the religious hope of resurrection and the Victorian concept of an evolutionary progress towards a New Jerusalem on earth.[8] In his lecture to the Church Congress of 1897, 'Religion and Art', Hunt presents the refinements of evolution as testimony to the organising hand of God.[9] A letter to Tupper criticises Darwin and other scientists as imperfectly informed 'know alls', but he says, 'I in fact never got far enough to conclude that Darwin's theory was irreconcilable with the idea of a divine Father's merciful presiding.'[10] This notion is shared by contemporaries whom Hunt admired, such as Browning and Tennyson.[11]

Hunt's philosophy also echoes that of Ruskin, summarised here by Errington:

> [Like Hunt,] Ruskin went to great pains . . . to unite the known facts of modern science as to the condition and structure of the physical world with the traditional idea that all was a visible embodiment of the divine maker's personality. He read the world as a graphologist might interpret a text, seizing upon the indications provided by a curve, a series of proportions, the brilliance of a distant horizon, or the veins in a lump of marble, and like the Tractarians, he employed the old word, type.[12]

Hunt's adoption of Ruskin's system of natural 'types' anchors the spiritual within the material; a natural or historical event manifests a sacred one.[13]

Hunt writes to Ruskin in 1880 about his state of belief in 1847. He claims that before finding *Modern Painters* he had been

> a contemptuous unbeliever in any spiritual principles but the development of talent, and Shelley and Lord Byron with Keats were my best modern heroes – all read in the light of materialism, or sensualism . . . It was high time I got something, and this something thus strangely gained was what first arrested me in my downward course. It was the voice of God. I read this in rapture and it sowed some seed of shame.[14]

Ruskin's exhortation to go to nature is re-expressed in the language of Hunt's letter. He defines his thinking as initially merely sensual, then dramatises his new understanding of a seamless relationship between the material *and* the sacred through his choice of natural imagery, 'some seed of shame'. Hunt's faith expresses itself as an augmented perception which can synthesise the physical and the metaphysical.

The last sentence of the second volume of *Modern Painters* foreshadows that of *Pre-Raphaelitism*, valorising the prophetic role of the artist and charging him to attend to 'all things that God has created to be beautiful and pronounced to be good'.[15] In 'Religion and Art', Hunt says, 'when the artist looks at the beauty which crowns every fresh line of effort in nature, he recognises the Master Artist's work'.[16] There are two significant points here. Firstly, an interest in historical and biblical evidence is deepened to construct all aspects of the natural world as manifestations of divine ordering. Secondly, the artist is defined as a visionary, one who can distinguish this divinity, expressed as 'beauty', from that which is fake, 'flaunting and meretricious' (2, 493). Paintings are essential proofs, empirical acts of witness of a spiritual hierarchy not just in their subject matter, but in *every natural detail*. They are also testaments of the visionary powers of the painter.

Hunt's memoir is a demonstration of this thinking. It ascribes a self-evident spiritual order to the world and to the life of the artist. The experiences in the autobiography are presented as a history which reflects and exemplifies the philosophy of the author as if it were natural; not made, but found. The artist is presented as one who is able to perceive evidence of God in the real and to re-present this order and beauty. Works of art are presented as records of the sacred meaning that the visionary has detected in history (including the Bible) and nature. Although this construction of art and the artist is not unusual in Victorian literature, it is in this case more than mere convention or propaganda. It links the act of perception and representation to issues of faith and self-definition and informs every aspect of Hunt's output.

As we have seen, this position is not unproblematic; the memoir betrays doubts about representation. Difficulty arises where 'data' or experience does not accord with the moral system and self-image of the author, or when an act of describing it involves authorial intervention. The implication that a spiritual system is not self-evident, that the perception and description of it are in some way delusional, a product of 'fantasy' or 'manipulation', casts doubt upon the integrity of Hunt's faith and of his persona. I shall show that the actual process of describing nature can also disrupt intellectual, or religious, preconceptions, fuelling religious doubt and destabilising artistic self-image. This can be demonstrated through an analysis of the representation of the sacred in a particular aspect of nature, the landscape of the Holy Land. I shall compare literary descriptions from *Pre-Raphaelitism* with journal accounts. Both reveal familiar anxieties about the construction of meaning through processes of description and representation. These concerns are most evident when nature is most closely addressed, during painting.

The published landscape

Pre-Raphaelitism offers vivid accounts of the protagonist's explorations of landscapes of all kinds. These underline his skills as a 'pioneer . . . of historic truth' and chronicler of the world, and support his image as a perceptive, mimetic painter. Concern is expressed about the differences between the artist's own visual experience of nature and that offered by the art of the time. Hunt asserts that other images lack both realism, 'true' light effects and colour, and a spiritual quality, an 'undying appeal to the hearts of living men' (1, 48). These visual and spiritual truths are constructed as mutually dependent. The memoir complains that 'Much of the favourite art left the inner self untouched' and concludes that this missing quality, a transcendent apprehension of divinity, is due to distortion of real appearances.

Hunt portrays himself as seeking the spiritual outside the arts, through his energetic explorations of nature and experience. As a youth, he skips Sunday services and heads for the countryside: 'I had no further misgivings in hearkening to the birds' call and the clang of the bells of Chingford Church rather than to the tinkling [the sermon] of the Lady Huntingdon Chapel' (1, 25). A later passage in *Pre-Raphaelitism* (2, 16–21) reiterates this idea. Hunt is described, during his first visit to Jerusalem in 1854, sitting at the window of the tower of his friend, Graham. Graham is reading aloud a religious tract, 'a kind of literature for which I cared little'. Hunt's attention wanders to the view, 'the centres of mystic reflection which enchanted the eye' (figure 2.2). At the close of the extended contemplation of the landscape which follows (covering three pages), Graham, unaware of the beauty of the scene or Hunt's distraction, asks whether he has 'ever heard such an eloquent sermon'. Hunt's reply, 'Never!', invites the reader to share his irony, privileging what is seen over what is read and voicing the distrust of eloquence, or 'tinkling', that runs through the memoir as a whole.

This inscription of spiritual significance into landscape is a convention of nineteenth-century travel writing.[17] In particular, of course, it closely resembles the style of Ruskin. Hunt's description of Mount Hermon and the Jordan valley (2, 54–7) is, perhaps, dependent on Ruskin's description of a river and mountain scene at Geneva in his memoir, *Praeterita*, published twenty years before. Both occur at sunset. *Pre-Raphaelitism*'s protagonist exclaims:

> Think how all the angels may have brought each his most precious contribution in order to make this noble picture! See how the firmament above is sapphire, and how it melts into topaz and to amber behind the mountain line; and then the mountain itself is clear lapis lazuli, infused by the sun into ruby and fire, except where the milky snow . . . glows in the sun and intensifies every other gem. See how in the plain the water

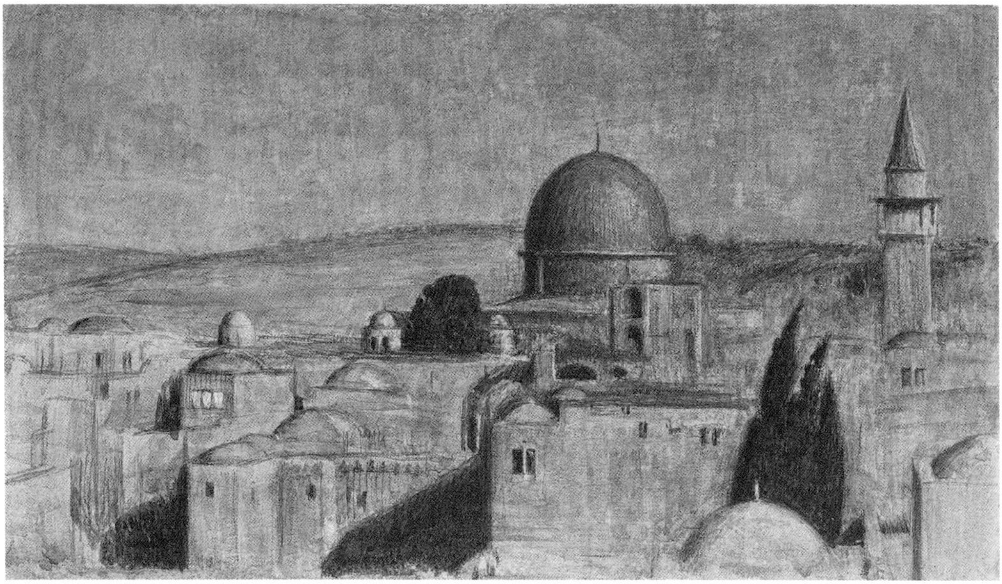

2.2
William Holman Hunt,
The Holy City,
1854

borders appear enamelled with emeralds, how the water is very jasper, and all the preciousness above is dropped molten into it, and the diamond stream of the Jordan carries its burden of colour along.

To Ruskin, Geneva is 'one lambent jewel', and the river around it, reflecting the Alps, is twisting 'the light into golden braids . . . inlaid with turquoise enamel'.[18] The location is different, but the language generalises nature into a similar vision of 'aquamarine, ultramarine, violet-blue, gentian-blue, peacock-blue, river-of-paradise blue glass of a painted window melted in the sun'.

Ruskin's 'unearthly' paradise matches Hunt's characterisation of his vision as a glimpse of 'some region of heaven'. Ruskin's earlier record of the Alps strikes a parallel chord: 'They were as clear as crystal, sharp on the pure horizon sky, tinged with rose by the sinking sun . . . the seen walls of lost eden could not have been more beautiful to us; nor more awful, round heaven, the walls of sacred death'.[19] Both writers repeatedly employ an imagery of precious stones to describe natural phenomena. For example, from Graham's tower 'the calm picture appeared as formed in mother of pearl' (2, 18). Their accounts thus recall the heavenly vision of the New Jerusalem in Revelation, also offered by an angel from the top of a mountain: 'And he carried me away in the spirit to a great and high mountain, and shewed me that great city . . . and her light was like unto a stone most precious, even like a jasper stone, clear as crystal . . . and the city was of pure gold, like unto clear glass'.[20] The Bible lists the foundations of the city as jasper, sapphire, emerald, topaz and quartz; the gates are pearl, and the streets of the city are 'of pure gold, as it were transparent glass'.[21] Hunt and Ruskin adopt a revelatory language to contribute a visionary, religious dimension to their descriptions of earthly phenomena.

The description of Mount Hermon is a clear demonstration of Hunt's conviction that nature provides its own sermon to the privileged artistic eye. This point is underlined by the quotation from Carlyle at the beginning of the chapter: 'The eye sees what it brings with it the power to see.' Hunt dramatises Carlyle's words by presenting his record in the form of a conversation with his local guide, Issa, beginning: 'men often fail to observe how beautiful God's works are'. 'See!' is repeated throughout the speech, but Issa sulkily refuses to acknowledge any beauty. The episode is summarised on the contents page, in fact, as 'Issa does not appreciate the scene' (2, v).

Hunt refines the vision of the landscape by employing Issa's blunt dismissal of his eulogy to remind the reader of the alternative, material, nature of the vision as 'rock, dirt and water'. Hunt's 'glory of these golden fields' and 'plain . . . enamelled with emeralds' are, to Issa, merely 'common maize and trees'. Issa's description is, of course, strictly valid, or 'true' and Hunt accepts this perspective: 'Yes! Yes! I am a madman', but, privately, he continues to enjoy the scene. He implies that he can perceive both his own *and* Issa's view. This addition takes the text beyond the topographical and emphasises the point that the artist/narrator has the capacity to see a higher meaning in the material, drawing the two together within his single viewpoint.

Hunt's prosaic appraisal of the landscape via the medium of Issa is reminiscent of Ruskin's physical analysis of nature in the first volume of *Modern Painters*, in particular his section 'Of the Truth of Earth'. This begins: 'By the truth of earth, we mean the faithful representation of the facts and forms of the bare ground.'[22] Initially, the text restricts itself to the geological nature of the earth's structure, using scientific language. On the subject of mountains it adopts metaphors of anatomy, introducing a degree of personification whilst preserving the scientific tone: 'Mountains are to the rest of the body of the earth what violent muscular action is to the body of man.' This is eventually elaborated into spiritual hyperbole, however: 'fiery peaks, which with heaving bosoms and exulted limbs, with the clouds drifting like hair from their bright foreheads, lift up their Titan hands to heaven, saying, "I live for ever!"' This reprises 'there shall be no more death', at the beginning of the passage from Revelation.[23]

Both Hunt and Ruskin unify their binary viewpoint through the common factor of authorial vision. The artistic eye is privileged and able to 'show' an extra spiritual dimension in the manner of the angel in Revelation. Ruskin proposes Tintoretto as an example of this artistic gift: 'Tintoretto's intensity of imagination is such that there is not the commonest subject to which he will not attach a range of suggestiveness almost limitless; nor a stone, leaf or shadow, nor anything so small, but he will give it meaning and oracular voice.'[24] *Pre-Raphaelitism* claims: 'It cannot be too clearly reasserted that *Pre-Raphaelitism* in its purity was the frank worship of Nature, kept in check by selection and directed by the spirit of imaginative purpose . . . [Its purpose was] in the fields of Nature and under the sky of Heaven frankly to picture her healthful beauty and strength' (2, 452). Horace Vernet's historically accurate 'Bible pictures' are, by contrast, dismissed as 'destitute of poetic fire' (1, 149). Mere realism, such as that of Issa, is not enough.

In the context of nineteenth-century respect for empirical observation, the artistic I/eye passes from scientific and objective to spiritual and subjective and the latter is able to borrow authenticity from the former. Thus, as Ruskin says, the scientific 'laws' of landscape 'become the foundation of all other truths'.[25] This notional category of 'truth' allows the particular vision of the narrator to be both specialised (more perceptive than Issa, Vernet or Graham) and generalised into an inclusive objectivity. The memoir's religious conception of a design in nature and its protagonist as one who can objectively 'recognise', describe and 'teach others to see'[26] are dependent on this position.

Just as the visionary element of the scene is ascribed to the special sensitivity of the artist, so the descriptions themselves are elevated in terms of art, in particular pigment and jewellery. For Hunt, both the view from Graham's tower and of Mount Hermon are *already* 'pictures'. The creative perceptions in the text represent the creation of the 'Master Artist', God. The reproduction of the landscape in the form of a secondary artefact is presented as a direct reflection of a scene that is divinely arranged. This conflation of describing and viewing authenticates a sacred reading of nature.

Hunt's expression of this idea differs from Ruskin's in one significant respect, however. *Modern Painters* deepens its description through a seamless evolution of language, but *Pre-Raphaelitism* separates material and spiritual readings through the introduction of Issa's subsidiary gaze. Ruskin makes extravagant claims for immortality, in keeping with the revelatory tone, but Hunt reminds us, 'It will not last long!' The use of two voices recalls the anxieties about alternative views and consensus discussed in Chapter 1. It creates a dislocation between the physical and the metaphysical and points to a discomfort with the relationship between the two kinds of perception; an awareness of the possibility of at least two appearances of natural form and two viewpoints of it, the one sacred, the other mortal.

The careful presentation of Issa's alternative, material point of view therefore simultaneously authenticates and undermines the protagonist's own inspired perception. The linguistic link that unites the factual and the spiritual within the single eye of the artist is 'Yes! Yes!

I am a madman.' This phrase is itself ambiguous, and boldly calls the reader's bluff, challenging him or her to agree and so to dismiss the previous two pages as insane fantasy. Hunt's integrity is dependent on his status relative to Issa's. The opinion of a servant, a heathen and a foreigner is weighed against that of the narrator, an Englishman, a Christian and an artist. The special eye of the artist is stressed by requiring the reader to acknowledge it in order to make sense of the episode within the context of the memoir of which he is the hero. The text admits the possibility of a perception of the material at odds with the Christian idea of nature as part of a divine plan, and thus effectively raises the stakes. The validity of the account focuses questions about Hunt's identity as a Christian and as an artist. A Christian, artistic viewpoint is asserted, but the alternative, mere 'rock, dirt and water', provides a background of anxiety about impermanence, relativism and about the artist's 'oracular' powers of sight and representation.

Any acknowledgement of the difference between seeing and describing will undermine belief and self-belief. The description of Mount Hermon constructs a spiritualised landscape through the manipulation of language, but elsewhere the memoir rejects manipulations, eloquence and fable: 'we saw no profit in relying on a vision, however beautiful it might be' (1, 159). Issa's intrusion reflects what Errington describes as a 'tension . . . between the perception of the scientist, anxious to explain and classify, and that of the artist or religious contemplative'.[27] The passage about Mount Hermon reflects the overall structure of the memoir in its attempt to represent a synthesis of sensual and imaginative vision, but the opposing voice is a reminder that the imaginative component is literally not visible, and brings with it anxiety that the description might represent not the inspired apprehension of truth, but 'fantasy', the invention of a 'madman'.

The private landscape

Hunt's diaries exhibit a similarly intense, but unstable, response to the landscape of the Holy Land. The assertion that the idea for *The Scapegoat* was suggested to him by the 'extraordinary scene of beautifully arranged, horrible wildness'[28] of the Dead Sea (plate 8) again constructs the sacred image as found in nature, while the tale of his lonely deprivations there privileges his heroic role and eye. A box in John Rylands Library contains a few large scribbled pages written during the second visit in November 1854, when the painting was executed. This informal journal has much in common with the description of Mount Hermon. It mentions the Old Testament associations of the place,[29] and a feeling of being in God's presence.

The surroundings are portrayed as having been 'arranged' by God to contain a moral message: 'if in all there are sensible figures of men's secret deeds and thoughts then is this the horrible figure of sin'. Hunt sees his own picture as 'undertaking a work of similar value in conveying important knowledge'. The landscape is again spiritualised through its characterisation as artefact and the artist is conflated with the Creator.

The distant mountains are described in familiar, revelatory terms: 'beautiful as precious stones', but the record is highly incoherent and also includes contradictory characteristics; they are 'dry and scorched':

> the rose colour is the burnt ashes of the grate the golden plain is the salt and naked sand. the sea is heaven's own blue like a diamond more lovely in a kings diadem than in the mines of Indes but as it gushes up through broken ice like salt on the beach, it is black, full of asphalt scum – and in the hand slimy, and smarting as a sting. No one can stand and say it is not accursed by God.

The sea is 'heaven's own blue,' the mountains 'beautiful as precious stones,' the sands 'golden,' but, the journal reminds us that, in *fact*, the sea is broken salt, slimy, stinging and black, the mountains are ashes and the golden plain is 'salt and naked sand'. This alternative, material identification is, however, then wound back on itself to become visionary again, but negative this time, a manifestation of 'deceit', recalling 'the lake which burneth with fire and brimstone: which is the second death', in *Revelation*[30]: 'earth joys at hand but hell gaping behind a stealthy terrible enemy forever'.

The physical and spiritual perceptions attributed to this landscape in 1854 are more confused than they are in the description of Mount Hermon. The three layers – metaphysical heaven, physical earth, metaphysical hell – alternate in a muddled fashion. In parallel to this, the gaze described by the text flits uncomfortably backwards and forwards from the distant sea, to actual physical contact, 'in the hand slimy, and smarting as a sting'. Within the same sentence, the sea is both intense blue (far), and black (near). The far connotes beauty and the near connotes ugliness, yet this spatial logic is reversed in the conclusion, 'earth joys at hand but hell gaping behind'.

Pointon notes how *Pre-Raphaelitism* re-presents the journey to the Dead Sea, inscribing a colonial and Protestant ideology into the tale of the hero's encounters with the local men.[31] The description of the place itself is also modified. In comparison to the journal, the memoir is surprisingly reticent about its appearance. Most detail is found in the account of an earlier visit with friends (1, 456–9), but even this is unusually brief and prosaic, comprising geological observations such as the shape of limestone outcrops. It lists place names and includes a map. Topographical actuality is further stressed by directing the reader to the published account of a travelling companion, William Beaumont's *A Diary of a Journey to the East, in the Autumn of 1854* (1856). Reminiscence is carefully grounded in fact and other texts, suppressing the imaginative augmentation displayed in the diary. Those intensely subjective, spiritual reactions are replaced by a reference to another text, the Bible: 'We had before our eyes the region, the very name of which has become a proverb of God's Judgment.' A rainbow conveniently acts as a 'celestial image of Heaven's mercy . . . while afar retreated the murmuring thunder, leaving peaceful beauty to reign instead' (1, 456). The journal experience of contrasting characteristics is put in order. The fluctuating gaze is now adjusted logically through accounts of the movements of the group. At a distance, the sea is still blue and the mountains 'amethystine' and the paradox of near and far is organised through a measured description of the arrival at the shore and a swim in the sea. The inviting water becomes stinging and dangerous once it is entered, but is, nonetheless, the eventual cause of the healing of cuts and scratches.

Negative material aspects are rationalised into a hierarchy dominated by Christian hope. God's message is nicely displayed through a construction of cursed desolation with redemptive accessories, rainbow and healing salt. The point is underlined by a repeated reminder that Hunt is all the time committing the scene to memory in order to assess its suitability as a background to *The Scapegoat*. The redemptive message of the picture itself therefore acts as an augmenting subtext. As in the description of Mount Hermon, the landscape is made meaningful by means of cultural associations, the Bible and Hunt's picture (figure 2.3).

The memoir's record of the second visit (1, 472–96) emphasises narrative action again, the practicalities of travelling, camping and the antics of the local men. Secondary literary references are used once more: 'that bitumous lake where Sodom flamed' (1, 495). The sense of wilderness is emphasised in this account because the artist is now alone. A constant stress on the dangers of the place promotes his valiant role in 'investigating' the 'heroic drama' which he seeks to represent (1, 349). Whereas the objective eye is buttressed by the initial geographical and historical explorations of the group, the special ability to see spiritual truths is reserved for the later, individual venture when the painting is being made. Hunt is described as telling instructive tales to his native servants while they beg him to become their leader. Their ignorance and superstition emphasise the bravery and clear-sightedness of the protagonist and prefigure the role of Issa and Max.

Both the diary and *Pre-Raphaelitism* insist that truth, a spiritual message, is literally inscribed within the physical landscape, placed there by God to be read by the true artist. In 1876 Hunt writes to Thomas Combe: 'the Dead Sea is I think the most extraordinary picture in

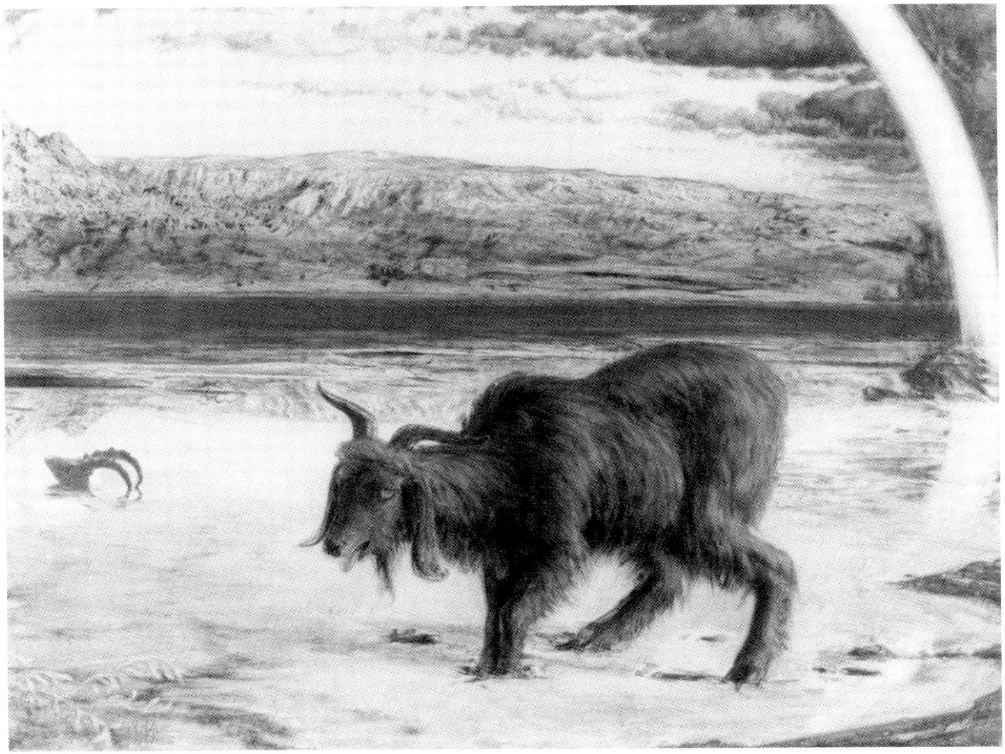

2.3
William Holman Hunt,
The Scapegoat,
finished sketch, 1854–58

the world'.[32] Hunt's diary does not, however, achieve the neatness displayed in *Pre-Raphaelitism*. Several constructions of the place exist simultaneously. Although the notes from the second visit were probably intended to be used for published accounts of his venture,[33] their rambling quality gives them some credence as a more spontaneous response to the scene itself. The account is no less religious, but the landscape insists on multiple associations, producing a confused description which is more vivid, but less rational and less securely optimistic. A sense of danger and ugliness alternates with a vision of heaven, rather than being subordinate to it. Hunt's dependence on the material to source his religious convictions is perhaps problematic; the very immediacy of the experience recorded in the diary leaves him susceptible to contradictory responses, not yet fully ordered into a coherently hopeful 'picture'.

This disordered structure and language continues throughout the account. Capital letters and punctuation are omitted, syntax is irregular and deletions are common. The content, too, is erratic. Vivid dreams are recorded, veering from idyllic meetings with friends to 'savage laughter'. The text itself swings from a conviction of safety in God's presence, to fear of attack from bandits and meditations on hell, self-doubt and loneliness: 'all works undertaken here partake of the curse of the country'. The bravery of *Pre-Raphaelitism* splits into alternate expressions of profound fear or fantasies of being 'chosen'. Discomfort becomes part of a 'ripening . . . for the masters hand if we have chosen to be graften ~~with~~ into His crabbed stock', but Hunt wonders, 'what shall follow these 27 years of disordered preparation?'[34] The redemptive interpretation, so firmly attached to the scene later on, is uncertain and the point of view fluctuates. The account is full of gaps, as if left to be filled in later. Both language and vision become fragmented and insecure.

The first lines of the diary parallel the artist's reading of the landscape with the reading of a painting. However, the landscape is not a work of art and the subsequent *process* of seeing and describing proves ambiguous. The relationship between material and religious truth proposed in *Pre-Raphaelitism* is perhaps less easily maintained at the site of immediate experience and direct representation in the form of the journal and the painting.

Hunt's diary of the following year contains notes about the scene of Mount Hermon described in the memoir. This record is entirely visionary and is almost interchangeable with the initial description of the Dead Sea from a distance: 'I seem no longer alone . . . but in God's audience . . . the sun is glowing to the pure hue of precious stones on the Mountain . . . I hear God speak in the solemn sunset hour'.[35] The similarity of these two accounts of different places, and the generalised literary language, suggests a disassociation of spiritualised vision from particular experience. This strengthens a sense that Hunt's Christian readings are conceptual, alternative to a close exploration of the real, and reinforces a sense of a tension between two modes of looking.

The journal has been ruminating on death shortly before and now adds, 'may I never lose one jot of such a charge as is in this dying sunlit journey'. It mentions giving Issa some opium as a medicine on the preceding page, and as Hunt, too, has been ill, it is possible that he is under the influence of the drug when he is writing. Whatever, this record of his experience of the landscape completely surpasses any measured incorporation of the rational and the material; it is openly fantastical, glorious, but redolent of death. This is acknowledged when Hunt recounts his dreams the following night and describes waking and 'lying with the pulse of strange waters beating the nights silence . . . I wonder which is the more like a dream'.[36]

The fantastical, revelatory tone contrasts with the vivid sense of hostile physical conditions of the Dead Sea diary. This is perhaps a product of the passive role of the narrator. The ride past Mount Hermon is undertaken in the character of traveller rather than painter. The experience is remote, not requiring the exacting scrutiny of visual representation. Precise observations do not disrupt the flight of fancy.

The published version introduces a balancing objectivity in order to construct the artist protagonist as sane, privy to the physical as well as the metaphysical.

Hunt's journal from his second stay in Jerusalem, while painting *The Shadow* in 1872, is the least literary in its tone and seems closer to a private diary than notes for a memoir. It features a repetitive structure and includes a great deal of material which would be inappropriate for publication, such as meal times and technical notes. This fascinating text constructs a particular kind of preoccupation with the environment which supports my contention that the above accounts reveal a way of seeing which attempts, but fails, to conflate the physical with optimistic metaphysical meanings during close confrontation with visual appearance and the mimetic painting process.

The journal comprises brief, daily jottings and is conspicuously dominated by notes on the weather. Each entry begins with an assessment of conditions outside, and even subtle hourly changes are recorded. In *Pre-Raphaelitism*, this is condensed into a familiar account of the difficulties Hunt has experienced in his pursuit of verisimilitude. His insistence on painting in a consistent dawn or dusk light necessitates rising before sunrise to set up on the roof in the hope of fine weather and results in loss of time and effort when it proves to be cloudy (2, 292–3). In fact, Hunt seems to have conducted a substantial amount of painting indoors. This makes the persistent obsession with the vagaries of light and temperature in the diary seem eccentric. Observations about the weather are also often couched in vivid language: 'clouds like ploughshares and misshapen overhanging rocks'.[37] 'Before the sun rises there is a break in the clouds in the east but this closes like angered lips and the rain comes again.'[38] The emphasis is on ugliness, flux and unpredictability. The personification in these quotes suggests a reading of environmental conditions which is rooted in practicality but which expands into a sense of abstract malice that goes beyond the picturesque. In a letter to William Bell Scott at this time, Hunt even describes his painting materials as hostile; everyday implements become weapons and turn against their owner.[39]

The diary lists frustration after frustration in attempts to complete *The Shadow*. When sun is predicted, he gets up early to find it cloudy; when he has despaired of sun, he is cruelly awakened by its rays to find that he is too late to prepare for a perfect morning. When he has painted indoors, viewing in the sun shows him that he has got it wrong, and so on. This exaggerated sense of elemental hostility recalls the Dead Sea record. One wonders whether Hunt's choice of uncomfortable locations and fleeting light effects, such as those of dawn, dusk and moonlight, for many of his pictures, is not related to a preoccupation with the inevitable difficulty of their capture, or whether a sense of adversity is exaggerated. Either way, there is a clear textual obsession with the vagaries of nature and a frequent construction of material conditions as disordered and dark, producing unreliable, changeable perceptions and undermining the completion of the image and the authority of the artist.

A contrastingly positive concept of environment is provided by verbal sketches of excursions into the countryside about Jerusalem. These take place, by definition, in the context of leisure rather than labour, like the trip to Mount Hermon. Their tone is one of timeless, fruitful beauty rather than changeable and destructive grotesque. An account of an escape from the studio, in the midst of struggles against wind, cold and cloud, is typical. The environment suddenly becomes benign and healthy and intense delight is expressed at 'the freshness of the air and the beauty of the tender herb covered hills'.[40] Hunt writes to Stephens, 'a ride down to Jaffa will be regarded by me as a reprieve from Death or worse'.[41] This kind of description is common to all reports of rides during this period, repeatedly noting the golden corn, verdant hills and luminous skies.

Such accounts reprise relations of other tours about Palestine, such as an 1855 trip to Nazareth, which again produces tributes to the loveliness of the fertile countryside.[42] The first view of the Sea of Galilee is described as 'like a precious sapphire, a precious gift, an espousal gem to confirm a bridal of some more righteous age'.[43] These words again recall Revelation: 'And I saw a new heaven and a new earth . . . and I, John, saw the holy city, New Jerusalem . . . as a bride adorned for her husband'.[44] The following lines, where God promises 'no more death, neither sorrow, nor crying, neither shall there be any more pain', underline the consolatory nature of these excursions. This sense of overcoming death is explained in a letter to Combe, where Hunt portrays his rides into the countryside as an antidote to his hardship and illness and describes a feeling of invincibility as he faces down hostile Bedouins.[45]

The stress on potency and health associated with these scenes contrasts sharply with the constant fears that adverse conditions are undermining fitness and strength in the studio. There, letters and diaries speaks constantly of 'pain',[46] and illness. Like the Dead Sea, the place is 'fearful', Hunt's body is 'disordered',[47] and he continually fears death. Nature is, therefore, alternately identified as beautifully ordered, promising health, rest and redemption, or as hostile, dangerous and disordered, a wilderness.

Negative readings of the elements are always associated with times when Hunt is actually painting. The passive enjoyment of roaming about the countryside eliminates the issue of clear vision, the close grappling with the real effects of light and weather demanded by his work. Pointon notes Hunt's 'sinister and contradictory' description of the Dead Sea, and detects 'extreme polarities' in all his journals, which she generalises into an overall response to the Middle East.[48] Chapter 8 will suggest that the phenomenon is also symptomatic of a dislocation between interior and exterior perceptions prompted by mimetic examination.

In very simple terms, these texts reveal a general difficulty in reconciling a whole and benign image of God with the inconclusive and threatening experience of his creation. Hunt's diaries indicate a tendency to respond to landscape in a less coherent way than in *Pre-Raphaelitism*, offering responses which vary from religious ecstasy to despondency. In the memoir these alternating sensations of grandiose oneness with God and confusion, fear and threat are replaced by an artistic self-image which attempts a balanced accommodation of both the visionary and the objective. Later rewritings, however, only partly disguise this difficult relationship with perception and immediate experience. Facts continue to haunt and undermine the synthetic I/eye of the text. Meaningless material evidence intrudes. Just as the 'golden plain' is revealed as 'salt and naked sand', at the Dead Sea, so 'the glory of these golden fields', at Mount Hermon, is disturbed by Issa's identification, 'rock, dirt and water'.

The journals reveal processes of description at a stage of greater incompleteness and insecurity than in published versions. They dramatise the doubts about authenticity of viewpoint and interpretation and the discomfort with evidence which have been detected throughout *Pre-Raphaelitism*. The disturbed viewpoint and self-image at the Dead Sea gives us insight into the unstable narrator of the memoir and its undertone of 'madman'. The internal contradiction within the phrase, 'beautifully arranged, horrible wilderness' encapsulates this. The Dead Sea is at the same time 'arranged', implying the hand of 'the Director who directs all', and a 'wilderness' implying absence and exile.[49] Beauty implies access to God's plan, a privileged, artistic view, whereas horror is a manifestation of disorder, mortality and alienation from God.

Hunt's constructions of landscape are associated with a state of belief and sense of self in special relation to a divine format. The materialism of his religious thinking, the need for the abstract to be manifest in the physical, creates a paradox. The artist's observations represent an inspired apprehension of truth. However, the diverse and random nature of immediate perception does not ally itself easily to a desired and imagined sense of authority and order. The alternatives presented by the 'beautifully arranged, horrible wilderness', or changeable light and, more importantly, by the varying subjective and deductive gaze of the witness, fracture the quality of absolute coherence, wholeness, safety and hope which Hunt attributes to creation and to his own sense of seeing clearly.

The memoir and the paintings attempt to repair these anxieties. The artefact performs a consoling function, ordering 'disordered' experience and neutralising the doubts about physical and spiritual safety that are implied by an experience of non-alignment between sensual and spiritual perceptions. In this way, they attempt to reconstruct the artist, and the eye of the artist, as authoritative.

Hunt's diary describes his first sight of Nazareth:

> Sweet Nazareth of Galilee, never did I imagine thee so lovely in all the many times that I have tried to picture the abode of our Lord. The sight of it this night crowds into my mind a thousand remembrances from the days of my schooltime when I first read the history of the Master who lived here humbly and in sorrow, with these bitter days when I lost my blind childish trust till the time when again God brought me ~~in sorrow~~ to kneel before him and with this all my friends who live in the hope he brought us.[50]

It is implied that faith has actually been found in the concrete view of Nazareth. However, the deletion of 'in sorrow' and its replacement with 'in the hope he brought us' seems to re-enact the difficult process of translating the visual, physical and emotional discomforts of experience into an optimistic, sacred vision. It recalls the addition of the symbolic goat to the Dead Sea shore. In both instances, landscape is modified into a hopeful type of redemption.

Art-making is presented as an oracular 'reflection' of the original act of creation, a concrete witness to religious fantasy. Like the memoir, the painting becomes a site at which an attempt is made to align the subjective and the objective, the visible and the invisible. Hunt's private writings exhibit an unusual tendency to rail against the vagaries of experience, however: setbacks, illness, lack of money, support, models, and, in particular, changing light and weather parallel the preoccupation with difficulty and criticism displayed in the memoir. I believe that this sensitivity is a response to the threat that these phenomena imply to self-image and faith. In particular, those conditions which actively hinder painting frustrate a need to enact and picture order.

The next two chapters will establish the importance of Christian hope to Hunt's self-image and its vulnerability to evidence and experience. An interrogation of the religious conviction set out in Hunt's work dramatises the troubled relationship between belief and reality. These issues, in turn, inform the actual handling of the materials of his paintings, which I shall explore in the final chapters.

Notes

1 Williamson, *Hunt*, p 17
2 Maas, *Hunt*; Wheeler, M., 'The Light of the World as "True and Sacred Art": Ruskin and William Holman Hunt', in *Ruskin's Artists: Studies in*

the Victorian Visual Economy, Papers from the Ruskin Programme, Lancaster University, ed. R. Hewison (Aldershot: Ashgate, 2000), pp 111–30

3 Vidler, A. *The Church in an Age of Revolution* (1961) (Harmondsworth, Middlesex: Penguin,1990), pp 112–13

4 Errington and Landow cite a broad range of theological texts, both biblical and contemporary, which Hunt seems to have studied in order to glean inspiration for the complex ideas of his paintings of the early 1850s; Errington, L., *Social and Religious Themes in English Art 1840–1860* (London: Garland, 1984), chapter 7; Landow, *Typological Symbolism*, pp 39–45

5 Errington, *Themes*, pp 457–8

6 Vaughan, W., 'Realism and Tradition in Religious Art', *'Sind Briten hier?' Relations between British and Continental Art 1680–1880* (Munich: Wilhelm Fink Verlag, 1981), p 208; also Pointon, 'Artist as Ethnographer', p 30

7 Vaughan, 'Realism', pp 218–19

8 'Hope' is a recognised theological term at this time, used by Paul, 'the hope and resurrection of the dead', Acts 23: 6, Wheeler, M., *Heaven, Hell and the Victorians* (Cambridge: Cambridge University Press, 1994), pp 6–7

9 'Religion and Art', *Contemporary Review*, 71 (1897), p 43

10 Letter to Tupper, 17 September 1872, *Correspondence*, p 167

11 Landow, *Typological Symbolism*, p 132

12 Errington, *Themes*, p 265

13 Ibid., and Landow, *Typological Symbolism*, pp 5–10

14 Letter to Ruskin, 6 November 1880, quoted M. Allentuck, 'William Holman Hunt, Monk and Ruskin: An unpublished letter', *Apollo*, 97 (1973), p 156

15 Ruskin, *Modern Painters*, 2 (1846), in *Works*, 4, p 43

16 'Religion and Art', p 43

17 Pointon, 'Artist as Ethnographer', pp 23–5

18 Ruskin, *Praeterita* (1885), in *Works*, 35, p 327

19 Ibid., p 115

20 Revelation 21: 9–18

21 Ibid., 19–21

22 Ruskin, *Modern Painters*, 1 (1843), in *Works*, 3, pp 425–30

23 Revelation, 21: 4

24 Ruskin, *Modern Painters*, 2, in *Works*, 4, p 262

25 Ruskin, *Modern Painters*, 1, in *Works*, 3, p 425

26 'Religion and Art', p 43

27 Errington, *Themes*, p 271

28 Journal, November 1854, John Rylands University Library of Manchester (hereafter JRL), MS 1210, 4v

29 Ibid., 4v–7v

30 Revelation 21: 5–8

31 Pointon, 'Artist as Ethnographer', p 23

32 Letter to Combe, 19 October 1876, JRL, MS 1213, 30

33 Pointon, 'Artist as Ethnographer', p 23

34 Journal, November 1854, JRL, MS 1210, 6

35 Journal, 1 November 1855, JRL, MS 1211, 73–4
36 Ibid., 2 November 1855, 75v
37 Journal, 16 February 1872, JRL, MS 1212, 3
38 Ibid., 20 February 1872, 11v
39 Letter to Scott, 20 February 1871, Scott, W.B., *Some Autobiographical Notes*, ed. W. Minto (2 vols, London: Osgood, McIlvaine, 1892), 2, pp 102–3 (hereafter cited as *Notes*)
40 Journal, 10 March 1872, JRL, MS 1212, 14
41 Letter to Stephens, 24 July 1871, BL, MS Don. e 67, 66, also letter to Scott, 30 September 1871, *Notes*, 2, p 104
42 Journal, May 1855, JRL, MS 1211, 69–77
43 Ibid., 27 May 1855, 70v
44 Revelation, 21: 1–2
45 Letter to Combe, 6 May 1870, JRL, MS 1213, 22
46 Journal, 2 March 1872, JRL, MS 1212, 12v
47 Ibid., 9 April 1872, 19. In his analysis of Mark Twain's *The Innocents Abroad* (1869), Sander Gilman suggests that the confident Anglo Saxon sense of the otherness and inferiority of the peoples of the Holy Land can be destabilised by direct experience of it and be associated with hysterical apprehensions of illness, *Health and Illness: Images of Difference* (London: Reaktion Books, 1995), pp 100–2
48 Pointon, 'Artist as Ethnographer' p 39
49 Journal, November 1854, JRL, MS 1210, 4v–6
50 Journal, 23 April 1855, JRL, MS 1211, 69v

3

Self-image: child and prophet

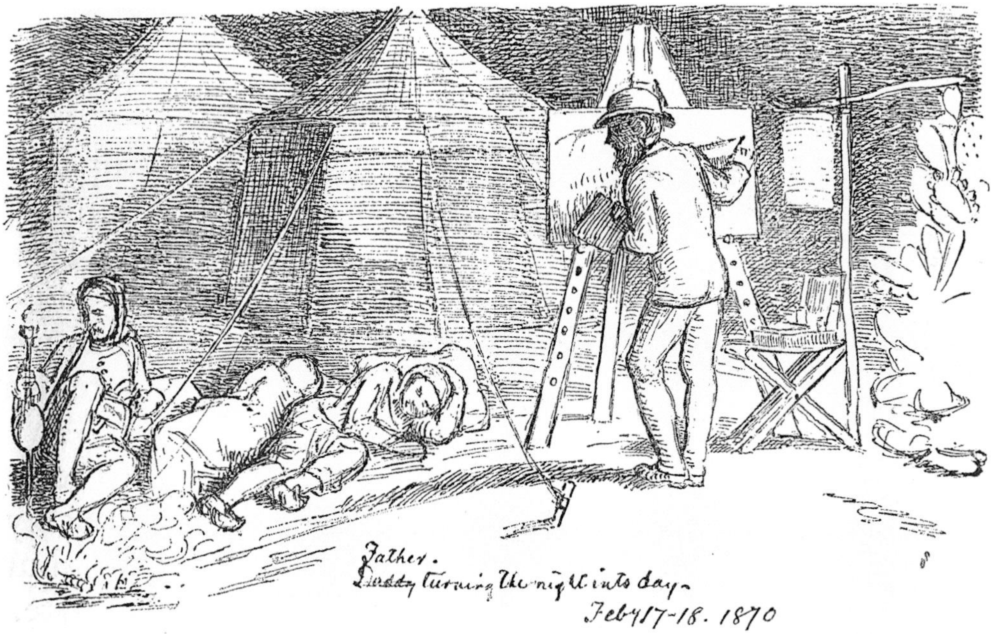

LETTER TO MY CHILD.

3.1
William Holman Hunt,
Letter to My Child; Father/Daddy turning the night into day Feb 17–18 1870,
Pre-Raphaelitism, 2, 299

Pre-Raphaelitism constructs art-making as prophecy, 'a priest's service in the temple of Nature, where ampler graces are revealed to those who have eyes to see' (1, xv), and Hunt's sacred interpretations of the Palestinian landscape imply an equally sacred construction of self. Revelation exhorts the visionary:

> Write: for these words are true and faithful . . . I will give unto him that is athirst of the fountain of the water of life freely.
>
> He that overcometh shall inherit all things; and I will be his God, and he shall be my son.[1]

This priestly aspect of Hunt's public artistic identity has been explored by several writers,[2] but the letters and journals reveal a more fragile sense of prophetic authority, very different from the rigid dogmatism by which he is usually characterised. The sage alternates with a different, childlike persona which informs the unstable narrator of the memoir and the ambivalent perceptions of environment illustrated in the previous chapter, as well as the iconography of the paintings of this period.

The prophet

Hunt's concept of the artist/prophet is elucidated by his response to meeting the Zionist, Henry Wentworth Monk, in Jerusalem in 1855. His letters of the time echo Monk's literal conception of the Old Testament as a practical 'mandate' for modern men to follow the example of its prophets, and his portrait depicts the bearded Canadian bearing a rolled-up copy of *The Times* as though it were a biblical scroll (plate 9) as Christ does in *The Beloved* (1898, Royal Collection, figure 9.2). Hunt, like Monk, constructs modern events as part of a millennial progress towards God's kingdom on earth (1, 434).[3] The memoir alludes to Carlyle's popular conception of history as a cyclical process culminating in the modern day by heading chapter 13 with a quotation from *Signs of the Times* (1829):

> The Christian religion under every theory of it, in the believing or the unbelieving mind, must ever be regarded as the crowning glory, or rather the life and soul of our own modern culture. How did Christianity arise and spread among men? It arose in the mystic deeps of man's soul; and was spread abroad by the preaching of the word; by simple, altogether natural and individual efforts; and flew, like hallowed fire, from heart to heart, until all were purified and illuminated by it, and it's heavenly light shone, and it still shines, and (as sun or star) will ever shine through the whole dark destinies of man. (2, 337)

Hunt's inclusion of this extract, his readiness to take Monk's millennial predictions seriously and his interest in Strauss and Renan's 'biographies' of Christ[4] illustrate a specialised version of Carlyle's idea: a belief in the Bible as a material history continuing into the present.

Hunt's lifelong fascination with Jerusalem can be seen as an attempt to explore the biblical promise of a New Jerusalem, and his prophetic relation to it, in surprisingly concrete terms. As I have shown, metaphors from Revelation haunt descriptions of the surrounding landscapes. Most, if not all, of Hunt's works deal with enlightenment and the role of prophesy.[5] In particular, depictions of Christ and prophetic types are continually informed by millennial ideas from Revelation and scriptures which contain other important references to the resurrection and Last Judgement, such as Job, Isaiah, the Gospels and Corinthians: the frame of *The Scapegoat* bears a quotation from Isaiah which looks forward to Christ's second coming (plate 1). The juxtaposition of the old and new law in *The Finding* alludes to an overturning of the established order in favour of a 'new dispensation',[6] recalling the artist's role in establishing a new dispensation in art and thus relating to Monk's understanding of the modern prophet. *The Shadow* also looks forward to the future; it is intended to be a subject which 'will be prized in the Millennium'.[7] The king's gifts in the chest refer to the Old Testament prophesies of the coming Messiah, just as the globes in *The Triumph* image 'the millennium which was to be the mature outcome of the advent of the Messiah'.[8]

These iconographical and literary themes extend, moreover, to embrace real events. In *The Pursuit of the Millennium*, Norman Cohn sets out the essential tradition that the 'last days', a time of war, disorder, suffering and temptation of Christians, during which many will succumb, will be followed by the establishment of a New Jerusalem and the redemption of the faithful, or more strictly, of the martyrs.[9] Hunt, like Monk, represents his own times as the 'last days'. He writes to Stephens in 1863: 'The prophet [Monk] is here on his way to Palestine again with a firm expectation of seeing the millennium commence in a year or two. I am sure it is wanted for you and me.'[10] The apocalyptic tone of the last chapter of *Pre-Raphaelitism* presents the nineteenth century as corrupt and war-torn. It attacks the French, critics, copyright law, modern art's 'lack of sanity and reverence', 'sickly' literature, the press, and finishes up with 'Constable's prophesy' that British art will soon die out despite its vital role in averting 'the ruin of the nation' (2, 492–3). This unpleasant combination of personal grievance and aggressive, social comment is typical, but becomes more meaningful if viewed in the context of a literal preoccupation with the disorder which traditionally precedes the Last Judgement.

Cohn notes that the millennial 'phantasy' often thrives amongst people who feel persecuted.[11] Although he is speaking of a general social phenomenon, it seems apt to Hunt's individual expressions of embattlement. The private writings clearly construct the artist as at odds with a society which is in the throws of the 'last days'. At the Dead Sea, he writes that 'the time has not yet come' for his 'valuable illustrations of scripture'.[12] In the following year, after meeting Monk, the usual grumbles are supplemented with millennial allusions and a nervous preoccupation with the Crimean War. England has 'no strength to bear judgment', and is undermined by misguided politics and moribund Christian conventions, suitable only 'to keep old cracked tea drinking ladies quiet'.[13] During the same period, Hunt complains to Combe of the irresponsibility of *The Times* and again voices his 'horror' of the war.[14] These concerns are repeated frequently. An undated fragment from his second stay in Jerusalem in the early 1870s speaks of the Prussian war as a fulfilment of 'providence': 'It seems the eternal judgments are fulfilled, at first in humiliation, and then in destruction.'[15] In 1878, Hunt again presents local unrest, and the 'stupidity and dishonesty' of men in the East and in England, as an anticipation of the 'millennium'.[16] He also continually reiterates his scepticism of the established church. He condemns the Jerusalem clergy during both visits to the East, generalising their wealth and showiness into evidence of 'the pomps and vanities of the world'.[17] Their complacency recalls that of the rabbis in *The Finding* in relation to the artist's own Christlike role as a 'signpost of men'.[18]

It is notable that the letters and journals relate the millennial view of the world to individual discomfort, dislocation and difference. The above letter to Combe is typical, mentioning Judgement Day in the context of personal dissatisfactions with social and physical environment: 'I never knew such unceasing bothers as mine. I never get a chance of comfort or repose.' An extraordinary note to Tupper, of the same month, clearly demonstrates a connection between Hunt's ideas of pre-millennial corruption, his own imagined role as God's representative and his consequent persecution. He is concerned that Tupper has been ill:

> – away with it for ever and grow strong . . . I think Jack that God cannot spare any man who calls himself His servant.
>
> Some say we have grown old enough to ~~know~~ /hear/ the sixth trumpet and that we are in the midst of the beginning of the troubles that follow. I don't know that our present battle is part of the great Battle Armageddon.[19] – and there are but few /to whom I would mention such a thought lest/ I should be an instrument of conveying an idea to our army that they had God to fight with; but in good truth our troubles come upon us like a scourge from God and I have the many abominations of which England has been guilty brought to my mind, and I think more often than ever, if not more effectually, of some means of doing my part towards purifying London of some of the impurities therein.[20]

The letter goes on to repeat grievances against the Jerusalem clergy, and then mentions failing to complete *The Scapegoat* in time for sending to the Academy Summer Exhibition because of 'accidents', adverse weather and the fact that 'February cheated us of three days'.

The familiar fixation with weather appears as one aspect of a general and a personal adversity.

This letter is one of the first to exhibit the bitter tone which was to become so common and which habitually constructs a continuum of 'disorder' (a favourite word of Hunt's) which embraces world events, society, accident and environment. A vivid sense of specific surroundings as hostile has been noted in the last chapter. Here, we see a general sense of danger and disagreement between the artist and his circumstances being rationalised as a paradoxically ordered, divine plan which predicts the discomfort suffered by the upholders of the faith in the 'last days'. The artist is identified with the faithful, and even Christ himself. An 1854 description of the journeying Saviour, 'walking with dusty feet along this way, wondered at by some, and laughed at by others',[21] seems to echo Hunt's own predicament in relation to mocking critics in England and his pilgrimage on the same road. A Christlike separation, similar to representations of Christ's agony in the garden, is imaged in a sketch in *Pre-Raphaelitism* (2, 299, figure 3.1). It shows the artist 'turning the night into day' as he paints in the dark while his servants sleep.

Codell observes that *Pre-Raphaelitism* constructs a heroic persona through a range of masculine Victorian paradigms: 'martyr, professional, rebel, Englishman, male, businessman, sage'.[22] Like Pointon, she analyses the way that these virtues are often defined through their difference to that which is foreign.[23] However, the fantasy of a millennial imposition of a Christian order upon a corrupted world can be seen as a function of the *individual*, an extreme realisation of the colonising ideology, an ultimate civilising act which separates the faithful from all others and transcends national boundaries. Hunt tells Ruskin that he has more hope of this coming to pass in Palestine (the site predicted in prophesies) than in England, 'insanely confirmed in all vanity'.[24] His millennial understanding of the corrupted state of society places the modern world *as a whole* as other to the state of the hero, a context of singular, prophetic exclusion and trial.

As James Eli Adams has noted with respect to Victorian writers, this polarisation between individual and social context expresses a crisis of authority at this time which resulted in a masculine ideal of autonomous self-mastery and self-fashioning.[25] The version of the prophetic persona exhibited in Hunt's writings represents a particular dramatisation of Adams's notion of 'inner-worldly asceticism', which differs in one significant respect. Unlike his protagonists, Tennyson, Kingsley or Pater, it takes the familiar Carlylean metaphor of artist/priest[26] to literal lengths, acting out a part in the 'last days', in words and deeds, in a physical wilderness, on the actual stage of the Holy Land. Succeeding chapters will show that this materialisation of the prophetic metaphor has several important implications for Hunt's work.

Codell notes, however, that Hunt's self-characterisation is not secure. The constantly shifting, unstable multiplicity of roles adopted by the memoir's protagonist, the attempt to counter relativism by building a universal basis for authority, being all things to all men, is counter-productive.[27] Adams presents tension within varieties of the prophetic persona as a conflict between private mastery of the self and the performance of that mastery. Codell observes a similar opposition between the singular and the collective persona in *Pre-Raphaelitism*. She notes the phenomenon discussed in Chapter 1, that the memoir portrays its hero as affiliated with a variety of characters, such as Rossetti, but is careful to systematically construct the artist as different from, and superior to, all these other participants, even Millais.[28] She connects Hunt's paradoxical interpretation of persecution as a symptom of Christlike privilege, to a basic contradiction within his array of masculine postures, a contradiction between the respected insider and the rebellious outsider, victor and victim. The solitary and misunderstood martyr, or rebel, alternates with the Englishman, the businessman, and the Pre-Raphaelite leader.

Hunt's millennial fantasy is the definitive valorisation of these masochistic exchanges between victim and victor. It relocates the prophetic performance to the stage of the 'last days' before the audience of final Judgement; material difficulty and social non-alignment become rationalised by an interpretation of environment and circumstance as the adversity which is the context of pious 'trial'[29]. Visions of revelatory promise in nature correspond to fantasies of prophetic authority, validation and eventual security. The negative expressions of place noted in the 1854 and 1872 journals are, nonetheless, accompanied by equally negative expressions of self. Behind the memoir's 'Hero as Man of Art . . . braving the hostile landscape',[30] lies a decidedly unheroic, private discourse of fear, humiliation and pain. The representations of the artist which are found in *Pre-Raphaelitism* are more than a manipulation of biographical details into Victorian conventions of heroism. The protagonist's posturings as adventurer, mentor and entrepreneur are also refracted versions of a fundamental fantasy of absolute prophetic singularity which answers privately expressed alienation, hurt and weakness.

The child

Adams, Sussmann and Codell explore public statements of the self, or the inner self, in history, literature and philosophy. The privately constructed persona of letters and journals represents another kind of performance to other kinds of audiences. It is an important facet of the prophet type which casts further light on its instability. Adams makes a powerful call for the recognition of exchanges between traditionally polarised and oversimplified ideals of the masculine and the feminine.[31] Equally important exchanges can be detected between the masculine and the childlike.

Hunt's output is as notable for a proliferation of children as for a proliferation of prophetic types. *The Finding*, *The Triumph* and *May Morning at Magdalen Tower* (1888–91, Lady Lever Art Gallery) are joined by his many portraits of children, such as *Master Hilary the Tracer* (1886, private collection, plate 16). Errington notes that early works, such as *Rienzi* (1849, private collection, plate 19) 'deal with the underdog, or outsider, and . . . an innocent child victim' and that other works, such as *The Eve of St Agnes* (1848, Guildhall Art Gallery, plate 17), *Lorenzo at his Desk in the Warehouse* (1848–50, Musée du Louvre, figure 7.1) and *The Finding*, also situate young protagonists at odds with society.[32] Their resistance against authority imitates the memoir's accounts of the artist's resistance against his father's objections to a vocation as an artist,[33] and his reforming campaigns against the art establishment. Hunt's other writings also stress childhood experience. His 'Notes on the Life of Augustus Egg' emphasises his friend's carefree younger years,[34] just as the memoir contrasts Millais' supportive upbringing and his own difficult family relations. This phenomenon is unexceptional in post-Rousseau, Victorian autobiography, which tends to dwell on formative experiences,[35] but the preoccupation goes deeper than this.

The issue of artistic authority, 'Who is truly an artist?' (1, xiii), is linked to artistic youth and nurture in the memoir's preface. It suggests that the individual artist, and civilisation as a whole, may only reach command and 'maturity' by inheriting the accomplishments of previous masters (1, viii–ix). As Codell notes, however, English art history is portrayed as having, so far, failed to provide such support, producing a 'series of individual efforts and discontinuities'[36]. The memoir's account of the protagonist's life and works is offered as a remedy for future artists. Hunt is proposed as the hero of the Carlylean vision of history, a progressive evolution catalysed by the example of great, sage-like men. But the protagonist has not benefited from any such mentor. He is, therefore, placed in the contradictory position of being a teacher who is himself untaught. This contradiction is neutralised by recourse to the prophetic persona. The true artist gains his insights from heaven, tutoring 'the unordered and anarchic' world into 'wise rule' by virtue of his 'priests service in the temple of nature, whose ampler graces are revealed to those who have eyes to see' (1, xv–xvi).

This paradox of the un-led leader is fleshed out in the first chapters of the memoir. They describe the Vasari-esque legend of the artist's lack of support, the 'obstinate silence' of the father when the twelve year old admits his determination to become a painter (1, 13–14) and the withdrawal from school in favour of work in a warehouse. The lad is depicted as managing to gain employment that is more conducive to his vocation, but the narrative stresses the inappropriateness of the boy's 'juvenility' for this 'trial' and his 'slowness of growth', often making gentle fun of his attempts to educate himself. These 'bunglings' are, at the same time, translated into an aspect of the prophetic role. Again, the transition from child to master is implied to be a function of prophetic singularity. Each incident in the boy's progress is presented as a mechanism of providence. Just as the narrator blames 'fate for having taken me away from school so early', so 'a special fate always kept open my artistic prospects'. The persecution of the actual father and the hostility of patriarchal structures in general (the workplace, the Academy), are presented as the protection of a fantasised father in heaven. Lack of earthly guidance is made up for by a heavenly guide. Worldly insecurity and punishment are once more interpreted as 'trial', paradoxical guarantees of other-worldly security and reward. The young protagonist plays a double, Christlike role, both child and prophet, victim and victor.

The memoir's confident construction of the unnurtured artist going on to nurture English art is, however, undermined by the shrill tone of the final chapters. The books' depiction of a crusading career is eclipsed by the flurry of reprints of negative reviews and by the apocalyptic picture of an unredeemable society, headed for 'ruin', referred to above. The motif of the uncared-for child used to emphasise the heroism of the protagonist, now tends to contradict it. An account of the 'child-like' ideals and 'innocence' of the Brotherhood are, tellingly, imaged through a reference to Millais' *L'enfant du Regiment* (1854–55, Yale Center for British Art): 'the child sleeping on the warrior's tomb amidst surrounding violence and bloodshed' (2, 465). This persistence of child/victim identification sits uncomfortably with the hero's 'robust and manly' image.[37] The exchange between worldly insecurity and punishment and other-worldly security and reward, between child and prophet, is incomplete.

A parallel pattern can be seen in the private writings. Here, the grandiose otherness of the prophet which I have identified also often degenerates into the forlorn otherness of mere neglect. While painting *The Scapegoat* the consoling idea that 'there must be some purpose' in hardship and exile 'as it comes from God',[38] often falters. The journal of work on *The Shadow* also expresses frequent doubts about God and a sense of being hopeless, weak and 'trapped'.[39] The following analysis of these journals and the letters will show that the prophetic persona is both a response to, and destabilised by, another self-image which is vulnerable and confused, which is not sufficiently differentiated from the disorder of the world at large, which doubts God, is unguided and hence powerless to guide. This alternative persona recalls the memoir in that it is often expressed through an obsession with poor parenting and the condition of the child.

The journal of work on *The Scapegoat* describes the picture as the delayed beginning of an artistic and prophetic career. Hunt's achievements before this date, encompassing the establishment of the Pre-Raphaelite movement and the production of at least half a dozen major paintings such as *The Light of the World* (1852–53, Keble College), are, incredibly, dismissed as '27 years of *disordered* preparation' (emphasis added).[40] This raises an important point: the prophetic role referred to in the diary is a *potential* persona, a fantasy of the future. The completion of the painting in hand represents the completion of the man, but this completion remains elusive. In the meantime, present worldly struggles and difficulties, couched in the terminology of the 'last days' are related to a state of incompletion, of childhood.

Throughout Hunt's private writings, a perceived late start and continuing failures of skill are blamed bitterly on a poor upbringing and education similar to that presented in the memoir.[41] Despite further successes after 1860 (for instance, the extraordinary popular and financial success of *The Finding*), references to backward development multiply. Correspondence regularly complains of a lack of 'father's provision', and bemoans the difficulty of negotiating life like a boat 'less than half made'.[42] A letter of 1866 asks Frederick Stephens to gloss over the artist's early hardship in a forthcoming pamphlet, but, in private, it claims that relations always treated him as a 'miserable ne'er-do-well', and speaks ironically of 'the precious flesh and blood trait of family amiability'.[43] In correspondence written during 1870, Hunt continues to describe himself as a 'pleb',[44] denied 'proper training', or 'advantages', and to repeatedly express undifferentiated rancour at the neglect and inadequacies of his family and society.[45] The astonishing frequency of these complaints strikes the reader as, in itself, childish, demonstrating a sense of helplessness and a refusal to accept autonomy or responsibility for the adult condition. The unguided artist becomes victim of, rather than victor over, the disorder of an unguided world.

The pre-millennial world-view contributes to, or at least informs, this sense of personal neglect. An idea of society as trivial and corrupting renders social participation and domestic comfort no less detrimental to artistic vocation than social disregard.[46] Hunt complains to Stephens of loneliness and a desire to have the leisure and income necessary to be with friends or afford the comfort of a 'nice wife and children, & quiet lazing on the sea-sand like other *heathens*' (emphasis added),[47] but sees this luxury as incompatible with the singularity of his pious profession. Family responsibilities are often the subject of acrimony, especially after the death of Hunt's father.[48] Success is dependent on leaving home and country.[49] As Codell says, quoting Kaja Silverman, 'Hunt's masochism is a "drama of the familial structure, which interlocks with the whole social order".'[50]

The attitude to marriage exhibited in the letters reflects this ambivalent attitude to social participation, demonstrating both a child's desire to be included and cared for and a defensive determination to be detached and different, the authoritative other. Happiness at engagement to Fanny Waugh fills Hunt's letters of the summer of 1865,[51] but, five weeks later this has turned into frustration with the new social and financial responsibilities that it brings.[52] He expresses concern about delays to his work, and in autumn 1866, seven months after the wedding, he whisks his heavily pregnant wife away from her family, bound for the Holy Land. They become stranded in Florence, due to a cholera outbreak and the closure of the ports, and Hunt writes from there that he has made arrangements for Fanny, but complains that his painting 'ought to be the first thought'.[53] Fanny dies from puerperal anaemia after the birth of a child, Cyril, shortly afterwards in December 1866. Hunt's letters express both anger that she has not fulfilled her duty of ministering to the artist and the surviving baby, leaving him free to paint, and the intense loneliness and remorse of a man who is 'tragically solitary'.[54] There is, similarly, both resentment and genuine concern over the difficulties of attending to the baby. Hunt insists on caring for his son himself and working on in Florence, refusing to let him be taken by relatives, but complains of the interruption to painting that he causes. The child fails to thrive and is near death when, nine months later, Hunt finally delivers him into the care of Fanny's family in England.

Hunt spends three of the next four years of his son's childhood abroad (August 1869 to July 1871), painting *The Shadow of Death*. Alone in Jerusalem, he writes, 'In my mind all domestic life to me is cursed and hopeless I strove hard to find it not so now while I can direct myself I live only for my work'.[55] In this picture, the appeal of Jesus to God, his back to his mother, echoes the artist's renewed commitment to a fantasised Holy Father and his prophetic role. This shift of identity is expressed in the deletion of 'Daddy', in the inscription of the Christlike sketch 'Father/~~Daddy~~ turning the night into day', which he sent to Cyril (figure 3.1). At other times, however, the conviction that the execution of *The Shadow* is a 'trial', is doubted as only a consoling response to 'struggle'; a letter to Tupper asks whether he has ever really 'had the true painter's instinct'.[56]

The vicissitudes of experience become polarised, alternately interpreted as signs of a childish vulnerability and ineptitude *in* the world and of prophetic otherness *to* the world. The childish self-image both fuels and frustrates the prophetic fantasy. When the artist is included in social and familial structures, he resents the way that business, banality and 'the claims of the weak and the dissatisfied'[57] inhibit the prophetic role. When he is outside them, however, this fantasy fails fully to answer immediate physical, emotional and social insecurities. This pattern illuminates the tension between the collective/singular, victor/victim personae in the memoir.

Hunt's correspondence about Cyril exhibits an analogous confusion between the parental role and that of the child. The artist's inadequacy as a father is related to his neglect as a son. Failure to provide for the child is blamed on an artistic, financial and social precariousness which is seen as a result of the irresponsibility of his own parents and the art establishment. Cyril, in turn, takes on an oddly parental role. His separation is presented as a deprivation to *Hunt*, of the love, comfort and 'teaching which comes as a . . . father, . . . the ~~crowning~~ main class of all in God's school'.[58] The artist's nurture is again linked to that of his child in a letter to Tupper in 1872. This conflates the loss of a wife with Cyril's loss of a mother. The child still 'wears upon him the sign of starvation in his first year' and Hunt worries that he will, like himself, be blighted by early neglect: 'failing health [might] make any genius he may have fruitless'.[59]

Hunt criticises the way the Waughs are bringing up Cyril: 'Coddling and crushing him dreadfully and he was already too advanced for them. They would have either broken his spirits or made him rebel. The old gentleman had ruled his family with a rod of iron. I am indebted to them for the care of him in his infancy.'[60] This confused construction of old Mr Waugh as both strict and caring, crushing and coddling, good and bad parent, pivots around autonomy and dependence. Independence is opposed to familial inclusion and nurture, but the exchange is incomplete. *Pre-Raphaelitism* describes Hunt's rebellion against his father's refusal to tolerate his vocation in a similarly confused way, stressing the kind intention of his tyranny: 'I did not think my father wrong in using all his authority to restrain me' (1, 30).

Despite Hunt's marriage in 1875 to Fanny's sister, Edith, her successful voyage with him to the East and her ministrations to himself, Cyril and two more children, doubt and complaints about parental and social irresponsibility increase. A letter to Tupper in 1877[61] develops these familiar grumbles into a heartfelt plea to know why man remains untaught and hence unable to teach: 'school books and slates of the learner . . . are in most cases broken and often cancelled and thrown away . . . A student dies leaving his developed talents still untried, having realised nothing here but just his practice bunglings.' It wonders why mankind cannot be helped to progress, why the individual is left weak and confused to fend for himself, and the long passage becomes a telling lament for the silence and obscurity of God. The parenting of the next world becomes confused with the parenting of this. Eventually, the letter offers a solution to its questions and proposes that: 'The ~~God~~ Father [is] proving the mettle of his children, refusing aid that would in any way nullify the trial.' This reference to a 'trial' re-establishes faith in divine leadership and transforms the artist from child to prophet. Worldly neglect becomes a sign of other-worldly privilege, but the reconstruction is tentative.

This letter foreshadows the paradox presented in *Pre-Raphaelitism*: in a society that fails to nurture, how can the 'student' inherit from the 'learner'? The reference to a silent God and bungling child echoes the tale of the artist's relation with his real father. The memoir's contradictory assertion of the heroic role of its protagonist culminates in a chaotic vision in the final chapters, whereas the letter's chaotic world-view is eventually rationalised into a hesitant sense of being a privileged participant in a divine plan. This polarity between security and neglect is distilled in the ambiguous term '~~God~~Father', where the abstract concept of God is replaced by a more worldly version of him. It implies a reciprocal self-identity as ~~Prophet~~Child that responds to the more immediate needs and discomforts that are set out in letters and journals.

The fantasy of security and transcendent authority in the next world is hampered by the insecurity of participation in this. The same letter links the neglected and bewildered artist to a disordered and equally neglected environment: 'marbles broken that were the glory of a temple chipped into rude shape to build the later savage's hut, colours that have changed while the varnish is drying, words that have lost their original meanings'. The 'glory' of the temple given over to the 'savage's hut' recalls Carlyle again,[62] and seems to relate to a notion of the Holy Land as neglected paradise, given over to uneducated inhabitants. Both Pointon and Codell draw on Edward Said's theorisation of the Oriental 'other' to demonstrate that *Pre-Raphaelitism* promotes an authoritative persona in relation to a familiar construction of the peoples and places of Palestine as ignorant, primitive, or as a crumbling remnant of past glories.[63] This patriarchal orientation is imaged in several of the drawings in *Pre-Raphaelitism* (2, 286, figure 3.2) but it is essential to note that this world-view is, here, not restricted to the East, it is a universal disorder. Correspondence frequently refers to the unenlightened 'savagedom' of English society, whose leaders do not provide 'some better system of training for youth'.[64] More importantly, patriarchal or prophetic otherness to this disorder is, as we have seen, not consistently maintained. The above passages in the 1877 letter *include* the artist and his art in its description of immaturity and neglect.

The passages also conflate the neglected environment with the neglect of art: the temple, the word and 'colors that have changed while the varnish is drying'. The persistent construction of world and self as

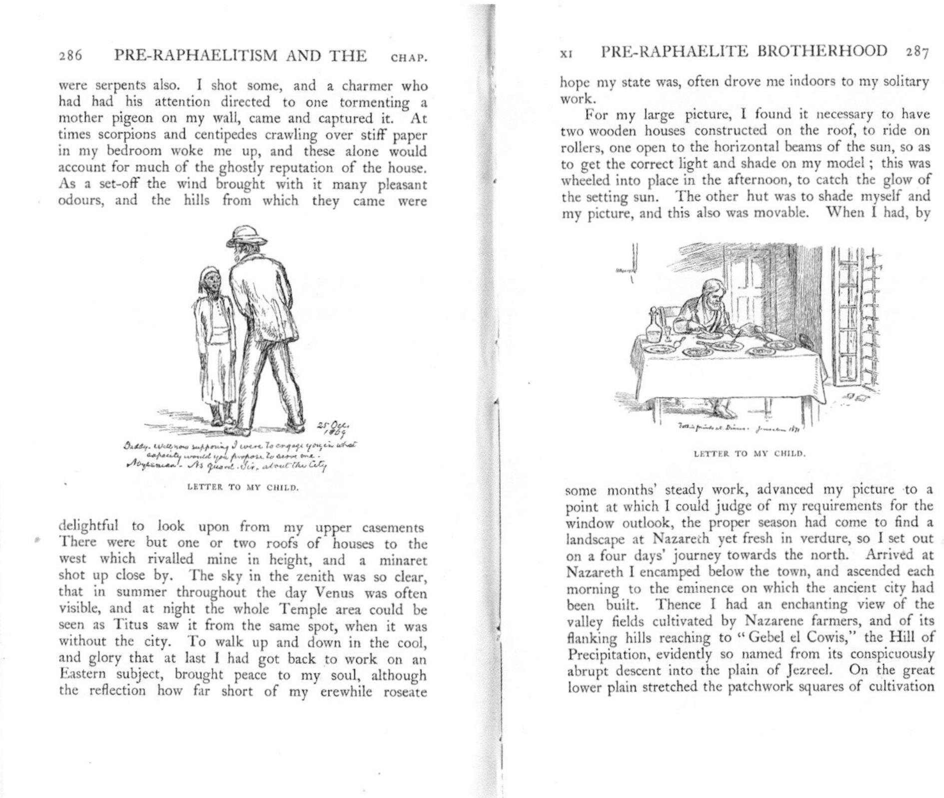

286 PRE-RAPHAELITISM AND THE CHAP.

were serpents also. I shot some, and a charmer who had had his attention directed to one tormenting a mother pigeon on my wall, came and captured it. At times scorpions and centipedes crawling over stiff paper in my bedroom woke me up, and these alone would account for much of the ghostly reputation of the house. As a set-off the wind brought with it many pleasant odours, and the hills from which they came were

LETTER TO MY CHILD.

delightful to look upon from my upper casements There were but one or two roofs of houses to the west which rivalled mine in height, and a minaret shot up close by. The sky in the zenith was so clear, that in summer throughout the day Venus was often visible, and at night the whole Temple area could be seen as Titus saw it from the same spot, when it was without the city. To walk up and down in the cool, and glory that at last I had got back to work on an Eastern subject, brought peace to my soul, although the reflection how far short of my erewhile roseate

XI PRE-RAPHAELITE BROTHERHOOD 287

hope my state was, often drove me indoors to my solitary work.

For my large picture, I found it necessary to have two wooden houses constructed on the roof, to ride on rollers, one open to the horizontal beams of the sun, so as to get the correct light and shade on my model; this was wheeled into place in the afternoon, to catch the glow of the setting sun. The other hut was to shade myself and my picture, and this also was movable. When I had, by

LETTER TO MY CHILD.

some months' steady work, advanced my picture to a point at which I could judge of my requirements for the window outlook, the proper season had come to find a landscape at Nazareth yet fresh in verdure, so I set out on a four days' journey towards the north. Arrived at Nazareth I encamped below the town, and ascended each morning to the eminence on which the ancient city had been built. Thence I had an enchanting view of the valley fields cultivated by Nazarene farmers, and of its flanking hills reaching to "Gebel el Cowis," the Hill of Precipitation, evidently so named from its conspicuously abrupt descent into the plain of Jezreel. On the great lower plain stretched the patchwork squares of cultivation

3.2
William Holman Hunt, *Letter to My Child*; Daddy. Well now supposing I were to engage you in what capacity would you propose to serve me. Abyssinian. As guard, Sir, about the City, 25 October 1869, *Pre-Raphaelitism*, 2, 286–7

immature, unguided and disorderly relates specifically to the 'unfinished' picture. Discussions of artistic and personal maturity are always accompanied by expressions of difficulty and delay in painting which are often couched in apocalyptic terms of environmental and personal 'ruin'. The language of this letter echoes a typical account of executing *The Shadow*: 'I labour incessantly . . . and lo! after bringing it to the last point the whole fabric topples down again and leaves me with the foundations to begin anew upon.'[65]

As I have suggested, each work of art represents the beginning of an artistic coming of age. The incomplete painting therefore connotes the incomplete artist. The 1854 and 1855 journal records of painting *The Scapegoat* contain references to repeated repainting and constantly express frustrations about finishing, especially over missing the Academy deadline. Nor does this tendency to constant dissatisfaction with work diminish with experience. *The Shadow* was laboured on exclusively for four years and *The Triumph of the Innocents* for twelve! The increasingly unstable and unresolved persona of the letters parallels an inability to resolve the work of art.

Although the artist constructs himself as other to a corrupt and misguided world, his practical participation within it, his actual human vulnerability and ineptitude, inevitably implicates him in its imperfection. The prophetic fantasy is both driven and destabilised by experience, creating a polarised persona. The heroic postures alternate with a childish, disenabled identity. The prophetic differentiation from a universal 'savagedom' proposed in private autobiographical texts is, like the painting itself at the time of writing, not yet complete. This subversion of a sense of difference and authority is expressed as non-differentiation. A career of 'disordered preparation' echoes a disordered world, creating a network of exchanges between the damaged or incomplete environment, the damaged or incomplete work of art and the damaged or incomplete artist, 'less than half made'.[66]

Vision

Hunt's pictures are tokens of a mature moral and artistic authority expressed as the fantasised state of the prophet – triumphant religious acts of vision. Their themes are, as Codell suggests, 'psycho-subjects', displaying a 'manly' persona.[67] *The Scapegoat*, *The Finding of the Saviour in the Temple*, *The Shadow of Death* and *The Triumph of the Innocents* depict prophetic types and can be considered, therefore, as manifestations of this persona. Yet these scenes simultaneously depict an animal, a child, a young man and a baby. I shall suggest that they represent an attempt to enact the fantasy that transforms childish weakness and alienation into aspects of the prophetic role. Hunt's practice of painting religious images on location, the reconstruction of the primitive, incomplete, disordered visual data of the Holy Land into a coherent image of divine events, complements this project.

Each scene as a whole embodies the special eye of an authoritative artist. In his essay 'Stories of the Eye', Daniel Pick links nineteenth-century destabilisations of identity to a 'problematic of vision', where dreams, memories and a fragmented, uncoded, 'childish' mode of sensual perception disrupt and complicate belief and a secure relation between the self and the observed world.[68] For Hunt, the transparent, perfect, completed image represents a reinvention of the confident observer. Its presentation of a sacred, ordered interpretation of the world validates the prophet/artist. As I have shown, artistic authority is, however, frequently superseded by self-doubt during the execution of the paintings. This weak, bewildered, childish self-image also coincides with diary records of disordered perceptions, nightmares, hallucinations and even blindness.[69] This tension between prophetic and actual seeing is manifested in the way the iconography of the pictures constructs the act of vision.

The raw materials of *The Scapegoat* (plate 1) are an epitome of the disorderly, the primitive and the mortal – a dying beast in an Eastern wilderness. Its predicament evokes the preoccupation with exile, loneliness and vulnerability in the writings of the time. An optimistic interpretation is secured by added references to the sacred in the form of the red fillet, the olive branch and the skull (relating the site to Golgotha), as well as the biblical text on the frame. The scull is circumscribed by a reflection of the moon to suggest a halo. A rainbow is also included in the Manchester Art Gallery version (completed 1858, figure 2.3). These motifs act like the words 'trial' and 'fate' in the autobiography: weakness and alienation are characteristically represented as prophetic sacrifice. The inscription of this fantasy has, however, to be represented by a symbolic, religious code. For the viewer, the detection of redemption in this image of literal suffering and desolation is dependent on a recognition and acceptance of this code. Like the memoir's transformation of 'bungling' child to sage-like artist, it requires a recognition of divine order, an act of faith. The painting offers an actual view of the material world and asks the observer to interpret it; to re-experience, and thus *validate*, the fantasised act of reading, or revelation, proposed by the artist.

Contemporary reviews of *The Scapegoat* do not always accept this transition from the real to the sacred. They suggest that the 'photographic' realisation of the picture is at odds with its symbolic content. The *Athenaeum* comments: 'Of course the salt may be sin and the sea sorrow, and the clouds eternal rebukings of pride, and so on, but we might spin these fancies from anything, from an old wall, a centaur's beard, or a green duck pool.'[70] Visible meanings subvert invisible meanings. Landow agrees:

> The iconographic problems we encounter in *The Scapegoat* . . . do not derive primarily from any obscurity, since a fairly large segment of Hunt's audience found such symbolism intelligible . . . *The Scapegoat* is a mere static emblem and one whose pictorial nature tends to struggle against the meaning the artist sought to impose upon it.[71]

Critics blame this sense of dislocation on a philosophical gulf between Hunt and viewers who do not accept the existence of transcendental correspondences between the visible and the invisible world.[72] However, as Michael Wheeler notes in *Heaven, Hell and the Victorians*, natural allegory was widely accepted at this time.[73] The *Athenaeum* reviewer is, as Landow says, not failing to 'read' the painting properly. He is responding to a genuine tension in a picture which juxtaposes a 'too realistic' scene with an emblematic spiritual message. The real problem with this image is not that it is too realistic per se, but that the specific depiction of physical *suffering and desolation* is at odds with its abstract notion of hope. It is the gruesome nature of Hunt's realism on which reviewers focus, the desolate landscape and the 'dying goat'.[74] The mimetic detail which is meant to authenticate the conception of promise in the goat's persecution subverts the fantasy.

Ruskin also suggests that the grimly material reality of the subject has undermined Hunt's Christian conception. He presents Hunt as over-literal, too 'excited by the circumstances of the scene'.[75] Hilton, by contrast, focuses on Hunt's obsessive, religious motivation for painting the picture, detecting the 'touch of the madman'.[76] The imaginative idea and the mimetic accuracy of *The Scapegoat* do not unite. Once detached from one another, they allow the painting to be viewed in two ways. Critics see it as a manifestation of unsophisticated, experiential pessimism and religious fantasy, a morbidly over-literal *and* a fanatically grandiose vision.

The painting dramatises the artist's apprehension of divine order in a fearful reality by demanding a similar process from the viewer. The subject of the picture is vision itself, the prophetic vision which finds positive meaning in worldly adversity, helplessness and disorder. This dialectic between the symbolic and the descriptive reprises the oscillating perceptions of self in Hunt's letters and journals, and corresponds with the tension between fantasy and reality, prophetic certainty and experiential, childish uncertainty. Critics' ambiguous, or incomplete perception of the goat as prophetic type echoes the instability within the artistic persona and the iconography of the work itself.

Hunt's interest in Christ reflects, as Codell suggests, a particular preoccupation with an unstable victor/victim identity. His project of reconstructing Christ's image from the 'primitive' races and locations of the Holy Land[77] reinforces the tension between prophet and child. Furthermore, his work specifically investigates the youthful aspects of Jesus: *The Finding* portrays him as a lost child, *The Shadow* as an exposed and naked young man about to leave home, and *The Triumph* as a persecuted baby. These particular Christs respond to anxieties about isolation, vulnerability and nurture and specifically compensate the unparented son. Jesus echoes the artist's embattled position, operating outside society; unprotected and without conventional support, other than a surrogate band of 'brothers', and *The Finding* and *The Shadow* explicitly depict the issue of separation from the worldly family in order to embrace the ~~God-~~Father.

The Finding (plate 6) dramatises a revolt against the conventions of an old establishment and society in favour of a higher ideal of heaven on earth, paralleling the Brotherhood's own determination on social and artistic reform. Its representation of the young prophet misrecognised yet admired by his family and by some elements of the establishment, recalls two of the memoir's descriptions of the early admiration received by Millais from parents and the Academy: the young, mop-topped lad being fêted by the older Academicians (1, 33), and Millais with his adoring family. '[With] fresh colour and blue eyes, with an apparently unguarded manner, . . . the son put one hand on his father's shoulder and the other on his mother's chair' (1, 61). The anti-establishment aspects of this picture are linked to *The Shadow* in a letter of 1872,[78] but the latter figure is more isolated and the additional elements of loneliness, weariness and an awareness of death reflect the concerns of an older artist.

The Shadow (plate 2) is a valorisation of Hunt's much publicised reputation for hard work and account of his own youth when, like Christ, he was subject to his parents, but rejected his father's profession and left home for a higher calling. The concept of the picture was prompted by the words of St Mark: 'Is he not the carpenter . . . ?' (Mark 6: 4; 2, 273). The preceding chapters of this gospel offer a negative portrayal of Christ's parents which parallels the construction of family in Hunt's writings. Jesus is travelling and teaching. 'When his family hears about this they set out to take charge of him: "He is out of his mind", they said' (3: 22). Christ refuses to obey them, but when he returns to preach in Nazareth, those who know his humble background there fail to listen: 'A prophet never lacks honour except in his own home town, among his relations and his own family' (6: 5). During the completion of the picture in London, Hunt complains of critical hostility and of family responsibility that 'shuts me out from the possibility of making my journey when I shall certainly have repose for my jaded soul'.[79] This repose echoes Christ's 'gratitude to His Father that the welcome hour of rest has come', depicted in the painting.[80] Hunt specifically connects the Virgin to his own mother in a wry comment to Edward Lear, 'many other reformer's mother has foreseen without supernatural revelation that the son's career would end under the hand of the public executioner'.[81] The reference to Christ's madness in Mark echoes his own nickname, 'the Mad' and his parents' label, 'ne'er-do-well'.

Just as Jesus' coming of age is enacted in the public sphere, the temple and the journey, so Hunt's authoritative role is enacted in the context of his public texts: his paintings and published writings. The concluding lines of the preface of *Pre-Raphaelitism* answer all the private concerns of the letters with a vision of the artist as saviour, traveller and educator, destined for immortality:

> The office of the artist should be looked upon as a priests service in the temple of nature, whose ampler graces are revealed to those who have eyes to see . . . , while declared law opens up wide regions unordered and anarchic, where selfish greed has yet to be tutored into wise rule. In the circle of the initiated responsive beings recognise the elimination of immature design in creation to be a triumph of patient endeavour, and they join in the chorus of those who 'sang together in joy' on the attainment

> of the ideal of Heaven's Artist, who in overflowing beauty endowed the colourless world with prismatic radiance, prophesying of Titians yet to be who should go forth to charm away scales from the eyes of the blind. (1, xv–xvi)

In *The Shadow*, Christ's gaze enacts the triumph of mature vision, prophetic apprehension of paradise ascribed to the artist in this passage, and in the final paragraph of the memoir: 'The windows of the edifice should be opened to the purity of the azure sky' (2, 492). As Jesus thanks God for his hour of rest, implying a more final deliverance, his gaze is directed through an open arch towards the distant beauty of the surrounding landscape. This motif echoes the revelatory descriptions of such scenes in the memoir and letters. The golden glow of the evening sunshine which floods in from outside, and the positioning of a window in place of the 'glory' of the conventional halo,[82] underlines these supernatural associations. The fruit on the window sill refers to the 'first fruits'; the notion that Christ's resurrection is the sign of eventual redemption for all (1 Corinthians 15: 20). The star and the green branches of the olive tree recall the promise of the olive branch in *The Scapegoat.* They also allude to resurrection: 'As of the green leaves on a thick tree, some fall and some grow; so is the generation of flesh and blood' (Apocrypha Ecclesiasticus 14: 18).[83]

These references to prophetic revelation outside in nature are juxtaposed with references to danger within the home of Jesus. The interior of the disordered room suggests highly physical aspects of toil and threat. Pointon notes suggestions of violence in the sharp implements, angular forms and severed contours surrounding the vulnerable body.[84] The shadow represents death itself and the exotic dress and accessories and back view of the Virgin dramatically disassociate her from conventional depictions of the nurturing Madonna. This painting constructs immediate worldly neglect, inside, and future, other-worldly safety beyond.[85]

This is again a picture about vision. The extraordinarily iconoclastic step of presenting the back of the Virgin sets her gaze in physical opposition to that of her son. Her view is a worldly one, focusing on physical death (the shadow imaging the crucifixion) and vain fantasy (the idea that her son will become rich and powerful represented by the king's gifts) (2, 273–5). The 'sermon' within the picture is described in a letter to Tupper, emphasising the role of the Virgin in wrongly thinking that her son's claims to 'royalty consist in the wielding of temporal power', implied by the crown in the chest.[86] The assignment of these misconceptions to the female figure recalls the antipathy towards domestic comfort/constraint in letters of this time.

The observer sees more than the Virgin, and is invited to look at Christ himself and thus transcend both the associations of death and disorder in the room and her limited understanding. In order to do this, a tired carpenter who is stretching and talking to himself must be read in terms of the conventions of traditional resurrection scenes. As with the scapegoat, Jesus' hostile worldly environment can only be superseded by a culturally informed translation of the religious symbols within it. However, nineteenth-century viewers of this picture again find that the materialistic rendering hinders imaginative interpretation. The *Art Journal* sees the figure as a mere vermin-ridden 'Galilean', wonders whether he is 'praying' or 'yawning', and fails to be convinced by the signs of resurrection: 'realistic art must give us the carcass alone, uninformed by the spirit'.[87] Pointon also suggests that the overtones of violence in the painting upstage its symbolic message.[88] Again, divine associations are superseded by the grim reality of the objects portrayed.

It is as though the transcendent prophetic vision is being tainted with the darkness, disorder and physical threats of the failures, weakness and exhaustion of the studio. As I have mentioned, Pick notes that cultural responses to nineteenth-century destabilisations of identity and faith are frequently expressed in terms of optical anomalies such as blindness and insanity. Although a letter to Tupper denies 'all shadow of doubt' about the 'higher idea' presented in the painting,[89] expressions of doubt and confusion dominate Hunt's writings during the image's execution, a period of struggle 'with the powers of chaotic darkness'.[90] Clouded weather is conflated with clouded vision,[91] 'everything looks bad and hopeless',[92] 'there is a curse on this picture'.[93] The untutored, immature, 'unordered and anarchic . . . colourless world' is not wholly overcome, as it is claimed to be in *Pre-Raphaelitism* (1, xv). The diary records nightmares and hallucinations, unreliable vision and periods of blindness.[94] A letter to Tupper admits these doubts about his vision and adds: 'His majesty of blackness [the Devil] certainly stands in our light in the studio at times.'[95] Another letter in the same year expresses fears of actual madness.[96] This dislocation between the optimistic, symbolic vision of the prophet and immediate, material manifestations of danger and lack of visual authority of the child is imaged by the shadow, the dangerous, domestic surroundings of Christ and the opposing delusions of the mother.

As I have demonstrated, a sense of childish neglect continues to alternate with a consoling fantasy of prophetic authority and immortality during work on *The Triumph of the Innocents* (1876–87). Whereas *The Shadow* images divine resurrection and transcendence ambiguously, however, *The Triumph*, for the first time, depicts it directly.

The Innocents specifically represent the child/victim. Hunt must have seen many Renaissance versions of the massacre of the Innocents during his time in Italy, possibly the most violent scriptural subject of the period. He viewed a version by Tintoretto (1565–87, Scuola di San Rocco, Venice), for example, with Ruskin in 1869 (2, 259–64). *The Triumph* offers a reassuring antidote to these as well as to the notions of childish neglect in his writings. It concentrates on the salvation of the children, rather than their death. The child in the foreground looks through the tear in his white clothes at his healed side (plate 3). This motif, and the white cloth, also alludes to and repairs other images of violence such as the spear wound in the side of Christ, often displayed in crucifixions, lamentations, pietàs and entombments, as well as the piercing and nailing suggested by the tools in *The Shadow*. The pose of the infant Jesus in all three final versions relates to Renaissance models where outstretched arms and crossed feet also reprise the crucifixion and the resurrection. The worldly danger which has haunted the career of Hunt's earlier Christs and types of Christ is, here, neutralised by the answering figure of the resurrected child immediately below his exposed body.

The mother's gaze is now aligned with that of her son and the Holy Family accompanies and supports the child away from danger. This danger is imaged by the anxious back view of Joseph, decked with one of the threatening tools in *The Shadow*. His exclusion from the revelation of the Innocents recalls the Virgin in the earlier picture. Where she focuses on the shadow, Joseph is looking for soldiers,[97] and his gaze is directed at two wild dogs skulking into the darkness before the entrance of a house like 'the wolf at the door'. This echo of the primitive and the disorderly underlines the consolatory nature of the image.

Unusually, *The Triumph* reconciles worldly nurture with a divine scheme. The parental role which has been opposed to the protagonist in the form of the rabbis and 'coddling' family in *The Finding*, and in the form of the mother and father (absent, but present in the evidence of his workplace) in *The Shadow*, is here harmonised with the role of the child as they guide him to safety. The prophet/child identities are reconciled by this combining of the previously opposing elements of protection and journeying out. The independent movement of the child in the Virgin's arms accentuates this. The setting is open countryside. The site of revelation is no longer a potential space. The ambiguous movement between materially dangerous social environments and abstract redemption, represented by doors and windows in earlier images of Christ, is resolved in the depiction of a single environment of actual safety: 'having left the colder climate of the high country, . . . the fugitives have descended into the rich and more balmy atmosphere of the plain. As they advance nearer and nearer to a place of safety they feel the blessed relief of peace after disturbance and terror.'[98]

This time, it is the harsh realities of Christ's material future that are reduced to a series of symbols – the torn, white drapery, the Eucharistic wheat, the crucified gesture – whilst the non-material phenomenon of the resurrection is, conversely, enhanced to a state of physical realisation in the form of the healed Innocents. In this picture, two poles of parental protection, that of the family and that of the resurrecting God, are harmonised and stressed, while negative aspects, trial, parental demands and absences, are suppressed.

This actual imaging of resurrected children may appear finally to reconcile the tensions between child and prophet, experience and faith. The promotion of eschatological fantasy to the realm of the visible removes ambiguity, and is perhaps intended to answer the critical incomprehension of earlier works. The 'triumph' format of the children's recognition of their Saviour seems to reinforce an authoritative identity, imaging a further fantasy of critical and popular applause for the artist and the picture, recalling Adams's idea of the role of the audience in the performance and authentication of self-mastery.[99] The recognition and co-operation of parents perhaps relates to a broader alignment of patriarchal structures such as the art establishment and society in general. The signal fires, illuminated cottages and well tended fields construct a civilised environment, benign at the level of society as well as nature. The prophet is validated and the child is parented. No uncomfortable movement from the material to the symbolic, from dying goat to type of Christ, or from vulnerable carpenter to resurrected Lord, is required. The picturing of abstract phenomena, the supernatural children, integrates fantasy, the invisible, with the visible. As Landow puts it, 'an image of this world that participates in eternity'.[100]

However, this family's safety and its triumph of vision have been achieved only through a relinquishing of a strenuous adherence to the real. As Hunt says, *The Shadow* is 'strictly – . . . as the Temple picture was – historic with not a single fact of any kind of supernatural nature'.[101] *The Triumph*, on the other hand, returns to the 'fantasy' of *The Light of the World*, 'invoking the model of fairyland'.[102] Mary Bennett cites several sources for this image[103] but the composition is, I think, also partly suggested by an actual fairy tale: *The Water-babies* by Charles Kingsley. Published in 1863, it was a popular book when Hunt's children were young and in 1872, he mentions admiring 'illustrations in children's books'.[104] The frontispiece of the book, by Noel Paton, is very reminiscent of the central group of Hunt's picture. The hero, Tom, is given a preliminary glimpse of an underwater afterlife, before being sent on his trials. He sits on the Good Fairy's lap in a Madonna and Child type composition, and is surrounded by happy water-babies who have already been admitted (figure 3.3).

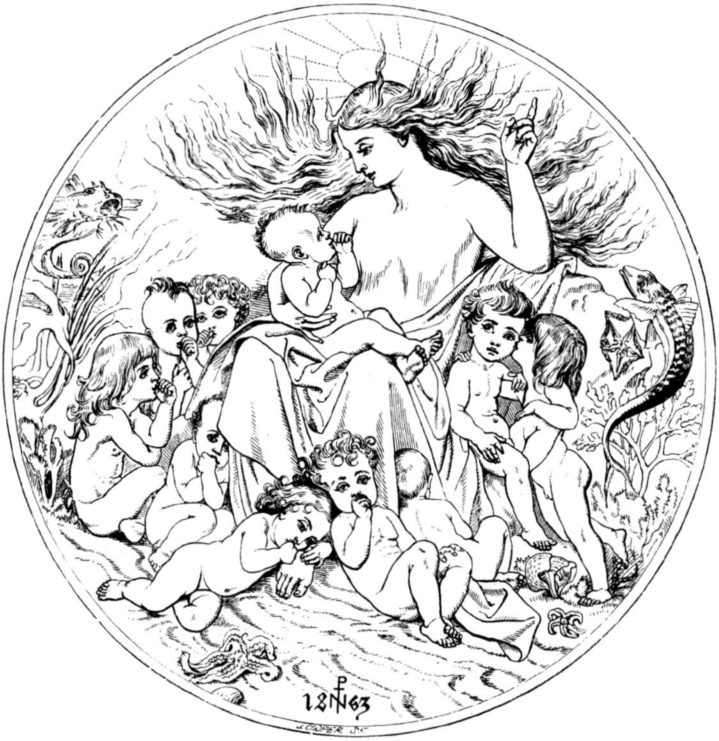

3.3
Joseph Noel Paton,
Water-babies,
1863,
frontispiece, C. Kingsley,
The Water-babies

The Good Fairy is, in every respect, an archetype of motherly nurture and Tom resembles Hunt's persona. Tom's vision of heaven helps him evolve from a savage into a guide. He seeks out his irresponsible master and saves him by showing him better ways. He is a neglected child/teacher whose providential travels and trials earn him a place in heaven. Hunt's scene may relate to a particular incident in the novel where a land baby, being innocent, is able to perceive Tom in the sea: 'the baby smiled and held out his hands, . . . kicked and leaped'.[105] His mother, at first blind to this, follows his gaze and, inspired by maternal love, also sees Tom and smiles. Shortly after this revelation, the ship sinks and they drown. The boat as a metaphor for the dark, perilous, unguided life, with 'no welcome till the land is reached',[106] is a favourite of Hunt's and is imaged in his contemporary work, *The Ship* (1875–79, Tate Britain, plate 11) and later sketch *Christ the Pilot* (1894, private collection, figure 7.3). The brief moment of grace of Kingsley's itinerant, doomed mother and baby recalls Hunt's description of *The Triumph* as a 'vision to the Virgin conjured up by her maternal love for her own child, the Saviour who is calling her attention to [the Innocents]'.[107] Adams argues that Kingsley's ideal of 'muscular Christianity' is an extreme example of the masochistic logic of 'conjoining self-mastery with the defiance of circumstance. Tom is an example of the 'figures of liminal or divided identity' that he often uses to explore this kind of masculine ideal.[108]

The Triumph is unusual in Hunt's work in that the type of vision that it constructs is fantastical, visionary, wholly that of the prophet. This does not imply, however, a stabilisation of the prophetic persona. It represents, rather, an increased reliance on this persona. The ambition of the image raises the stakes, and accelerates insecurity behind the scenes. The worldly woe contained in the letters written during the execution of this image contrasts sharply with its other-worldly hope. The religious and artistic doubts expressed in the 1877 letter to Tupper proliferate throughout the correspondence of this period. Concerns about atheism, war, social persecution, illness and particularly death create a repetitive, ironic counterpoint to the community, nurture and resurrection shown in the picture. Moreover, the completion of the image, the 'triumph' of prophetic vision, remains, as I have said, elusive, dragging on for twelve years and necessitating, oddly, its own resurrection in the form of new start on a second canvas, the first proving too weak to sustain the weight of paint or the constant cutting away and reworking.

This cycle of painting and scraping away the token of artistic maturity dramatises the oscillating self-image in the writings between the complete and the incomplete. Hunt's own tools literally enact the persecution implied by the tools in the image. This failure to finish perpetuates a long exile from London and the art world. The prophet/artist struggles to visualise a 'God whom he can't *trace*' (emphasis added) and, like a child, he asks: 'Why is it that in every truth revealed ~~lays~~ lies some sand or error of wrong? and that in every revelation there is a key taken with it which distorts . . . why is it that we cry in vain . . . ?'[109]

The next chapter will show that the resort to pure invention is highly problematic, requiring a privileging of interior, or subjective, vision over objective deduction which produces enhanced fears about that vision, and the artist's prophetic authority. I shall suggest that the conception and execution of *The Triumph* represents a failed act of reparation of belief and self belief, catalysed by an accelerating preoccupation with death.

Notes

1 Revelation, 21: 5–8

2 Farrar and Meynell, *Hunt*, pp 17–19; Landow, *Typological Symbolism*, pp 5, 113–14; Sussman, 'Artistic Manhood', p 158; Codell, 'Artist Colonised', p 216

3 Journal, 23–25 February 1855, JRL, MS 1211, 4v; Allentuck, 'Hunt, Monk and Ruskin', pp 156–7

4 Strauss, D.F., *The Life of Jesus Critically Examined* (1835), trans. M. Evans (London: Chapman Brothers, 1846); Renan, J., *The Life of Jesus* (1863) (London: Trubner & Co., 1864); Hunt mentions reading these in letter to Stephens, 25 July 1868, BL, MS Don. e 67, 22v and *Pre-Raphaelitism*, second revised edition (London: Chapman and Hall, 1913), 2, p 338
5 Landow, G.P., 'Shadows Cast by *The Light of the World*: William Holman Hunt's Religious Paintings 1893–1905', *Art Bulletin*, 65, 3 (1983), p 480
6 Journal, 20 February 1855, JRL, MS 1211, 4v
7 Letter fragment, 1870s?, JRL, MS 1213, 35
8 *The Triumph of the Innocents*, pamphlet (London: Fine Arts Society, 1885), quoted Bennett *Hunt*, p 54
9 Cohn, N., *The Pursuit of the Millennium* (London: Paladin, 1972), p 24
10 Letter to Stephens, 4 August 1863, BL, MS Don. e 66, 76
11 Hunt describes thoughts of the millennium to be 'rife in the minds of pious Jews, particularly . . . those in great tribulation', *The Triumph of the Innocents*, quoted, Bennett, *Hunt*, p 54
12 Journal, November 1854, JRL, MS 1210, 6
13 Journal, 20 February 1855, JRL, MS 1211, 2v–3
14 Letter to Combe, 11 March 1855, JRL, MS 1213, 3
15 Unidentified letter (to Combe, 1870?), ibid., 24–5
16 Letter to Tupper, 23 January 1878, *Correspondence*, p 283
17 Journal, 31 March 1872, JRL, MS 1212, 17v; letter to Combe, 17 March 1855, JRL, MS 1213, 4
18 Journal, November 1854, JRL, MS 1210, 6
19 Revelation 9: 16
20 Letter to Tupper, March 1855, *Correspondence*, pp 46–7
21 Ibid., 24 July 1854, p 45
22 Codell, 'Artist Colonised', p 216, also Sussman, 'Artistic Manhood', pp 158–61
23 Codell, 'Artist Colonised', pp 220–2, Pointon, 'Artist as Ethnographer', pp 22–5; also Sussman, 'Artistic Manhood', p 162
24 Allentuck, 'Hunt, Monk and Ruskin', p 157
25 Adams, *Dandies and Desert Saints*, p 11
26 Carlyle, T., *Sartor Resartus* (1833–34), (Oxford: Oxford University Press, 2000), p 44
27 Codell, 'Artist Colonised', p 227
28 Ibid., pp 216–20
29 Journal, 2 May 1872, JRL, MS 1212, 22v
30 Sussman, 'Artistic Manhood', p 161
31 Adams, *Dandies and Desert Saints*, p 8–9
32 Errington, *Themes*, p 242
33 1, chapters 1, 2; Holman-Hunt, *My Grandfather*, pp 33–7
34 'Notes on the Life of Augustus Egg', *Reader*, 1 (1863), p 462
35 Wather, L., 'The Invention of Childhood in Victorian Autobiography', in *Approaches*, pp 64–83
36 Codell, 'Artist Colonised', pp 221
37 Gissing, *Hunt*, p 217
38 Journal, Jerusalem, 16 March 1855, JRL, MS 1211, 7v

39 Journal, Jerusalem, 9 April 1872, JRL, MS 1212, 19
40 Journal, November 1854, JRL, MS 1210, 6
41 Letter to Lear, 24 April 185?, JRL, MS 1214, 40; also letter to Combe, 30 May 1855, JRL, MS 1213, 6
42 Hunt, letter to Stephens, 6 November 1864, BL, MS Don. e 66, 105v–106, also 4 January 1865, 109v
43 Letter to Stephens, 10 November 1866 and April 1867, BL, MS Don. e 67, 5; 9v
44 Ibid., 21 June 1870, 59v
45 Ibid., 2 October 1870, 62v; also letters to Tupper, 30 June 1870, *Correspondence*, pp 136–7; 9 October 1872, pp 172–3; 28 December 1876, p 214; 26 September 1877, p 236; letter to Edward Lear, 3 September 1872, JRL, MS 1214, 45; Journal, 12 March 1872, JRL, MS 1212, 15; 5 April 1872, 18v
46 Adams, *Dandies and Desert Saints*, pp 9–10
47 Letter to Stephens, 25 August 1863, BL, MS Don. e 66, 79v
48 Letter to Lear, 31 December 1856, JRL, MS 1214, 19; also letter to Tupper, 11 August 1857, *Correspondence*, p 50; letter to Stephens, 6 November 1864, BL, MS Don. e 66, 105v–106
49 Letter to Tupper, 7 January 1864, *Correspondence*, p 68
50 Codell, 'Artist Colonised', p 218
51 Letter to Stephens, 18 August 1865, BL, MS Don. e 66, 127–128v
52 Ibid., 28 September 1865, 132–132v
53 Letter to Stephens, 9 October 1866, BL, MS Don. e 67, 1
54 Ibid., 19 January 1867, 7v
55 Ibid., 31 October 1869, 46v
56 Letter to Tupper, 20 September 1874, *Correspondence*, pp 196–7
57 Letter to Stephens, 17 June 1867, BL, MS Don. e 67, 11v
58 Letter to Tupper, 22 February 1872, *Correspondence*, p 149
59 Ibid., 9 October 1872, p 173
60 Ibid., 2 June 1873, p 184
61 Ibid., 15 July 1877, pp 222, 232
62 Carlyle, *Sartor Resartus*, p 180
63 Pointon, 'Artist as Ethnographer', pp 25–6; Codell, 'Artist Colonised', pp 222–4, Said, E., *Orientalism* (1978) (Harmondsworth: Penguin, 1985)
64 Letter to Tupper, July 1870, *Correspondence*, pp 125–32
65 Ibid., 20 September 1874, pp 195–6
66 Letter to Stephens, 6 November 1864, BL, MS Don. e 66, 105v
67 Codell, 'Artist Colonised', p 219
68 Pick, D., 'Stories of the Eye', in *Rewriting the Self: Histories from the Renaissance to the Present*, ed. R. Porter (London: Routledge, 1997), pp 191–5
69 Journal, Jerusalem, 18 April 1872, JRL, MS 1212, 20
70 'The Scapegoat', *Athenaeum*, 1489 (10 May 1856), p 589
71 Landow, *Typological Symbolism*, pp 107, 111
72 Sussman, 'Scapegoat', p 90
73 Wheeler, *Heaven, Hell*, p 19
74 *Athenaeum* (10 May 1856), p 589

75 Ruskin, 'Academy Notes', in *Works*, 14, p 64
76 Hilton, *Pre-Raphaelites*, p 108
77 Codell, 'Artist Colonised', pp 211–29; Pointon, 'Artist as Ethnographer', pp 25–6
78 Letter fragment, 30 October 1872, BL, MS, quoted, Bronkhurst, J.E., 'The Shadow of Death', *The Pre-Raphaelites* (Tate Gallery, 1984), p 221
79 Letter to Tupper, 20 September 1874, *Correspondence*, p 196
80 *Mr Holman Hunt's Picture, 'The Shadow of Death'*, pamphlet (London: Thomas Agnew and Sons, 1873), quoted, Bennett, *Hunt*, p 49
81 Letter to Lear, 11 February 1873, JRL, MS 1214, 45
82 Derived from Leonardo da Vinci's *Last Supper* (1495–98, refectory, Sta Maria delle Grazie, Milan), which Hunt admired, letter to Stephens, 3 February 1869, BL, MS Don. e 67, 32
83 Royal Academy catalogue (1854), entry for *The Awakening Conscience* (1853–54, Tate Britain, London), quoted, Bennett, *Hunt*, p 35
84 Pointon, 'Artist as Ethnographer', pp 41–2
85 This formula is repeated in the finished gouache *Christ Appearing to Mary Magdalene*, 1892, Fogg Art Museum, a reworking of his first religious canvas *Christ and the Two Marys*, 1847–91, Art Gallery of South Australia
86 Letter to Tupper, July 1870, *Correspondence*, p 128
87 'Realistic Attempts at Sacred Art', *Art Journal*, 35 (1873), pp 86–7; also Colvin, S., 'The Shadow of Death', *Macmillan's Magazine*, 30 (1874), pp 219–21
88 Pointon, 'Artist as Ethnographer', pp 41–2
89 Letter to Tupper, July 1870, *Correspondence*, p 129
90 Letter to Combe, 4 September 1871, BL, MS, quoted, Bronkhurst, 'The Shadow of Death', *Pre-Raphaelites* (Tate Gallery, 1984), p 221
91 Journal, Jerusalem, 22 April 1872, JRL, MS 1212, 20v
92 Ibid., 12 March 1872, 14v
93 Ibid., 18 April 1872, 20
94 Ibid., 18 April 1872, 20
95 Letter to Tupper, 17 September 1872, *Correspondence*, p 168
96 Ibid., 24 February 1872, p 150
97 *The Triumph of the Innocents*, quoted, Bennett, *Hunt*, p 53
98 Ibid.
99 The stream of life recalls Hunt's reforming role: 'True judgment directed us to choose an educational outflow from a channel where the stream had no trace of . . . pollution . . . and was innocent' (1, 137)
100 Landow, *Typological Symbolism*, p 129
101 Letter fragment, BL, MS, quoted, Bronkhurst, 'The Shadow of Death', *Pre-Raphaelites* (Tate Gallery, 1984), p 221
102 Pointon, 'Artist as Ethnographer', p 34. Landow notes a departure from historical scenes and a reliance on revelation in Hunt's late religious works, 'Shadows cast by *The Light of the World*', pp 478–9
103 Bennett, M., *Artists of the Pre-Raphaelite Circle, The First Generation, Catalogue of Works in the Walker Art Gallery, Lady Lever Art Gallery and Sudley Art Gallery* (London: National Museums and Galleries on Merseyside/Lund Humphries, 1988), p 90

104 Letter to Tupper, 24 February 1872, *Correspondence*, p 150
105 Kingsley, C., *The Water-babies* (1863) (London: Macmillan, 1869), p 283
106 Letter to Tupper, 3 March 1876, *Correspondence*, p 205; the metaphor of the badly steered ship is used to describe society's 'modern degeneracy' in Hunt's subsequent letter, 23 September 1876, p 210. See also letter to Bodleian Library, 25 June 1894, Oxford MS Eng. lett. e 118; Landow, G.P., '"Christ the Pilot": A Panel from William Holman Hunt's Unfinished Triptych', *Journal of Pre-Raphaelite Studies*, 5 (1980), pp 81–91
107 Letter to Scott, 5 January 1880, *Notes*, 2, p 229
108 Adams, *Dandies and Desert Saints*, pp 17–18
109 Letter to Tupper, 15 July 1877, *Correspondence*, pp 232–3

4 *Death: materialism and mysticism*

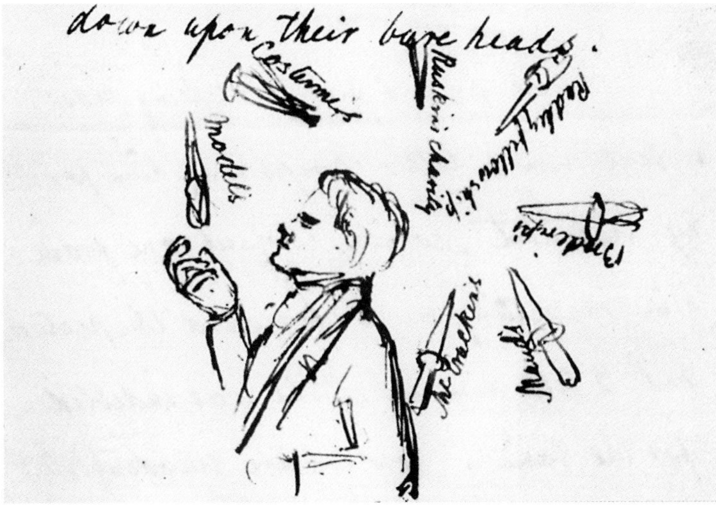

4.1
William Holman Hunt,
Letter to Lear,
24 January 1853

4

The generally accepted idea of Hunt as 'Holy Hunt' oversimplifies his faith and devalues his intellectual engagement with the emotional and spiritual issues raised by nineteenth-century materialism. The religious ideas presented in his work are not mere dogma or pious posturing; his faith is, as we have seen, both debated and doubted. As Wheeler demonstrates in *Heaven, Hell and the Victorians*, questions of 'death, judgment, heaven and hell' which so preoccupied Victorian artists and writers represent a direct confrontation with central issues of modernity, 'problems of evidence, authority and language'[1].

The Shadow and *The Triumph* distil these issues. They address a particular eschatological difficulty: 'how to represent the Christian triumph over death and suffering and how to depict the supernatural without violating material laws?'[2] The fulfilment of biblical promise in individual resurrection is, however, less easily dealt with than the more distant, millennial concept of the salvation of the world. Death presents the artist with the literal limits of the material, the end of the physical body, and hence the question of bodily resurrection becomes crucial, simultaneously testing the artist's physical and imaginative authority. In this chapter, the instability of the prophetic role manifested in the iconography of *The Shadow* and *The Triumph* is connected to profound anxieties about mortality, revealing a link between the integrity of the artist's vision and the integrity of his body.

Evidences

After the loss of Fanny in 1866, Hunt's correspondence begins to feature earnest discussions about life after death. Fears for his own health, that of Cyril, and, after 1875, that of his new family, are juxtaposed with anxious and restless attempts to assert the authority of his vision of a Christian eschatological hope.

The immediate aftermath of the bereavement coincides with a crisis of belief and self-belief. Hunt writes that he feels cursed[3] and tells Stephens that 'the still silence makes me dread that she knows all my unworthiness and despises me'. This remorse and unease is accompanied by a strong sense of alienation from an obscure and angry God: 'All the play is played out, the lights are darkened and I seem to be left alone to mind the vacant theatre . . . I thought my faith in and my realisation of God's supreme mercy so firm that I should not under any circumstance feel at enmity with Him.' The idea of suffering as a guarantee of status falters here: 'such frequent trials are more than my feebleness can bear'.[4]

In *Pre-Raphaelitism*, this religious disquiet is put into the mouth of Ruskin in the form of a discussion of the critic's temporary atheism during a meeting in Venice, shortly afterwards (2, 265–6). Ruskin claims that eschatological hope is a delusion: 'The whole story of divine revelation' is 'a wilderness of poetic dreaming', destructive of 'reason . . . There is no Eternal Father . . . I feel my loneliness in having no one to console me when I am overcome.' These words recall the loneliness and despair of Hunt's letters, but the memoir has him reply confidently:

> The evidence of the individuality of Christ and of His teaching is absolutely convincing to me, there is a record in the early books of the Bible of the advancing teachings of the prophets, without which Christ's evangel would have been impossible. So far the revelation is established in my mind; all the rest is extraneous and may be left in suspense.

The public text counters a ventriloquised accusation that belief is 'dreaming' by justifying the scriptures and prophesy as historical fact. However, the death of Fanny has posed a theological problem which can never be resolved by recourse to experience or data. The question of the afterlife *must* be 'left in suspense'.

A fear that immortality might be no more than a vain and self-deluding dream is more explicit in Hunt's private writings. His image of himself 'left alone to mind the vacant theatre', reprises Macbeth's soliloquy after the death of his wife:

> Life's but a walking shadow; a poor player,
> That struts and frets his hour upon the stage,
> And then is heard no more (*Macbeth*, Act 5, Scene 5)

Six weeks after Fanny's death, a letter to Combe complains about difficulties in thinking of her soul, rather 'than any other part of her . . . the shrunken but beautiful body', in the tomb, and expresses concern about the finite nature of Hunt's own 'physical qualities'.[5]

Despite these doubts, Hunt resolves to trust in faith and consoles himself with the idea that he can redeem himself through work.[6] At this time, he is working on both *Fanny Holman Hunt* (1866–68, Toledo Museum of Art, plate 12) and *Isabella and the Pot of Basil* (1866–68, Laing Art Gallery, plate 13). The latter depicts the moment in Keats's poem, *Isabella* (1820), where the heroine, driven to madness by the murder of her lover, Lorenzo, weeps over a pot of basil in which she has buried his decaying head. This image answers the uncertainty in the letters, relocating associations of self-delusion and insanity on to a *failure* to see beyond the physical. Hunt also plans *The Shadow* and *The Triumph*. These paintings will restate a fantasy of eschatological safety and reinstate the prophetic persona which both validates this hope and will answer the final judgement.

The reaction to death exhibits the polarisation demonstrated in the previous chapter. Eschatological belief is defended in public statements, in *Pre-Raphaelitism*, in the iconography of the paintings, and in some private writings, but the insecurity that underlies these declarations frequently prevails, especially in the letters and the diaries. These two positions are, like the prophet/child personae, often closely juxtaposed within the same text. If assertions of belief are disentangled and differentiated from expressions of doubt, however, each can be seen as an ongoing response to the other. The complex iconographical schemes of *The Shadow* and *The Triumph*, and the content of the writings associated with them, become more meaningful if they are viewed as *dialectical* texts, which manifest both hope and harm.

The letters written to Tupper and Scott while painting *The Shadow* discuss the question at length. Their main theme is an argument that faith can be validated by objective research. Hunt supplements clues gained from the Bible and from his travels by reading biographies of Christ. He rejects the characterisation of the Saviour as a mere native 'dervish' in J.E. Renan's *Life of Jesus* (published in English translation in London, 1864),[7] but admires D.F. Strauss's *The Life of Jesus* (published in English translation in London, 1846).[8] Though some thought this book heretical,[9] the careful realism of *The Shadow* represents a conviction that Jesus' divine and historical identities can be reconciled.

In 1870, in an interesting turn of phrase, Hunt tells Tupper that he has dismissed 'any shadow of a doubt about his [Christ's] spiritual authority'.[10] In the same year, he defends the historical reliability of the scriptures to Scott: 'You know that above all my life-affection is my love of Christ . . . I believe more defiantly than ever . . . Christianity, even in its highest pretensions, must be true. You know I am not saying this in ignorance of critical and scientific theories.'[11] The letter goes on to express conviction in the resurrection: 'I mean the direct supernatural origin and nature of Christ; that He really came down from heaven, from the dwelling place of divinity, that He performed miracles, that He rose from the dead and returned again into heaven – there! I have almost written out my creed.' The defiance and self-consciousness about stating the 'pretensions' of a 'creed' betray continuing doubt about them. Indeed, the letter's acceptance of the supernatural sits awkwardly with an accompanying emphasis on 'evidences'. It goes on to suggest that the difference between man and Jesus can be understood as like the difference between animals and man and that a divine origin is the only explanation for the existence of the world, as 'nothing comes of nothing'. Hunt's evidence for Christianity is anxiously reasoned.

Unlike Tupper, Scott does not share Hunt's religious convictions. Although he is a close friend, he represents the kind of alternative audience that might construct Hunt's view as subjective and deluded. It is necessary to offer proofs of belief, just as it was with Ruskin. Scott's scepticism simply draws out existing doubts and vulnerability to a materialist point of view.

Hunt also conducts discussions with Tupper on the religious implications of science. Both tend towards the opinion that a better informed scientific theory could reconcile science and faith.[12] Hunt expresses a powerful sense of the infancy of science, and writes of a time when 'we shall be able to hear what is said in other planets or suns . . . perhaps even get photographs made by the inhabitants thereof of past events in our planet'.[13]

In his letters to Scott, Hunt predicts a scientific explanation of spiritualist phenomena.[14] For a while, these seem to offer some proof of life after death, but by 1877 he has dismissed them.[15] He also discusses the related problem of the 'next life'[16] and Christ's resurrection: 'the physical absurdity of His body having been received into the clouds'.[17] He conjectures that an explanation will be 'perhaps recognised at a later time', suggesting that the ascension of Jesus has something in common with the physical transition of solids into gas!

A later letter of 1871, however, following a serious illness and 'dejection' with his work, admits that he is 'apt too much to trust the cheerless view of the end'.[18] It dwells on enemies in Jerusalem and in London and even sees the painting as a 'tenacious foe', describing his tools, weather and his whole life as set against him. Poor health produces a vivid picture of the physicality of death. Echoing the description of Fanny in her tomb, Hunt describes himself: 'my eyes sank so deep into my head, and I became green, and my body seemed such a heavy, stiff, unelastic corpse'. A preoccupation with illness and 'physical limitations' also dominates the 1872 journal and other letters of the period.

The Shadow (plate 2) presents Christ as a concrete and empirical reality at a time when Hunt's sense of authority and eschatological hope are not secure. The factual clues that Hunt has gleaned from the *New Testament*, biographies of Jesus, local settings, accessories and types,[19] are reproduced in extreme mimetic detail. In 'The Gaze and the Glance', David Clarke remarks: 'mimetic art is produced as if it were something (some thing) having a reality prior to, or independent from the image'.[20] The historical and visual accuracy of this painting is an attempt to answer fears about the subjective, non-empirical, nature of faith. It aspires to represent an act of witness which equates both to the religious sense of the word or prophetic vision and to the Victorian respect for fact.

St Paul plays an important part in nineteenth-century eschatological debate and offers a model of a prophet dealing with a sceptical world.[21] Hunt's 'creed' quotes 1 Corinthians[22] and his self-image is closely allied to Paul's definition of the struggling prophets and their 'trouble which came to us in Asia':

> We were pressed out of measure, above strength, in so much that we despaired even of life:

> But *we had the sentence of death in ourselves, that we should not trust in ourselves*, but in God which raiseth the dead. (emphasis added)[23]

Paul addresses the fatal implications of self-doubt and asks: 'If there is no resurrection then Christ was not raised; and if Christ was not raised, then our gospel is null and void, and so too is our faith, and we turn out to have given false evidence about God.'[24] He puts his finger precisely on the fear of delusion, and answers it in the form of data, a list of witnesses who have seen the resurrected Christ, including himself.[25]

Hunt tells Tupper that he regrets that he cannot also witness a resurrection, as did Paul, or as John witnessed that of Lazarus: 'It cannot to us be a light to reveal the truth /no miracle not seen can be/ this it was only as it was fresh glowing from the furnace of divine providence'.[26] The intense physicality and the conventionally 'risen' stance of Christ in *The Shadow* perhaps enacts this desire. Hunt's journal describes a vision of Christ in a dream while working on his picture and, interestingly, the Saviour appears in the form of a painting.[27] The wheat fields and fruits on the sill refer to Paul's analogy of Christ's resurrection as 'firstfruits of the harvest of the dead',[28] and the golden illumination recreates the sense of miraculous immediacy, 'fresh glowing from the furnace of divine providence'. This phrase, and the obsessive need for sunlight to light the model, recalls Paul's description of his meeting with Jesus as accompanied by bright light.[29] Hunt also records periods of blindness, echoing Paul's temporary blinding. Paul's text states: 'Last of all He appeared to me too . . . and his grace to me has not proved vain; in my labours I have outdone them all.'[30] This reference parallels the strenuous journeys and labours of the artist, as well as the subject of *The Shadow* itself.

Hunt's representation of Christ's physical body constitutes a re-witnessing of him, if not a kind of resurrection in itself. As Elizabeth Bronfen says in her essay, 'Risky Resemblances: On Repetition, Mourning and Representation', 'repetition can be seen as an attempt to counteract absence, loss and death . . . [A]s a double of the lost object, the first object can return in a new form, thus questioning the uniqueness of the first term and implying that the loss is not irrevocable'.[31] This is interesting in the light of the fact that Hunt completes a likeness of Fanny after her death, and subsequently married her younger sister, Edith, on 8 November 1875. *The Shadow* is perhaps another kind of 'double', or a precise likeness of the elusive Saviour to counteract wavering faith and thoughts of mortality.

Pointon reads Hunt's 'obsessive depiction of the body's surface' as a response to a 'fear of death' represented by the tools.[32] The substantial figure specifically answers preoccupations with physical deterioration and weakness. The Saviour's flawless, muscular body and brightly illuminated skin counter the sharp tools and the shadow. His attitude of 'repose and relaxation', and prayers of 'gratitude to His Father that the welcome hour of rest has come',[33] neutralises the exhaustion of the artist as well as fear of mortality. Hunt's journal contains frequent prayers of a similar kind, equating 'repose' to the final rest.[34]

The close association between Hunt's concept of Christ and his self-image as prophet, established in the previous chapter, reinforces the idea that the representation of the body of Jesus has a direct relationship to the physical intactness of the artist himself. Hunt used many models for the figure, including himself: a vision of 'defects' and 'great obliterations' in the picture drives him to get up and, bending double, to copy his own knee.[35] There are also precedents in the scriptures for a simultaneity between the body of Christ and that of the follower. Paul describes the prophet as being like a limb of Christ, recalling Hunt's metaphor of himself as a branch,[36] and also says, 'every man has Christ for his head'. In 1898, Hunt completed a replica of the head in the picture for Queen Victoria. This is entitled *The Beloved* (Royal Collection) and may relate to Edith's favourite appellation for her husband, 'Beloved Holman', as recalled by his granddaughter.[37]

The apparently far-fetched idea that the head of Christ might be conflated with the artist's own as a realisation of mutual resurrection is supported by the pattern of work recorded in his 1872 journal. He repaints or corrects the head almost daily and confides to Combe:

> The principle difficulty I have now is with the head of Christ. I must depend upon this to show the personage it represents, for the originality of the treatment would lead people away from recognising it – yet I want to get in the head too much that is different from the conventional head, which is always too weak to me. I have thus my need for God's help, for which I pray as for bread.[38]

The head of Christ must not be weak and it must be both divine and realistic. In this, it perhaps represents an antidote to the merely material, decaying head which haunts the story of Isabella, associated with the artist's fears of death.

Judgement and authority

The consoling nature of this image of Christ is dependent not only on the power of its corporeal perfection to neutralise physical concerns about weakness and death, but also on its role as a testament to the artist's Christ *like* prophetic status. The depiction of the head is the focus of the attempt to embody this special vision, which, as Hunt tells Combe, must be distanced from social convention. Hunt is, however, conscious of the audience of the painting and the possibility that it might fail to recognise 'the personage it represents'. This worry is focused on the 'originality' of the particular treatment. Hunt's privileged sense of self entails a rejection of the collectivity of convention, but, as in the memoir, this isolation generates fears about the singularity or relativity of his vision.

In the letter to Combe, the 'conventional' is dismissed as 'weak', but the journal, and other letters of this period, juxtapose familiar anxieties about the artist's corporeal weakness with anxieties about the soundness and sanity of his singular vision. The material evidences of immortality, surveyed above, are, correspondingly, accompanied by an equally repetitive defence of moral integrity. Fantasies of eschatological safety are threatened by fears of subjectivity and delusion, as well as fears of actual weakness. A discourse of damage and disease, and a particular vocabulary of mutilation, also accumulates around the issue of judgement and authority.

Fears of insanity are specifically related to doubts about the possibility of envisaging and depicting a sacred beauty. The correspondence of 1869 is preoccupied with Stephens's accusations that Hunt's recent picture, *Bianca – the patroness of Heavenly Harmony* (1868–69, Worthing Museum and Art Gallery, figure 8.2), is ugly. In one letter, Hunt vows to abandon his career and shut himself away in his own 'self conceit'.[39] In 1872, as *The Shadow* nears completion, he questions his artistic perceptions and wonders whether he is going 'mad'.[40] The journal reveals that he has relatively little trouble with the figure of Mary, but incessantly repaints the figure of Christ and is continually convinced that it looks 'bad and hopeless';[41] 'work all in doubt'.[42]

Hunt seems unable to assess the image and craves the validation of a collective opinion, yet he is nervous about exposing the picture to ridicule:

> I go to more violent extremes in my estimation of it than I have with any previous picture except perhaps the Temple picture which for the same reason I have no one to show it to I fretted over enormously Sometimes indeed I am in good spirits and I feel that it will silence all cavillers but in an hour seeing the impossibility of this, whatever merit it had, I see it as a future humiliation.[43]

This sense of being watched, judged and 'humiliated'[44] by God (and Fanny) is compounded by an acute consciousness of a more worldly audience, impatient for the belated return to London, 'where so many are waiting to denounce'.[45] This audience becomes associated with violence. Stephens's criticisms of *Bianca* are 'lacerating'[46] and the reception of *The Shadow* is dreaded, as 'a mortal wound . . . a knife in my liver'.[47] This vulnerability to public opinion is described as a feeling of helplessness and exposure 'to the power of the world . . . the ravages of the outside scramble'.[48]

Hunt's correspondence consistently links his concerns about the future critical and public reception of *The Shadow* to the lengthy and self-righteous complaints about fashion, rumour, critics, journalists, rival artists and the Academy, referred to in previous chapters.[49] These negative characterisations of 'the power of the world' foreshadow those in the memoir: 'cramping distortions of ephemeral tastes of the day . . . the fashion for such frivolity being the mark of the corruption of original sin . . . imperilling the vigour of the race' (1, xiv). This morbid language recalls the 'unbelieving, and the abominable, and murderers, and whoremongers, and sorcerers, and idolaters, and all liars', who are condemned to death in Revelation.[50] Hunt denounces the work of Rossetti's followers: 'hysteric grimacings, that would relegate healthy manliness to be a mark of childishness, or rudeness, and would deny the name of poetry to all that was not sickly and morbid' (2, 365).

As I have noted in Chapter 1, such attacks are a defensive response to the potential of opposing ways of seeing to deconstruct the integrity of the artist and cast his vision as aberrant; diverse judgements of the world are discredited and replaced with a single set of divine criteria. The idea of the artist set apart from, and persecuted by, a disordered society in the throes of the 'last days' is, in part, a Christianised rationalisation of modern mass society's natural heterogeneity and inevitable failure to consent uniformly to a personal vision. The language of immaturity, insanity, deceit, death and disease which permeates descriptions of unsympathetic critics and artists is a measure of the capacity of other views to contradict this sense of the artist as a privileged participant in eternity. The issues of integrity which underlie episodes in the memoir such as 'The *Pall Mall Gazette* letters', 'Issa does not appreciate the scene' and 'Max and the pistol', become, in this context, *actual* issues of life and death. It is significant that two of these incidents feature weapons, the gun and Valentine's sword, which are false. Worries about integrity centre on the act of exhibition. This fear of the critical audience is specifically evoked by the description of Stephens and his 'posse' gossiping in front of *Valentine* (2, 344).

In private writings, the artist's sage-like relation to his audience is even less secure. This manifests itself in the form of negative and dangerous constructions of performance. In an early letter to Lear, Hunt writes: 'I have for the last three weeks been like one of those street tumblers who spinning a wheel of sharp knives, are unable to look to the right or to the left, for fear of dangerous tools coming down upon their bare heads.'[51] This statement is accompanied by a sketch of himself surrounded by a halo of daggers (figure 4.1). They are labelled with the names of patrons, models, critics and other problems, representing a familiar construction of society as diverse and hostile, 'the ravages of the outside scramble'. The masochistic prophet/child exchange reappears as artist/performer. The prophet/artist is, as Adams says, 'implicated in the logic of the Dandy'.[52] Max Weber calls this paradoxical tension between private mastery of the self and performance of that mastery 'virtuoso asceticism':

> It is imperative for the virtuoso that he 'prove' himself before God, as being called solely through the ethical quality of his conduct in this world. This actually means that he must 'prove' himself to himself as well. No matter how much the world as such is religiously devalued and rejected as being creatural and the vessel of sin, yet psychologically the world is all the more affirmed as the theatre of god-willed activity in one's worldly calling.[53]

The tumbler reappears in the Dead Sea journal: 'heaven help me to escape from despair at the worth of my vocation. I would not for any world content myself to be a sort of caper-cutter upon canvas, an acrobat who turns and grimaces in the highroad to the thousand passing ~~busily~~ by busy to evil or good.'[54] The grimacing acrobat recalls the 'hysteric grimacings' attributed to Rossetti's followers. His descriptions of other 'false' artists relate to underlying fears about judgement of the integrity of his own work and person. The figure of the tumbler prefigures Hunt's image of himself as a lonely player after Fanny's death,[55] and his self-characterisation as a deluded 'fool' at the height of problems with *The Shadow*,[56] as well as Renan's unacceptable depiction of Christ as a mere 'dervish'.[57]

In his Romanes lecture of 1895, Hunt proclaims that Art 'is not the mere cross-mark of a clown, not the imprint of the thumb of the savage'.[58] The savage personifies the materialism of Issa or Scott, and the clown relates to the fantastical, the grotesque, the 'flaunting and meretricious' (2, 493), but both figures are unenlightened, childish and associated with damage, disease and death. The position of Christ in the midst of so many sharp, hostile objects in *The Shadow*, imitates Hunt's picture of himself surrounded by a halo of knives, and suggests that the painting responds to ambivalent characterisations of the artist as clown-like, as well as weak and mortal. The clear-eyed, adult figure of the Saviour answers threats to physical *and* spiritual integrity.

The interior setting of the picture contains overlapping references to both physical and moral hostility. The Virgin's shifting gaze represents the diverse and destructive viewpoints of the social context. It enacts the childish perceptions of the savage and the clown, embracing the literal fact of death (the shadow) and delusions of wealth and luxury (the kings' gifts). A letter to Tupper specifically likens her preoccupation with the treasures in the chest to the wrong-headedness of the London art establishment's artificial laurels, and her hidden face implies a literal obscuring of divine beauty. The use of a back view is perhaps a defensive reply to Stephens's complaints about the ugliness of *Bianca*. Hunt comments, disingenuously, 'it is unfortunate that there is no youthful female figure in it'.[59] The fact that Mary's pose echoes the shape and angle of the saw creates associations between alternative points of view, such as those represented by Stephens or the art establishment, and mutilation. Both the saw and her dress echo the cool, blue tones of the shadow. The shadow spear cast by the saw approaching Jesus' side alludes to criticism, 'like a knife in my liver'. The spiky crown and the Virgin's jewellery, representing artifice, ostentation and vanity, echo the sharp, shiny tools about the workplace and those on the wooden batten, intended to suggest 'the idea of the fingers nailed thereon'.[60] Christ's surroundings illustrate a continuum of persecution, embracing spiritual and corporeal danger.

This suggestion of a conflation of moral corruption and physical violence is reinforced by the stylistic pedigree of the painting. Mary's pose is partly derived from that of Ariadne in Titian's *Bacchus and Ariadne* (1522–23, National Gallery, London, figure 4.3), as she turns to see the god and his retinue. The dandiacal, deformed and drunken revellers seem to image Rossetti's grimacing followers. Their capers and their theatrical display of parts of a dismembered donkey underline the equation between performance, the grotesque and mutilation. *The Shadow* also echoes the poses of Christ and the kneeling female figure in Raphael's *The Transfiguration of Christ* (1517, Pinacoteca, Vatican, Rome, figure 4.4). *Pre-Raphaelitism* conspicuously condemns this image as pompous and false, and specifically rejects its fantastical depiction of Jesus. A very extended footnote pays morbidly close attention to medical and anatomical inaccuracies in the depiction of the convulsed, 'demoniacal' boy (1, 100–1). The notion of 'virtuoso', or showy artifice, focuses upon a grimacing, grotesque and demented child.

When artists are influenced by other artists they are unlikely to borrow directly; they tend, rather, to recombine, modify or even invert ideas or motifs. Hunt's use of references is generally dialectical rather than derivative. The relationship between his painting and these oddly inappropriate prototypes is like that between the image of the healed Innocents and depictions of Herod's massacre; gruesomeness and artificiality are corrected. *The Shadow* rejects Raphael's idealisations of Christ, the halo and 'the physical absurdity of His body having been received into the clouds',[61] preferring to imitate Leonardo's simpler representation of 'the highest type of humanity' (2, 268), the window echoing that which replaces the halo in *The Last Supper* (1495–98, refectory, Sta Maria delle Grazie, Milan).[62] *The Triumph* also refers to *Bacchus and Ariadne*. Unlike Titian's pagan scene, it presents a procession of unself-conscious, perfect children following the

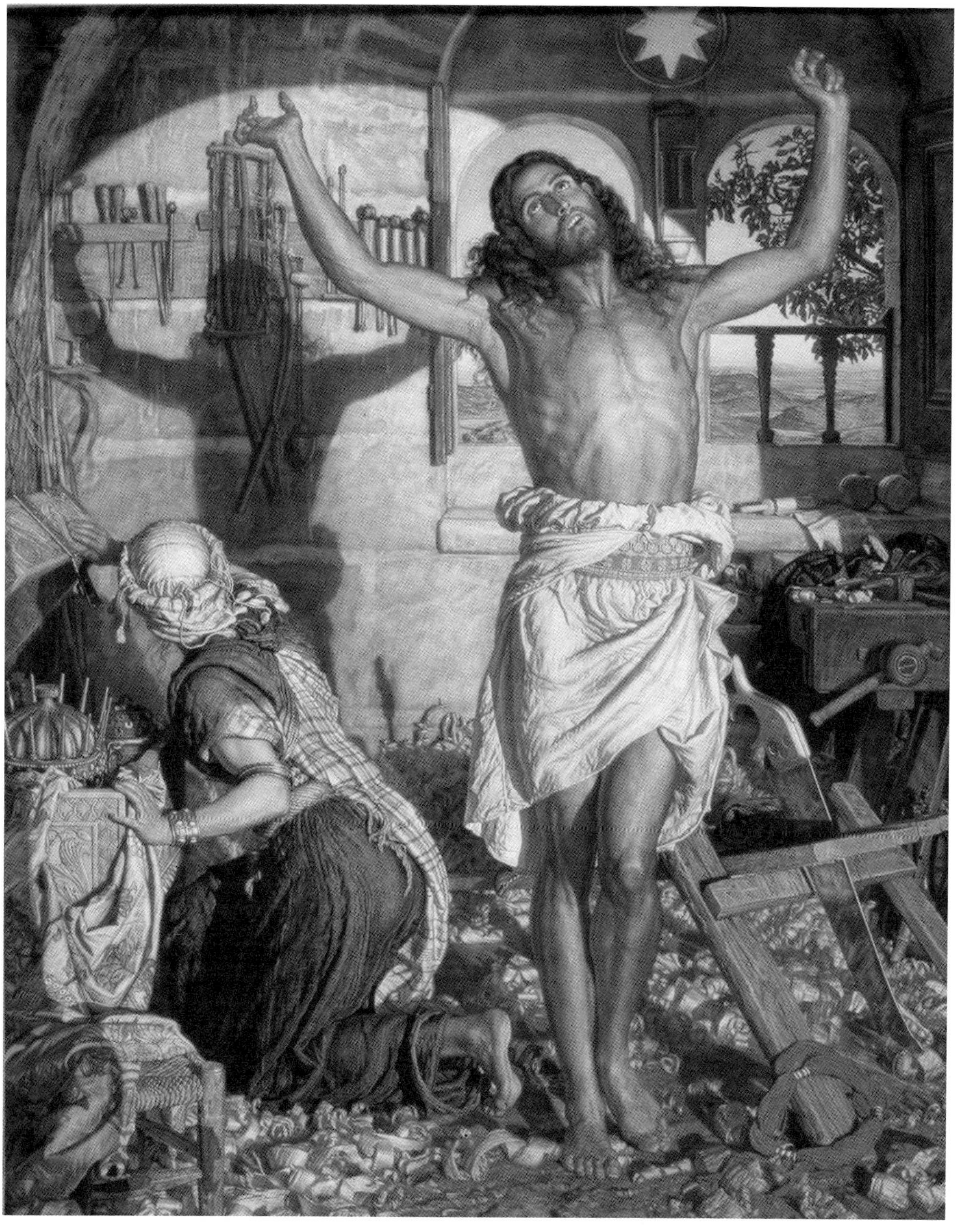

4.2
William Holman Hunt,
The Shadow of Death,
1869–73

true Saviour and bearing only garlands. The little satyr, blithely pulling along the head of a decapitated donkey, reappears in the pose and position of the Innocent who is looking at his healed wound, while the donkey itself is given sacred status as the mount of Christ.[63]

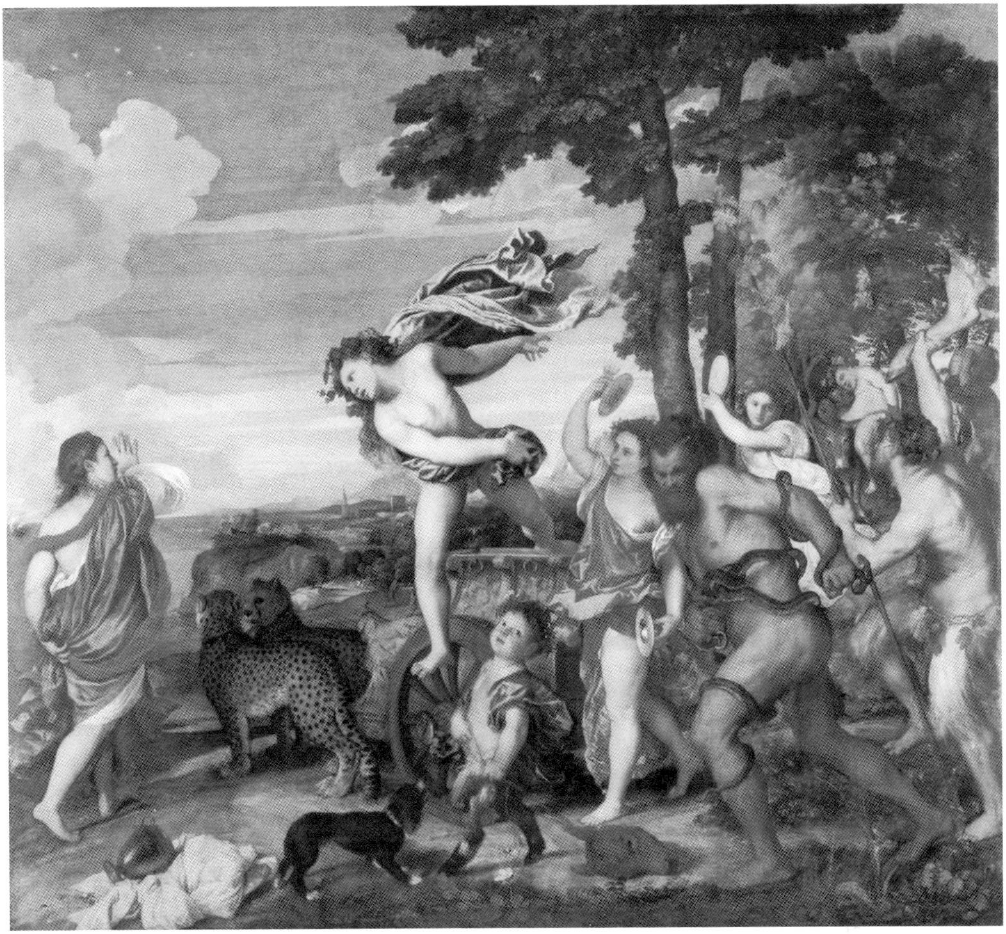

4.3
Titian,
Bacchus and Ariadne,
1522–23

The echoes of past art in *The Triumph* and *The Shadow* constitute self-conscious references to the potential of art to be naive, deceptive or morbid. These equate to the defensive discussions of alternative critical accounts in the letters of this period and look forward to the anxious awareness of manipulative and misleading literature in *Pre-Raphaelitism*. This preoccupation with the potential artificiality and danger of the written or painted text relates to more profound fears about authority: the veracity of the artist's prophetic fantasies; to fears that his 'trial' of labour and suffering is merely strutting and fretting;[64] and that his declaration of immortality is no more than 'a tale told by an idiot' (*Macbeth*, Act 5, Scene 5). As Hunt writes of Monk: 'he is a queer enthusiast, but only mad if believing in the bible implicitly denotes insanity, perhaps it does'.[65]

The preoccupation with deceit and delusion and association of them with the primitive, the grotesque, the sick and the violent, express the

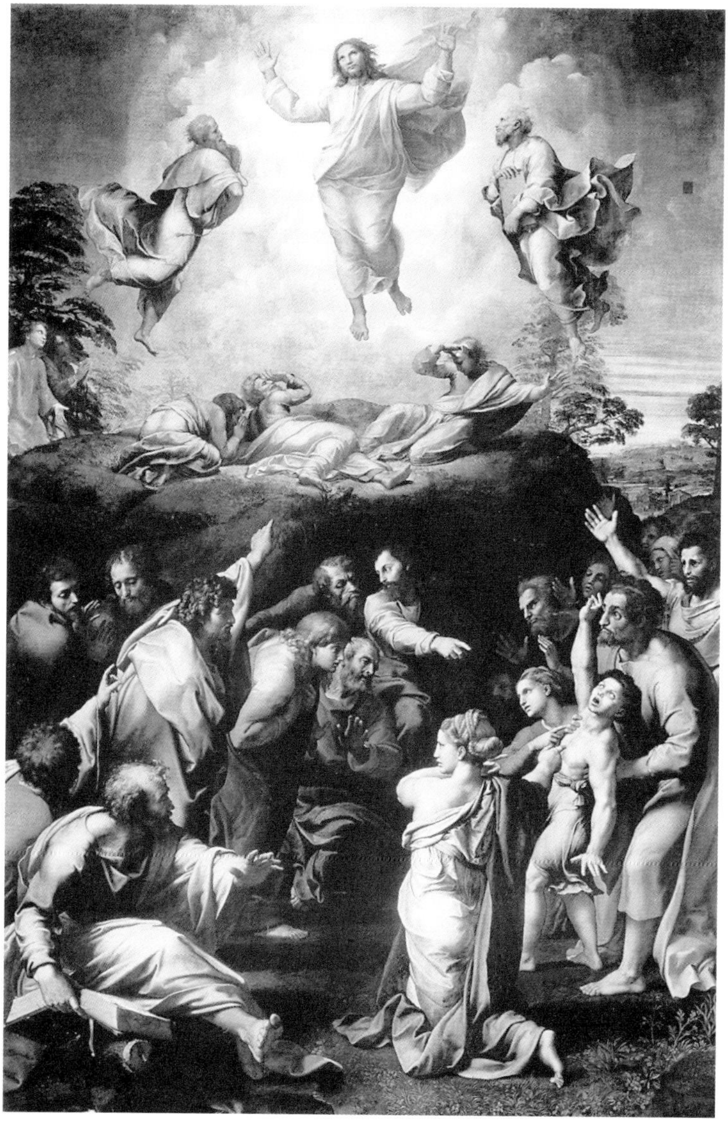

4.4
Raphael,
The Transfiguration of Christ,
1517

extent to which they threaten an interrelated sense of moral and physical integrity. The perfection of the figure of Christ relates to the safety of both the body and the soul of the artist. The potential success of *The Shadow* answers a range of anxieties about authority which relate to Hunt's reputation and social and financial security, as well as his prophetic status and his worthiness to God in the light of imminent judgement. It thus constructs the resurrection of the artist at levels of the circumstantial, the spiritual and the corporeal.

Triumph of the Innocents?

The realisation of the fantasy of resurrected children in *The Triumph* (plate 3) accords with Hunt's happier, more stable home life with his new wife, Edith, Fanny's sister, whom he marries in 1875. She cares for him and Cyril and is always presented as loyal and supportive.[66] The equation of the nurture of father and son is given an unusually positive expression in a jaunty letter to Tupper of 1876, in which Hunt imagines sharing Cyril's privilege of having a personal tutor. For the first time, Hunt is accompanied on his 'trial', his journey to the East, by a family. This seems to be imaged in the travelling family in the painting. He writes with uncharacteristic optimism (and clarity of punctuation), 'in spite of all my vexations here, . . . I can profess to being in a position happier than ever I was in my life, and even better in my health than for many years'.[67]

However, the illness and exhaustion experienced during work on *The Shadow* quickly return, and are augmented by concerns for the safety of the new family. By December 1876, Hunt is beginning to complain of 'difficulties' and 'headaches' and death again becomes a regular theme of the correspondence.[68] The sense of the artist as suffering and singular prophet emerges even more powerfully. He rails against critics and other artists who must fail to redeem the English public and describes his home threatened by violence due to local unrest. He is again plagued by nightmares.[69]

The familiar exchange between faith and security is demonstrated in the following letter of July. It amplifies worries about the family's safety before becoming an analysis of 'revealed religion'.[70] Hunt rehearses his arguments to Scott about the logic and use of religion, and goes on to give a long analysis (over seven hundred words) of biblical predictions to support belief in a 'vital force in the fulfilment of prophesy'. He then turns to John and the raising of Lazarus. In the nineteenth century, this was considered to be, like Paul's 1 Corinthians 1 and 15, important evidence that Christ physically rose from the dead and proof of the resurrection of the body.[71]

The letter focuses on the linked themes of authority and witness. It is interested in the record of the raising of Lazarus, rather than the miracle itself. It presents it as a vivid feat of memory of 'facts' fifty years after the event: 'It is by an eye witness of extraordinary intelligence.' The role of John as viewer and his unusual powers of recall parallel the claims of the memoir (p 24), but Hunt goes further: he presents the text by John as 'greater' than direct witness. This valorises his picture, another textual realisation of resurrection.

Again there are parallels between the painting and an oddly literal understanding of biblical account. The letter describes John's gospel as 'illumined' by 'a true light', and Hunt reports devising a new form of 'supernatural' lighting for his painting, 'an earthly light' made by experimenting with magnified moonlight to convey the 'celestial nature' of the children (2, 324).[72] This procedure of intensifying night light seems to be an interpretation of Paul's idea that revelation is only seen 'through a glass, darkly' (1 Corinthians 13: 12).

The point of the letter's lecture on the reliability of reported, or textual, prophesy is to get round the lack of a clear record of Christ's resurrection. He concludes that there is no 'distinct and methodical' account of this because 'the Apostles preached the resurrection of Christ'. In other words, he now valorises prophetic witness as a substitute for proof, paralleling his promotion of the text of John over the witness itself. This liberty is essential when dealing with the unverifiable issue of life after death, but it heightens the importance of the integrity of such records. Hunt even suggests that the scarcity of details of the resurrection proves that the Gospels were contemporary, not written in the third century as some German scholars were suggesting,[73] because a later account would have felt the need to add embellishments to back up the unlikely story.

This long and convoluted defence of the historical actuality of resurrection dramatically underlines the challenge which the concept poses to Hunt's reliance on material corroboration of belief. He now accepts the absence of concrete evidence and is driven to cite the lack of it, a silence in the Gospels, as proof itself! *Pre-Raphaelitism* constructs its author's honesty in a similar way, including opposing evidence in order to suggest an unbiased survey. The validation of religious vision is shifted onto a valorisation of the viewer. The sincerity of the witness stands in for the sincerity of the account. The letter is at pains to defend the value of records by witnesses who, like himself, aspire to the status of prophet, and thus prop up the unseeable fantasy of specific bodily resurrection and Hunt's picturing of it.

In the next letter to Tupper, material proof is again admitted to be inadequate and faith and vision are called upon instead:

> I no more than others can say that I have found any proof that can upset the arguments of materialism against mortality I have in fact come to the conclusion that there are none yet my confidence in a day of judgment and an after life are stronger than ever. While I am forced to admit my own inability to adduce proof of the existence of God Almighty.[74]

Despite this abandonment of the 'evidences' offered to Scott six years earlier,[75] the letter goes on to repeat, at length, the same reasoning. The dependence on proof cannot be completely abandoned: 'Revelation is a matter of detail of decreasing value in later days – I think – altho I believe that science itself will justify what seems amiss when science is complete.'

Eschatological hope cannot be completely supported by material evidence or by mere faith. Private correspondence continually interrogates both of these, but belief is increasingly dependent on the integrity of the prophetic self-image, the interior, self-fashioning role of Carlyle's prophet/hero. The challenge to the reader to either accept the revelations at Mount Hermon, or dismiss the artist as a 'madman', becomes tragically significant, a defiant dare to death itself.

The picturing of Christ as a baby ratifies prophetic perception by aligning the prophet and the child, previously opposed, through a valorisation of their shared purity of gaze. As Gissing puts it: 'in a great painter there is always something of the child'.[76] Hunt is not, now, being deprecating when he calls his faith 'childish'.[77] Paul recommends that the prophet combine a childish innocence with an adult intellect,[78] and Hunt reprises his words: 'The man who is tempered to appeal to an inner monitor is . . . ready for higher service – when he will see things more clearly than now.'[79] The Innocents' 'martyrdom on the path of their *recognised* Lord' (emphasis added), seems to describe an understanding of the artist's own developing vision: 'they progressively mark their understanding of the glory of their martyrdom . . . Behind . . . babes are as yet hardly awakened to their new life . . . Towards the front are other spirits of children *triumphing* in completer knowledge of their service' (emphasis added).[80] In the absence of 'tangible evidence' of life after death, an innate childish instinct towards good, echoing Kingsley's Tom, acts as a substitute for 'a God that he can't trace'.[81] *The Triumph* departs from earlier works in its attempt to reconcile prophetic inspiration and the innocent, instinctive perceptions of the child.

However, Hunt's new reliance on a childish, unreasoned faith is not secure. As I have shown in Chapter 3, the childish persona tends to undermine prophetic authority and optimism. The doubt and distress which dominate the period of painting *The Shadow* continue. The incoherent structure of Hunt's discussions of hope, the falling back on proofs between admissions that there are none, the odd repetition of the excuse that failures are due to difficulties and a poor start, the continued preoccupation with death, illness and with critics, all betray insecurity. The disorder described in correspondence contrasts with the benign vision of the picture: 'Why is it that man's laws are never yet perfect enough to reach all treachery and infamy – and the fates permit the wicked to profit by their honesty and vice? To me there is no explanation . . . but the life hidden behind the veil.'[82]

The more the prophetic vision is relied upon, the more the issue of its perfection and, with it, the perfection of its token, the image, becomes paramount. The painting, imaging the invisible, that which cannot be traced, 'behind the veil', represents a fantasy of redemption which is all too flimsy. The orderly and perfect picture must be seen as a response to confusion rather than a complacent refuge in dogma. Despite the subject matter, the actual imaging of the unknown is an attempted act of autonomous prophesy, not an acceptance of childish, incomplete understanding, and is tied more closely than ever to the authority of the artist.

The defensive role of *The Triumph* is, like that of *The Shadow*, underlined by the way Hunt's letters construct the picture's uncanny relevance to the themes of physical safety in his correspondence. In 1876, he tells Tupper that, during the birth of a child to Edith, he has re-experienced anxieties similar to those provoked by Fanny's confinement and death. The birth is a success and the new baby is described as 'a darling rolly poly dolly with a very sensible determination to lose no opportunity of sucking and sleeping'. Relief is imaged in the flow of Edith's milk, 'I dismiss my fear her milk has come in good quantity, and baby is thriving on it'.[83] This echoes the positive aspects of nurture in the picture and suggests an association between the maternal flow, the rolling sequence of Innocents in white, swirling draperies and 'the flood upon which the spiritual children advance'[84]. The plumpness of the babies and the generous, outflung arms of Jesus, originating from the breast of the Virgin (shown naked in a preliminary sketch, 1876, Walker Art Gallery, figure 4.5) reinforce this link. Hunt made use of sketches of his family in painting this group (1879, Walker Art Gallery) and mentions that his new baby is 'free from any sort of blemish',[85] recalling the intactness of the Innocents.

However, the iconography of the picture also alludes to the longer-standing sense of threat and neglect which continues to dominate Hunt's writings. Hunt's first conception for the design, in 1868, was orientated specifically towards the feeding of the Christ Child by angels and coincided with his anxieties over the feeding of the motherless Cyril.[86] Bennett cites Tintoretto's *Flight into Egypt* (1565–87, Scuola di San Rocco, Venice) as one source for the composition.[87] Hunt may also have been familiar with engravings of Tintoretto's *The Origin of the Milky Way* (1578, figure 4.6), acquired by the National Gallery in 1890, which features an expansive gesture on the part of Juno, flowing, milk-like draperies and a wreath of attendant putti. It combines two figures in front and back view, as do *The Shadow* and *The Triumph*. The angry goddess's rejection of the suckling Hercules might relate to Fanny's withdrawal and Hunt's sense of her stern judgment of him from heaven (she was meant to wear a peacock shawl, Juno's motif, in her posthumous portrait.) Hunt's design makes good the associations of rejection and starvation in *The Origin*, just as it corrects the massacre of the Innocents.[88]

The picture also neutralises other physical threats. Hunt believes a 'massacre' of Christians to be imminent in the area, and organises the escape of his own family on horseback by night.[89] The dogs in

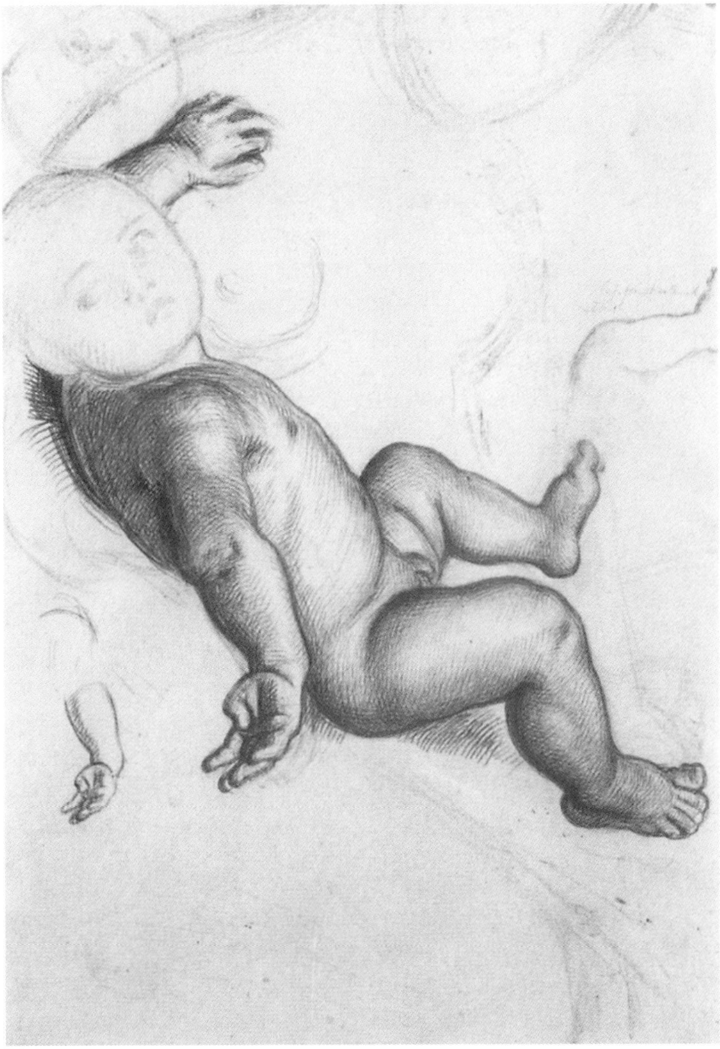

4.5
William Holman Hunt,
Study for the Christ Child in the Virgin's arms for 'The Triumph of the Innocents',
1876

the image recall his idea of hostile Moslems who 'foam at the mouth against all Christians',[90] as do the 'soldiery' anxiously looked for by Joseph. In addition, the image answers concerns for the spiritual safety of Hunt's children, representing an ability to demonstrate faith to them. The way this is expressed again shows a conflation of their nurture and the artist's own. Hunt records that he is 'clinging' to faith and a few lines later, says, 'I look forward therefore with great eagerness to find out reasons to give my children for clinging fast to the last to revealed religion'.[91] The phrasing implies the desperate and inconclusive nature of this belief, and a corresponding threat of danger to himself and offspring.

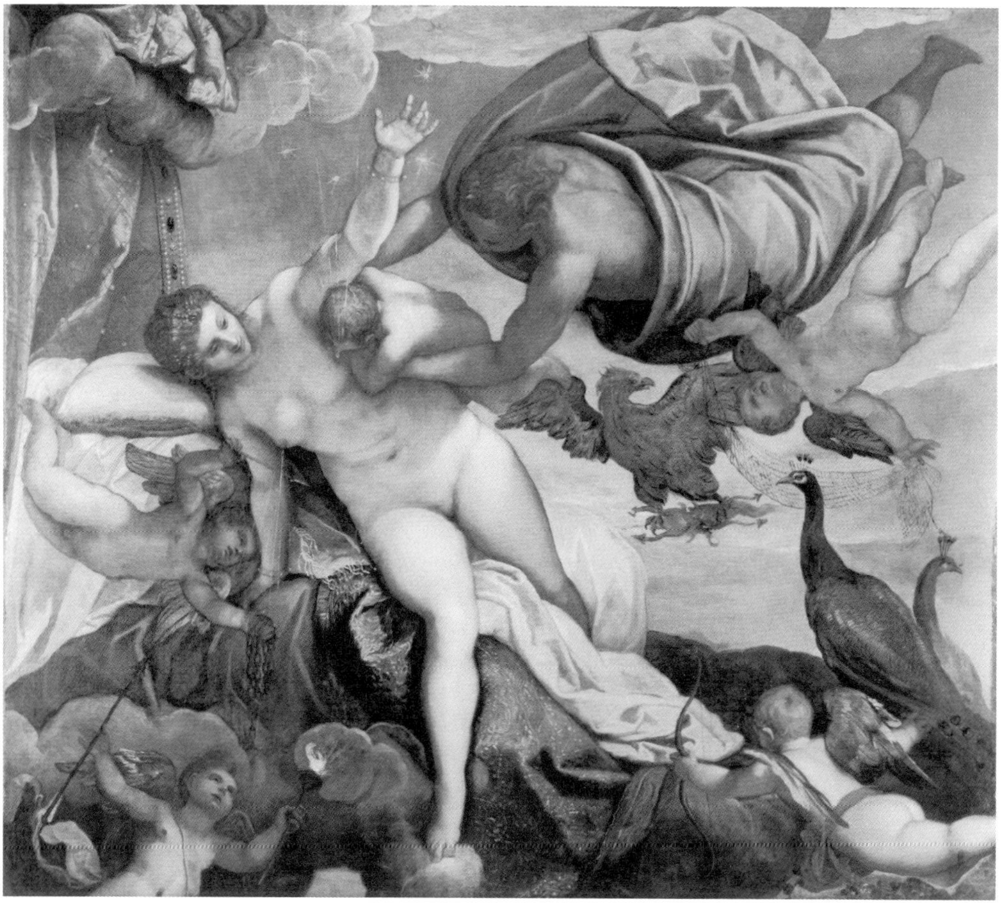

4.6
Jacobo Tintoretto,
The Origin of the Milky Way,
1578

As I noted in the previous chapter, *The Triumph* also images an ideal of the return of the household to the safety of London, about which Hunt is already talking in 1876.[92] Adams presents tension in the prophetic persona as a contradiction between private mastery and its authorisation through public demonstration. *The Triumph* represents this performatory component, the virtuoso element of Weber's 'virtuoso asceticism'. The picture's completion thus addresses broader issues of safety. It will remedy Hunt's sense of not being provided for in financial terms, repair reputation and the sense of childish incompleteness in skill and education. Complaints about these are prevalent at this time.[93]

In this role, the picture participates in the contingent and enacts just the material, circumstantial dangers it is meant to answer. It stubbornly eludes completion. Hunt is only able to finish it in1887, after twelve years. Subjective, abstract hope becomes a bluntly objective, concrete disappointment, a 'terrible curse of hopeless struggle when most of all man wants to feel relief from the anxiety about his position and prospects'.[94] 'I feel the thing has well nigh ruined my best chances of shewing myself to posterity at my best'.[95] A 'ruined' picture implies commercial and artistic 'ruin',[96] and the word 'difficulty' is frequently used to describe the obstinacy of the painting as well as general misfortunes. Letters that record illness and bad weather, also record painting 'the picture all wrong',[97] demonstrating the inevitable problems that will result when an ambitious ideal is attempted in a world that is not ideal. Hunt acknowledges this, 'yet I will hold to my dream as long as possible'.[98]

Hunt's use of vocabulary constructs an intimate relationship between the imperfections of the painting and the imperfections of the world, the artist and his family. A preoccupation with the uneven surface of the ground[99] (he had had similar problems with the sandy texture of *The Shadow*)[100] is generalised into a symptom of the human condition: 'in every truth revealed there lies some sand of error and wrong'.[101] In August 1879, he tells Stephens that 'I have lately had to upset the picture all again',[102] recalling the boat metaphor and his 'clinging' to religion. The problem relates to damage to the canvas caused by a soaking it received during storms in Jerusalem. At the time, Hunt recounts the deluge in apocalyptic terms familiar from his 1872 journal, and perceives himself as almost shipwrecked.[103] He describes later flaking of the paint surface as a heavy snowstorm, and reiterates his own difficulty in weathering 'this last storm', and 'the effort to be calm under this constant trouble'.[104] This repeated metaphor relates to the idea of the perilous voyage depicted in his contemporary work, *The Ship*. It also reinforces the construction of the incomplete state of the painting as relating to Hunt's own sense of childish neglect and inadequacy, left like a boat 'half made'.[105] The deluge imagery subverts the constructive, liquid flow of the composition. The canvas turns out to be too weak for its purpose and is itself described as undulating 'like the sand ripple of the sea shore'.[106]

Difficulties with models and with the inappropriate support cause Hunt to repaint even more than usual. The image of the sealed-up wounds of the Innocents is thus re-enacted in the filling in of breaks in the ground and gaps in the image, which can be seen in the form of black blemishes in X-rays of the Fogg Art Museum version (figure 9.5), worked on in parallel with the Walker Art Gallery picture. The painting process is described in corporeal terms: a letter of August 1878 describes struggling to 'cure' the 'blistered and twisted canvas', which in the end seems 'healed'.[107] In October a 'great fissure' is being repaired.[108] In April 1879, he is 'covering many distracting white spots'[109] and in May, 'serious sores'.[110] In August he writes that he is still filling up 'weak places'[111] and continues to do so until he is forced to begin on a new canvas the following year (now in Tate Britain).

A letter to Tupper reports that baby Gladys is ill, robbed of her physical 'glory', and also that the 'glory' of the painting is set back.[112] The wholeness of the Innocents stands in for the wholeness of the painting and the wholeness of the artist and his children. It also connotes the wholeness of prophetic maturity. Its refusal to become complete, however, suggests that the material is still subverting the fantasy, recalling the image of the undeveloped child amidst chipped and broken marbles 'that were the glory of a temple'.[113]

As time wears on, this notion of safety is extended to a simple alternative between the work's success, with all the comforts it will bring, and death. It will either secure 'name and position', or 'kill me outright'.[114] The demise of career, body and spirit are conflated with the failure of the image. Correspondence claims certainty that life is almost over (although Hunt lives another thirty years) and presents *The Triumph* as a last chance.[115]

The completion and exhibition of the picture focuses issues of authority and integrity. The words of critics are, once more, potentially 'fatal'.[116] The work is hidden and letters acknowledge the repetitious nature of failed promises to display it. Hunt tells Stephens in 1880, 'Had an eye seen it till I had got the evil fairly cured I don't think I could have answered for my sanity.'[117] Again public exposure brings fears of madness. Each time Tupper is due in London, Hunt writes that he expects to have it completed ready for his viewing, but never does.[118] Tupper dies in 1879 without seeing the picture, and Hunt's short notes to him during his last illness seem callous in their obsession with finishing his work and gaining his approval before it is too late.[119] This need is perhaps fired by the imminence of another death. The judgement of his friend and posterity stand in for an imminent judgement and eternity of a spiritual kind.

The attempt to construct prophetic security and authority through *The Triumph* is undermined by experience. One letter displays a painful awareness of this dislocation, distinguishing between 'our moral decisions for we are absolutely free in these', and the 'conditions under which we have to prove our patience, and make our decisions'.[120] Hunt's lengthy, but muddled, rationalisations of conviction in his personal vision of divinity, point to the inevitable limitations of dependence on material 'proofs', including the picture itself, in the face of a growing need to gainsay death.

The only resurrected bodies that Hunt will see are those he invents. Prophetic sight is thus energetically constructed, through an equation of hardship, trial and Christlike sacrifice, an invocation of the innocent gaze of the child and the participation of another privileged mortal, the Virgin. The imaging of the healed Innocents fills the silence of preceding designs. The unavoidable tension between symbols of hope and material manifestations of danger in the analogous imagery of previous work is here answered by a resurrection which is not read, but seen.

Despite the valorisation of the child in this painting, the act of seeing such an abstract event is an entirely prophetic one, on a par with John's witnessing of Lazarus, or Paul's confrontation with the risen Christ. The aim is to promote the incomplete comprehension of the child into a triumphant, prophetic understanding. As Paul says:

> For we know in part, and we prophesy in part.
> But when that which is perfect is come, then that which is part shall be done away.
> When I was a child, I spake as a child, I understood as a child: but when I became a man, I put away childish things.
> For now we see through a glass, darkly; but then face to face; now I know in part; but then shall I know even as also I am known.[121]

The imaging of a fantasy, that which is hidden behind the veil, as material, face to face, requires the privileging of interior, or subjective, vision over objective vision, which produces enhanced fears about that vision and the artist's prophetic identity: 'then shall I know even as also I am known.' It could be argued that the execution of *The Triumph* represents Hunt's artistic coming of age, but the refusal of the picture to become complete and the continuing fear of death and judgement during its production, suggests discomfort with the flight of fantasy which it represents.

Hunt reproduces his own gaze with unusual intensity, but, as we shall see, it is never quite clear and complete. As Adams notes, paraphrasing Lacan, the fantasized identity is inevitably mediated, or 'self-estranged' by its externalisation or performance, in language, or in this case, paint.[122] Hunt writes that in the afterlife he 'will see more clearly than now', but in the meantime, lack of visual control in the worldly realm, lack of skill, opportunity and health, threaten his claim to be witness to, and a participant within, a divine order. His 'realisation of God's supreme mercy'[123] becomes dependent on the successful construction of the image. His difficulties with the work, however, re-enact an alternative experience of confusion and weakness in a meaningless, disordered and hostile world, and bring with it an alternative, endangered self-image.

Hunt's mimetic style confronts reality, but never completely tames the nineteenth-century doubt that nature is not a promise of heaven, but 'rock, dirt and water', that death is merely death. The Victorian 'double awareness', a tension between the deductive and the prescriptive, identified by Landow,[124] haunts all aspects of Hunt's output and causes a profound and sustained crisis of faith and authority, and a preoccupation with physical harm, which is fundamental to an understanding of his work.

Reparation and repetition

When texts are placed side by side, a pattern of metaphor emerges. Again and again, Hunt's writings invoke the neglected child, the savage, the sailor cast adrift in storms; or the grimacing madman, the dervish, the clown, the deceiver and the decadent. I have confined my analysis to two paintings, but these preoccupations inform all of his works, most notably in the spectacle of primitive and superstitious riot, *The Miracle of the Holy Fire* (1896–99, Fogg Art Museum); the examples I have cited are just a few of many. These interrelated identities, savage and clown, threaten the authority of the artist and are associated with death and an incomplete or damaged persona, expressed as the state of the child. The paintings and the memoir attempt to synthesise an adult, whole self-image which reconciles experience and imagination, where fantasy and reality validate each other.

Melanie Klein's exploration of the relationship between the physiological and the psychological describes a similarly dialectical sense of self originating from actual experiences of gratification and frustration. Her idea that this results in a splitting of the subject[125] recalls the polarised prophet/child persona that is exhibited in Hunt's writings. The attachment of exaggeratedly negative and positive values to objects and environment in these texts can be equated to Klein's notion of the individual's corresponding tendency to characterise external objects as idealised and 'good', or persecutory and 'bad'.[126] As I have shown, environment can be interpreted in terms of extreme, even apocalyptic, hostility. Fearful personal qualities, the victim/child and the madman/clown, are projected through the personification of objects and circumstance: Hunt's tools turn against their owner and February 'cheats' him of three days (pp 59, 66). In the midst of this, positive qualities are intermittently introjected to create a sense of oneness with highly subjectified, visionary environments, such as Mount Hermon, which coincide with a conviction of autonomy, omnipotence and being chosen.

The attempt to unite and resolve the experiential and rhetorical voices of the memoir, or the 'materialism and mysticism' of the paintings, may be understood in relation to the Kleinian act of 'reparation'. It represents a negation of damage, putting 'dispersed bits back together again, bringing what has been killed back to life'.[127] This definition seems to express the battles against 'disorder'. As we have seen, the collation and assembling of fragmentary perceptions and clues into the ordered image, and the constant sealing and repairing of the wounded paint surface, answer fears about the artist's own physical and mental wholeness. As Klein says: 'the effort to undo the state of disintegration to which [the object] has been reduced presupposes the necessity to make it beautiful and perfect'.[128] Klein asserts that the origin of the split object is the breast. *The Triumph* repairs apprehensions of environmental hostility and lack of nurture, associated with death and mutilation, with an imaging of motherhood, a generous flow of milk, healed children and triumphant immortality. Klein's assertion that this process is central to mourning[129] is singularly appropriate to the resurrection fantasy discussed in this chapter.

However, Hunt's practice seems to enact a defective mechanism of reparation in that he exhibits an obsessional compulsion to repeat the reparative act and anxiety about its completion. Repetition is a singular feature of his output. Issues such as education, criticism and illness are returned to regularly; parts of the painting are reworked numerous times. A certain vocabulary peppers his writings in the same way that certain motifs are reused in his iconography. In addition, Hunt's overall iconographical schemes exhibit an unresolved, internal set of dialectical relations which reflect the divided identities that are found in the writings. This is most conspicuous in the failure to synthesise the depiction of actual physical danger and a symbolic message of metaphysical safety in *The Scapegoat* and *The Shadow*, discussed in Chapter 3.

There is much more to say on this subject, but to do so would distract from my primary objective of relating the characteristics of iconography and written texts to those of the art object. However, this brief reference to psychoanalytical theory does underline the main point of the last four chapters. That is, that there exist complex patterns of similarity between constructions of the self and the image, and that these are often expressed in terms of corporeal safety and harm. I shall now go on to explore Hunt's artistic practice and will demonstrate that the dislocations evident in his writings and iconography relate to both the stylistic and the physical characteristics of the paintings, resulting in other forms of damage or fragmentation.

Notes

1 Wheeler, *Heaven, Hell*, p 3
2 Errington, *Themes*, p 275
3 Letter to Combe, 23 July 1869, JRL, MS 1213, 19
4 Letter to Stephens, 19 January 1867, BL, MS Don. e 67, 7v
5 Letter to Combe, 1 February 1867, JRL, MS 1213, 17
6 Letter to Stephens, 16 January 1867, BL, MS Don. e 67, 6–6v
7 *Pre-Raphaelitism* (1913), 2, p 338
8 Letter to Stephens, 25 July 1868, BL, MS Don. e 67, 22v
9 Vaughan, '*Realism*', p 210
10 Letter to Tupper, July 1870, *Correspondence*, p 129
11 Letter to Scott, 7 April 1870, *Notes*, 2, pp 89–90
12 Tupper, letter to Hunt, 3 February 1870, *Correspondence*, pp 105–6; letter to Tupper, 17 September 1872, pp 167–8

13 Ibid., 21 April 1879, p 275
14 Letter to Scott, 10 August 1870, *Notes*, 2, p 94
15 Letter to Tupper, 26 September 1877, *Correspondence*, p 234
16 Letter to Scott, 20 February 1871, *Notes*, 2, pp 98–9
17 Ibid., 10 August 1870, p 96
18 Ibid., 30 September 1871, pp 102–5
19 Ibid., 10 August 1870, p 96
20 Clarke, D., 'The Gaze and the Glance: Competing Understandings of Visuality in the Theory and Practice of Late Modernist Art', *Art History*, 15, 1 (March 1992), p 81
21 Wheeler, *Heaven, Hell*, pp 8–9
22 1 Corinthians 15: 3–4
23 2 Corinthians 1: 8–9
24 1 Corinthians 15: 13–15
25 Ibid., 5–8
26 Letter to Tupper, 15 July 1877, *Correspondence*, p 226
27 Journal, 3 March 1872, JRL, MS 1212, 13
28 1 Corinthians 15: 20
29 Ibid., 8–10
30 Journal, 2 March 1872, JRL, MS 1212, 9; 18 April 1872, 3, 22; May 1872, 12v, 20, 19v, 25
31 Bronfen, E., 'Risky Resemblances: On Repetition, Mourning and Representation', in *Death and Representation*, eds S.W. Goodwin and E. Bronfen (London: Johns Hopkins University Press, 1993), p 106.
32 Pointon, 'Artist as Ethnographer', p 42
33 *The Shadow of Death*, quoted Bennett, *Hunt*, p 49
34 Journal, 9 May 1872, JRL, MS 1212, 24
35 Ibid., 28 January 1872, 5v
36 1 Corinthians 12: 27; Journal, November 1854, JRL, MS 1210, 6
37 Holman-Hunt, D., *My Grandmothers and I* (London: Hamish Hamilton, 1960), p 29
38 Letter to Combe, 10 May 1871, JRL, MS 1213, 27
39 Letter to Stephens, 20 December 1869, BL, MS Don. e 67, 52
40 Letter to Tupper, 24 February 1872, *Correspondence*, p 150
41 Journal, 12 March 1872, JRL, MS 1212, 14v
42 Ibid., 22 April 1872, 20v
43 Letter to Tupper, July 1870, *Correspondence*, pp 129–30
44 Letter to Stephens, 19 January 1867, BL, MS Don. e 67, 6v–7; this theme is often repeated
45 Letter to Tupper, July 1870, *Correspondence*, p 128; also Journal, 30 January 1872, JRL, MS 1212, 6; 19 February 1872, 10v; 26 February 1872, 11v
46 Letter to Stephens, 21 June 1870, BL, MS Don. e 67, 57
47 Letter to Tupper, 3 April 1875, *Correspondence*, pp 199–200
48 Letter to Stephens, 3 May 1875, BL, MS Don. e 68, 147
49 Letter to Tupper, July 1870, *Correspondence*, pp 125–32; also 3 August 1871, pp 137–8; 2 June, 1874, pp 193–4; letter to Stephens, 3 February 1869, BL, MS Don. e 67, 32
50 Revelation, 21: 8
51 Letter to Lear, 24 January, 1853, JRL, MS 1214, 6

52 Adams, *Dandies and Desert Saints*, p 10
53 Weber, M., *Max Weber: Essays in Sociology*, eds H. Gerth and C. Wright Mills (New York: Oxford University Press, 1958), pp 290–1
54 Journal, November 1854, JRL, MS 1210, 6
55 Letter to Stephens, 19 January 1867, BL, MS Don. e 67, 7v
56 Letter to Tupper, 11 August 1875, *Correspondence*, p 201
57 *Pre-Raphaelitism* (1913), 2, p 338
58 *The obligations of the Universities Towards Art, The Romanes Lecture, 1895: Delivered in the Sheldonian Theatre, May 30 1895* (London: H. Frowde, 1895), pp 18–19
59 Letter to Tupper, July 1870, *Correspondence*, p 129
60 Hunt, *The Shadow of Death*, quoted Bennett, *Hunt*, p 49
61 Letter to Scott, 10 August 1870, *Notes*, 2, p 96
62 Hunt admired this, letter to Stephens, 3 February 1869, BL, MS Don. e 67, 32
63 Hunt copied *Bacchus and Ariadne* in 1846 (private collection, reproduced, Witt Library, University of London). Kathryn Smith notes that Joseph is also derived from Titian's muscular satyr, 'The Post-Raphaelite Sources of Pre-Raphaelite Painting', *Journal of Pre-Raphaelite Studies*, 5 (1980), p 45
64 Letter to Tupper, July 1870, *Correspondence*, p 130
65 Hunt, letter to Stephens, 25 August 1863, BL, MS Don. e 66, 79
66 He even speaks kindly of his mother and sister during this period, letter to Tupper, 3 April 1878, *Correspondence*, p 239
67 Ibid., 9 March 1876, p 206
68 Ibid., 28 December 1876, p 213
69 Ibid., 26 January 1877, pp 216–17
70 Ibid., 15 July 1877, pp 223–7
71 Wheeler, *Heaven, Hell*, p 22
72 *The Triumph of the Innocents*, quoted Bennett, *Hunt*, p 53
73 *Correspondence*, p 230, note 31
74 Letter to Tupper, after 15 July 1877, *Correspondence*, p 231
75 Letter to Scott, 7 April 1870, *Notes*, 2, p 90
76 Gissing, *Hunt*, p 219
77 Letter to Tupper, 15 July 1877, *Correspondence*, p 225
78 1 Corinthians 14: 20
79 Letter to Tupper, July 1870, *Correspondence*, p 131; 1 Corinthians 13: 9–12
80 *The Triumph of the Innocents*, quoted, Bennett, *Hunt*, p 53
81 Letter to Tupper, after 15 July 1877, *Correspondence*, p 232; a central theme of *The Water-babies*
82 Ibid., p 233
83 Ibid., 23 September 1876, p 209
84 *The Triumph of the Innocents*, quoted, Bennett, *Hunt*, p 53
85 Letter to Tupper, 23 September 1876, *Correspondence*, p 209
86 Bennett, *Pre-Raphaelite Circle*, p 87
87 Ibid., p 90
88 Letter to Tupper, 15 July 1877, *Correspondence*, p 222
89 Ibid., 23 September 1876, pp 210; 212, note 12

90 Ibid., 26 January 1877, p 217
91 Ibid., 15 July 1877, pp 224–5
92 Ibid., 28 December 1876, p 213
93 Ibid., pp 213–16
94 Letter to Stephens, 16 August 1879, BL, MS Don. e 68, 51v
95 Letter to Tupper, 11 March 1879, *Correspondence*, p 268
96 Ibid., 15 July 1877, p 222
97 Ibid., 23 January 1878, p 238
98 Ibid., 16 January 1877, p 217
99 Letter to Stephens, 5 August 1879, BL, MS Don. e 68, 50
100 Journal, 1 June 1872, JRL, MS 1212, 26–26v
101 Letter to Tupper, after 15 July 1877, *Correspondence*, p 233
102 Letter to Stephens, 5 August 1879, BL, MS Don. e 68, 49
103 Letter to Tupper, 23 January 1878, *Correspondence*, p 238
104 Ibid., 2 August 1879, pp 290–1
105 Letter to Stephens, 6 November 1864, BL, MS Don. e 66, 105v–106
106 Letter to Stephens, 15 February 1880, BL, MS Don. e 68, 76
107 Letter to Tupper, 28 August 1878, *Correspondence*, p 254
108 Ibid., 16 October 1878, p 278
109 Ibid., 10 April 1879, p 270
110 Ibid., 5 May, 1879, p 279
111 Ibid., 2 August, 1879, p 290
112 Ibid., 26 September 1877, p 235
113 Ibid., 15 July 1877, p 232
114 Letter to Stephens, 26 November 1879, BL, MS Don. e 68, 62–62v
115 Letter to Tupper, 15 July 1877, *Correspondence*, p 223
116 Ibid., September 1879, p 292
117 Letter to Stephens, 15 February 1880, BL, MS Don. e 68, 76; also 5 August 1879, 49
118 Letter to Tupper, 2 September 1878, *Correspondence*, p 234; 10 April 1879, p 270
119 Ibid., 2 June 1879, p 228; July 1879, pp 289–90
120 Ibid., 15 July 1877, p 223
121 1 Corinthians 13: 9–12
122 Adams, *Dandies and Desert Saints*, p 11
123 Letter to Stephens, 19 January 1867, BL, MS Don. e 67, 6
124 Landow, *Approaches*, p xiii
125 Klein's ideas are summarised by Juliet Mitchell in *The Selected Melanie Klein* (1986), ed. J. Mitchell (Harmondsworth, Middlesex: Penguin, 1991), pp 19–21
126 Klein, M., *Contributions to Psychoanalysis* (London: Hogarth Press, 1950), pp 282–90
127 Laplanche, J. and J.-B. Pontalis, *The Language of Psychoanalysis* (London: The Institute of Psychoanalysis, Karnac Books, 1988), p 389
128 Klein, *Contributions*, p 290
129 Ibid.

5

Practice: materials and technique

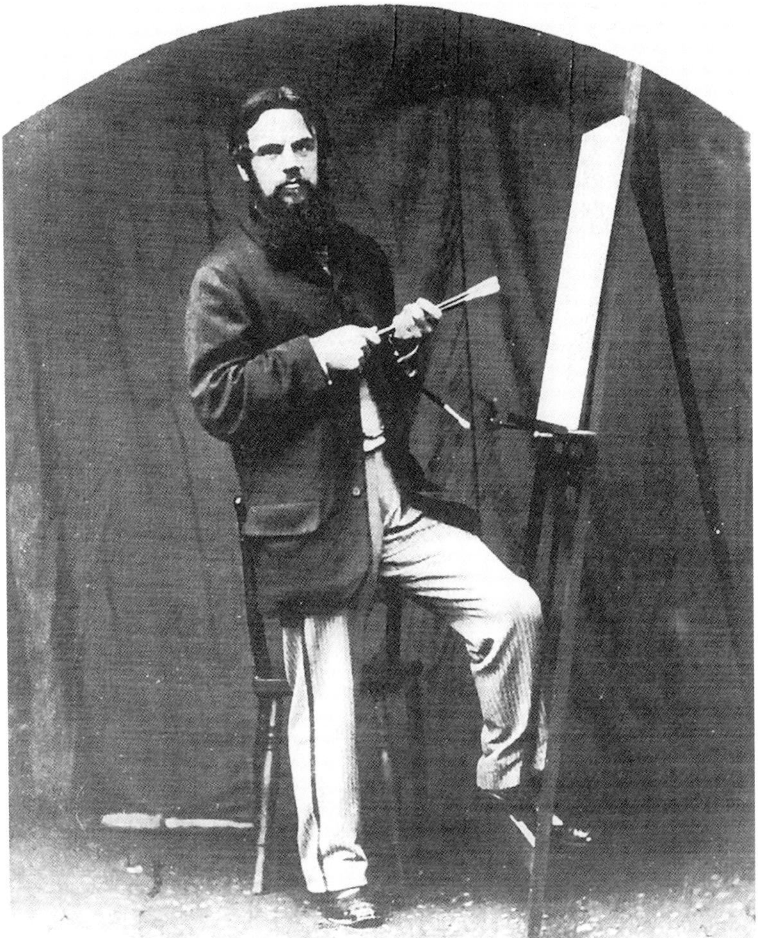

5.1
Lewis Carroll,
William Holman Hunt at an Easel

5

The production of all artists involves a continual negotiation with the characteristics and limitations of materials which is often disregarded by art historians. As Peter Dormer says in *The Art of the Maker*: 'The modern orthodoxy is that conception and execution are separate activities and that execution – mere making – can take care of itself.'[1] Hunt's writings and practice reveal a profound preoccupation with technique. He publishes copiously on the subject and regularly brings it into other discussions of art. His practice exhibits a pattern similar to that seen in his writing and the iconography of his paintings: an elaborate concern for realism and control, accompanied by an underlying anxiety about its absence.

Art historical treatments of Hunt's work make little reference to his craft, restricting themselves to stressing the use of *plein air* verisimilitude and the 'wet white method', as a source of brightness.[2] Technical analysis tends to be the province of texts on painting conservation, conservation records, or painting manuals, such as P.G. Hamerton's *The Graphic Arts* (1882) or A.P. Laurie's *The Painter's Methods and Materials* (1960),[3] Melissa Katz's more recent 'William Holman Hunt, Artist's Materials and the 'Pre-Raphaelite Technique' (1995),[4] and Townsend, Ridge and Hackney's *Pre-Raphaelite Painting Techniques* (2004).[5]

'Craft knowledge' and 'aesthetic judgments' are, as Dormer says, often separated.[6] In Hunt's case, the problem is compounded by the highly figurative nature of his images and their tendency to conceal their means of production. Misunderstandings about his technique have also arisen from a literal reading of his memoir, as Katz has noted. She calls for a more comparative approach which combines a critical investigation of the writings with technical analysis of the paintings.[7] This chapter attempts such an analysis.

Campaigner

The experimentation or negligence of artists of the late eighteenth and early nineteenth centuries produced an array of deteriorated and technically inadequate work which presented a grim lesson to the generation that followed, and catalysed concern for more reliable practices and materials.[8] The Victorian period was also a time of accelerated developments in the science of artists' materials, resulting in a plethora of research and publication on the subject. Many new pigments became available due to industrial and chemical advances.[9] The chemist, George Field, published various books on pigments from the 1830s onwards,[10] and Frederick Barff, Assistant Professor of Chemistry at University College, London, gave a series of presentations on the subject to the Society of Arts called 'On Artists' Colours and Pigments', in late 1870 and 1871.[11] Hunt was actively involved in, and well informed about, these changes. He read Sir Charles Eastlake's *Materials for a History of Oil Painting* (1847), an edition of Goethe's *Theory of Colours* (1810, translated 1840), Mary Merrifield's *Original treatises in the Arts of Painting* (1849)[12] and Theophilus's *Essay Upon Various Arts* (translated by R. Hendrie in 1847),[13] and hailed Cennino Cennini's *The Craftsman's Handbook* (1437, translated by Merrifield in 1844) as 'the great mouthpiece of the new Italian living art'.[14] He bought his colours from Field and corresponded with him and Barff.[15] He is one of the artists featured in Hamerton's 'Technical Notes' series in the *Portfolio* and his 1882 book *The Graphic Arts*[16] frequently refers to Hunt as an expert.

Painting methods had previously been considered an area of craft and these publications represent an emerging consciousness of science, professionalism and historical continuity. Hunt's contributions to the field exhibit a pioneering but ambivalent response to this transition. By the time he began to paint in the 1840s, commercial suppliers, or colourmen, had already taken over a large part of responsibility and expertise in the field. *Pre-Raphaelitism* dates interest in materials from the 1870s (2, 455–6), after problems with unstable pigments in *The Shadow*.[17] Private letters of this time propose an artist's co-operative to take control of supplies, and rail at the indifference of colleagues. They also record the beginnings of personal research into commercial paints.[18] Hunt goes public in 1875 when he co-operates with Hamerton in 'Technical Notes – William Holman Hunt, an interview with the artist'. On 23 April 1880, he addresses the Society of Arts with 'The Present System of Obtaining Materials in use by Artist Painters as Compared with that of the Old Masters', reprinted in the *Architect* in the same year and later summarised in *Pre-Raphaelitism* (2, 453–6).

These texts marginalise other interested parties and present Hunt as singular and unassisted in his campaign for better practice. The address mentions Field 'feeling aggrieved that he had so few signs from artists themselves of their appreciation', adding that 'the old gentleman was quite affected' by Hunt's own acknowledgement.[19] The memoir claims to report Millais scoffing, 'If we had gone bothering about, waiting till we had proved that the materials were perfect, we would never have done anything to this day' (2, 375). Three letters to *The Times* in 1880 construct the art establishment as equally lethargic about the 'security in the character of materials' and neglecting to insure against the deterioration of the nation's heritage. In typical manner, Hunt 'quotes' an unidentified academician declaring that 'such work is beneath the dignity of the Royal Academy'.[20] The final letter announces the formation of a painters' guild at the Grosvenor Gallery.[21]

Material expertise is presented as a characteristic of the old masters and the Academy is blamed for breaking this custom: 'The traditions and practical skill, which as we've seen old masters husbanded, . . . had been thrown away by the previous generation as too troublesome to keep: and so the second hand had no gift for the new English Art.[22] Hunt himself is thus again presented as, by contrast, on a par with great men of the past. A parallel is implied between the address and the *Handbook* of Cennini, recording the 'life experience' and 'practical prescriptions' of the artist (1, 2),[23] and *Pre-Raphaelitism* is introduced as a substitute for the loss of 'the system of apprenticeship under which was produced all the great art of past ages' (1, x). Hunt claims that his campaigning has already brought about improvements (2, 454). His approach is valorised as authentic, the experience of the art labourer, but the address is also defensive about his participation in 'everyday' practicalities. Criticism of the Academy and alignment with the old masters mediates this ambivalence.[24]

Hunt's construction of himself as reintroducing both scientific objectivity and old master authenticity into practice is clearly related to his broader self-image. It manifests his habit of setting himself up against commerce and an establishment associated with deception and national peril. The proliferation of contemporary publications on materials and technique suggests that his representation of his campaigning in the field of materials as a solitary quest is a characteristic exaggeration. It is, however, exceptional to find such a well-known artist conducting experiments and enquiring into the science of materials.[25] Irwin notes that 'Hunt's communications on the subject were with scientists, Mr Stewart, Mr Barff, Richmond and Dr Sim, not with fellow artists',[26] although he did co-operate with the amateur painters John Wharlton Bunney and Mrs Hugh Blackburn.[27]

A 'Present System'

The address to the Society of Arts is an important but neglected source. It sets out a clear philosophy on the material aspects of art and, when placed alongside scientific examination of the paintings, dramatically clarifies our understanding of Hunt's technique. It was delivered in two sessions, but even so, it must have been of exhaustive, and exhausting, length (the text extends to 16,000 words). It was supplemented with numerous visual aids in the form of variously aged canvas and ground samples and pigment samples in different media. Its primary theme is a fierce belief 'that the artist should master a thorough knowledge of . . . materials'.[28] *Pre-Raphaelitism* also pleads for 'that vital branch of art':

> The painter, not being properly educated in the nature of materials, is not able to judge of and use wisely the preparations supplied to him; the artists' colourmen, on their side, prepare their wares without knowledge of the uses to which their customers will put them; each may be working inimically to the other. (2, 452–3)

A characteristic attempt is made to counter the commercialism, depersonalisation, flux and relativity of nineteenth-century art-manufacture with a reliable code of practice based on scientific and historical certainties. Both the address and the memoir re-present the history of making to coincide with the personal beliefs and practice of the artist, however. As we shall see, this practice tends to involve selecting techniques and materials which conform to an aesthetic based on smoothness, rigidity, brilliance and precision.

Hunt tends to favour the ritual care over methods and materials of mediaeval and early Renaissance painters. The memoir traces this interest in quattrocento handling to a meeting with Claude Lorraine Nursey, a pupil of David Wilkie, in 1847, while copying Wilkie's *The Blind Fiddler* (1806, Tate Britain):

> [Nursey] said that Wilkie painted it without any dead colouring, finishing each bit thoroughly in the day . . . I tried the method, and I now looked at all paintings with the question whether they had been so executed. I began to trace the purity of work in the quattrocentists to the drilling of undeviating manipulation with which fresco-painting had furnished them, and I tried to put aside the loose, irresponsible handling to which I had been trained, and which was nearly universal at the time, and to adopt the practice which excused no false touch . . . [T]he taste for clear forms and tints and for clear handling grew in me; while at the same time I wished to guard myself against a slavish imitation of the quattrocentists. (1, 53)

In the address, Hunt admires the uniform grounds and unfaded colours of the quattrocento paintings in the National Gallery, which he claims to have examined with a magnifying glass.[29] Their technique is represented as a guarantee of smoothness, brightness and longevity.

Pigment

The address claims that Hunt also imitated old master practice in preparing his paint himself,[30] maintaining that in earlier times, pigments 'were sold in their unmanipulated state'.[31] As I have mentioned, the concern for materials dates only from the 1870s; before this he used commercially prepared products and Roberson's ledgers record that he continued to purchase ready-made paints after this date.[32] Several of these are referred to in the Society of Arts address, but are recommended only after testing. The lecture is a plea for a reduction in the control given to the commercial colourmen, and the re-enfranchisement of the artist over his materials, old and new.

The choice of pigments in the address also reflects concerns for brightness, strength and control, and a distaste for 'lower harmonies of light and colour' or 'old master glow'. Veronese's *The Consecration of St Nicholas* (1562, National Gallery, London) is described as covered by 'a wash of some dark concoction administered by the dealer at the beginning of this century (because before it was refused by purchasers as too bright for their perfect taste)'.[33] Hunt records displaying his own research and ageing tests, conducted to supplement the findings of Field and Barff,[34] in order to demonstrate the brilliance and durability of available pigments. As a result of these, he advocates traditional tints: flake (lead) white, Naples yellow, yellow ochre, raw sienna, Chinese vermilion, Venetian red, Indian red, crimson madder, Indian lake, burnt sienna, raw umber, burnt umber, cologne earth, burnt lake (madder), Antwerp blue, cobalt blue, blue black and ivory black. His eulogy of genuine ultramarine recalls that of Cennini: 'the heavenly colour . . . its nobility, its beauty, its perfection'.[35] The address warns that colourmen often supply one pigment under the name of another, or diluted with another (2, 455). New unreliable pigments, cadmium and chrome yellow, have, for example, been found mixed with lead white and sold as traditional Naples yellow.[36]

Hamerton comments that Hunt rarely mixed tints except for flesh[37] and Irwin concurs, noting that even here, he used a mixture of white, orange vermilion and cadmium yellow as a base, with pure glazes over the top.[38] Optical microscopy and energy dispersive X-ray (EDX) investigation at the Tate has recently confirmed an unusual absence of mixed pigments in his work.[39] This practice exhibits an understanding, shared by Cennini, that the combining of pigments to produce a colour reduces intensity.[40]

The reluctance to reduce intensity by mixing, narrows the choice of hue and leads Hunt to experiment with more modern pigments. Bright yellows and greens, essential for the representation of vivid vegetation, are notably unavailable in this traditional list, as are the purples evident in many of Hunt's paintings. Chemical advances in the nineteenth century produced a range of alternative hues: chrome reds, oranges and yellows, cadmium yellow, cobalt yellows, greens and blues, cerulean blue, viridian, emerald green, and artificial ultramarine violet. The choice of purples and reds was further expanded by the aniline dyes, based on coal tar, including the alizarins which tended to replace natural madders.[41]

Scientific analysis of *The Awakening Conscience* (1853–54, Tate Britain) reveals the use of traditional and expensive natural ultramarine blue and rose madder alongside artificial cobalt blue and emerald green.[42] Experiments with these new materials are dramatised in the diary made at the time of painting *The Shadow*:

> 3 March – Find the cheek and chin have not brilliancy enough in them. Scrape off the colour of yesterday, put a little white in part and paint again with more transparent colour.
> 1 May – [Hunt is still worried about the flesh tones] Paint the left shoulder and the breast with, as usual, Naples Yellow, Raw Sienna, Vermilion, Oxide of Chromium and later in the day a little Cadmium to make the green golden enough.

> 24 May – the breast on left is still wanting in light and warmth so I scrape down to the white preparation . . . I have a great deal of anxiety about my work, fearing the flesh may become opaque – but in the end I think I succeed – if so it is owing to the use of two new colours, cobalt green and cadmium, instead of O[xide] of Chromium and Raw Sienna – which for this part are too dull.[43]

Here we can see the important role played by modern cobalt green and cadmium in achieving accuracy and brightness.

As I have noted, problems with adulterated and unreliable modern pigments were causing concern, during the 1870s. Difficulties in completing *The Shadow* were found to be partially due to the impurity of Roberson's Orange Vermilion.[44] Hunt had every brand of vermilion in London analysed and found all to be contaminated with 'foreign matter' except some imported Chinese Vermilion, which was in fact the pure, traditional pigment. Another traditional red, Madder Carmine, was discovered to be a new and unstable aniline dye.[45] The blackening properties of the red lead with which the Roberson's vermilion was mixed, and the unstable aniline dye masquerading as madder carmine, ruined the subtle glazing of the flesh tones.

The memoir insists that the new manufactured pigments are to be suspected as they have not stood the test of time (2, 453) and the address demonstrates a detailed scientific understanding of their problems. It notes that aniline dyes sometimes fade and others are chemically unstable and therefore recommends natural madders, as seen in the mountains and red fillet of *The Scapegoat*, for instance.[46] Cobalt green is tested and approved, but found less vivid than emerald green: 'a quality of tint contained by no other green'.[47] Samples of chrome pigments which were 'put on trial canvases in 1860 are still [in 1880] incomparably superior in brilliancy to cadmium, lemon and strontium yellow of the same date' (2, 456).[48] Hunt claims to avoid cadmium yellows because he knows them to be regularly adulterated with chrome yellows, preferring to buy chrome colours directly so that he can verify their quality and avoid the lighter, least stable shades.[49] He finds 'carmine yellow' to be particularly alkaline, rendering paint layers easily washed off.[50]

Irwin notes that 'Hunt himself never mentions black. No doubt he only used very small amounts of it where absolutely necessary.'[51] Just as white tends to desaturate, or undermine the purity of, a colour's hue when mixed with it, black undermines its brightness, and would therefore have also been used sparingly. The 'prismatic colour'[52] of Hunt's painting can be seen to be the result of a strenuous and conscious pursuit of the brightest pigments, used in their purest, unmixed form, in thin layers which will allow maximum illumination from the reflective white ground below. This has to be balanced with the desire for stable tints, and Hunt's research and experiments reveal concerns about his departure from traditional pigments in the search for brilliance.

Support

Hunt's choice of painting supports reinforces the preference for smoothness. At this time, supports were supplied ready-made by colourmen. During his address, Hunt displays samples of canvas and recommends strong, firm fabrics, such as sailcloth.[53] Their rigid quality ensures an even, hard surface. A robust canvas is also required to sustain the habitual, repeated rubbing downs and repaintings demonstrated in the 1872 journal.[54] Hunt mentions a canvas which, 'on any scraping out and corrections has had its ground broken up into facets, on account of the weakness of the cloth'[55].

The address acknowledges, however, that sailcloth is no longer popular, having been superseded by lighter, finer fabric. Hamerton makes no objection to ordinary linen canvas and acknowledges some artists' preference for a coarse texture not admitted by Hunt. This, Hamerton says, can break up outlines, and 'makes hard precision impossible and naturally encourages a rich style of painting'.[56] A prominent weave distracts the eye from the image and the dimples harbour shadow which undermines the brilliance of pigments. Texture and slackness also hinder the controlled pressure of the brush and the ability to make thin, precise strokes. Hunt's particular advocacy of strong, even cloth reveals a personal aesthetic preference.

Hunt's consciousness of the flatness of his works is eluded to in an early letter to Stephens where he asks him to arrange the lighting of some pictures for viewing in his studio so that they 'will not . . . be seen as bad bas relieves'.[57] *The Triumph* (Walker Art Gallery version), painted on a cotton support, due to no other being available, suffered from poor tension. Hunt had it lined (adhered to a second canvas), but found that 'the defective part of my canvas proved that the wrinkled linen had been distended by the restorer over some soft composition which gave way under the slight pressure of painting' (2, 340). He eventually began on a new canvas (Tate Britain version). His concern about flatness is again revealed in his elaborate solution to repairing the old one:

> I subsequently called in my reliner to confer upon a scheme for cutting out the defective centre of the Jerusalem painting, and replacing it with a new piece of sound canvas. This could have been done before but I had observed that many pictures so treated with apparent thorough success had in the course of twenty years or so revealed the join by the two sharp edges of the canvas turning upwards. My plan was to make the inserted square an inch or so larger than the aperture, to unravel the edges of this and also of the surrounding cloth, to weave them together and lay them down on a sound backing, so that there would be no edges anywhere. (2, 342)

The smooth, hard surface preferred by Hunt is described by Hamerton as 'like that of a panel'.[58] Panel supports were traditionally used in the fifteenth century and by Hunt throughout his career for smaller pictures, such as the replica of *The Shadow* (1873, Middlemore Estate). Hunt's travelling and location work probably made panels too unwieldy for larger paintings. By the mid-nineteenth century, variations such as blind stretchers (where the frame is filled in behind with a wooden barrier) and loose linings (a second layer of canvas stretched under the first) were facilities on offer. Hunt often had canvases lined before, during, or shortly after painting. *The Awakening Conscience* is lined on to a blind stretcher, *The Afterglow in Egypt* (1854–63, Southampton City Art Gallery, plate 14) and *The Finding* have been painted over paper tape added at the time of lining.[59] *The Scapegoat* is loose lined on to a blind stretcher.[60] All three versions of *The Triumph* are both lined and panelled in.

These measures contribute to the firm look of the paint surface. Hunt describes *The Triumph* being lined in the hope that it could be made as 'tight as a drum' (2, 339). It is impossible for the art historian to assess the subtle differences in the appearance of lined and unlined paintings because most non-contemporary works in galleries have been lined as a conservation measure and share this hard quality whether or not it was the painter's intent. Hunt too would have experienced old master canvases in their lined form and would have perhaps associated them with a firmness which was in fact more recently acquired. Whether or not this was the case, we see Hunt taking great pains to give his canvas paintings the rigidity of a panel.

Ground

Supports supplied by colourmen often already had a commercial lead white ground, usually white or off-white, to which Hunt tended to add several extra layers. This again represents an attempt to treat the canvas support like a gessoed, quattrocento panel. Although Hunt usually used a conventional lead white primer, the address compliments gesso.[61] He calls this a 'tempera' ground, the traditional ground for tempera paintings, and regrets that 'the tempera ground has disappeared, which was the delight of the Florentines and Venetians, when painting pictures that have best retained their purity'.[62] Hunt writes from Florence to Stephens saying that he intends to have the canvas for 'my principal picture in Jerusalem' (*The Shadow*) prepared by a local man in 'best English cloth' and with a traditional Italian tempera ground.[63] *The Triumph* was also prepared with a tempera ground and transported back from Jerusalem without rolling.[64]

The address comments that Vasari approves lead white priming and says: 'White lead as a ground is perhaps worthy of comparison with gesso, but it has not so long and certain a testimony to recommend it.'[65] Oddly, it does not mention the unsuitability of gesso for canvas, even though this is stressed in the same passage by Vasari: 'Unless canvases are to remain stationary, they are not coated with gesso, which would interfere with their flexibility, seeing that the gesso would crack if rolled up.'[66] This omission underlines the need to present idiosyncratic preferences as authoritative orthodoxy.

The address attributes the dull look of many paintings to the use of earth pigments in the ground layer and prefers the brightness that results from light grounds: 'The use of much umber with the white may be the main reason that no Georgian pictures vie in vividness with those painted three centuries earlier.'[67] Hunt, himself, purchased canvases that were 'extra-primed'[68] and/or covers the existing ground with a fresh white priming of his own. The use of extra ground layers enhanced both the rigidity and smoothness of the support, eradicating any hint of canvas weave, as well as covering any marks or smudges gained in storage or transport. The concern for a clean, even surface is demonstrated in the 1872 diary entries:

> 1 June – Find the left breast unpleasantly rough and sandy in texture, so . . . shave off some of the disagreeable roughness and have to paint in the white parts exposed.
> 2 June – I can't resist scraping off remaining grittiness of surface.[69]

Despite the defensive alignment with old master practice, the preparation of the grounds found in Hunt's pictures again exhibits an innovative and sensitive manipulation of material characteristics. He often mixed lead white (flake white) with the new pigment, zinc white (introduced 1834). He was aware of Barff's conclusion that zinc white was more stable than lead white and had also conducted his own tests.[70] Zinc white tends to absorb a higher proportion of the oil/varnish medium than lead white and would therefore dry to a glassier layer.[71] Lead white, however, has a greater drying effect on the oil film which would have speeded up the preparation time of grounds. Hunt tended to use both pigments, mixed with oil and varnish, to render the surface both smooth and opaque.[72]

Hunt was probably attracted by the brighter, less creamy colour of zinc white, as well as the crisp, hard surface. Tests at the Tate have shown that lead white has the highest reflectance of the whites, but zinc white reflects less only in the red/yellow end of the spectrum. By combining them, Hunt gains the bluest white at maximum reflectance.[73] The result of this was that most of the light that penetrated through the thin paint layer would be bounced back, illuminating the colour from behind like a stained-glass window. The principle is an old one, outlined by Goethe, for example, but the use of a lead-zinc ground is experimental, the first known instance.[74] Hunt also often took the unusual step of mixing his ground pigments in poppy oil instead of linseed oil because it was known to yellow less.[75]

It was important that the ground did not dull with age and continued to reflect the maximum amount of light.

Pre-Raphaelitism's account of other experimentation, in 1851, with a third local priming applied on the day of painting, known as the 'wet white' method (1, 276) has been readily referenced. *Pre-Raphaelitism* aligns the wet white with quattrocento fresco, but the technique is probably more akin to that of Wilkie (1, 53). Hunt's journals make frequent references to renewing specific areas of a white ground:

> 25 May – It was a fools' paradise that I was confiding in yesterday, for this morning I find the only thing to be done is to lay a new ground.
> 26 May – After breakfast I feel compelled to make preparation surer, to make my ground of yesterday brighter.
> 4 June – About noon put *a* little white on the chest of the big [picture] as it must be dry tomorrow. I lay it out on the roof in the hot sun, covering up all the other parts. It seems hard by sunset.[76]

The word 'ground' is used to encompass priming and underpainting, however, and as we can see, it was left to dry. In a letter to Tupper during work on *The Triumph* Hunt again mentions being 'obliged to wait long for the drying of the paint I put on to form a fresh ground' and the delay caused by the length of time it takes to become 'workably even and dry'.[77] Hamerton says that Hunt only used the 'wet on wet' system between 1850 and 1854 and that, by 1882, he had adopted 'a stone-coloured ground'[78] It is clear, I think, that in his later career, Hunt applied discrete areas of a white underpaint/ground layer, as described for the wet white method, but waited for them to dry in order to provide a smooth base. No mention of a wet ground is made in Hunt's interview with Hamerton in 1875, either.[79] In the light of my discussions in Chapter 1, the occurrence of the story in the memoir, over fifty years after the event, suggests that the 'wet white' tale might be just that, a late manipulation of the facts intended to underline Hunt's experimental originality. No confirmation of a consistent use of the wet ground has arisen from technical analysis of cross-sections of Hunt's work, to date.[80]

Hunt's actual technique is fundamentally dominated by a need for a white reflective underpainting to promote brilliance. His application and re-application of new grounds in localised areas is a result of his habit of repeatedly scraping down and repainting specific parts. Evidence of this can be seen in paint cross-sections. A sample taken from the sunlit carpet of *The Awakening Conscience* shows a second lead white ground over remnants of earlier paint. Twenty-two years later Hunt summarises his technique for Bunney:

> [*The Triumph*] was first laid with tempera [ground] and I got all my outline and rough effect in water [colour] putting amber [copal] varnish on in a very thin state for later paintings. It is a good system for work

> which has need of much balancing and drawing – if much light be needed and the previous alterations have lost the original white, it is well before the further work in oil to paint one, two, or three coats of flake [lead] white over leaving the first work to show through faintly only.[81]

Paint

Hunt's method of applying the pigment to the ground also represents a catholic management of materials orientated towards maximum luminosity. He emulates fifteenth-century practice in its care to paint 'fat over lean' (quick-drying, low medium-content paint beneath paint with higher medium content) and to allow each layer to dry before going over it. Hamerton states that 'In the intervals of different stages he makes an important point of drying and baking the picture well in the sun, according to the old Venetian practice.'[82] This careful management of paint layers caused considerable delay. Hunt writes to Tupper from Florence of an (unidentified) picture which must be left to dry for a week before renewed painting.[83]

It has already been established that white tends not to be used as a means of lightening other shades as this would have the effect of reducing vividness. Instead, lighter hues are achieved by thinner layerings which allow the ground to illuminate them from behind like stained glass. Close observation of the pictures reveals that even the works coinciding with the memoir's account of wet white experiments (1850–54) are only partially painted in transparent layers, however. Hunt's handling is flexibly diverse. Opaque paint, such as lead or zinc white, is used for the highlights and some flesh, like body colour in watercolour painting. Some areas are brushed in a precise technique variously akin to watercolour or quattrocento tempera painting. A fine building-up of linear strokes, typical of early Renaissance handling, tends to be found in sections with textural interest, such as fabric, hair, grass or wool. Sometimes these are supplemented with a form of impasto that literally imitates actual texture. A broader, blended building-up of transparent layers supplements this.

Hunt paints in a mixed oil and varnish medium. The address advocates nut or poppy oil with a little copal.[84] He advises Mrs Blackburn to use copal with nut oil in a ratio of one to three, combining it by boiling it together for a day. Interestingly, he recommends pure nut oil for flesh, in keeping with the tendency to employ opaque mixtures of white for these areas, and pure copal for the eyes, presumably to reproduce their particular glassy, transparency.[85] Scientific analysis at the Tate seems to indicate an astute use of glaze pigments which have a refractive index close to that of the oil/varnish medium.[86] This maximises colour saturation and minimises surface scattering, thus improving absorption and increasing the amount of light reflected back from the white ground below.

Although Hunt used Roberson's 'amber colours' containing linseed oil, copal and mastic varnish, in his early career,[87] he became increasingly suspicious of commercial media. Both Barff and Hunt comment that contemporary linseed oil was commonly adulterated with up to 20 per cent hemp seed oil.[88] An anxious letter to Stephens in 1879 asks for help in finding an old, tried and trusted bottle of poppy oil that Hunt has left stored somewhere while away: 'I dread to finish with colour ground in colourman's oil.'[89] Hamerton states that, after 1853, Hunt carefully used an old stock of high-quality copal and oil varnish diluted in turpentine, manufactured in 1842.[90]

Hunt's reliance on tried and trusted concoctions relates to the fact that the exact nature of the problems and ageing properties of mixed media was obscure: 'Varnish painting was almost, if not quite, lost [by Georgian times]'.[91] The address tracks the practice of mixing oil and varnish from Van Eyck to Van Dyck, and thence via Dobson into English practice.[92] It commends Reynolds for his attempts to rediscover the secrets of mixed media and attributes his many failures to the vacuum of information and experience then existing in English art.[93] Hamerton takes a similar line on the traditional importance of resin varnishes as part medium, even going so far as to state that the term 'oil painting' could equally be named 'oil/varnish painting'.[94]

Hunt goes on to accept that pure oil is less problematic: 'varnish is often mischievous', but says that it is also less able to preserve the 'brilliancy' of certain pigments than oil/varnish when properly used.[95] Laurie agrees that the addition of varnish to an oil medium protects it from moisture which contributes to the tendency of the oil to yellow as it ages.[96]

Hunt's particular method aims at the 'enamelled surface' and the minimal, microscopic craquelure that he admires in Dutch artists and Van Eyck. His address specifically advocates their perfect surface, describing it as 'glassy' and the colours safely 'shut up in amber [copal]'.[97] He describes the kind of surface he is after to Scott:

> I seldom mix my copal and turpentine [a diluent] together, not because there would be any danger to the permanency of the work . . . but only because the character of the surface obtained thereby is not so pleasant to my taste as the fat full firmness got by paint in its pure state as mixed with oil, or when compounded only with copal.[98]

Hunt recommends that Mrs Blackburn 'keep the effect uniform' to avoid the 'catch'em olive oil character which I feel we both dislike'.[99] Conservation scientists at the Tate have recently calibrated this effect, showing that the copal component maximises smoothness and further minimises surface scattering.[100] This accords with the desire for a glassy effect indicated by Hunt's choice of ground. The result is to produce a mirror-like texture in keeping with his idea of painting as 'the reflection of heaven's beauty in nature' (1, 488).

The copal/oil combination is slow drying and therefore aided a precise blended technique; as Hunt says: 'varnish . . . permits each touch to spread, though very slightly, . . . and may be accounted for'.[101] Hamerton records that:

> Mr. Hunt's purpose in using varnish is not to attain the very rapid drying which Landseer valued for pictures painted quickly. On the contrary, Mr. Hunt lessens the drying quality of his copal medium by gently simmering it with so much linseed oil that a touch on the bare canvas remains wet two days or more. He is always anxious not to use too much of the medium, putting the smallest possible quantity into the dipper, and avoiding a general glaze at the beginning of the days work until the last painting, when it becomes necessary to bring out the tints to their full value.[102]

Hunt confirms this in a letter to Scott in 1859, but admits problems:

> I confess it [copal] does often hamper me very much. It clogs my brush so as to make fine work impossible. Of late years I have used some made by Webster in his own garden which is more difficult to handle than that you get from the colourman, which dries quicker: I remember that the rapidity with which that dried allowed me to use a layer of tint over another even on the same day, while my present medium will not allow me to do so.

In order to execute his work in layers he starts off in a quicker-drying, diluted paint: 'To avoid the excess of this quality when it becomes difficult to work, I often begin by modelling all out with a turpentine dilution of the copalled pigment. When I repaint over old work, I often too soften the surface of the dry ground, and modify the colour with washes of turpentine.'[103]

Here we witness the artist struggling to achieve control. The opportunity to blend his paints at length before they dried and so avoid the 'false touch' (1, 53) requires a 'fat', slow-drying medium. The journal complains that while painting *The Shadow*, 'The paint is too dry by the time it's ready for blending.'[104] However, the ability to build up transparent, glassy layers requires a 'lean', quick-drying medium, otherwise it is necessary to wait a long while before the last application has dried. The choice of medium plays an important role in allowing the artist control of his brushstroke. In Hunt's case he requires it to facilitate a 'fine' blending technique as well as his pedantic alterations, modifications and layering. Both these are necessary to achieve the extremes of mimesis that I will be discussing in Chapter 8.

Varnish

The varnish content of the paint layer tends to raise its refractive index and saturate and protect it enough to make a final, overall varnishing unnecessary. Many of Hunt's works remain unvarnished, or bear only a very thin layer, without appearing chalky or unfinished.[105] Hunt was well informed about the dulling or yellowing properties and tendency towards degradation of varnish layers.[106] The memoir mentions Tintoretto's series at San Rocco as having 'lost some of their original richness, from the desiccation of the varnish and mildew' (2, 488). An inscription written on the back of *Valentine* in 1861 notes that in the intervening ten years its mastic varnish has reduced the 'intensity' of the picture.[107] Hamerton mentions that Hunt would only varnish as a protection against dirt and vapours if the client was not prepared to put glass in the frame.[108] *The Scapegoat* is glazed in this way and bears only a very thin varnish layer.[109]

In August 1879, Hunt tells Stephens that he is restoring *Claudio and Isabella* (1852, Tate Britain) and *The Awakening Conscience* (1853–54, Tate Britain, figure 5.2); 'both so out of order through premature varnishing'.[110] The spandrels of the latter picture contain a typically pedantic, self-conscious note:

> Painted with Copal (oil) weak originally in use with R.S. of turps
> for drawing out parts. Emerald Green & Gamboge in transparent
> part of foliage: picture retouched with same vehicle in 1864
> W Holman Hunt
> Please copy the above
> Note before
> obliterating it.
> THE PICTURE WAS VARNISHED with
> MASTIC IN 1864 ON ALL PARTS BUT
> THE GIRL. AFTER A FEW YEARS ALL THE
> VARNISHED PARTS WERE /CRACKED/ THE
> REST NOT AT ALL. A RESTORER
> FILLED UP THE CRACKS
> WITH COLOUR AND MASTIC
> THIS HAS NOW BEEN
> TAKEN OFF AND
> I HAVE NOW
> FILLED UP WITH
> AMBER
> 86[111]

The pains Hunt takes to preserve the painted surface intact, even years after completion, are symptomatic of the importance of the smooth, unbroken skin to his aesthetic. The use of oil/varnish media and rigid supports produce a glass-like paint layer. These combine to promote a sense of the painting as window, or mirror, and the illusion of a rectangle of real vision circumscribed by the frame. Where the paintings are glassed in, as Hunt recommends, this effect is further enhanced. The use of unmixed, bright pigments, such as

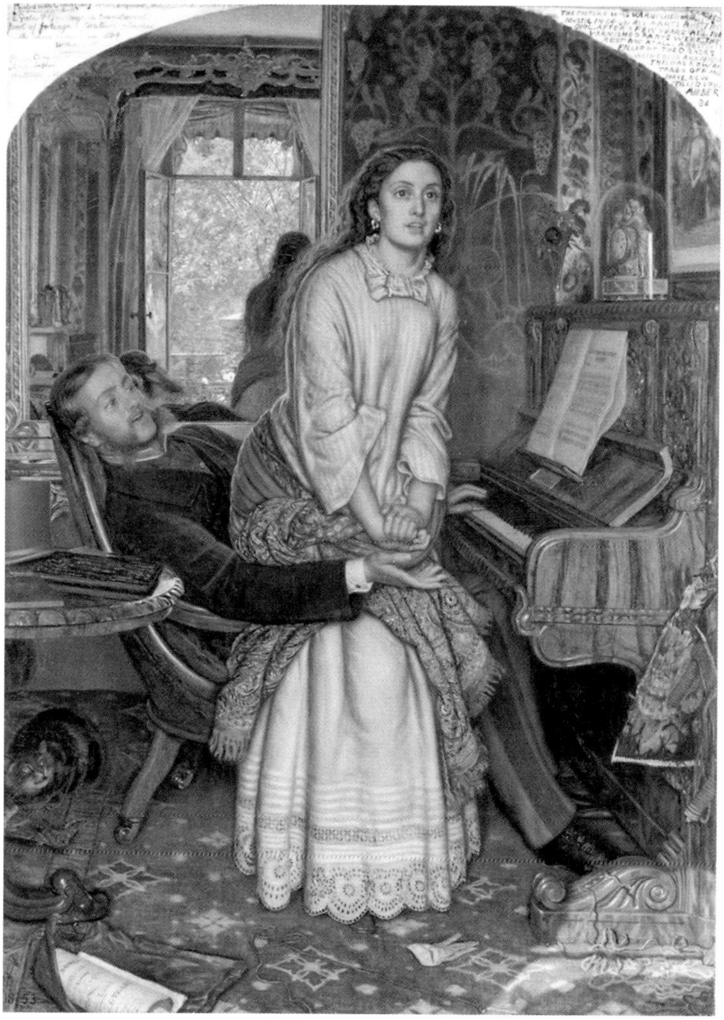

5.2
William Holman Hunt,
The Awakening Conscience,
1853–54

emerald green, also contributes to the imitation of the light effects of nature. As Hunt describes his intention with regard to *Rienzi*, he aims 'To paint . . . every detail I can see, and with the sunlight brightness of the day itself' (1, 91).

Both *Pre-Raphaelitism* and Hunt's address to the Society of Arts express his exhaustive and serious approach to the business of 'mastering' his materials and moulding them to meet a certain aesthetic. The final appearance of his paintings is carefully manipulated to disguise their means of production, and yet his texts and practice construct a highly self-conscious, complex perception of the art object's material identity and the process of making. This paradox will be pursued in the following chapters.

Notes

1 Dormer, P., *The Art of the Maker* (London: Thames and Hudson, 1994), p 7
2 Hilton, *Pre-Raphaelites*, p 56; *The Pre-Raphaelites* (Tate Gallery, 1984), p 15; Prettejohn's *Pre-Raphaelites* draws on more recent sources on technique, and presents a more elaborate discussion of these themes, chapter 4
3 Laurie, A.P., *The Painter's Methods and Materials* (1960) (New York: Dover, 1967), pp 71–2, 240. Also, Laurie, A.P., 'The Late Mr Holman Hunt's Experiments in the Permanency of Artists' Oils and their Colours', *Journal of the Society of Arts*, 70 (5 May 1922), pp 432–8; Sitwell, C.L., 'William Holman Hunt, "Our English Coasts", 1852 (Strayed Sheep)', in *Completing the Picture, Materials and Techniques of Twenty Six Paintings in the Tate Gallery* (London: Tate Gallery, 1982), pp 57–60
4 Katz, M.R., William Holman Hunt, Artist's Materials and the 'Pre-Raphaelite Technique', *Historical Painting Techniques, Materials and Studio Practice* (Marina del Rey, California: Getty Conservation Institute, 1995), pp 158–65 . See also Irwin, L., 'The Painting Materials and Techniques of William Holman Hunt', diploma paper, Courtauld Institute of Art, University of London, 1977. Roberson's ledgers are accessible through the Fitzwilliam Museum, Cambridge), these survey Hunt's choice of pigments and collate several useful primary sources on the subject, such as Hunt's accounts with his supplier, Roberson and Co.
5 Townsend, J., J. Ridge and S. Hackney, *Pre-Raphaelite Painting Techniques* (London: Tate Gallery, 2004). See also Hackney, S., R. Jones and J. Townsend, *Paint and Purpose: A Study of Technique in British Art* (London: Tate Gallery, 1999), chapter 11
6 Dormer, *Art of the Maker*, p 8
7 Katz, M.R., 'Holman Hunt on Himself: Textual Evidence in Aid of Technical Analysis', in *Looking Through Paintings: The Study of Paintings Techniques and Materials in Support of Art Historical Research: Leids Kunsthistorisch Jaarboek 11*, ed. E. Hermens (Leiden, Netherlands: Uitgeverij de Prom and Archetype Publications, 1998), pp 415–44
8 Carlyle, L., 'The Artist's Anticipation of Change as Discussed in British Nineteenth-century Instruction Books on Oil Painting', *Appearance, Opinion and Change* (London: United Kingdom Institute of Conservation, 1990), pp 62–7
9 *Completing the Picture*, pp 19–22; also Harley, R.D. *Artists' Pigments 1600–1835: A Study in English Documentary Sources* (London: Butterworth Scientific, 1970)
10 Irwin draws attention to Roberson's ledgers which record Hunt buying Field's *Grammar of Colouring (Rudiments of the Painter's Art)* (London: John Weale, 1850) on 17 September 1856, 'Painting Materials', p 4
11 Barff, F., 'On Artists' Colours and Pigments', *Journal of the Society of Arts*, 19 (30 December 1870), pp 109–12; (6 January 1871), pp 120–4; (13 January 1871), pp 134–9; (20 January 1871), pp 156–62; (27 January 1871), pp 179–87
12 'Materials', p 486

13 Ibid., p 487
14 Ibid., p 485
15 *Completing the Picture*, p 57
16 Hamerton, P.G., 'Technical Notes – William Holman Hunt, an interview with the artist', *Portfolio*, 6, 1 (1875), pp 45–8; Hamerton, P.G., *The Graphic Arts* (London: Seeley, Jackson and Halliday, 1882)
17 Letter to Tupper, 11 August 1875, *Correspondence*, p 201; 'Materials', p 495
18 Summarised in Katz, 'Hunt on Himself', pp 427–31
19 'Materials', p 492
20 'Pigments and Artists' Colours', *The Times* (28 April 1880), p 8
21 *The Times* (2 June 1880), p 12; this did not come to anything
22 'Materials', p 489
23 Ibid., p 486
24 Ibid., pp 486–7
25 Carlyle, L., 'A Critical Analysis of British Handbooks, Manuals and Treatises in Oil Paintings Published in Britain Between 1800–1900: With Reference to Selected Eighteenth-century Sources', Ph.D. Thesis, Courtauld Institute of Art, University of London, 1991
26 Irwin, 'Painting Materials', p 2
27 Letter to Bunney, 19 December 1875, quoted Bennett, M., 'Footnotes to the Holman Hunt Exhibition' *Liverpool Bulletin*, 13 (1968–70), pp 43–5; letter to Blackburn, 17 November 1857, JRL, MS 1268
28 'Materials', p 497
29 Ibid., p 487
30 Irwin, 'Painting Materials', p 2; Hamerton, 'Technical Notes', p 45
31 'Materials', p 485
32 Katz, 'Hunt on Himself', p 430
33 'Materials', pp 487–8
34 Ibid., pp 492–3, 495
35 Ibid., pp 485–6. Hunt preferred to use genuine ultramarine (Hamerton, *Graphic Arts*, p 250), but it was expensive and he displays tests on artificial 'French' ultramarine. He finds that all but Winsor and Newton's product tend to effloresce (form a whitish bloom), 'Materials', pp 495–6
36 Ibid., p 496. The adulteration of artists' pigments was surveyed six years later in Standage, H.C., *The Artist's Manual of Pigments showing their Composition, Conditions of Permanency, Non-Permanency, and Adulterations; Effects in Combination with Each other and with Vehicles; and the Most Reliable Tests of Purity* (London: Crosby, Lockwood and Co., 1886)
37 Hamerton, *Graphic Arts*, p 250
38 Irwin, 'Painting Materials', p 12. The pigments added to white underpainting of flesh vary; he also uses cobalt green, Journal, 25 May 1872, JRL, MS 1212, 25
39 Ridge, Hackney and Townsend, 'Pre-Raphaelite Technique and its Consequence', Tate Gallery, 13 September 2002; one exception is the mixing of emerald green and yellow glaze
40 Cennini, C., *The Craftsman's Handbook* (1437), trans. D.V. Thompson (New York: Dover, 1960), pp 20–37

41 *Completing the Picture*, p 57
42 Hackney, Jones and Townsend, *Paint and Purpose*, p 82
43 Journal, 1872, JRL, MS 1212, 13, 21v, 25
44 Townsend, Ridge and Hackney, *Pre-Raphaelite Painting Techniques*, p 42
45 Letter to Tupper, 11 August 1875, *Correspondence*, p 201; *The Times* (4 May 1880), p 6
46 Conservation records, National Museums and Galleries on Merseyside
47 'Materials', p 495. Hunt's notes on the canvas of *The Awakening Conscience* confirm that both emerald and chrome green were used, conservation records, Tate; also used in *The Scapegoat*, Journal, 24 March 1855, JRL, MS 1211, 8
48 'Materials', p 494
49 Ibid., p 492
50 Ibid., p 486
51 Irwin, 'Painting Materials', p 69
52 Hilton, *Pre-Raphaelites*, p 88
53 'Materials', pp 496–7
54 Scientific analysis has confirmed this habit, Townsend, Ridge and Hackney, *Pre-Raphaelite Painting Techniques*, p 53
55 'Materials', pp 492–3
56 Hamerton, *Graphic Arts*, p 229
57 Letter to Stephens, undated, BL, MS Don. e 66, 13–14. In fact Hunt showed the guests around the studio himself, in order to position the painting according to the light of the actual hour of the day!
58 Hamerton, *Graphic Arts*, p 229. *The Blind Fiddler* is also on panel.
59 Conservation records, Birmingham Museums and Art Gallery and Southampton City Art Gallery
60 Conservation records, National Museums and Galleries on Merseyside
61 'Materials', p 490. Hamerton states that only three of Hunt's pictures bear a 'tempera ground' and that the rest are oil and lead or zinc white, *Graphic Arts*, p 250
62 'Materials', p 490
63 Letter to Stephens, 22 June 1869, BL, MS Don. e 67, 31
64 Letter to Stephens, 2 May 1878, BL, MS Don. e 68, 11
65 'Materials', p 490
66 Vasari, G., 'The Three Arts of Design', *Lives of the Painters* (1550), quoted Laurie, *Painter's Methods*, p 68
67 'Materials', p 490
68 Hackney, Jones and Townsend, *Paint and Purpose*, p 80
69 Journal, 1872, JRL, MS 1212, 26–26v
70 Barff, 'Artists' Colours' (6 January 1871), p 123; Hamerton *Graphic Arts*, p 226
71 Laurie, *Painter's Methods*, p 88
72 Both lead white and zinc white have been detected in *The Finding*, conservation records, Birmingham Museums and Art Gallery
73 Ridge, Hackney and Townsend, 'Pre-Raphaelite Technique'
74 A practice outlined in Goethe, J., *The Theory of Colours*, trans. C. Eastlake (London: John Murray, 1840), para. 247, Townsend, Ridge and Hackney, *Pre-Raphaelite Painting Techniques*, pp 57–8

75 'Materials', p 491; confirmed by Laurie, *Painter's Methods*, p 133
76 Journal, 1872, JRL, MS 1212, 25–26v
77 Letter to Tupper, 16 October 1878, *Correspondence*, p 258
78 Hamerton, *Graphic Arts*, p 250
79 Hamerton, 'Technical Notes', p 45; Katz, 'William Holman Hunt', pp 162–3
80 Townsend, Ridge and Hackney, *Pre-Raphaelite Painting Techniques*, pp 59–62
81 Letter to Bunney, 11 July 1876, quoted Bennett, 'Footnotes', p 46
82 Hamerton, *Graphic Arts*, p 250
83 Letter to Tupper, 16 June 1869, *Correspondence*, p 91
84 'Materials', p 491
85 Letter to Blackburn, 17 November 1857, JRL, MS 1268
86 Ridge, Hackney and Townsend 'Pre-Raphaelite Techniques'; see also Townsend, Ridge and Hackney, *Pre-Raphaelite Painting Techniques*, pp 66–7
87 Katz, 'Hunt on Himself', p 430
88 'Materials', p 496; Barff, 'Artists' Colours', p 159
89 Letter to Stephens, 5 April 1879, BL, MS Don. e 68, 40
90 Hamerton, *Graphic Arts*, p 250
91 'Materials', pp 490–1
92 Ibid., p 487
93 Ibid., p 490
94 Hamerton, *Graphic Arts*, p 199
95 'Materials', pp 486–7, 495
96 Laurie, '*Painter's Methods*', p 130
97 'Materials', p 487
98 Letter to Scott, 11 February 1860, *Notes*, 1, p 49
99 Letter to Blackburn, 17 November 1857, JRL, MS 1268
100 Ridge, Hackney and Townsend, 'Pre-Raphaelite Technique'
101 Hamerton, 'Technical Notes', p 45
102 Hamerton, *Graphic Arts*, p 251
103 Letter to Scott, 5 December 1859, Troxell Collection, Princeton University, quoted Landow, G.P., 'William Holman Hunt's Letters to Thomas Seddon', *Bulletin of the John Rylands University Library of Manchester*, 66 (1983), p 154
104 Journal, 1 March 1872, JRL, MS 1212, 12v
105 Technical analysis reveals an absence of a varnish layer on *The Finding*, conservation records, Birmingham Museums and Art Gallery. Also, *The Miracle of the Sacred Fire, Church of the Holy Sepulchre* (1899, Fogg Art Museum), Katz, 'Hunt on Himself, p 442
106 'Materials', p 490
107 Katz, 'Hunt on Himself', p 433; confirmed by technical analysis of the work by Townsend, Ridge and Hackney, *Pre-Raphaelite Painting Techniques*, p 71
108 Hamerton, *Graphic Arts*, p 249
109 Ultraviolet examination, conservation records, National Museums and Galleries on Merseyside
110 Letter to Stephens, 16 August 1879, BL, MS Don. e 68, 52
111 Conservation records, Tate. Hunt's note added 1882

6 Eye: object and image

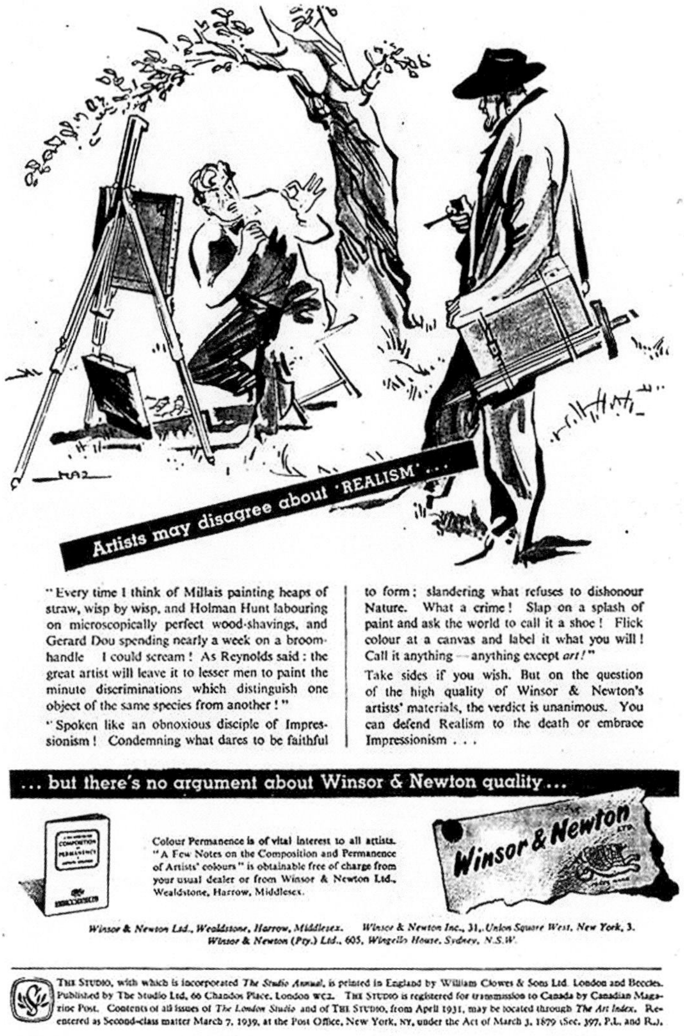

6.1
'Artists may Disagree about REALISM . . .'
Winsor & Newton advertisement, 1949

Pre-Raphaelitism offers itself as a straightforward re-presentation of evidence in order to authenticate its beliefs, in particular its construction of the artist. This emphasis on authenticity buttresses a similar claim for the truthfulness of Hunt's paintings; the work of art is a 'reflection of heaven's beauty in nature' (1, 488). The memoir's pursuit of literary realism is, however, self-conscious, revealing awareness of, and anxiety about, the performance of textual fabrication and the artificiality and relativity that this implies. As we've seen, Hunt's writings and the iconography of his paintings contain references to false views and false art. Hunt's painting practice exhibits a similar awareness of the process of artistic fabrication. I shall suggest that his unusual interest in controlling the materials and manufacture of his work is a defensive response towards a modern understanding of their potential to undermine the illusion of the image, and, by extension, the authority of the artist's eye.

Editing the object[1]

The post-war orthodoxy of Modernism now seems as dated and vulnerable as the slightly shabby works that it once championed, but the art historical hierarchy that proceeded from its retrospective logic of development has proved remarkably robust. Clement Greenberg's 'Modernist Painting' (1961) and Michael Fried's 'Three American Painters' (1965), equated modernity and value with progress towards abstraction and acknowledgement of the demands of the medium.[2] This marginalisation of subject painting (tainted, as it was, with historically specific contingencies) had began fifty years earlier with Roger Fry and Clive Bell and most collections still roughly reflect the modernist pedigree immortalised in Alfred Barr's 1930s chart 'The Development of Abstract Art.[3] Paintings such as *Our English Coasts* (1852), admired by the French avant-garde at the *Exposition Universelle* of 1855, are now housed in Tate Britain, separate from their more canonical, continental contemporaries in the National Gallery.[4]

My specific concern, here, is with the polarisation of art historical approaches to nineteenth-century painting that has ensued. Greenberg's conflation of abstraction with acknowledgement of materials has resulted in highly representational paintings such as Hunt's being excluded from both the adventure of modernism *and* consideration as made objects. This is illogical. All painters deal with the physical difference between a representation and that which is represented. Deconstruction is not the sole invention of abstraction or the post-Saussurean age; the word may be new in its twentieth-century usage, but the practice must always have been with us; the inevitable flip side of construction. A painted image deconstructs itself simply by being flat and made of varnish, pigment, canvas and wood. Viewing

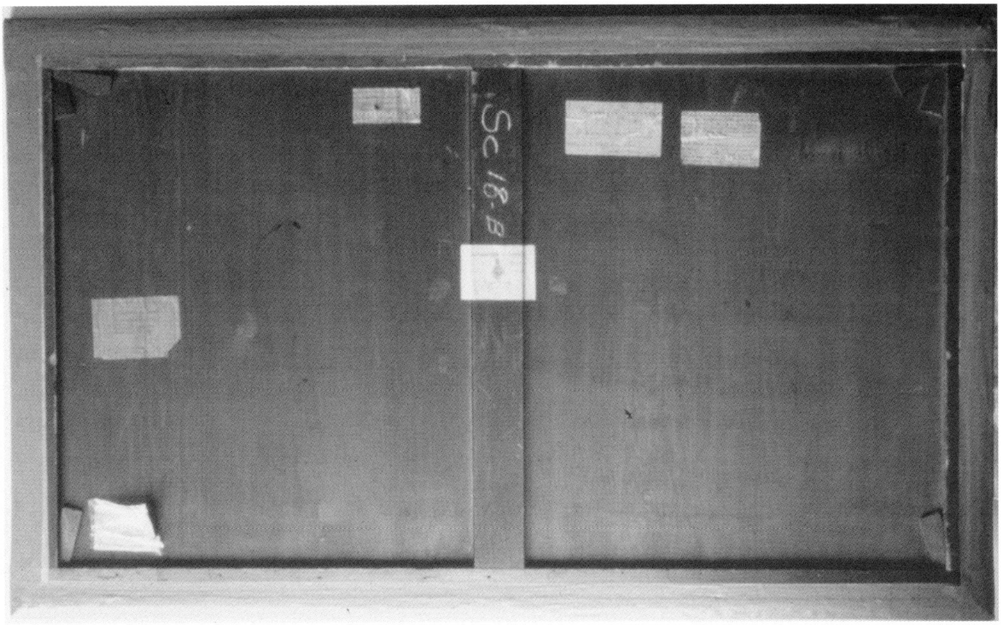

6.2
William Holman Hunt, rear view, *The Triumph of the Innocents*, finished sketch, 1870–1903

it closely, or from the back, will achieve a total deconstruction, even destruction, of the illusion that it is anything other than these materials (figure 6.2). The deconstructing gaze is, moreover, as characteristic a symptom of the materialism of the age as the preoccupations with visual and scientific evidence discussed in previous chapters.

Hunt's writings frequently exhibit this kind of gaze. The Society of Arts address describes a Rembrandt self-portrait in terms of its materials and manufacture: 'painted, probably, with simple earths mixed with white and perhaps a little Naples Yellow – there are touches of tempered vermilion on the eyes which would suggest that this had been put on cautiously in a final glaze'.[5] Of course, in the context of the address, it is perhaps not surprising that perception of a painting embraces both the image and its constituents. This double perspective is, however, also demonstrated in *Pre-Raphaelitism*, in the record of his sojourn in Venice with Ruskin, where they view Tintoretto's *Life of the Virgin* series (1565–87, Scuola di San Rocco, Venice) (2, 259–64).

The memoir begins by noting the physical decay of the paintings. This sets up a moment of simultaneity between image and object as it goes on to describe the 'dilapidation and ruin' portrayed within the setting of *The Annunciation*. The material view is then balanced by a list of iconographical features and their 'symbolism' (2, 260). All this is juxtaposed with an extract about the picture from Ruskin's *Modern Painters* (2, 262).[6] Ruskin is described as reading aloud his earlier account as they scrutinise the other works, and they compare this commentary with their present viewing. At *The Crucifixion*,

Hunt's text steps away from the image and returns to the object, identifying the technique and materials that he supposes Tintoretto to have used (2, 263).

The quotation from *Modern Painters* is characteristically both compared and contrasted with what the memoir presents as immediate experience. Showing the two spectators agreeing with Ruskin's critique puts Hunt's text on a par with Ruskin's already famous book. As Ruskin says, 'the words are all justified' (2, 262). However, at the same time, the reprinting of part of Ruskin's description accords to the author's own 'eyewitness' narrative a directness, which goes beyond Ruskin's iconographical view to reveal the painting as both image and object.

The account describes Tintoretto's technique: 'first painted in tempera medium, and this, for final painting, had been floated over with oil varnish, almost certainly amber, and while each space was drying, he had glazed and painted what was necessary in oil colours' (2, 263).[7] The text dissolves the image to bring process and materials into focus, foregrounding the active artist. This passage subtly diminishes Ruskin's text. Ruskin's early role as mentor is reversed and Hunt is now 'showing' to Ruskin, re-establishing the primacy of the artist and the act of painting, and laying claim to a broader, more active, scientific, or 'real', vision than that exhibited by the critic.

A dual perception of paintings as both object and image is often found elsewhere in *Pre-Raphaelitism*. These instances again serve to highlight the apparent realism of the text, as well as valorising artistic experience and industry. However, where Hunt's own pictures are being discussed, references to materials are not allowed to dissolve the image, as they do in the case of *The Crucifixion*. The record of painting *The Shadow* stresses the artist's labour, but does not speak of it in terms of a manipulation of materials, despite his problems with pigments. Process is reduced to 'imitation', and the description is restricted to beginning with a blank canvas, setting the model to pose, and the race against time and weather to 'complete' a portion of work before sunset (2, 293–4).

When the material nature of the art object is mentioned later in his chapter, it is accompanied by a balancing account of the illusionistic power of the picture. The narrative of a visit of some local people to the studio in Jerusalem presents *The Shadow* as both mundane object and miraculous vision (2, 306–7): one person begs to touch it, 'to feel what is the difference between the linen and the flesh, the sky and the shavings'. Hunt tells his guests that it is only paint which is still wet. The visitor wants to see the back of the picture so that he can see Mary's face. Hunt refuses to move it, but shows him the back of another: 'It is just like this, a mere framework of wood.' On a later occasion, some Moslem ladies are described looking at the oil sketch for *The Triumph* and exclaiming: 'It looks like paper on the surface but on the margins outside it is cloth' (2, 327). This is followed by another detailed explanation of iconography and symbolism.

The memoir frequently deconstructs (in the general sense of the word) the work of other artists, such as Tintoretto and Rembrandt, or, more brusquely, Whistler: 'a life-sized canvas loosely smeared with paint, which professed to be a ballet dancer' (2, 361). The protagonist's own pictures, however, are not taken apart in this way. A painting may be 'a mere framework of wood' *and* a likeness of the Virgin and Christ, but the one does not challenge the other. An image is never described in a state of incompleteness, or 'half made'. In Hunt's case, the transformation of bare materials into a representation of something else, the artist's practice, is presented as apparently miraculous. *Pre-Raphaelitism* shows us the art object in order to stress the precise objectivity of the artist and the skill and labour of art-making, but the exact relationship between it and the representation which it bears is elided in order to preserve the integrity of the image.

This dual view, stressing both the material (physical components) and the image (its meaning and spiritual value) is reminiscent of the juxtaposition of the physical and the spiritual explored in Chapter 2, where the 'heavenly vision' of Mount Hermon, concludes with a restatement of its geological characteristics: 'rock, dirt and water' (2, 54). All these examples privilege the gaze of the Christian artist, both scientific *and* spiritual. His vision is valorised as superior to the limited, literal gaze which he ascribes to local people, embracing the material, the representational and the spiritual elements of art and nature.

Greenberg's definition of modernist sensibilities seems relevant to Hunt's acute consciousness of his materials:

> Illusionist art had dissembled the medium, using art to conceal art. The limitations that constitute the medium of painting – the flat surface, the shape of the support, the properties of pigment – were treated by the Old Masters as negative factors that could be acknowledged only implicitly or indirectly. Modernist painting has come to regard these same limitations as positive factors that are to be acknowledged openly.[8]

Hunt's response to materialism tests this polarised definition. His writings exhibit a variation of the modernist, materialist perspective, one that is ambivalent. His statements about technique, such as the Society of Arts address, do 'acknowledge openly' the physical nature of the art object, but apply this to the work of other artists. The only direct mention of his own work's physicality is to two unnamed early pictures.[9] Writings which promote the realism of his painting, such as *Pre-Raphaelitism*, draw our attention to 'wet paint' and the 'framework of wood', but place equal emphasis on the total illusionism of the image.

Obscuring the object

In the context of the memoir, it is possible to place the view of the object and the view of the image side by side without the one undermining the other. They are reconciled through a textual construction of a privileged, all-seeing, artistic eye. This is not possible, however, when viewing the picture itself. How is this paradox dealt with? Courbet, for example, extends the materialist gaze implied by his so-called realistic treatment of subject matter into a display of the *facture* of the paint surface.[10] Hunt does not. Both artists seek authority in terms of material truth, and both, to this end, consciously explore the material relationship between paint and image, but they respond to it in different ways. Hunt's practice represents no less of an engagement with surface properties, but this engagement is strenuously orientated towards their disguise. One aspect of the objective, materialist gaze is suppressed in order to preserve visual materialism of other kinds.

Every detail of Hunt's practice represents a precise negotiation with the relation between image and paint, a relation which is, as we have seen in Chapter 5, at all stages rigorously regulated. Lined, finely woven canvases conceal any residual texture beneath secondary grounds which are carefully renewed whenever they become rough, so that the exceptionally smooth plane does not interrupt the paint layer or draw attention to itself. Early work, such as his sketches after Titian and the 1845 *Self-Portrait* (Birmingham Museum and Art Gallery, plate 10) follows the sensuous display of bravura brushstrokes and buttery paint found in the work of Reynolds and followers, such as Etty, but this is rejected by 1849. Millais returns to it later in the century but Hunt consistently expresses dislike for 'pomatum-y texture'.[11] Reynolds's loose treatment strikes the eye simultaneously as image and as paint, thus dramatising the personal, performatory elements of process and the activity of the brush. Hunt abjures this kind of 'loose' impasto and strenuously conceals his materials, and his hand. The memoir mentions admiration for Etty as a 'veteran master of colour', but accompanies this with a sketch of him wielding a comically large brush (or palette knife) over a small nude (1, 94, figure 6.3). It gently criticises his use of 'accentuated prominences of pure white' and muddled layering of opaque tints, preferring his paintings in their less worked, early stage (1, 93–5). Hunt's own highlighted areas are usually added in thicker, opaque mixtures of white, but they lie flat, or imitate the texture of the object being depicted, such as the the dress in *The Awakening Conscience* (figure 5.2), or the embossing on Mary's bracelet in *The Shadow*.

Reynolds and later artists experimented with rough grounds and media additives to enhance the identity of the paint surface.[12] The

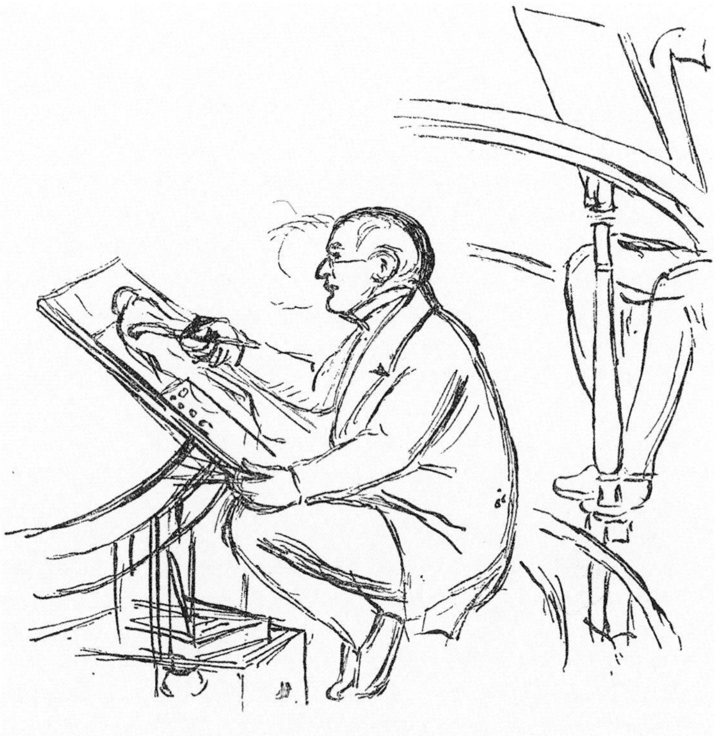

6.3
William Holman Hunt, *Etty in the Life School*, *Pre-Raphaelitism*, 1, 94

Cubists display the physical properties of their art as 'positive factors', using coarse canvases, sandy grounds and media additives in order to create texture and to draw attention to the two-dimensional, material nature of the painting.[13] Hunt also experimented with additives, but in order to minimise texture, employing glazes of slow-drying copal mixture. The touch of the artist is further concealed by the use of soft, small strokes of a sable brush (1, 198).

The use of a blended brushstroke and the addition of varnish to the oil medium also renders the paint layer semi-transparent so that it is illuminated by light bouncing off the white ground beneath. This 'crystalline lustre of varnish' (1, 121) shares the qualities of glass and enhances the sense that the image is viewed through a window rather than on a plane. Hunt's picture frames literally act as window frames in that they often have glass insets which further distract our attention from the picture surface. Hunt seems deliberately to explore this idea in his image of his son tracing against a window pane, *Master Hilary the Tracer*.

Greenberg portrays the developments of modernism as a series of experimentations with flatness, colour and the role of other media effects. He stresses that the significance of these experiments lies *not* in their being traditional or otherwise, but in the awareness, or 'self-criticism', of the qualities that they imply.[14] Although Hunt's experiments with the material aspects of the art object are pursued in order to align them with the image, the very strenuousness of this process suggests a modern confrontation, if not acceptance, of its physical properties. The Modernist logic of art as overt performance of material characteristics is not so far from Hunt's performance of non-performance. His 'virtuoso asceticism', extended to the art object, is merely the flip side of what might be termed modernism's 'virtuoso aestheticism'.

Greenberg sees materialism and rationalism as undermining both art and religion in the nineteenth century, threatening to relegate them to roles of 'entertainment' and 'therapy' respectively.[15] As we have seen, Hunt's output exhibits an acute awareness of this potential of modern perspectives to trivialise painting and belief: 'Art is generally regarded as a light and irresponsible pursuit' (1, vii). *Pre-Raphaelitism* defends Hunt's art as a sane and serious service to the nation, but private writings reveal a fear that his work may be self-indulgent delusion, mere 'caper-cutting'. The memoir champions a notion of spirit common to art and religion, but, again, in private writings, faith falters in the face of science and a lack of consensus. The logic of materialism is perceived, but the slippage between text and reality that it implies is fundamentally opposed to a creed and self-image which is firmly dependent on art bearing witness to something beyond itself, a universal, pre-modern religious hope. Whereas Greenberg sees art's salvation from trivialisation to have lain in the acknowledgement of its particular material nature and in the expelling of 'every effect that might conceivably be borrowed from . . . any other art', Hunt's preoccupation with the rational, scientific aspect of the materials of his work is, conversely, rigorously *allied to* other fields – religion, patriotism, poetry and literature.

Hunt's paintings are a focus of defence against a modern perspective. They represent a paradoxical attempt to recreate the certainty of faith in a nineteenth-century context of scientific relativism. A post-Enlightenment cognisance of the constructed nature of both artistic and religious texts accelerates and problematises this need for authentification, resulting in an unparalleled exploration and testing of the extremes of pictorial realism.

Space

Greenberg cites the limitation of the frame as a pictorial property which has been interrogated by modern artists: 'the norm of the picture's enclosing shape or frame was loosened, tightened, then loosened once

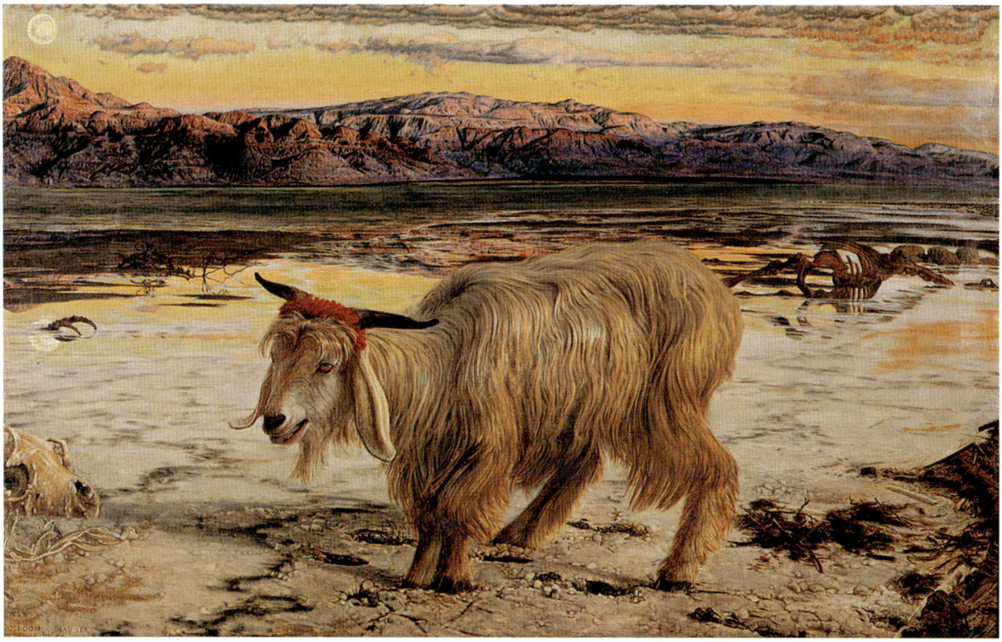

1
William Holman Hunt,
The Scapegoat,
1854–55

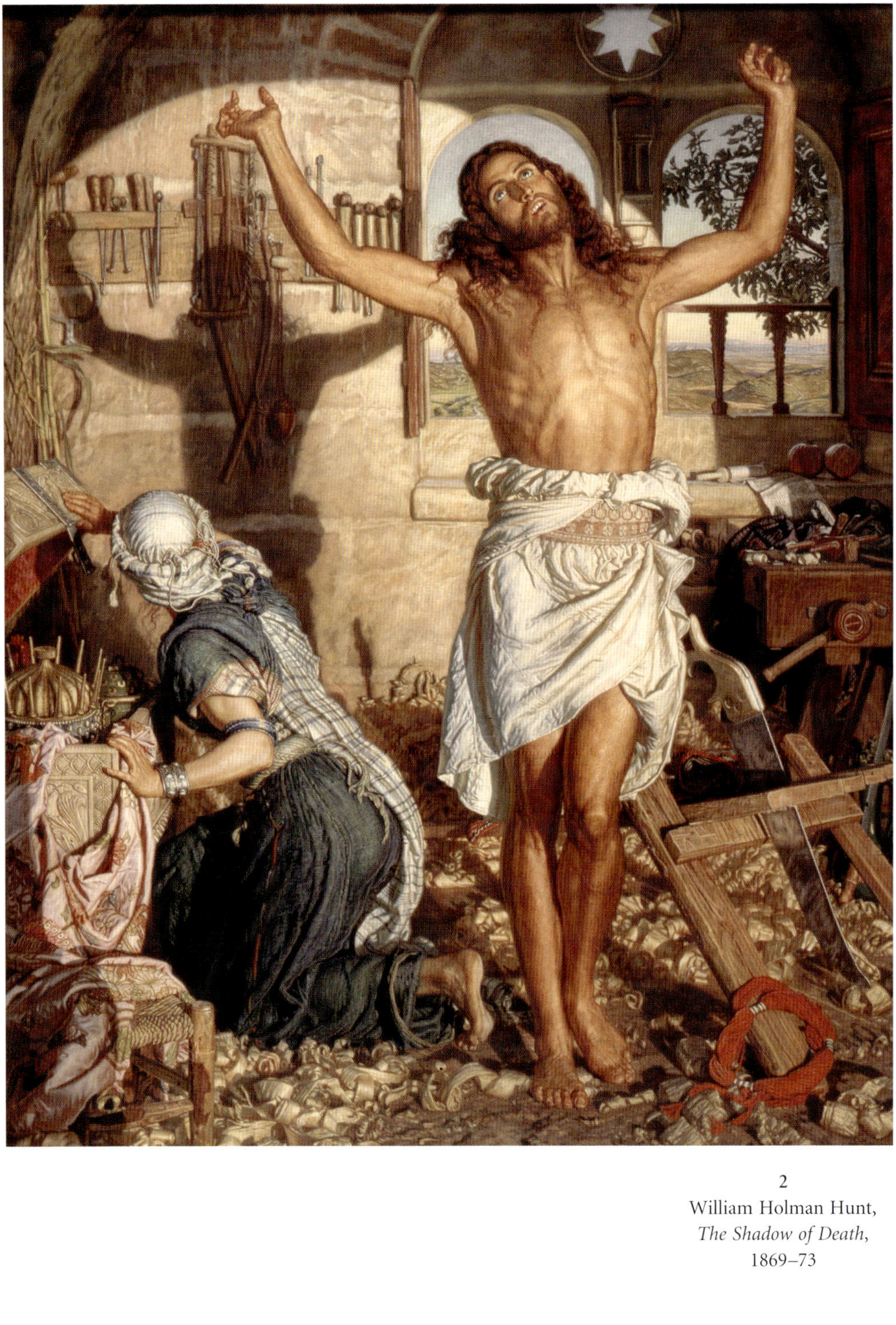

2
William Holman Hunt,
The Shadow of Death,
1869–73

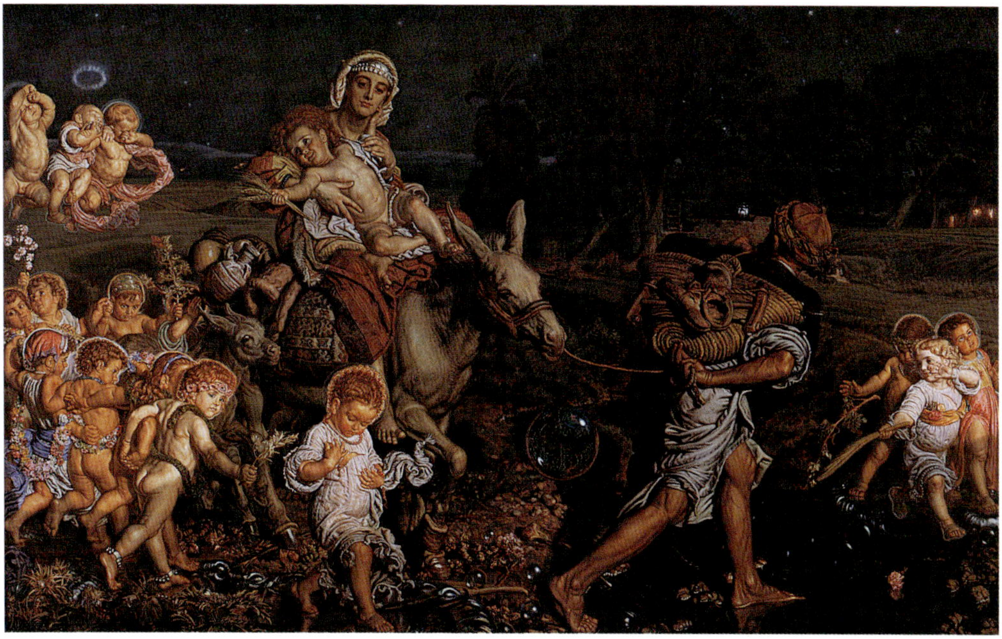

3
William Holman Hunt,
The Triumph
of the Innocents,
1876–87

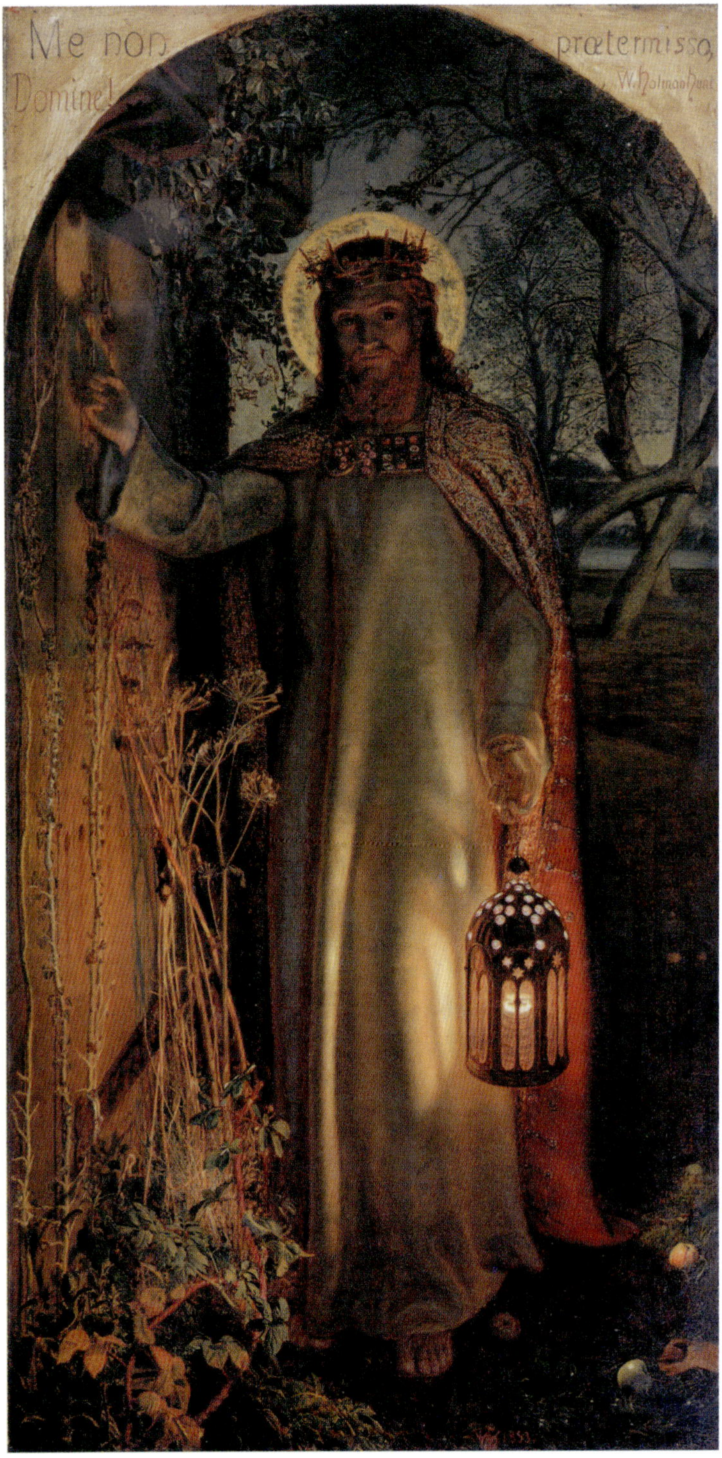

4
William Holman Hunt,
The Light of the World,
1852–53

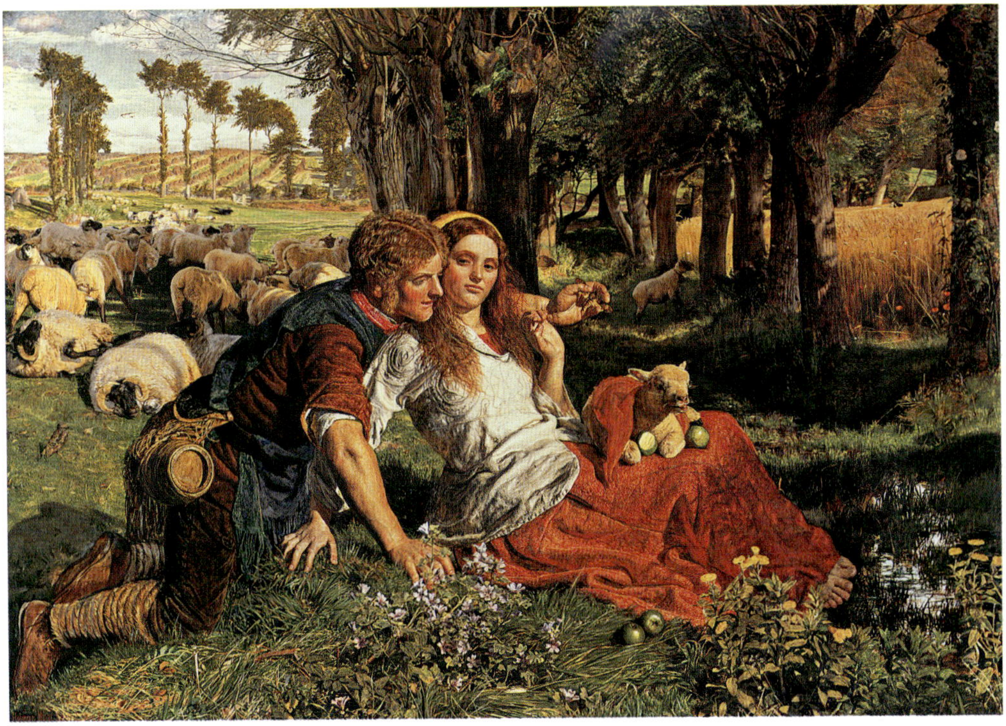

5
William Holman Hunt,
The Hireling Shepherd,
1851–52

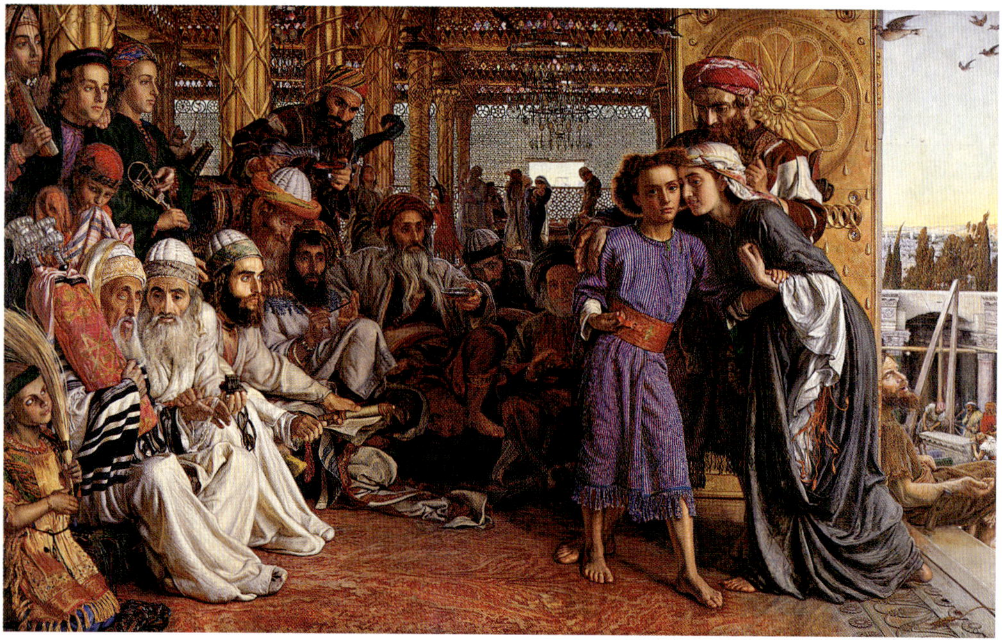

6
William Holman Hunt,
The Finding of the Saviour in the Temple,
1854–60

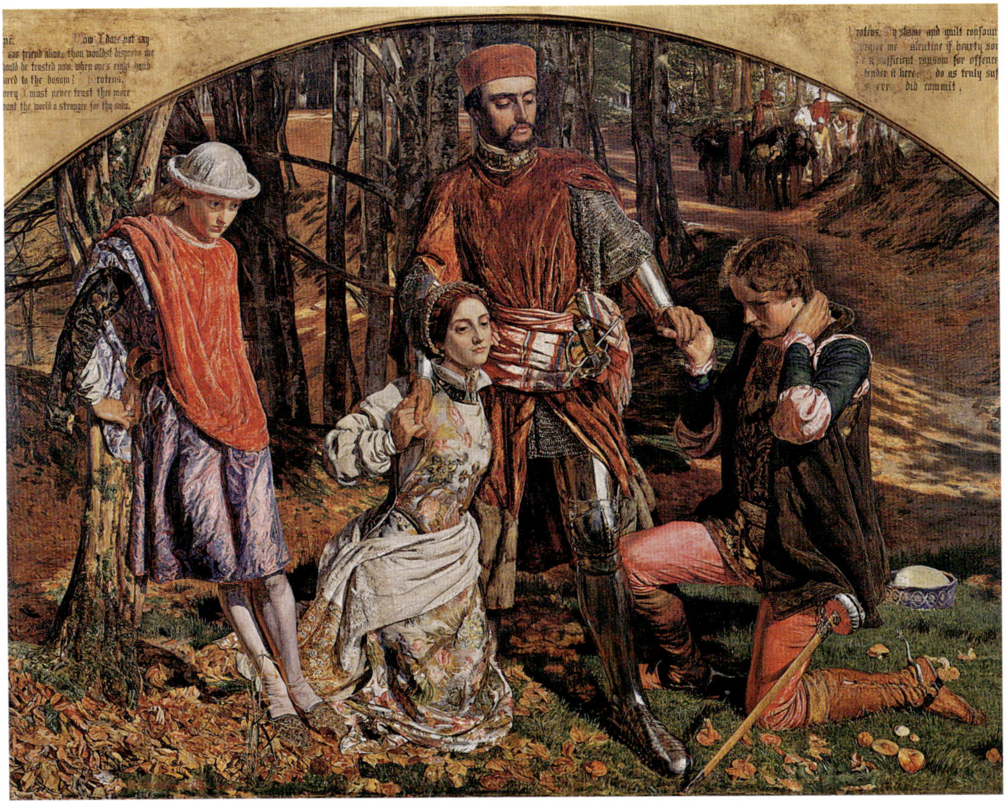

7
William Holman Hunt,
Valentine Rescuing Sylvia from Proteus,
1850–51

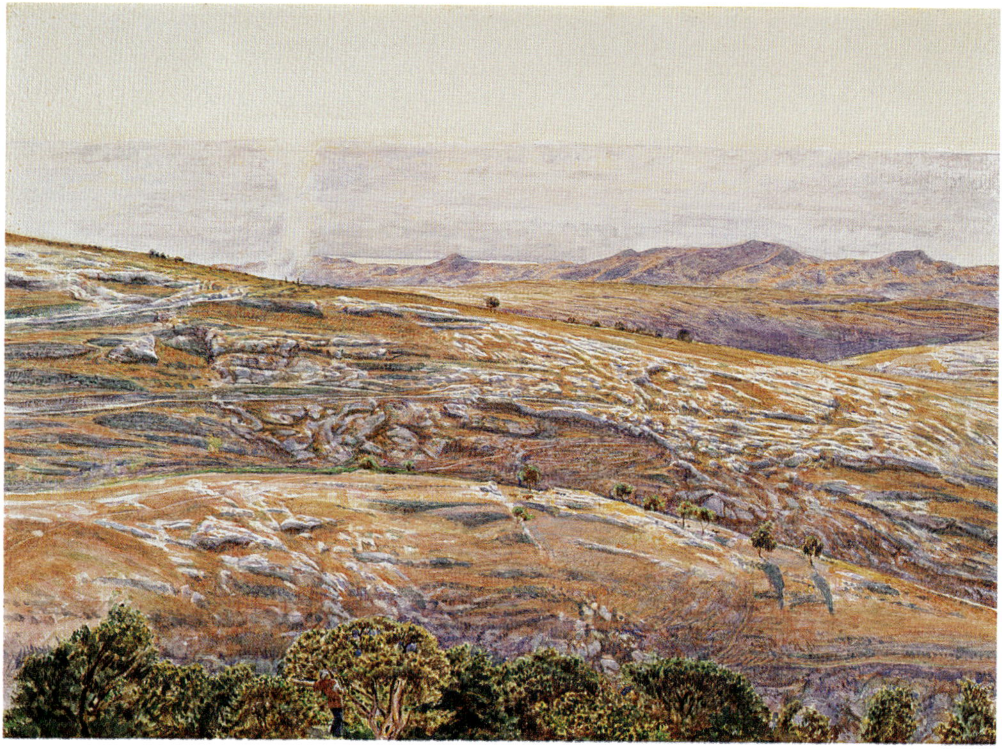

8
William Holman Hunt,
The Dead Sea from Siloam (View from the Mount of Offence looking towards the Dead Sea and the Mountains of Moab),
1854–55

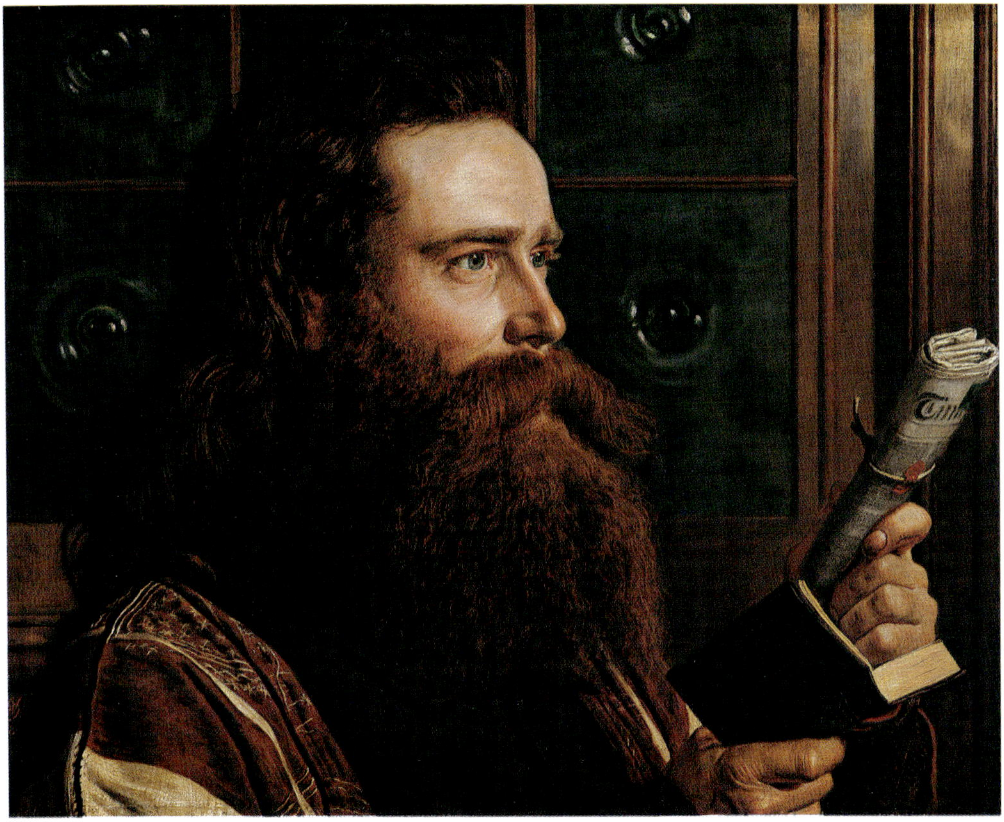

9
William Holman Hunt,
Portrait of
Henry Wentworth Monk,
1858

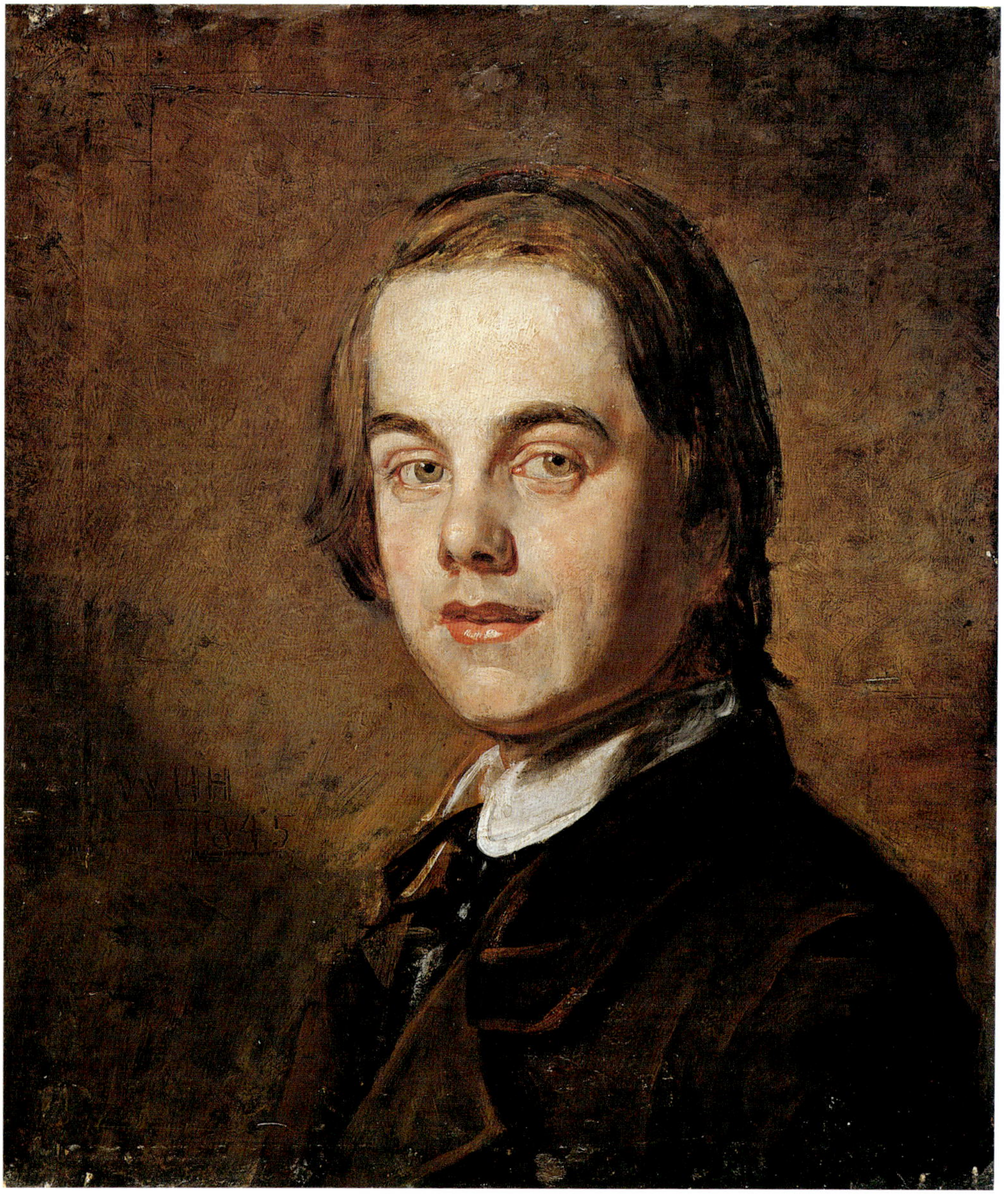

10
William Holman Hunt,
Self-Portrait,
1845

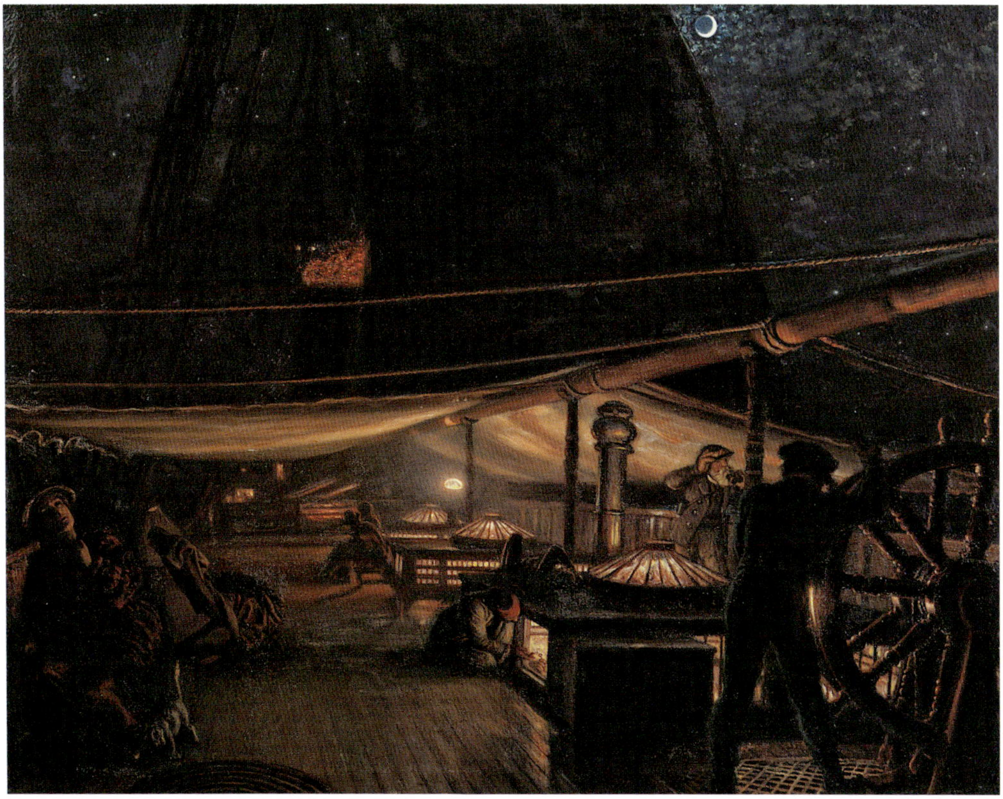

11
William Holman Hunt,
The Ship,
1875–79

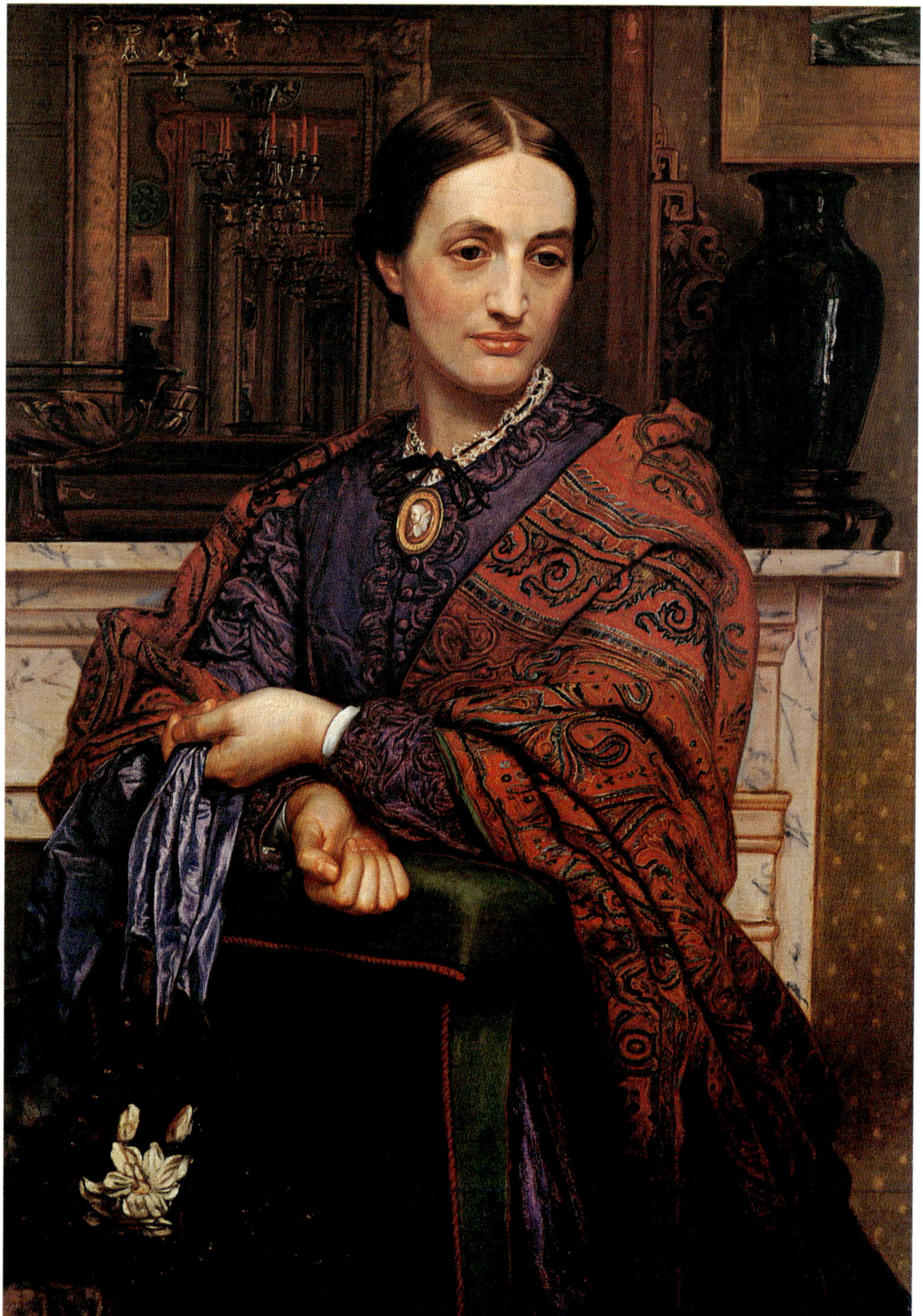

13
William Holman Hunt,
Isabella and the Pot of Basil,
1866–68

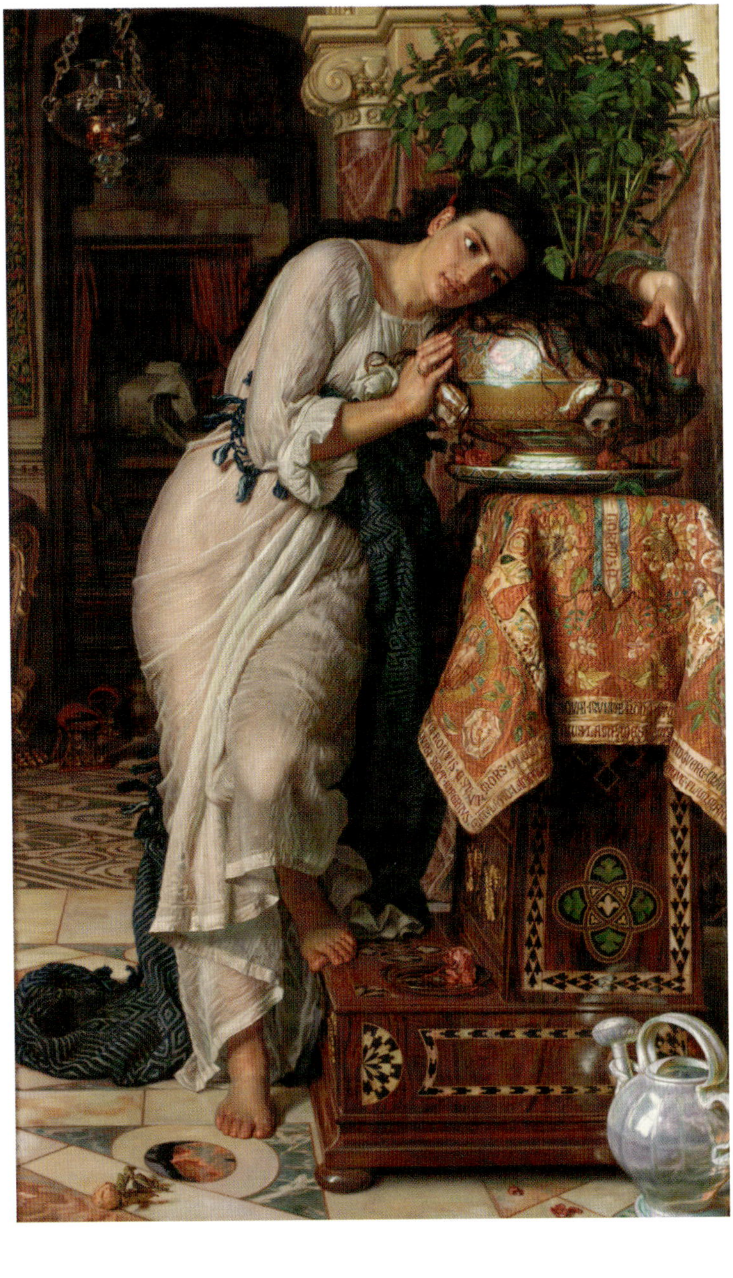

12
[*left*]
William Holman Hunt,
Fanny Holman Hunt,
1866–68

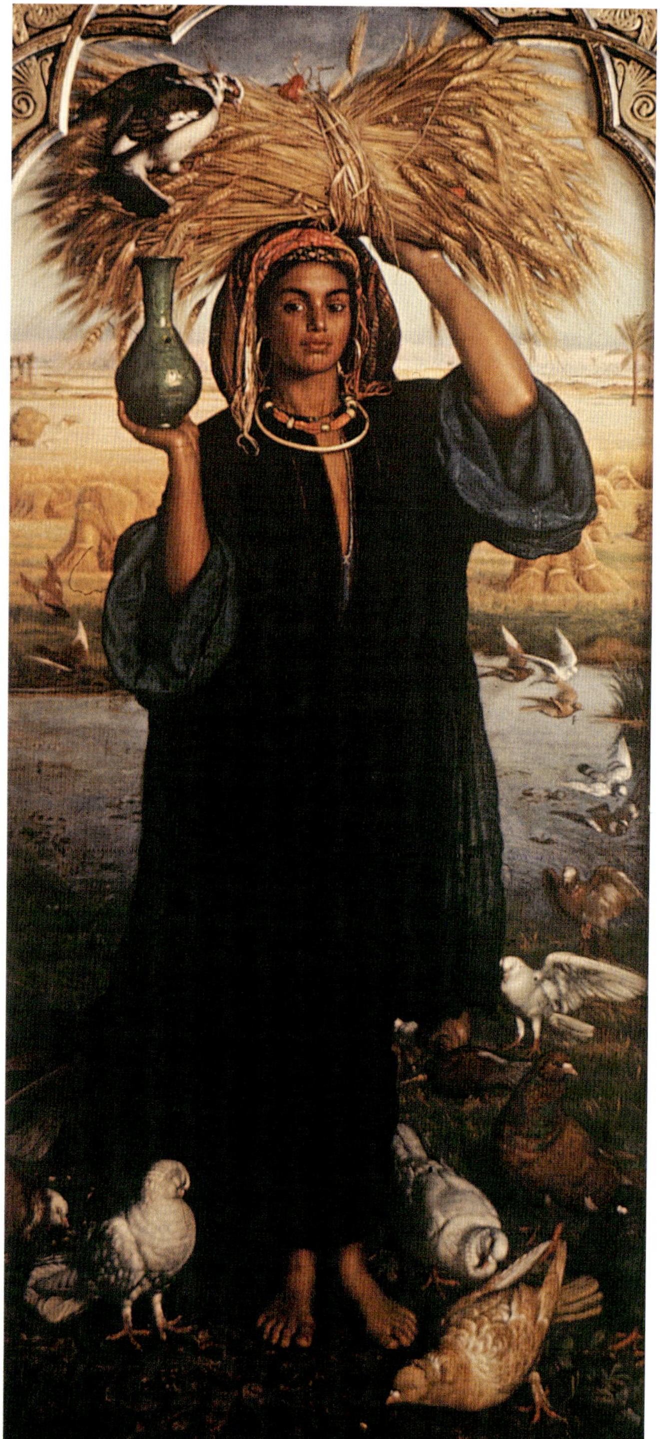

14
William Holman Hunt,
The Afterglow in Egypt,
1854–63

15
[*right*]
John Everett Millais,
Autumn Leaves,
1856

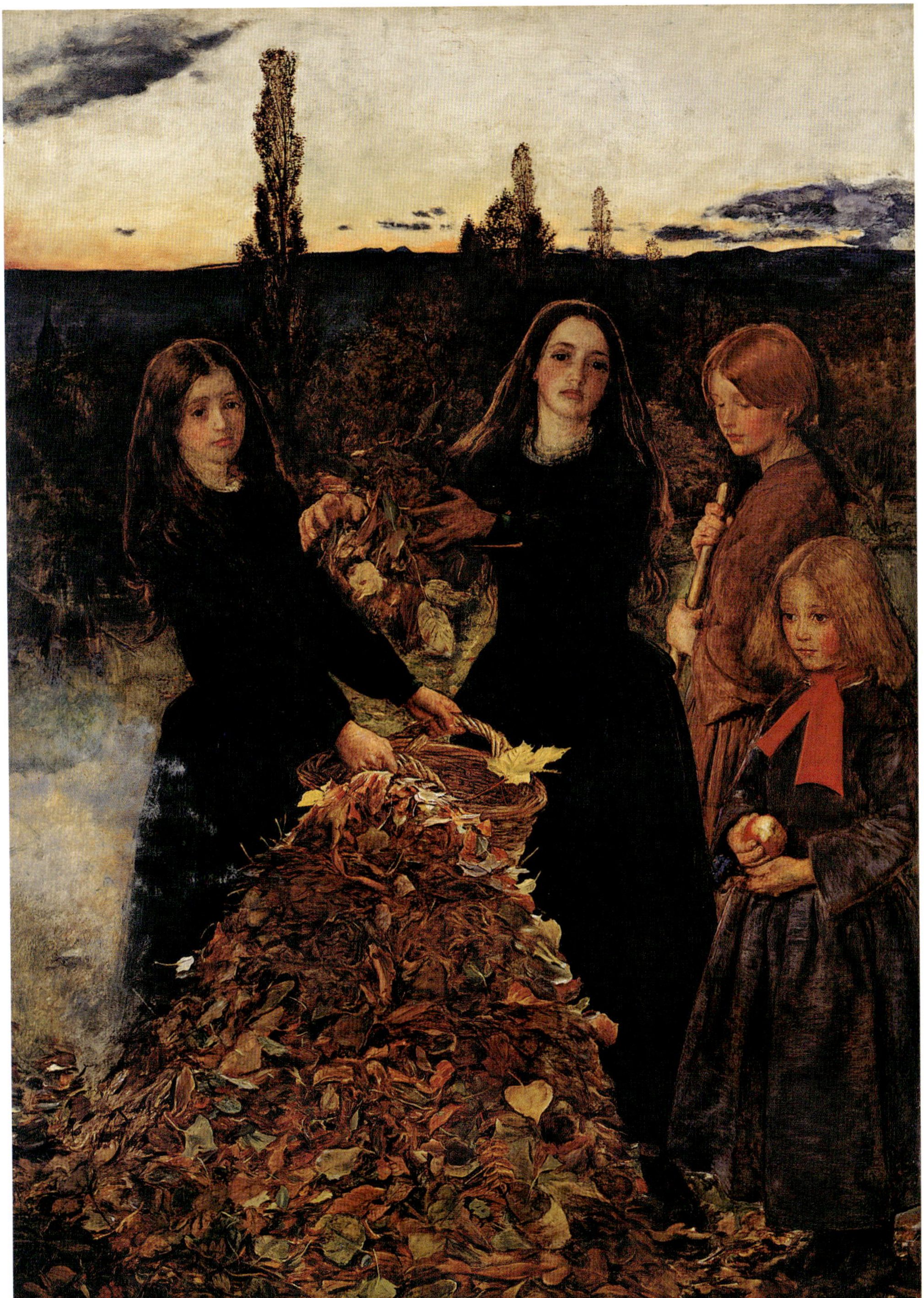

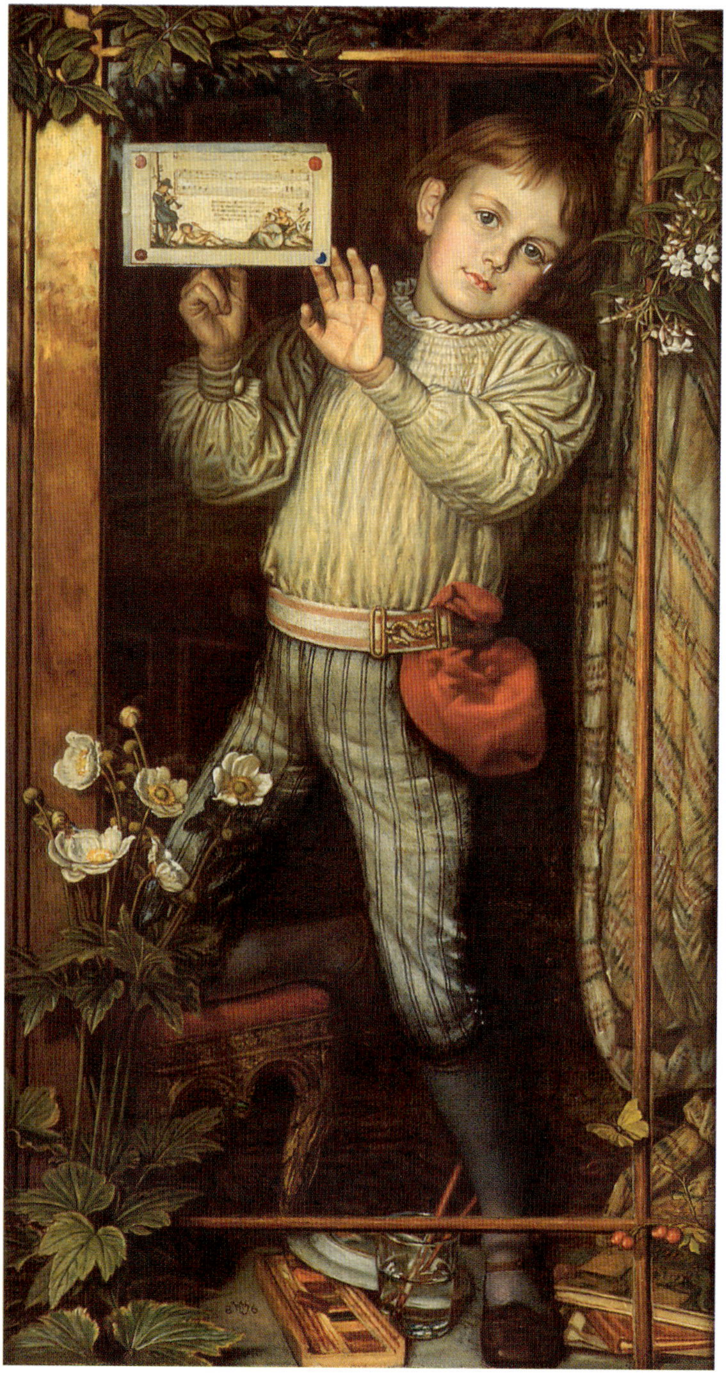

16
William Holman Hunt,
Master Hilary the Tracer,
1886

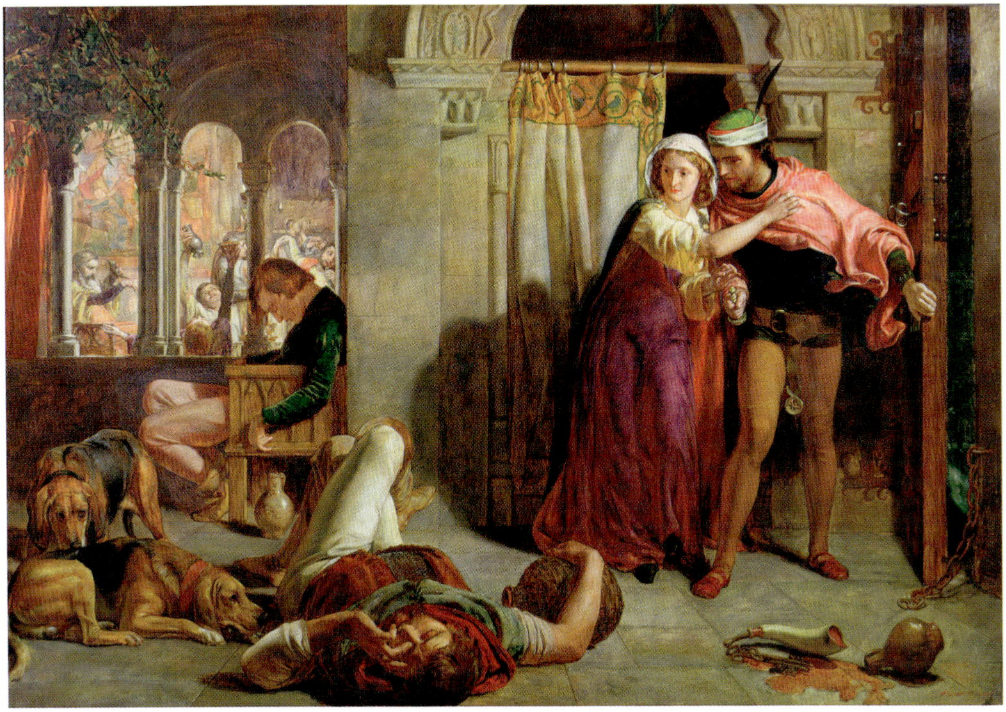

17
William Holman Hunt,
The Flight of Madeline and Porphyro during the drunkenness attending the revelry (The Eve of St Agnes),
1848

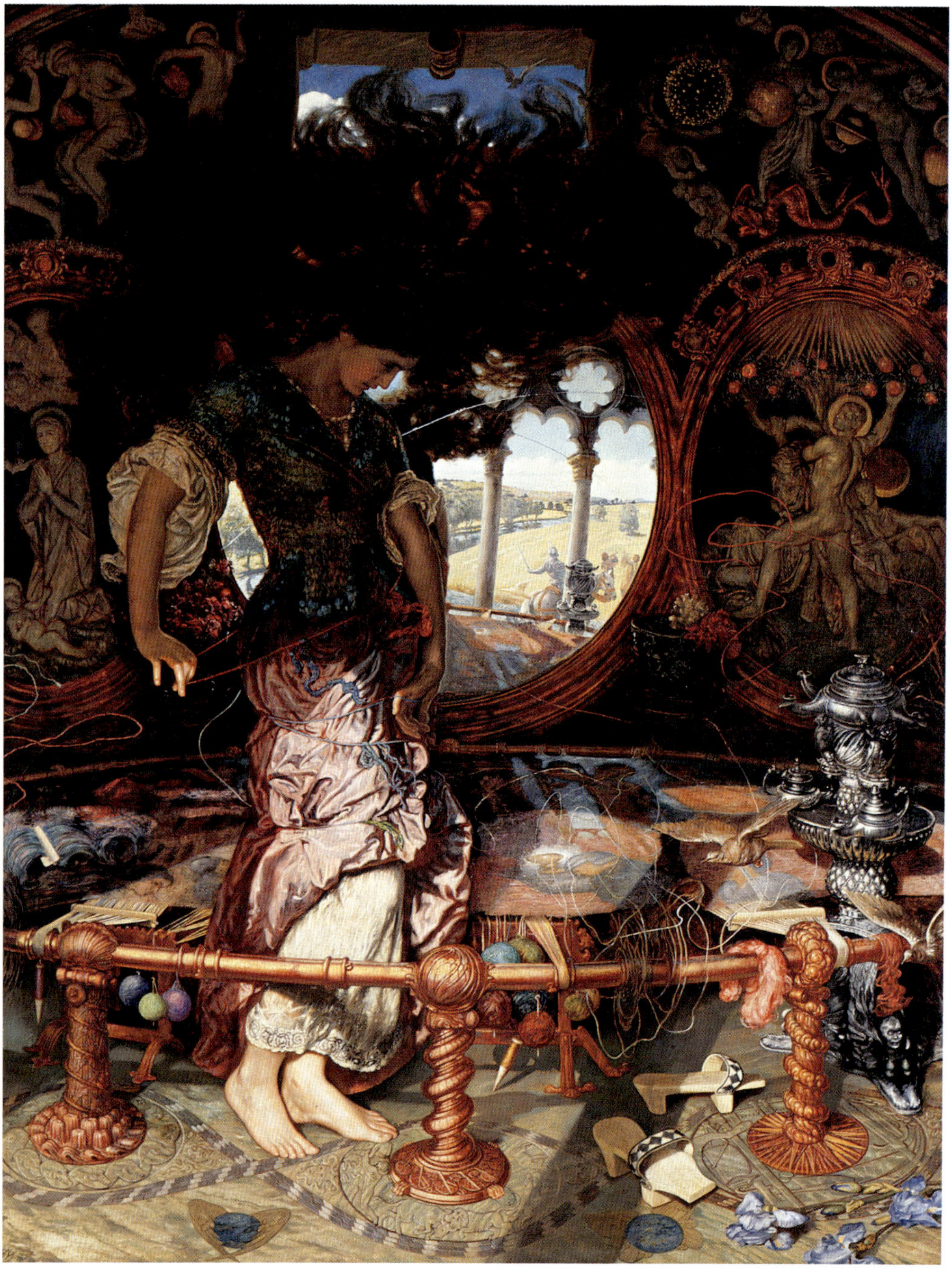

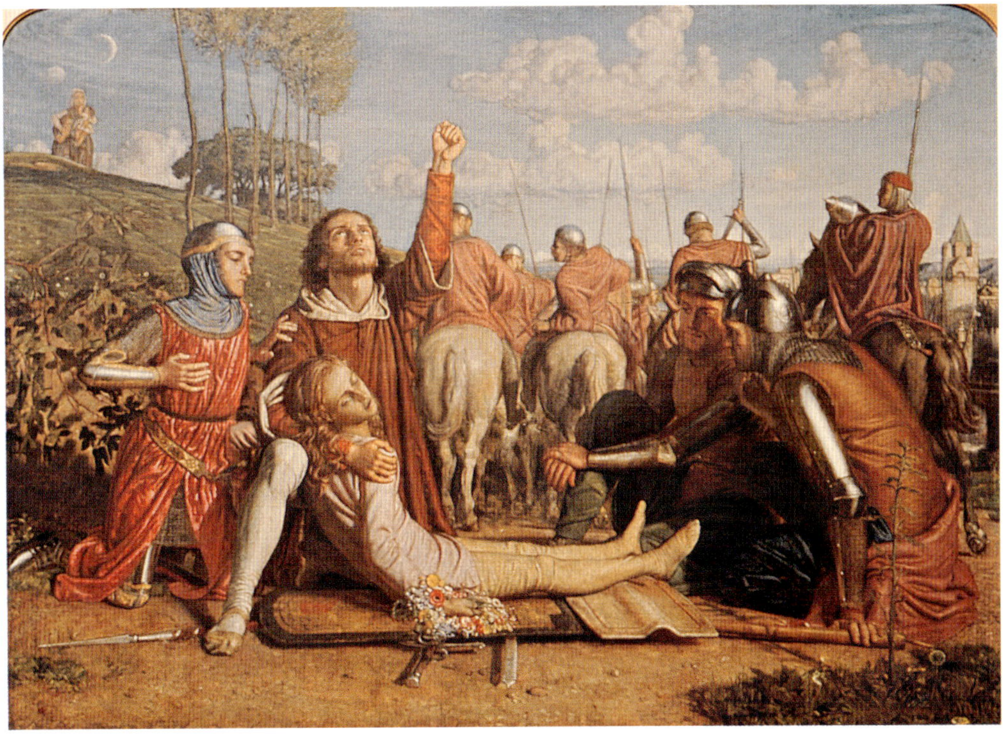

19
William Holman Hunt,
Rienzi vowing to obtain justice for the death of his young brother, slain in a skirmish between the Colonna and the Orsini factions,
1848–49

18
[*left*]
William Holman Hunt,
The Lady of Shalott,
1886–1905

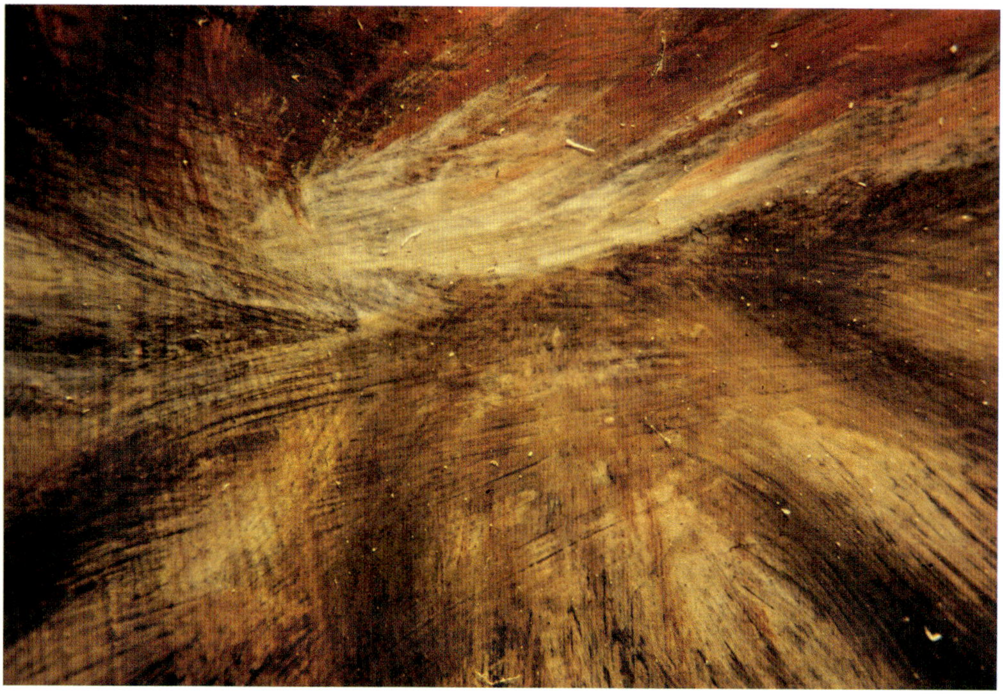

20
William Holman Hunt,
The Afterglow in Egypt,
magnified detail, parting in
feathers of brown bird,
lower left-hand side

21
William Holman Hunt, *The Afterglow in Egypt*, magnified detail, eye of brown bird perched on wheat sheaf

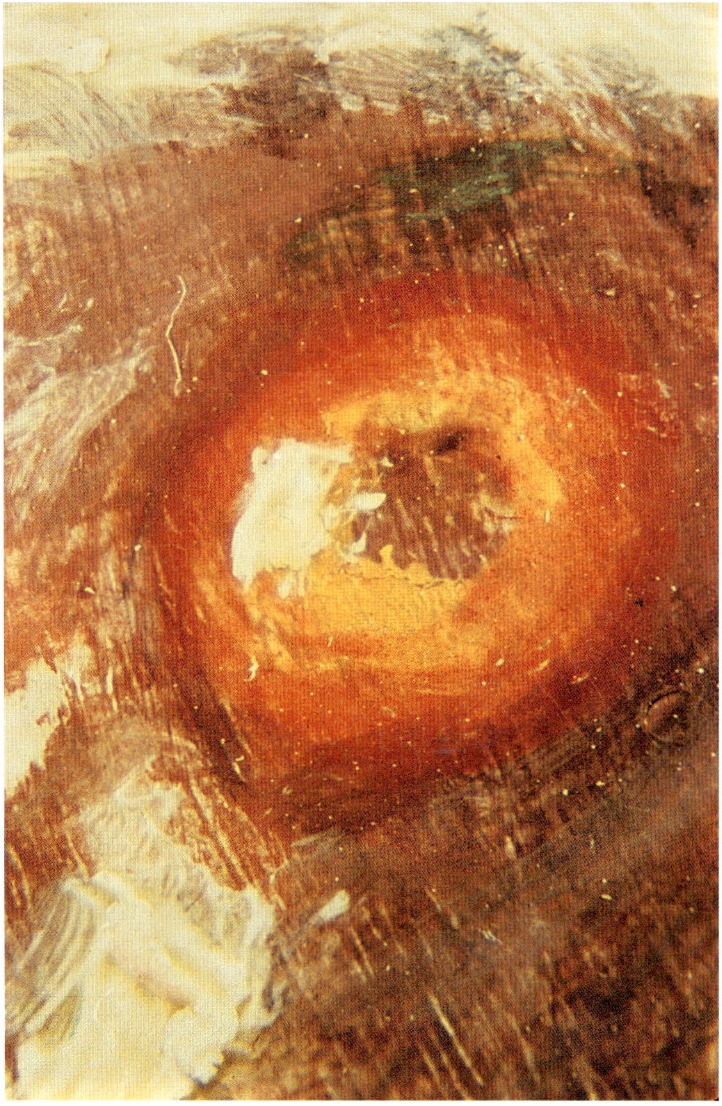

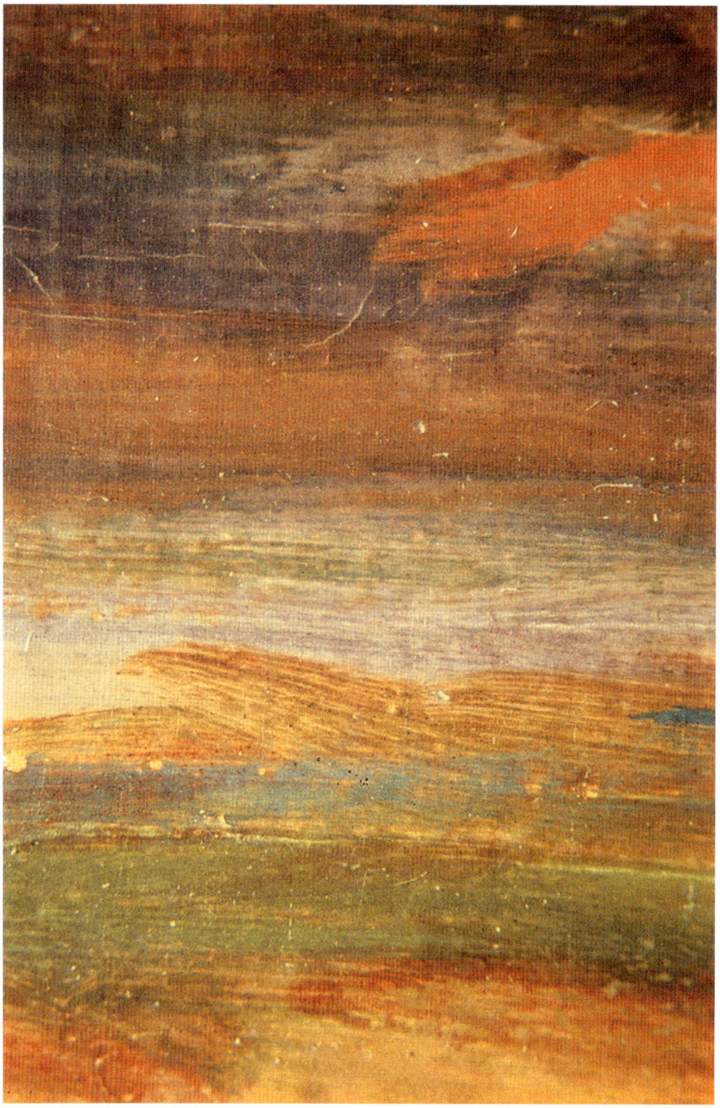

22
William Holman Hunt,
The Afterglow in Egypt,
magnified detail, margin of
river, middle left-hand side

23
Pierre Auguste Renoir,
Boating on the Seine, detail,
1879–80

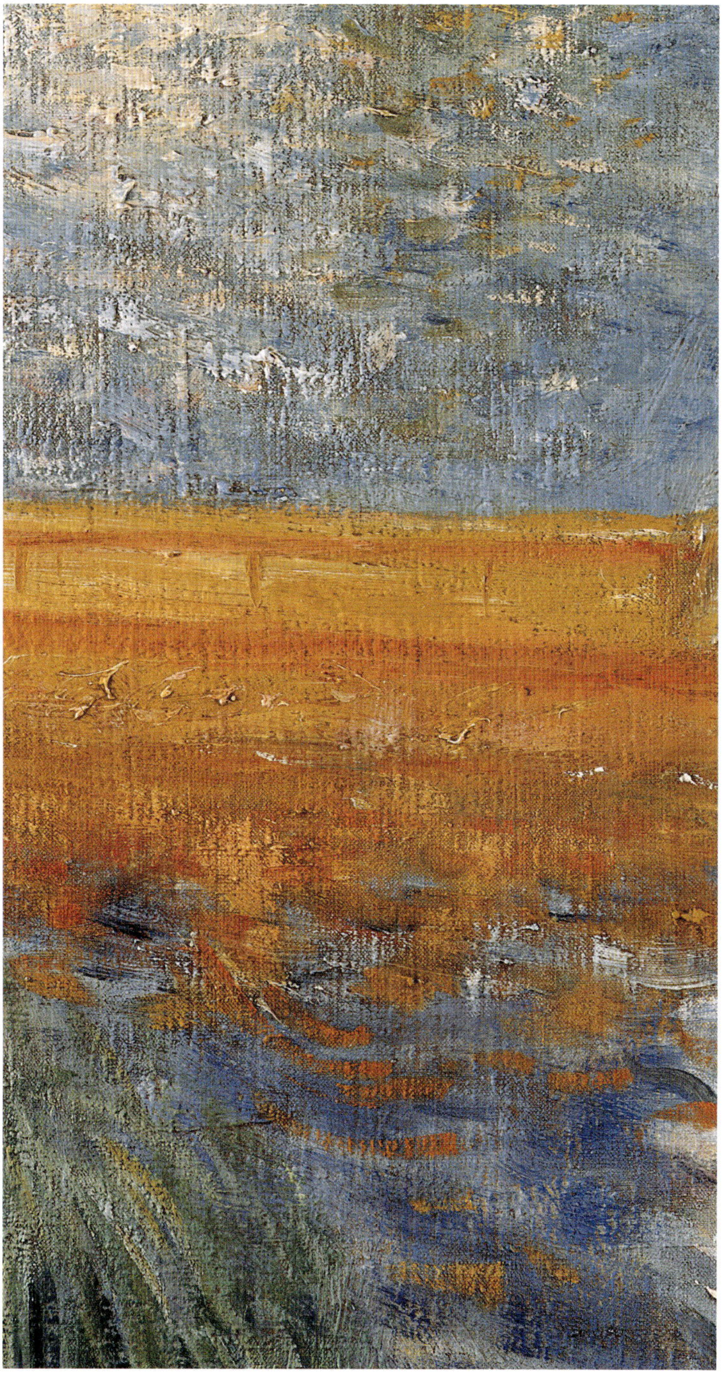

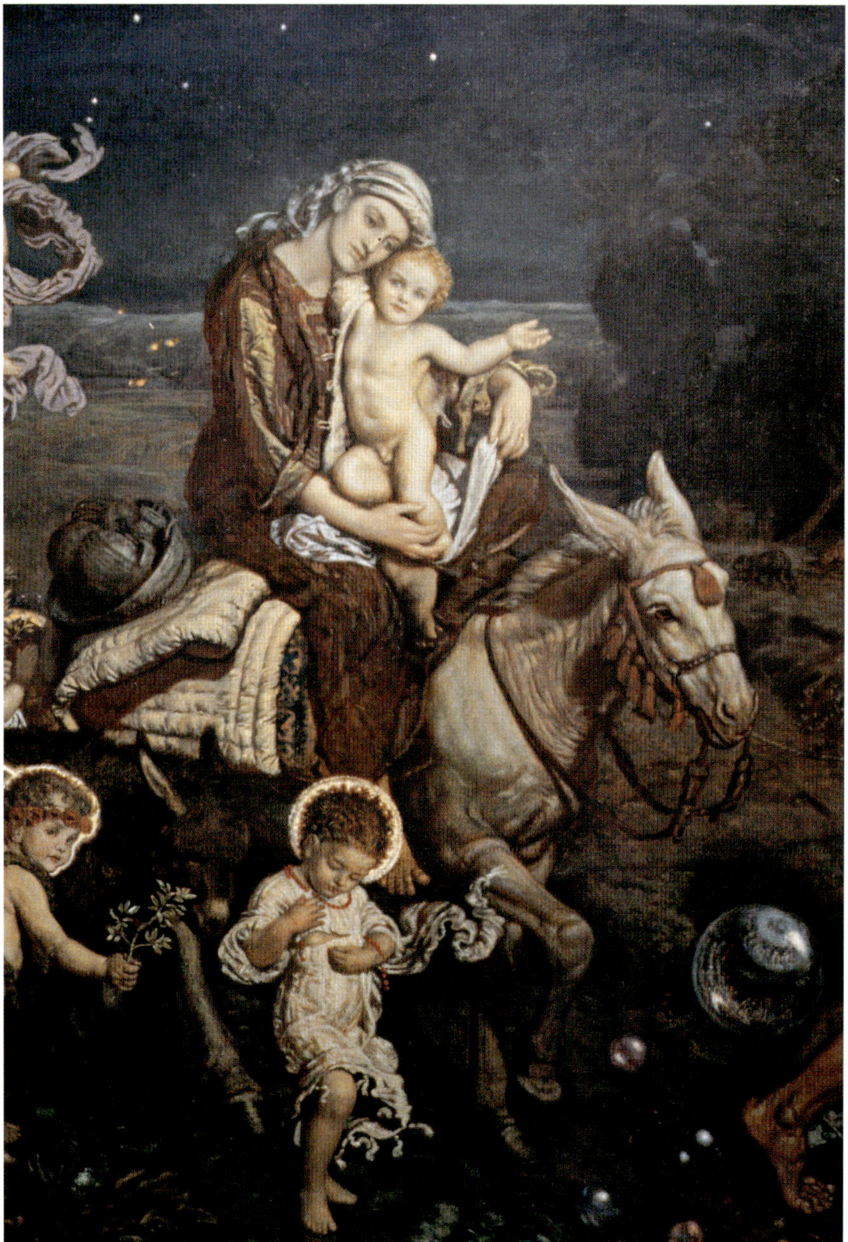

24
William Holman Hunt,
The Triumph of the Innocents,
finished sketch, detail,
1870–1903

again'.[16] Hunt's inclusion in the 1996 exhibition *The Art of the Picture Frame*, at the National Portrait Gallery, London, points to his 'controlling interest' in this aspect of the painting.[17] Bronkhurst's article, 'Holman Hunt's Picture Frames, Sculpture and Applied Art', surveys Hunt's practice of designing his own frames and notes that, unlike Millais, he specialises in frames which 'comment on the action within the picture space'.[18] This interest represents a concern about the way the frame curtails the image; an attempt to use symbolic motifs and inscriptions to extend the content of the picture beyond the edge of the canvas. This recalls Picasso's use of a piece of rope to enclose *Still Life with Chair Caning* (1912, Musées Nationaux, Paris), to complement the found object, a piece of oilcloth, within the picture. However, Hunt's intervention at the limits of the image lacks Picasso's self-critical irony. Whereas Picasso is drawing attention to the collage materials of his art, Hunt's frames reinforce iconography.

The arched tops of works such as *The Light of the World*, enhance the sacred meaning of the subject matter, but later paintings, such as *The Shadow* and *The Triumph*, are painted within rectangles. This shape contributes to a sense of the painting as a window on to a three-dimensional scene. *Pre-Raphaelitism* quotes Walter Crane's description of the 'daylight effects' of Pre-Raphaelite pictures of the mid-nineteenth century as 'apertures in the wall of exhibitions' (2, 351).

Greenberg sees the open acknowledgement of the two-dimensional canvas as a fundamental feature of modernism, but Hunt's work systematically stresses the three-dimensional. Unusually strong modelling emphasises the so-called 'pre-modern' quality which Greenberg calls 'the sculptural'.[19] For example, commentators on *The Finding* complained of an excessive use of 'lights scattered all over the canvas in a manner most distracting to the eye'.[20] These highlights are necessary to compensate for the lack of dull tones in Hunt's palette; in the absence of shadow, three-dimensional effects of light and dark must be achieved by using extra white. His occasional use of a precise, raised surface is also intended to promote the illusion of textural fabrics, metalwork, hair or grass. In *The Triumph* (plate 3), the heads of Mary, Jesus and the Innocents are executed in a thicker layer of paint, 'giving an effect close to low relief'.[21] Hunt often made sculpted models of parts of his figures, such as the heads of Christ in *The Light of the World* and *The Shadow*.[22]

Hunt's compositions also are carefully orientated towards the creation of a three-dimensional effect. The conspicuous use of conventions of literary realism exhibited in *Pre-Raphaelitism* is echoed by an equally profuse array of conventions of pictorial realism. The works are cluttered with a range of devices which construct depth – overlapping, perspectival orthogonals, diminishing forms and oblique,

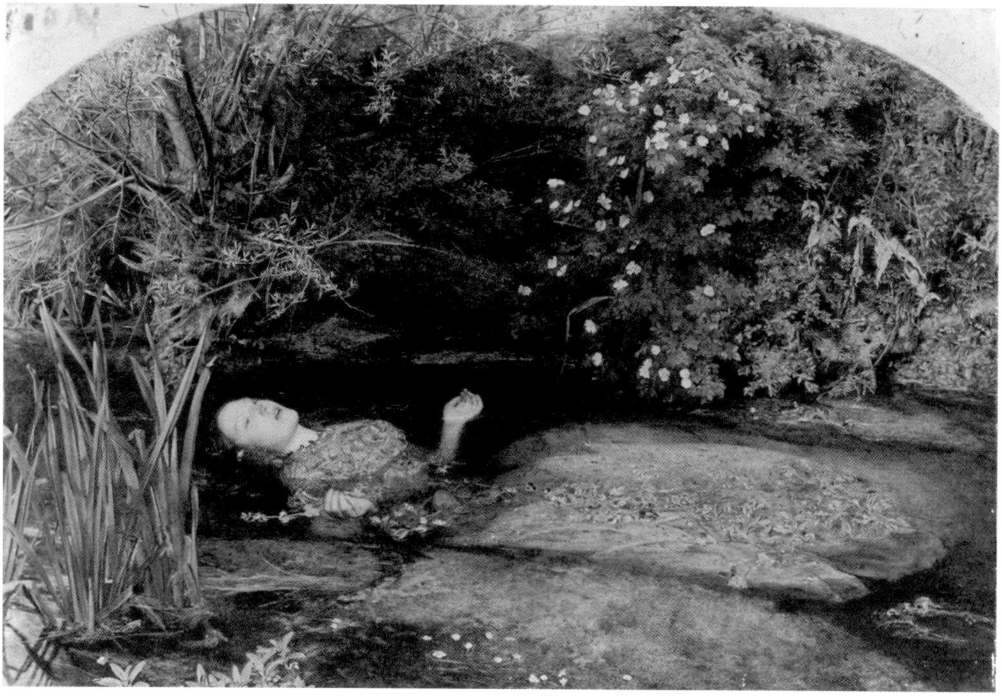

6.4
John Everett Millais, *Ophelia*, 1851–52

foreshortened objects. The very elaboration of this process again seems to reveal an experimental consciousness of the devices themselves, a paradoxical mobilisation of artifice, reminiscent of the carefully contrived 'naturalism' of the memoir.

Hunt's figures are almost always set at an angle to the picture plane; an arm or a knee comes forward in overstated *contrapposto*. This is exploited in the poses of the Christs in *The Finding* (plate 6) and *The Shadow* (plate 2). Often, the whole body is bent, as in the case of Mary in both *The Finding* and *The Shadow*, and Joseph and the children in *The Triumph*, clearly defining the space it inhabits. Millais also positions the figures in *Ophelia* (1851–52, Tate Britain, figure 6.4) and *Autumn Leaves* (1856, Manchester Art Gallery, plate 15) at a three-quarter angle, but foreshortening and modelling are minimised, offering a more elegant, flattened profile. Hunt emphasises the modelling of foreshortened limbs, sometimes to the point of ugliness. His hands and feet sacrifice grace for the sake of plasticity. This can be seen by comparing the curled fingers of Christ in *The Shadow* to those of Ophelia. Christ's arm pushes awkwardly towards the viewer in *The Light of the World* (plate 4) and even more so as he pulls on his buckle in *The Finding*.

Objects are also placed obliquely, and are often strategically positioned in the foreground. The chair and saw in *The Shadow* act as conspicuous depth clues. These familiar and relatively geometric shapes are easily read as foreshortened, and serve a similar function to that of the diminishing patterns of marble in quattrocento painting, also used by Hunt in *The Finding* and *Isabella* (plate 13). Scenes are often staged in an architectural box which is again reminiscent of perspectivally self-conscious fifteenth-century painting. *Isabella*, *The Finding* and *The Shadow* are examples. In outdoor subjects, artificial orthogonals are offered instead, such as the leaves, cracks in the salt and reflections in *The Scapegoat* (plate 1).[23] The chest, the foremost plank and the saw in *The Shadow* are similarly aligned with the picture's vanishing point (somewhere around Christ's heart). The gazes of figures are also often orientated along receding diagonals which draw us into the painting. The most dramatic instances of this are where a figure faces away from the viewer, as in *The Shadow* and *The Triumph*.

Master Hilary the Tracer (plate 16), a painting about painting, clearly exemplifies this virtuoso, multiple construction of three-dimensional illusion. The overall conception of the design is obviously concerned with promoting the picture frame as window frame. The texture and orientation of the paint surface equates it to the pane of glass behind which Hunt's son leans. The window frame is exactly aligned with the edges of the canvas. Hilary's body is twisted away so that our eye is drawn up his leg and into the space he occupies. Both arms are foreshortened. His hand comes forward and his palm and fingers are distorted as they press against the glass. His diagonal gaze echoes the angle of his body, reinforced by the parallel arm and stripes in the curtain. The curtain itself is a conventional means of obscuring the artificial cut-off of the frame and producing a sense of 'looking in', common since the Renaissance. The simple geometric shapes of paintbox, glass, plate and books on the ground, all placed obliquely, are clear perspectival clues. The painstakingly rendered foliage defines layers of depth through the simple process of overlapping and the flowers bend forward into our space. The glass of water is, like the curtain, a motif drawn from Dutch art, displaying the painter's mimetic skills. The picture which the boy is tracing is a design by Crane, and seems to refer to his reference to Pre-Raphaelite paintings as windows (2, 351).

In his essay 'Pre-Raphaelitism and Post-Raphaelitism: The Articulation of Fantasy and the Problem of Pictorial Space', Paul Barlow detects a similarly complicated investigation of pictorial space in *The Eve of St Agnes* (plate 17), and contrasts it with the unconcerned conviction of transparency of some contemporaries, such as Henry O'Neil. He suggests that Hunt's interest in spatial conventions represents an acknowledgement of the essential flatness of the medium. Barlow points out that Hunt's space is characteristic in its fussy reluctance to allow the eye a clean sweep past the picture surface. Secondary spaces are generally viewed through apertures, windows or mirrors. The abundant spatial clues which I have identified above tend to be isolated from each other, inhibiting a homogeneous perspectival reading. Orthogonals are interrupted, and Barlow notes that the corners of *The Eve of St Agnes* are hidden by shadows and that 'the base of the pillar . . . is scarcely differentiated from the stone flags of the hallway'.[24]

This kind of composition is typical. The bases of the columns in *The Finding* are covered by the figures and we construct a logical idea of depth from separate scraps of information, such as the orthogonal of the temple step, and the diminishing of the figures and architectural features. Similarly, it is the angle of the saw and the chair and the positioning of the figures which communicate depth in *The Shadow*. This isolation of self-contained depth clues strengthens the argument that they are being used consciously. Their distribution about the canvas recalls the arrangement of discrete references to depth in Cubist pictures, Georges Braque's *Clarinet and Bottle of Rum on a Mantelpiece* (1911, Tate Modern, figure 6.5), for example.[25] It contains isolated instances of modelling in light and shade, brief orthogonals, the corner of an oblique object or one object overlapping another. Both artists are exploring these conventions, but whereas Braque deliberately dislocates his clues to interrogate pictorial space, Hunt uses them in harmony, to reinforce the three-dimensional illusion.

Hunt's use of the visual language is no less self-conscious than his use of literary language in *Pre-Raphaelitism*. I would contend that in both cases he displays an anxious awareness of the process of fabrication. Barlow argues that this awareness is deliberately revealed. He suggests that *The Eve of St Agnes* 'stresses the contradictions involved in the mythic dissolution of the picture surface'[26] by contrasting a flat, two-dimensional, archaic background (the tapestry setting of the revellers), with the potent depth clue of the heavily foreshortened porter in the foreground. He sees this as a response to Keats's poem in that it plays on ideas of fantasy and reality that correspond to inside and outside, flat, pictorial space and real space beyond the painting (articulated by the open door). The theme of escape from an interior associated with false art which is featured in *The Eve of St Agnes* he believes reoccurs in many of Hunt's designs, such as *The Finding* and *The Shadow*. I agree with Barlow's assertion that Hunt is aware of the artificial nature of pictorial three-dimensionality, but do not accept his suggestion that *The Eve of St Agnes* itself, as a complete work of art, deliberately advertises its own artifice.

This awareness is signalled clearly in *Pre-Raphaelitism*. It dramatises an argument with Gladstone over a design on a teacup:

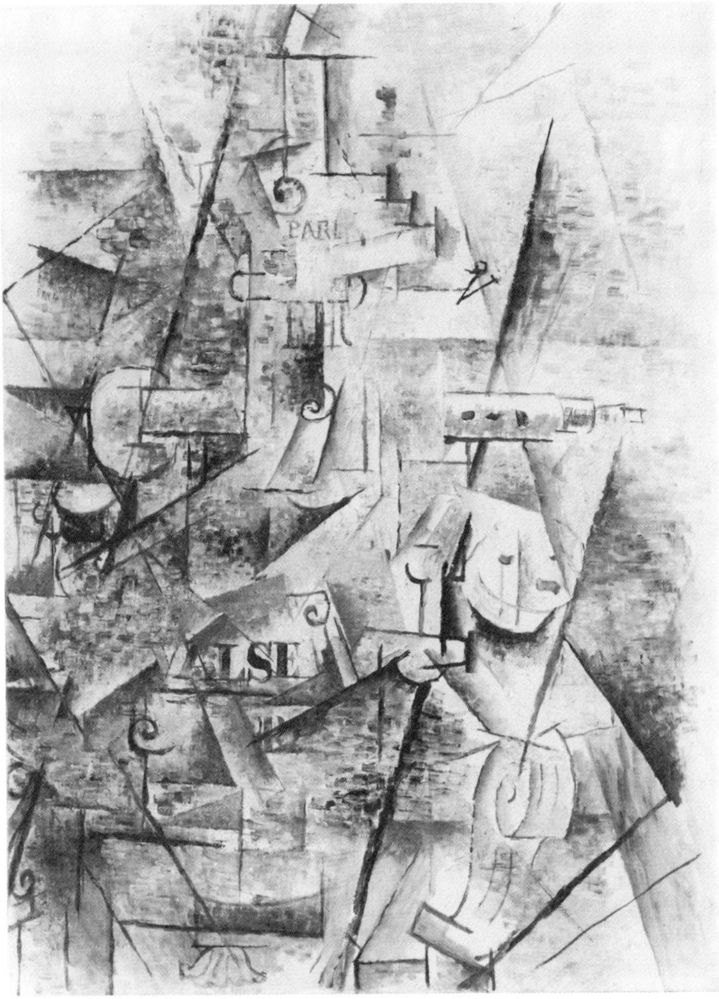

6.5
Georges Braque,
Clarinet and Bottle of Rum on a Mantlepiece,
1911

'I must admit that Sèvre and Dresden porcelain cause me pain in their elaborate determination to defy the principles of sound design,' I said.
'But how do they do that?' he inquired.
'By disregard of the fitness of things.'
'In what way does "fitness" enter the question?' he asked.
'It is not my personal theory I am propounding, it is often spoken of now as "Ruskin's principle,"' I said; 'but in fact many before him tacitly or openly declared it. Socrates, as an artist, where he lays it down that beauty depends upon fitness, and all true artists have recognised the law.' Seeing him hesitate, I said, 'allow me to explain,' and I took up a cup. 'This is a vessel out of which a man drinks, and it should give an undisturbed impression as to its purpose, but when the cup is in our hands, observing it on the outside we see a picture of linear and aerial perspective, with full light and shade of distant mountains, of a great

> plain of trees and a platform of steps in the foreground; we turn it forward and under the teacup is a distant bay, a ruined temple, a fountain close at hand, with statues, and cavaliers and dames dancing about. Our mind is in a state of discord to reconcile opposite impressions, one impression being that this is a half-globe to hold the liquid that is within it, the other being that of distances and buildings, on concave or convex surfaces, which could only be rightly depicted and intelligibly understood when seen on a flat surface; the cup and the pictures are perfectly incongruous, and elegant manipulation is misplaced.'
> 'But,' said he, 'Oriental porcelain sometimes has representations of objects and landscape painted on its surfaces.'
> 'It is true,' I said, 'but these are not portrayed with the aid of elaborate perspective and light and shade. The objects are represented as ornaments, controlled by design fit for the nature of the thing in use.' (2, 202)

The text exhibits an astute understanding of the problem of three-dimensional space rendered two-dimensionally, but this objectivity does not extend to the 'flat surface' which presumably means the picture surface. Despite the detail of this speech, it omits to explore the question of 'fitness' in more ambiguous categories such as flat decorative objects, like the tapestry in the background of *The Eve of St Agnes*. It makes a swift, sharp distinction between the teacup (decorated object) and the picture (not decorated object), implying that the illusion of a view, 'a distant bay, a ruined temple, a fountain close at hand, with statues, and cavaliers and dames dancing about', is appropriate only to the latter.

The portrayal of the scene in his hands is so vivid that we see it in our mind's eye as real. In particular, the phrase 'close at hand' implies a continuity between the onlooker's space and pictorial space. Thus, when the speaker reminds us that what we are really considering is 'a half-globe to hold the liquid', we are struck by the absurdity of the contrast between the two. He shifts the reader's focus and illusion becomes overt fantasy, in keeping (again) with the trivial revelry that is depicted. Although the lecture executes a masterful deconstruction of this landscape, it does not acknowledge the possibility of a corresponding deconstruction were such a view on a flat surface not designated as mere decoration. The passage demonstrates a modernist awareness of the tension between the material object and the illusion it bears, but this tension is elided when it comes to the kind of object that the artist, himself, produces.

The structure of the teacup passage itself offers an interesting corollary to the general tendency of texts by Hunt to deny their own constructed nature. Acknowledgement of the intervention of the author, that the proposition is motivated by an authorial point of view, is suppressed by the way his opinion is presented as being elicited by

Gladstone in the form of repeated questions. It is also presented as Ruskin's idea. The names of these two great men, Ruskin's agreement and Gladstone's eventual agreement, lend historical proof to the protagonist's opinion. The use of minute observation of a single object, the cup, to demonstrate the argument is also characteristic of both Hunt's literary and painting style.

The passage is presented as direct speech, painstakingly described with all the 'but's and initial short questions, constructing the words as vivid, unmodified 'evidence', like the cup. The inverted commas act in a similar way to the secondary frames (pictures, doors, windows) so prevalent in Hunt's pictures: *The Awakening Conscience*, *The Shadow*, *Master Hilary* for example. These secondary brackets lead the observer to forget the primary bracket, which is, in the case of the painting, the real frame, and in the case of the book, the quotation of the narrator. Frames, like that through which the revellers are seen in *The Eve of St Agnes*, are included to promote the real frame as a window rather than part of an artificial designation of the scene.

Barlow suggests that the foreshortened man in *The Eve of St Agnes* is the final stage in a 'systematic analysis' of a series of spatial models developing from the 'mediaeval' (wall decorations) to the 'Renaissance' (revellers) to the 'modern' (porter) and that it suggests a further, notional, category of 'reality' which is beyond the open door, outside the picture space altogether.[27] However, I think that Hunt's production reveals no acknowledgement of this final step. I propose a simpler, binary, spatial categorisation similar to the one expressed to Gladstone: two-dimensional artefacts (such as the wall decorations) versus the three-dimensional (the actual scene shown in the picture). The painting is a manifestation of the artist's inclusive perception, the ability to distinguish fact from fiction which is dramatised by the above conversation. It presents itself as an equivalent of real vision, 'close at hand' which includes, *within* it, specimens of the false and the true, just as *The Shadow* does.

Hunt's elaborate use of spatial clues is a defence against the inherent flatness of the picture surface. As I have noted above, dramatically foreshortened figures are common in his work and not confined to one 'level' or category of spatial realisation, as Barlow argues the porter to be in *The Eve of St Agnes*. This figure is simply an especially virtuoso example of illusionism, similar to the flowers in the foreground of *Master Hilary*. This is an artist declaring his power to create form and space, in much the same way as Mantegna did with his *Dead Christ* (1506, Brera, Milan). As Hunt said in later years of his Christ in *The Light of the World*, 'he was to be firmly and substantially there'.[28]

Barlow's assertion that *The Eve of St Agnes* 'proposes the absence of nature as a necessary condition of art',[29] may apply to the art depicted in the painting but cannot apply to the intentions of the painting itself. The artifice identified by Hunt in past art (such as that of Raphael), in much art of his time (Whistler) and in decorative objects, is included in the form of works of art in pictures such as *The Eve of St Agnes* or *The Shadow* in order to ascribe a contrasting realism to the overall scene. Like the quotations in *Pre-Raphaelitism*, they point up the artist's *completer* vision.

The problems of fantasy and reality in Keats's poetry do indeed haunt texts by Hunt (as shown above), but, as I have shown, the status of his art as visually equivalent to, and a revelation of, nature is paramount. His concern is always to repudiate fears that his images represent mere 'poetic dreaming'. The manipulation of conventions of depth does not necessarily imply a conscious questioning of them. I would prefer to change the emphasis and propose 'the systematic analysis of stages from artifice into reality' that Barlow observes in *The Eve of St Agnes* as a symptom of an underlying anxiety about the status of art in relation to the real; an anxiety already evident in both the form and content of Hunt's writings and in his iconography. As Greenberg says, awareness of the dishonesty of the three-dimensional illusion does not necessarily lead to an engagement with it. Hunt's careful denial of this dishonesty is a kind of acknowledgement of it in itself.

The recent reintroduction of Hunt into art historical debate has been brought about through the agency of a critical methodology which has rejected modernism's formalism in favour of historical readings. This approach has, however, tended to represent a continuation of the marginalisation of material aspects of his work noted in my introduction. Rather than reject the narrative of modernism outright, this chapter has sought to initiate something approaching a Derridean deconstruction of Greenberg's model, especially its polarisation of the pre-modern and the modern. The margins, that which has been excluded, are returned to the centre and found, as I shall show, to be implicit in the mainstream.[30]

Authorities of the eye

Hunt's exhaustive pursuit of realism is fundamental to the status of his work as religious witness rather than subjective peformance; a recreation of the privileged vision of the artist. This myth is supported by the propagandising of the artist's powers of sight in *Pre-Raphaelitism*, as exemplified by the story of the protagonist identifying a distant eagle while on a walk with Tennyson (2, 173). The legend has persisted: Wood reports, in 1981, that Hunt could see the moons of Jupiter with the naked eye![31]

This promotion of the artist's vision is clearly demonstrated by Hunt's discussions of perspective. In 1876, he tells Tupper that he prefers to observe the diminishment of actual forms, rather than construct them according to mathematical theory:

> I had never worked out the problem about the side perspective of a circle, or a circular column, and I feel ashamed that I had not as I must often have been near to the necessity of doing so. Once I remember distinctly that painting on an outline which I had drawn by rule hastily ~~or perhaps always~~, it was in the Temple picture where the bases of the columns were hidden by figures, I was dissatisfied with the proportions of the columns and not seeing the opportunity for getting the result better by rule I added to the bulk until this satisfied my eye . . . Many painters of acute perception – Millais to wit – would go from an outline given them by a shallow rule and say afterwards 'The thing looked all wrong till I gave my eye the reins.'[32]

This passage also goes some way towards explaining Hunt's almost defiant inclusion of perfect spheres in *The Triumph*, on which he was working at the time of writing. He comments, 'the globe ~~in perspective~~ is certainly the best object to choose as a test of the problem how to draw a circle in perspective'.[33]

Although the letter from Tupper to which Hunt is replying is lost, he seems to have been comparing a diagram with a photograph. In 1870, Tupper published a paper 'On an Optical Illusion' in the *Philosophical Magazine*, and, in 1874, 'On the Centre of Motion in the Human Eye' in the *Royal Society Proceedings*. He corresponded with Hunt about his findings.[34] In her essay, 'The Elusive Depth of Field: Stereoscopy and the Pre-Raphaelites', Lindsay Smith draws attention to the fact that a general atmosphere of scientific approaches to the act of looking, catalysed by photography, manifests itself in Pre-Raphaelite painting in the form of an awareness of the limitations of single point perspective and the two-dimensional format: 'a singular crisis point in visual perception and representation'.[35]

Like Barlow, Smith suggests that Pre-Raphaelite art and contemporary poetry react to questions of the limits and subjectivity of perception thrown up by Romantic poets, and she identifies a 'cultural shift from Romantic to Victorian inscriptions of optical agency'.[36] She confirms that the Pre-Raphaelite reaction to this was to promote the artist's eye, not to embrace flatness, but to try to approximate real vision even more closely. Hunt's depiction of perfect spheres in *The Triumph* is a direct response to this challenge. They augment the triumph of vision the work is meant to represent.

Hunt expresses distrust of the lens and a valorisation of the eye in a comment to Stephens about a photograph of his godson: 'One has to make allowances for the distorting character of the lens as in all photographic portraits.'[37] According to Smith, Ruskin is also suspicious of the distorting lens, approving the magnifying glass, but not the microscope which 'transgresses its [the eye's] so-called natural bounds'.[38] Hunt writes to Stephens in 1864 about a stereoscopic photograph of elephants that he has seen:

> The stereoscopic photography will be of great value to me. What the clerk, Woodthorpe, says I cannot understand for I saw the Elephants on the most conspicuous plans, and draw them in my sketch. I am old enough, it is true, to admit my eyes may have deceived me, but then there is the illustration in the London News with the objects on the top of poles, whatever they may be called, with four legs, a heavy/rounded body and a large head with tusks and a trunk, possibly you have written 'Elephants' for 'Ravens', the photograph will settle all I hope.[39]

We are not privy to the private joke which seems to be being shared, but we get a sense that Hunt prefers not to take photography too seriously. It is commitment to the eye of the artist which explains this bravado about the new invention. The attitude to traditional perspective reveals a move away from the mathematical construction of the viewer as a single stationary eye, as Smith suggests, but Hunt replaces this with a general valorisation of sight. Hunt's scientific interest is directed towards the manipulation of materials into a reproduction of his own vision (more will be said about perspective in Chapter 8).

Ruskin describes Hunt's technique as a direct 'transportation' of visual impressions. He stresses colour, that which the camera cannot record (at this time):

> [*Our English Coasts* (1852, Tate Britain) shows] us for the first time in the history of art, the absolute faithful balance of colour and shade by which sunshine might be transported into a key in which the harmonies possible with pigments should yet produce the same impressions on the mind which were caused by the light itself.[40]

Ruskin's eulogy to Hunt's fidelity to his material vision is in some ways justified, as I shall illustrate in Chapter 8. However, it again represents the myth of the artist's eye, and its unproblematic re-presentation in paint, which has grown up around Hunt's technique. Landow identifies Hunt as one who attempts to 'plumb the limits of painting', but he, too, submits to this eclipsing of process and material properties by the mimetic illusion, seeing Hunt as a 'man of the idea', like the modern artists who conceptualise, but do not execute their work.[41]

Hunt's successful performance of the mimetic power of his eye through writings and via the style of his paintings can again be construed as defensive. As I have shown in Chapter 4, private statements express deep concerns about the limits and subjectivity of perception. Where public texts emphasise the artist's sanity and his 'staring propensities' (2, 63), the journals reveal a stark awareness of the anomalies of vision, such as those experienced at the Dead Sea. During work on *The Shadow*, Hunt suffers from headaches and overwork which confuse his sight: 'my eyes will scarcely serve me'.[42] The picture seems to look different from day to day, optical decisions are difficult: 'I am so bewildered now that I can see nothing.'[43] A temporary blindness occurs during work on *The Triumph* in 1879,[44] and the disability returns in his sixties.[45] The fact that he is almost totally blind by the time he is writing the memoir underlines the mythical nature of its all-seeing hero.

Hunt's public demonstrations of a precise, objective focus on the materials of painting, discussed at the beginning of this chapter, and his pursuit of a painstaking pictorial illusionism may seem to be contradictory. They are, however, both related to investment in the authority of the artist's eye. In 'The Gaze and the Glance', Clarke points out that 'Greenberg's formalism yearns for the tangible certitude of the literal in an analogous way to realism's desire for pure mimesis, the copy indistinguishable from the original.'[46] The prioritisation of the eye through the mimetic reproduction of the artist's visual experience, relates to the opposite extreme of modernist attempts to gain visual authority through pure abstraction, where materials reveal themselves as themselves. Both seek unambiguous vision.

Clarke dramatises the modernist focus on materials by citing Frank Stella's remark, 'what you see is what you see': 'I didn't want to record a path. I wanted to get the paint out of the can onto the canvas . . . I tried to keep the paint as good as it was in the can.'[47] *Pre-Raphaelitism* narrates Hunt's own youthful experience of his materials in terms that express a similar pleasure in, and focus upon, them: 'How I idolised these implements when they were in my possession! The camel-hair pencil, with its translucent quill and rosy-coloured silk binding up its delicate hair at the base, all embedded together as in amber, was an equal joy with the gem-like cakes of paint' (1, 5). He recalls being allowed to watch an artist painting the burning of the Houses of Parliament: 'the conflagration grew in volume to such an extent that two or three times the palette was put down, and the painter set to work with the muller on the slab to grind a fresh supply of vermilion and chrome yellow' (1, 10–11). Ruskin, who shares Hunt's valorisation of the eye, describes having his portrait painted: 'I sat contentedly motionless, counting the holes in the carpet, or watching him squeeze his paint out of its bladders.'[48] Clarke notes that the foregrounding of materials in Stella's remark asserts the integrity of the eye because it is the eye and the gaze which is the point of interest, not the paint itself. Each of these accounts is asserting optical control, recalling the memoir's use of the protagonist's detection of the material nature of Tintoretto's paintings to privilege his visual authority over that of Ruskin.

The dual vision exhibited in Hunt's output represents an ambiguous nineteenth-century response to some of the aesthetic concerns which were to come to characterise modernism. It is an attempt to achieve a modernist *and* a nineteenth-century form of absolute focus, a precise perception of the object (the 'framework of wood' and 'cloth') and the image ('the flesh, the sky and the shavings') (2, 306–7). This can be constructed in *Pre-Raphaelitism* by a textual separation of the two kinds of gaze, but the painting itself cannot be apprehended as object and image without the partial destruction of one or the other.

As Greenberg notes, most art presents the viewer with some form of compromise, a 'dialectical tension' between the physical properties of the picture and its representational role. 'Whereas one tends to see what is *in* an Old Master before seeing it as a picture, one sees a modernist painting as a picture first.'[49] However, as Clarke says, the extremes of mimetic and abstract art are exceptions to this. In order to achieve a total optical authority, they elide process and promote either the representational or the material to an absolute, each excluding the other. Hunt puts himself in the paradoxical position of simultaneously attempting two kinds of optical authority.

Furthermore, *Pre-Raphaelitism* constructs a third kind of perception, an equally absolute apprehension of imaginative truth. The 'framework of wood' and 'cloth' and 'the flesh, the sky and the shavings' which is *The Shadow*, is also meant to represent a transcendental perception of the resurrected Christ. The dislocation is, as I demonstrated, in the Introduction, expressed by reviewers of *The Scapegoat*, *The Shadow* and *The Triumph* and modern commentators also identify 'slippage between the literal and symbolic'.[50] A tension between 'sight and insight' is fundamental to Victorian understanding of seeing, as Kate Flint establishes in *The Victorians and the Visual Imagination*,[51] but in the case of Hunt, the spiritual vision is at odds with two types of literal gaze, that which beholds the image and that which beholds the object, themselves at odds with each other.

Pre-Raphaelitism separates out these three kinds of perception. In it the unpainted canvas for *The Triumph* is described by the Moslem ladies as paper and cloth. They then view the study and see 'a woman on a donkey' and 'a lot of babies'. Hunt supplements their 'primitive', twin, literal understandings of object and image with an explanation of the scriptural significance of the figures. The Moslem lady then recognises that 'Jesus was the only being ever born on earth who possessed the soul of God' (2, 327). Hunt's particular ideal of complete, prophetic apprehension constitutes the sum of each type of looking.

This construction of the eye refuses to compromise either the spiritual, the optical or the material. Landow seems to allude to this multiple gaze in the following passage, where he refers to purely abstract art, as well as to Hunt's odd combination of mimetic and spiritual spectacle: 'Placing a black square on a black ground may not say anything true about anything beyond the way we perceive in a specific context – but then it does not say anything false either. The painting of William Holman Hunt, in contrast, makes explicit, detailed reference to both material and spiritual worlds.'[52] Landow admits the discontinuity between mimetic and spiritual content, but Hunt's illusionism perhaps obscures the equally significant dislocation between image and object.

Landow explains Hunt's attempt to synthesise the material and spiritual as a refusal 'to accept the loss of belief, the cultural fragmentation and the sheer lack of confidence that made the Victorians the progenitors of the modern age'.[53] Sussman, too, equates the Pre-Raphaelite mimetic style with visual authority.[54] Clarke sees the yearning for the literal certitude of both mimesis and pure abstraction as a reaction against relativity of meaning, what he calls 'the unstable world of signification', common to both centuries.[55]

Hunt's paintings are exemplars of visual and textual control. Their function in repairing the self-image of the artist is condensed in their role as manifestations of an absolute visual authority. This authority is multiple: the imaginative authority of the prophet, representing the divine; the mimetic authority of the eye, representing nature; and the scientific authority of the eye, perceiving the material actuality of things. The pursuit of each of these represents Hunt's struggle for 'tangible certitude' in the face of relativism and religious doubt.

Greenberg stresses that modernist 'self-criticism', the awareness of the properties and limitations of the work of art, arises from 'the actual practice and experience of art'.[56] A further investigation of Hunt's painting technique will reveal the origins of the anxious and disruptive modernist perceptions which I have outlined here. The final three chapters will investigate the way that Hunt's method of production attempts to synthesise all three forms of control, beginning with the definition of spiritual meaning and belief, going on to deal with mimesis, and concluding with an exploration of the role of the artist's materials. The practical failure to achieve a synthesis of these forms of visual authority contributes to the tensions exhibited in Hunt's writings and the fragmented and uncomfortable appearance of his work.

Notes

1 The reciprocal interrogation of material self-consciousness as exhibited in Hunt's work and theorised by modernism was first presented as 'William Holman Hunt: Revealing and Disguising the Object' at the conference, 'Work and the Image', April 1998, University of Leeds; in *Visual Culture in Britain*, 14, 2 (2003), pp 1–20

2 Greenberg, C., 'Modernist Painting' (1961), in *Art in Theory 1900–1990*, eds C. Harrison and P. Wood (Oxford: Basil Blackwell, 1993), pp 755–7; Fried, M., 'Three American Painters' (1965), ibid., pp 770–2
3 Barr, A., *Cubism and Abstract Art* (New York, Museum of Modern Art, 1936)
4 Elizabeth Prettejohn draws attention to the potential of re-viewing the Pre-Raphaelite group in the light of broader continental developments in *The Art of the Pre-Raphaelites*, p 65; as does Paul Barlow in 'Millais, Manet, Modernity', in *English Art 1860–1914: Modern Artists and Identity*, eds D. Peters Corbett and L. Perry (Manchester: Manchester University Press, 2000), pp 49–64. Prettejohn interrogates Greenberg's ideas of the avant-garde in relation to Leighton's aestheticism in 'The Modernism of Frederic Leighton', ibid., pp 31–48
5 'Materials', p 488. Hunt is probably accurate in his detection of a narrow palette based on earth pigments, although Rembrandt seems to have employed red lakes to glaze, rather than vermilion which he tended to use mixed into opaque layers. He used lead tin yellow which is very similar to Naples yellow, Bomford, D., et al., *Art in the Making: Rembrandt* (London: National Gallery/Yale University Press, 1989)
6 Ruskin, *Modern Painters*, 2, in *Works*, 4, pp 264–5
7 These comments probably reflect a rough grasp of Tintoretto's general technique and a desire to show off, rather than sharp observation; such information can only be accurately deduced from scientific analysis. Investigation of another large Tintoretto, *Christ Washing His Disciple's Feet* (*c.* 1566) at the National Gallery, reveals a thin gesso ground typical of the artist but only scant traces of any varnish medium, Plesters, J., 'Tintoretto's Paintings in the National Gallery', *National Gallery Technical Bulletin*, 4 (1980), pp 36–7
8 Greenberg, 'Modernist Painting', pp 755–6
9 'Materials', pp 493–4
10 A discussion of the various significances of *finis* and *facture* in painting between 1840 and 1880 appears in Rosen, C. and H. Zerner, 'The Ideology of the Licked Surface: Official Art', in *Romanticism and Realism, The Mythology of Nineteenth Century Art* (London: Faber and Faber, 1984), pp 183–232
11 'A Fight for Art', pp 475–7. Hunt also prefers Titian's smoother, earlier style
12 Kirby Tally Jr, M., '"All Good Pictures Crack": Sir Joshua Reynolds's Practice and Studio', in *Reynolds*, ed. N. Penny (London: Royal Academy/Weidenfeld and Nicolson, 1986), pp 62–4
13 Perry, R., 'Pablo Picasso "The Three Dancers"', in *Completing the Picture*, p 88
14 Greenberg, 'Modernist Painting', pp 755–6
15 Ibid., p 755
16 Ibid., p 757
17 Simon, J., *The Art of the Picture Frame: Artist, Patron, and the Framing of Portraits in Britain* (London: National Portrait Gallery, 1996), pp 104–5, 173–4

18 Bronkhurst, J., 'Holman Hunt's Picture Frames, Sculpture and Applied Art', in *Re-framing the Pre-Raphaelites: Historical and Theoretical Essays*, ed. E. Harding (Aldershot: Scolar Press, 1996), p 233
19 Greenberg, 'Modernist Painting', p 757
20 *Illustrated London News* (28 April 1860), p 411
21 Bennett, *Pre-Raphaelite Circle*, p 90
22 Bronkhurst, 'Holman Hunt's Picture Frames', p 238
23 The spears on the ground in *Rienzi* (plate 9) mimic the broken lances that draw out perspective lines in Uccello's *Battle of San Romano* (*c.* 1450, National Gallery, London)
24 Barlow, 'Pre-Raphaelitism', pp 74–5
25 In subject matter too, *Clarinet and Bottle of Rum on a Mantlepiece* is like *Master Hilary the Tracer* (and, I would contend, most of Hunt's work), art about art
26 Barlow, 'Pre-Raphaelitism', pp 74–5
27 Ibid.
28 Letter to Tupper, 20 June 1878, *Correspondence*, p 247
29 Barlow, 'Pre-Raphaelitism', p 73
30 Derrida, J., 'Structure, Sign and Play in the Discourse of Human Sciences', *Writing and Difference* (1978), quoted in *Modern Criticism and Theory: A Reader* (1988), ed. D. Lodge (Harlow: Longman, 1997), p 108. Derrida's term for this invading or enfolding of the core by the margins is 'invagination', Derrida, J., *Of Grammatology* (Baltimore: Johns Hopkins University Press, 1976), p 158
31 Wood, *Pre-Raphaelites*, p 41
32 Letter to Tupper, 23 September 1876, *Correspondence*, p 208; Hunt also advises Stephens, 'perspective is certainly one of the least things one requires', letter to Stephens, October 1852, BL, MS Don. e 66, 16
33 Letter to Tupper, 16 January 1877, *Correspondence*, p 217
34 Ibid., 12 January 1874, p 189
35 Smith, L., 'The Elusive Depth of Field: Stereoscopy and the Pre-Raphaelites', in *Pre-Raphaelites Re-viewed*, p 84
36 Smith, 'Elusive Depth of Field', p 92
37 Letter to Stephens, 31 October 1869, BL, MS Don. e 67, 47v
38 Smith, 'Elusive depth of field', p 86
39 Letter to Stephens, 7 January 1864, BL, MS Don. e 66, 81–2
40 Ruskin, J., *The Art of England, Lectures Given in Oxford* (Orpington: George Allen, 1884), p 11
41 Landow, *Typological Symbolism*, p 2
42 Journal, 2 March 1872, JRL, MS 1212, 12v
43 Ibid., 9 April 1872, 19v
44 Letter to Stephens, 16 August 1879, BL, MS Don. e 68, 52
45 Maas, *Hunt*, pp 101–3
46 Clarke, 'Gaze and the Glance', pp 81–2
47 Stella, F., 'Questions to Stella and Judd', *Minimal Art: A Critical Anthology* (1968), quoted, ibid., pp 82, 96, note 10
48 Ruskin, J., *Praeterita* (1885) (Oxford: Oxford University Press, 1990), p 13

49 Greenberg, 'Modernist Painting', p 756
50 Smith, 'Seed and the Flower', p 111
51 With particular reference to *The Light of the World*, Flint, K., *The Victorians and the Visual Imagination* (Cambridge: Cambridge University Press, 2000), pp 72–4
52 Landow, *Typological Symbolism*, p 1
53 Ibid.
54 Sussman, 'Artistic Manhood', p 116
55 Clarke, 'Gaze and the Glance', p 81
56 Greenberg, 'Modernist Painting', p 759

7 Design: icon and symbol

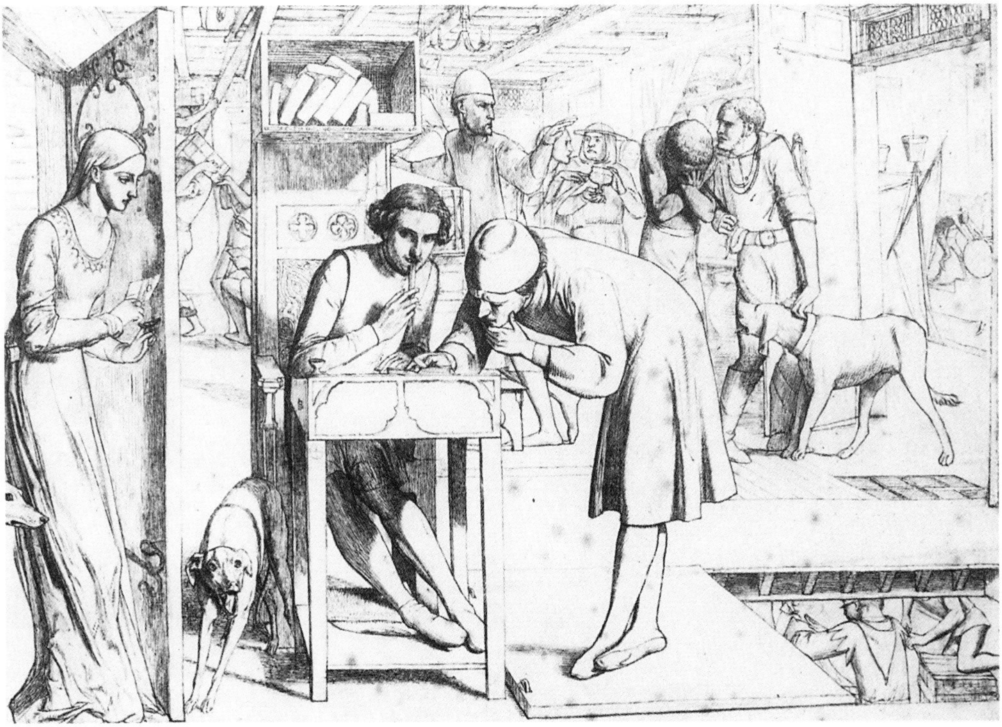

7.1
William Holman Hunt,
Lorenzo at his Desk in the Warehouse,
1848–50

Hunt's detailed style and elaborate accounts of the act of painting have resulted in an increasingly entrenched acceptance of his technique as an exercise in extreme mimesis of found appearances. His reputation as a painter tends to stand and, more frequently, fall by this myth, depending on the critical approach. The trend has been to perceive a dogmatic, even fanatical motive for his pursuit of 'Pre-Raphaelite practices of observation',[1] and to understate imaginative input. The description of his style, by himself as well as others, as 'Pre-Raphaelite', encourages a conflation of his approach with that of Millais and Rossetti and a false comparison between developments in their later careers and the apparent conservatism of his own. An interrogation of these assumptions is long overdue.

Imitation and imagination

Hunt presents painting as more than imitation; he tells Tupper:

> I can't tell how far my pictures convey an elevated idea of the object to the spectator I wish them to do so but I should not be so nearly content if I did not sometimes observe that from the same nature other artists often make what seems to me an offensive representation, as for instance in pictures done by painters who come out to the East with the idea that they have merely to copy the nature they find.[2]

He insists, in other words, on a simultaneously optical and spiritual act of looking that is only available to some artists. For example, Millais's 'worship of nature led him to love the intangible beauty she offers to them that can see' (2, 405), but Vernet lacks this 'poetic fire' (1, 149).

The conviction that his artistic vision might approach an augmented truth, a prophetic sight of 'God's order' in nature, complicates Hunt's claims to realism. The memoir maintains that empirical evidence, 'Nature's teachings', contribute to and validate perception of the spiritual (1, 134), but is not specific about the exact relationship between the two. It betrays an awareness of this difficulty when it refers to Rossetti's conviction that fact can undermine the poetry of art (1, 147). Hunt writes:

> It will be seen that we were never realists . . . art would have ceased to have the slightest interest for any of us had the object been only to make a representation, elaborate or unelaborate, of a fact in nature. Independently of the conviction that such a system would put out of operation the faculty making man 'like a God,' it was apparent that a mere imitator gradually comes to see nature claylike and finite, as it seems when illness brings a cloud before the eyes. Art dominated by this spirit makes us esteem the world as without design or finish, unbalanced, unfitting, and unlovely, not interpreted into beauty as true art makes it.

The argument is demonstrated by describing an unidentified landscape which 'made God's sky look hideous, although his handling and surface were careful; we once all agreed that a bright March sky was too crude, and too much like man's work to be painted' (1, 150).

The mortal and the meaningless are characteristically associated with the unaugmented materiality of natural appearance, the 'March sky', and of the art object itself, 'handling and surface'. Both are 'claylike and finite'. The antidote to this is astonishingly indistinct, especially considering that it is written at the end of Hunt's life and not during the early search for a philosophy of art which he is describing in these chapters. The extra element which might provide abstract meaning is expressed most specifically as *that which is lacking in the material*, but present in the poetic interpretations of the material by the successful artist. It can be only awkwardly demonstrated through an oblique reference to the faculty making man 'like a God' and through an example of a work of art which *fails* to manifest this. The 'handling and surface' and the 'March sky' fail to transcend their physical identities and signify 'God's sky'.

The focus of this passage is divided in three ways between the physical object, an image of the physical world and an image of the metaphysical. However, it is able to focus clearly only on the two sensual aspects of the work of art. Imaginative transcendence, through 'beauty' and 'design', is elusive, dependent on the familiar, but vague, construction of the divinely inspired 'true artist'. This text elides the exact method by which paint on a surface, or an objective imitation of nature, might include a spiritual element by constructing a notion of a privileged, artistic eye, alert to both the visible and the invisible. During the execution of the painting, however, the problem becomes a practical one, requiring an actual mechanism which relates the material and the imagined.

One practical solution is offered. *Pre-Raphaelitism* asserts that spiritual value is conferred upon a work of art by a recognition and choice of beautiful and moral subjects. As Landow notes, 'one means of preventing his art from presenting nature "claylike and finite" was to depict emotionally powerful scenes from literature and from sacred and secular history'.[3]

An example of this thinking can be found in the memoir's consistent denigration of gruesome topics, demonstrated by the retrospective survey of pictures viewed in Paris in 1849. Thomas Couture's tableau of revelry, drunkenness and delusion, *Romans of the Decadence* (1847, Musée d'Orsay) is condemned as the creation of 'a well trained workman without the breath of life in his nostrils' (1, 186). Similarly, Paul Delaroche is approved only when he is not 'indulging his taste for bloodshed and murder' (1, 187). The artist is described as admiring the draughtsmanship of Géricault's *The Raft*

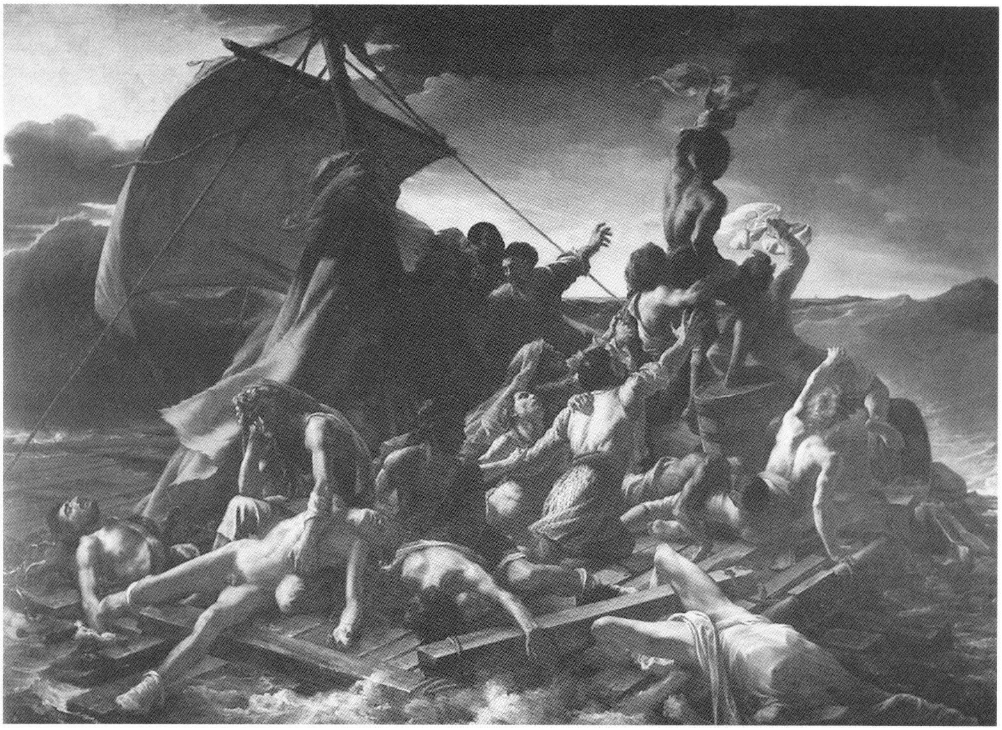

7.2
Théodore Géricault,
The Raft of the 'Medusa',
1819

of the 'Medusa' (1819, Musée du Louvre, figure 7.2), but searching in vain for 'further grace either of human love or artistic charm', in the spectacle of 'maddened men, famished and dying' (1, 186). If Hunt's unfinished *Christ the Pilot* (1894, private collection, figure 7.3) is a response to Géricault's image, as suggested by Landow,[4] it is one that conflates its violence with insanity, and corrects both of them (a practice noted in Chapter 4). The unusual inclusion of a mother and children in a scene traditionally associated only with Jesus and his disciples, furnishes associations of nurture which neutralise Géricault's focus on starvation. According to the memoir, poetry is as poetry shows, or rather as the poet shows. A work of art is spiritual because it depicts a scene which is beautiful and sacred, promising life or redemption.

Hunt's complex use of typology is basically a manifestation of the simple idea that a picture is as sacred as its subject. Spiritual worth is imported into the painting by representing aspects of the concrete world which convey an extra symbolic significance, such as the scapegoat. Each depicted object is augmented by an interpretation informed by scripture. Imaginative intervention occurs through the process of selecting such subjects, accessories and models: 'For ideas of a typical kind I feel a great value in every indication of the varying

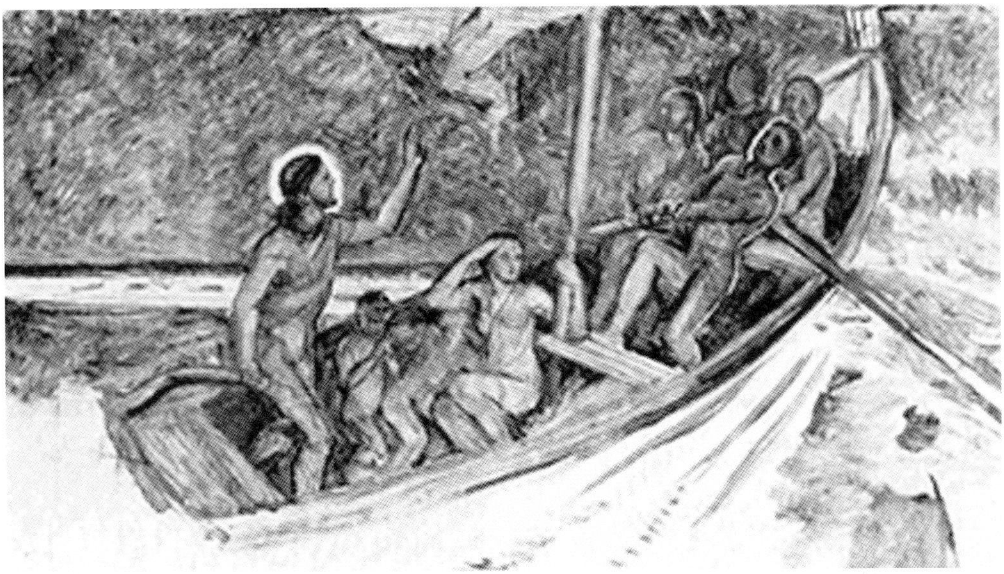

7.3
William Holman Hunt,
Christ the Pilot
(The Life Boat),
1894, sketch

natures of each object in the picture . . . but every distracting accident is an impertinence and should be avoided.'[5]

A construction of the prophetic sight of the artist is not only central to a consoling system of belief, the fantasy that the artist is part of, and privy to, a divine plan in nature, it is also central to the *practical* problem of representing it. Its function is expressed as an act of reading. 'A fact in nature' is read as poetic, selected and thus 'interpreted into beauty'. Hunt cannot discern 'God's sky' in the work of the unknown landscapist, or 'grace' in the work of Géricault. The failure of those artists to recognise and select is associated with a lack of moral and spiritual inspiration, decadent or maddened men, spectacle and mortality.

Hunt's own paintings present aspects of nature, often scenes of imminent death, elevated by a symbolic message of hope. They dictate and valorise the kind of selective/interpretive process which is being proposed as a means of combining the sensual and the imaginative gaze. As a contemporary said of *The Triumph*: 'The difficulty . . . is that the painter is trying to raise us to do what, as an artist and seer, he habitually does – to see with two eyes at once; with the bodily eye and the soul's; to gain one vision of two worlds; to read one system in two spheres.'[6]

As Sussman notes, Hunt's conceit is dependent on a philosophical characterisation of nature as a divine text, already arranged.[7] The Dead Sea landscape is a 'picture'; thus, the re-presentation of it can be rationalised as an act of selective reflection. I wish, however, to interrogate Sussman's explanation of Hunt's work in terms of a Ruskinian sacred naturalism. The philosophical construction of nature as already textual, 'God's message', is, as we have seen, possible only within textual descriptions of it. It is not always available at the point of direct experience where the gaze becomes contradictory and disordered, apprehending a 'beautifully arranged, horrible wilderness'. The mimetic/spiritual gaze is not unproblematic. It is necessary to investigate Hunt's actual practice in order to question his notion of synthetic perception and to clarify its role in the manufacture and appearance of the paintings.

Manufacturing the design

As I have noted in the previous chapter, the writings of Hunt and Ruskin stress the mimetic aspect of his technique and his dependence on visual research. *Pre-Raphaelitism* catalogues a methodical appropriation of visual and historical evidence, 'attention to chronological costume, to the types of different races of men, to climactic features and influences', for example (1, 149). It provides a narrative which takes the reader to each of the locations in which Hunt says he painted his major works, offering proof that they were executed in front of his subjects, like a photograph.

Scenes such as *The Shadow* were, of course, not available to be witnessed in their entirety, however. Hunt's subject matter is initially derived from biblical and literary texts rather than from life; models, accessories and landscapes were assembled into the desired tableau. Errington notes that the individual motifs themselves were also frequently derived from literary language and metaphor, Hunt finding ideas and symbols culled from Ruskin and other writers, as well as from the Bible.[8] Despite Hunt's emphasis on the historical veracity of his sources, it is significant that the choice of subject matter *and* detail, the act of 'selection' in other words, is initiated by textual rather than visual research.

At the Dead Sea, the fear of the journal is associated with direct physical contact with the danger of the environment, hope derives from a more considered and organised translation of the scene in symbolic, biblical terms in the memoir. Nature becomes a divine artefact, and it is its textual coherence which makes meaning. Hunt's painting practice also involves an initial arrangement of nature at a distance, without direct reference to real appearances, through a design process which has more in common with the mechanisms of literary language than with visual observation. The actual manufacture of the image involves elements of contrivance which challenge the myth of straightforward reflection. Painting from life is only begun after a precise choice of subject, iconography and composition. This can be demonstrated by examining Hunt's use of preliminary drawings.

Hunt writes to Stephens from Florence in 1869: 'I have some good subjects in my head and these I shall design most carefully before I begin them.'[9] No full design for *The Shadow* or *The Scapegoat* exists, however, and only studies are recorded for *The Triumph*. This might seem to suggest that they were painted more or less directly from nature. However, the complexity of the later works suggests that detailed compositional lines were placed directly on to the white ground of the small, experimental canvases, and then transferred on to the larger version, as described by Hunt in his letter to Bunney about *The Triumph*.[10] Recent scientific analysis has confirmed this.[11] Infra-red photography has revealed such outlines on the ground of *The Awakening Conscience*, all save one coinciding exactly with the painted image above.[12]

Surviving drawings for other works provide a useful insight into the conception and execution of these plans. Although Hunt's drawing style is fulsome and three-dimensional in self-sufficient landscapes, for small portraits executed from life and preparatory studies from nature for parts of paintings, his designs are almost exclusively linear. Colour tends to be associated with works intended for completion and sale, transcribed from life in oils or watercolour, such as *The Dead Sea from Siloam* (1854–55, Birmingham Museum and Art Gallery, plate 8) or *The Plain of Esdraelon* (1870, private collection). Colour is not included in preparatory work for subject paintings other than in the form of written notes.[13] Tone is also limited. Chiaroscuro is found only in studies from nature for details of a painting, such as *Study from a Mecca donkey* for *The Triumph* (1876, Northampton Museum and Art Gallery, figure 7.4), but in these cases, modelling is confined within the boundary of a strong outline. Even the shadow on the leg is a self-contained shape.

Most casual or preliminary sketches for narrative subjects are worked out only in line. Hunt also tends to ink over 'right' lines and erase 'wrong' lines; even chalk or pencil drawings have the precision of those finalised in pen. Particular examples are the sketch of the porter for *The Eve of St Agnes* (1848, private collection, figure 7.5) and figure studies for *Rienzi*. A study of Rienzi's leg is rubbed out in an effort to achieve a convincing sense of foreshortening,[14] as is the head of Sylvia in a drawing of *Valentine* (1850, British Museum, figure 7.12). A precise metal point study of Joseph for *The Triumph* (1876, British Museum, figure 7.6), made almost thirty years later, indicates the consistency of this linear method. A chalk study of the head of Christ in *The Shadow* (1872?, private collection, figure 7.7) and an ink study for the Christ child in *The Triumph* (1876, Walker Art Gallery) juxtaposes a strong contour and hatching, like the drawing of the donkey.

The dominance of line increases with narrative content. Hunt's more finished illustrations and complete subject drawings, such as the

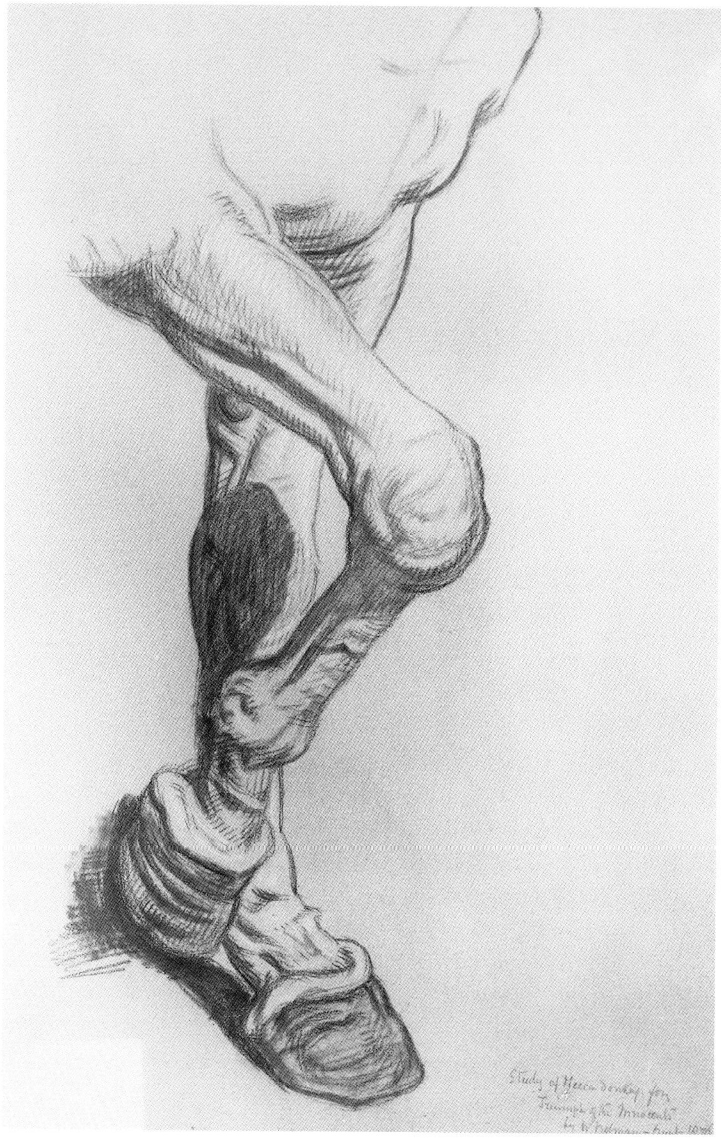

7.4
William Holman Hunt,
study from a
Mecca donkey,
1876

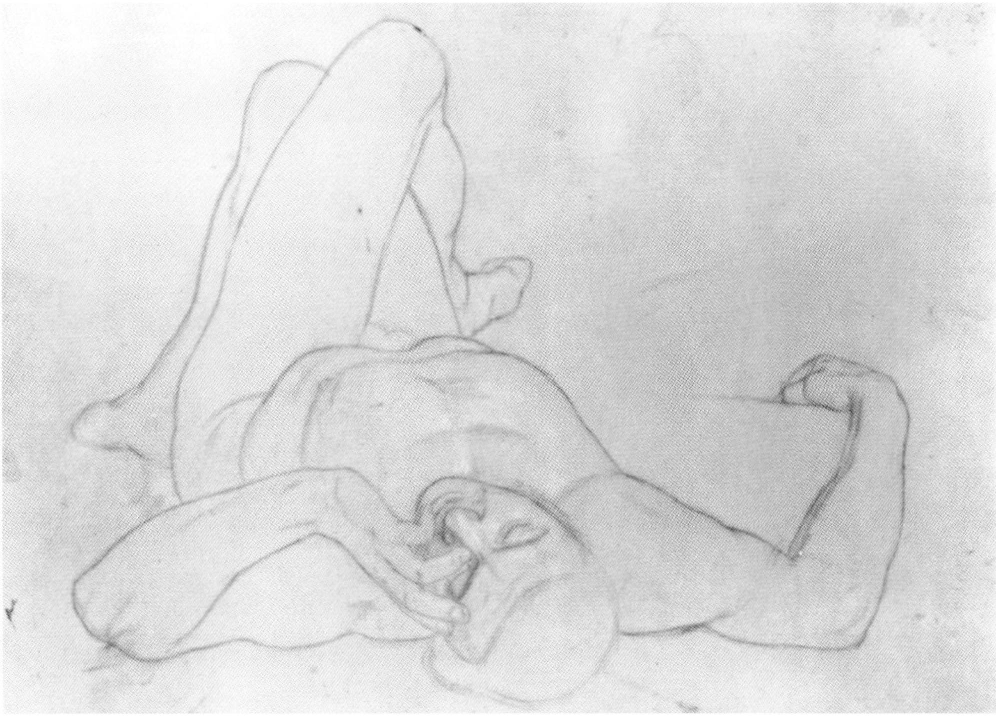

7.5
William Holman Hunt, life study of sleeping man sprawled on the floor, 1848

above design for *Valentine*, are particularly linear. The medium – pen or brush, ink and pencil – could easily lend itself to fluidity, texture or a blocking in of mass, but these are minimised. Hunt developed this 'hard edged outline'[15] during 1848, under the influence of Millais, particularly in his contributions to the Cyclographic Society, such as *In the Warehouse* (figure 7.1). Compositional sketches for designs are also linear. They vary from casual notes, such as those for *The Shadow* (undated, Manchester Art Gallery, figure 7.8) to detailed schemes. Studies for *The Eve of St Agnes* (1848, Guildhall Art Gallery, figure 7.9) are mere jottings of experimental poses for the two protagonists with abbreviated and generalised faces and limbs. More complete preliminary compositions for paintings, such as that for *Valentine*, also exhibit this stylised quality.

None of these linear designs refer directly to nature. The memoir describes the artist working out his compositions for *The Lady of Shalott* (National Gallery of Victoria, Melbourne, figure 7.16), *Claudio and Isabella* (Tate Britain) and *Ruth and Boaz* (Ashmolean Museum, Oxford, 1, 103 figure 7.10) in 1850 with no reference to models. In fact, it says that he conducted much of this work at night (1, 211).

Bronkhurst notes the 'medievalised' quality of Hunt's early drawings, 'in which the compositional coherence is emphasised by the

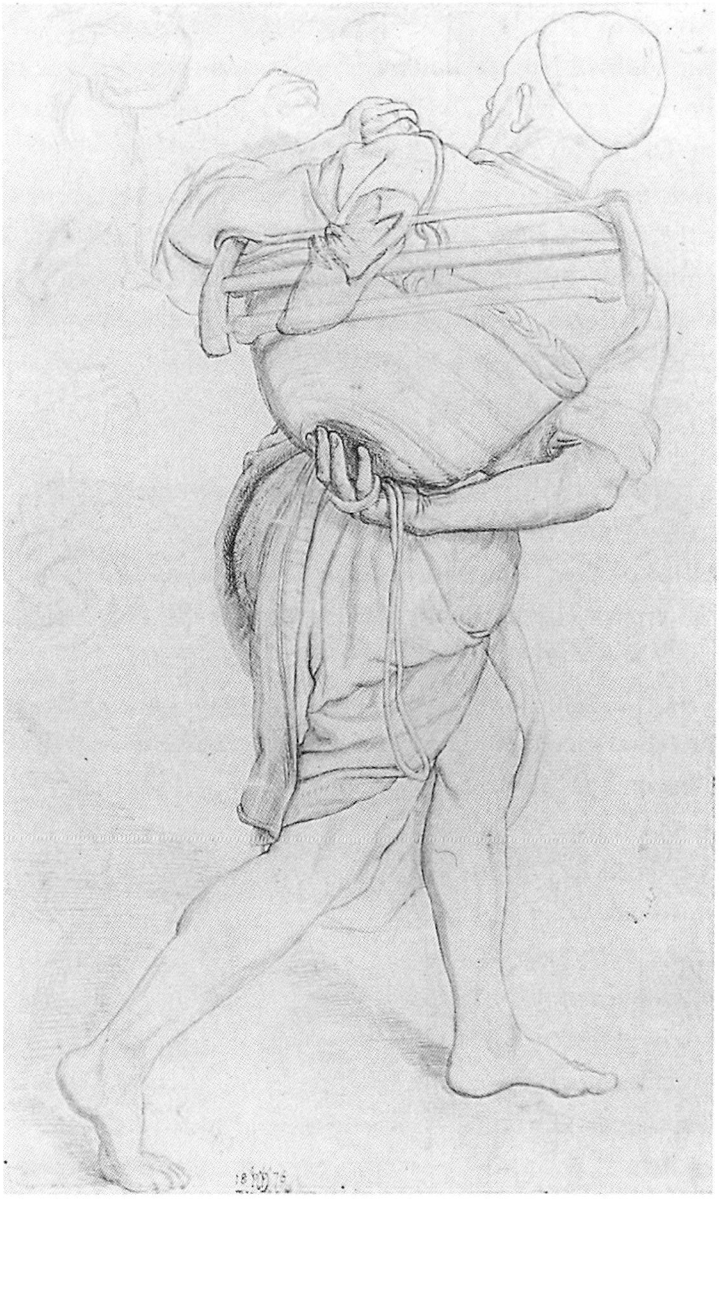

7.6
William Holman Hunt, study for Joseph for *The Triumph of the Innocents*, 1876

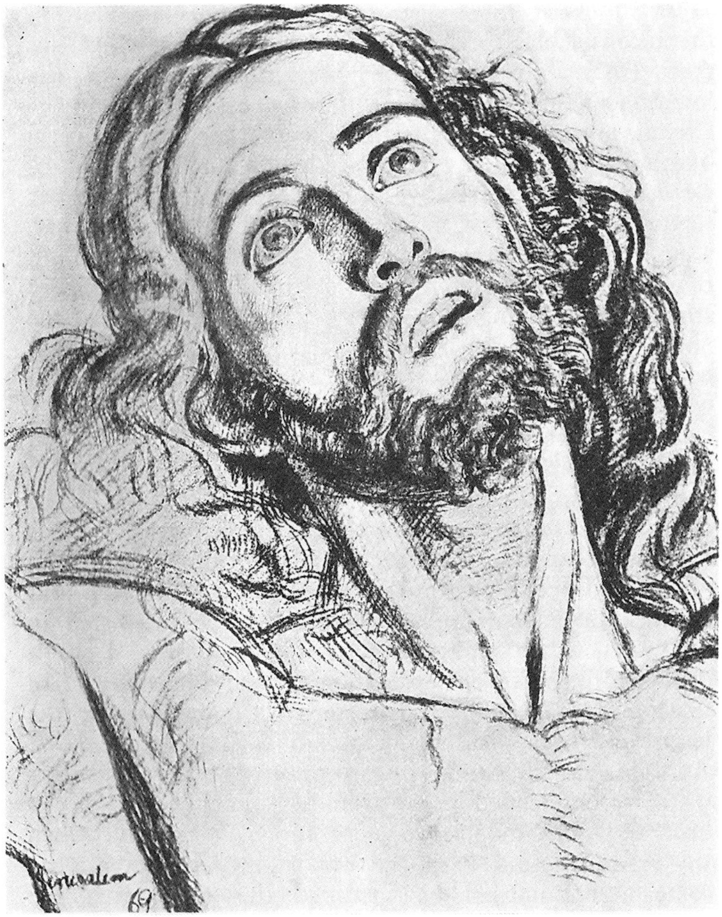

7.7
William Holman Hunt, study for the head of Christ in *The Shadow of Death*, 1872?

controlled use of diagonals played against strong verticals and horizontals'.[16] Hunt's rayed composition for *Ruth and Boaz* is a particularly geometrical example of this. He admired Flaxman's 'artistic devotion to decorative design' (1, 110) and these works display an interest in line as mere definition, as the edges of things, becoming an interest in it as a constructive tool, a means of relating objects to each other, and building the elaborate compositional layouts described in the previous chapter.

Rough figures are initially placed in the composition and posed like stick-people, as can be seen in a rough sketch for *Valentine* (1850, private collection, figure 7.11). The position of the trees in both the sketch and the design is governed by a diminishing arrangement, which signifies depth, and by their role as a framing device for the main figure. They perform the same function as the architectural features of the

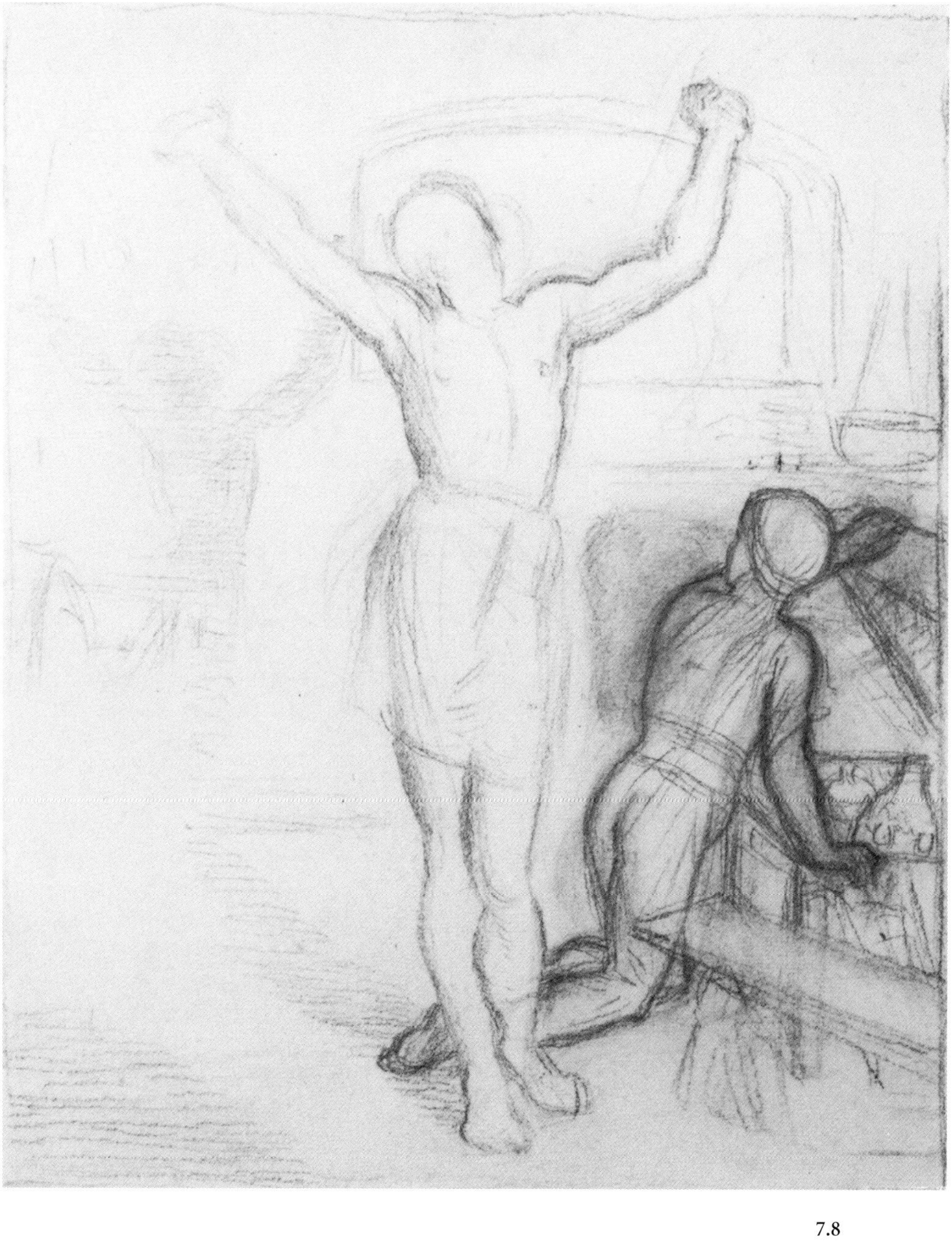

7.8
William Holman Hunt, sketch for the figure and composition of *The Shadow of Death*, undated

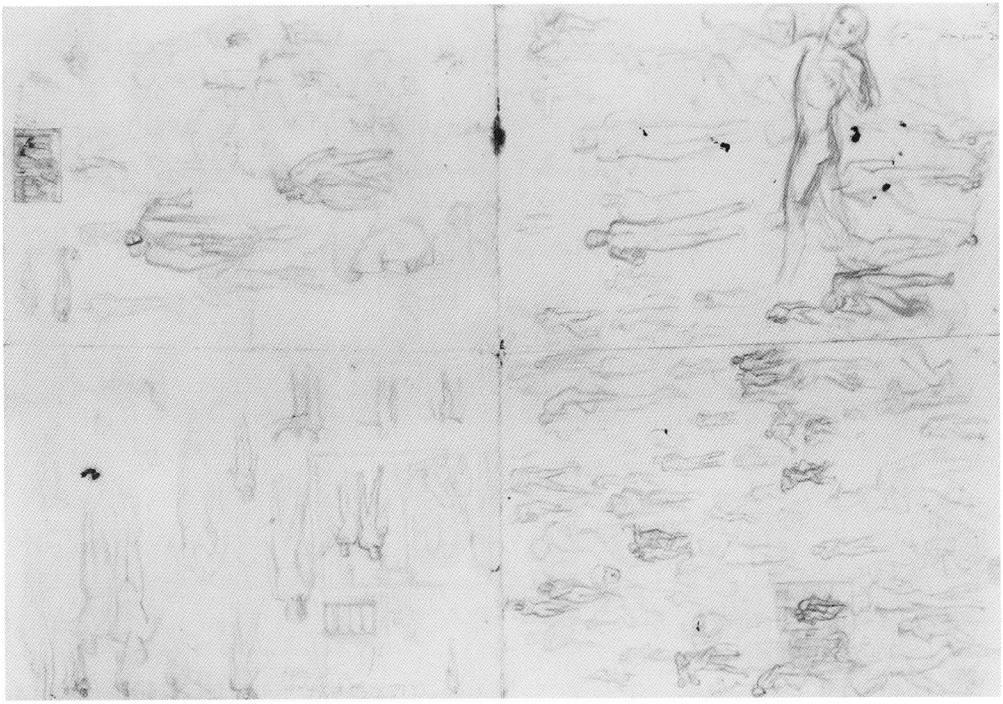

7.9
William Holman Hunt,
sketches for *The Eve of St Agnes*, 1848

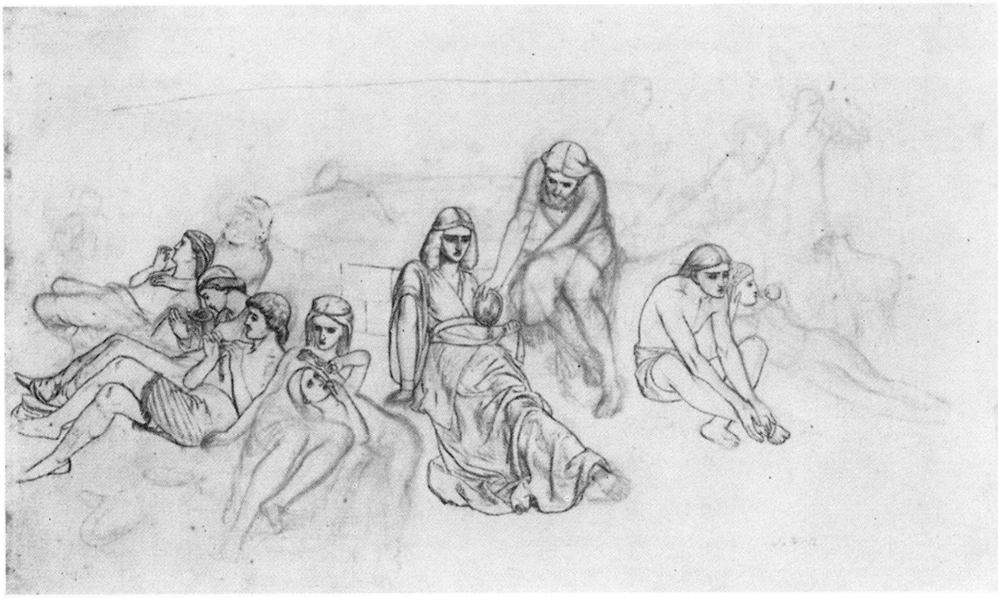

7.10
William Holman Hunt,
Ruth and Boaz, 1850

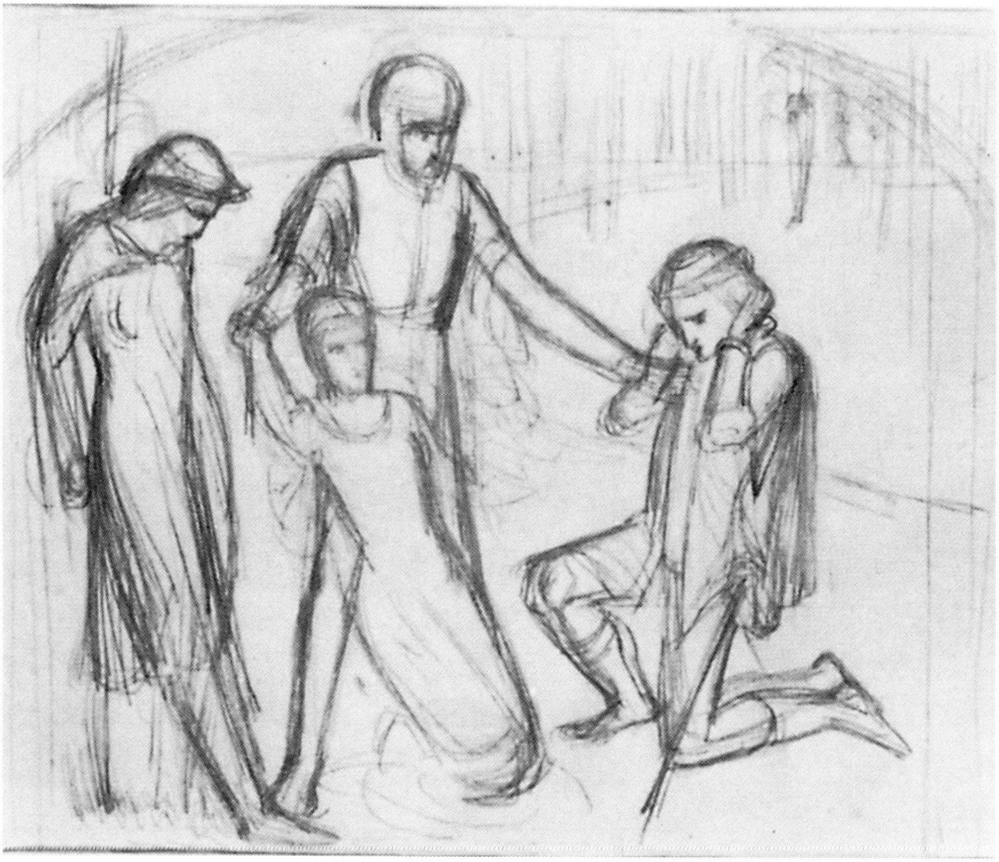

7.11
William Holman Hunt,
sketch for the composition
of *Valentine Rescuing Sylvia from Proteus*,
1850

frame, or within the image, in fourteenth- or fifteenth-century works, where a saint is separated from subsidiary characters, often kneeling, such as Hans Memlinc's *The Donne Triptych*, *c.* 1470, which Hunt would have seen in the National Gallery (figure 7.13). The trees and figures in the final painting (figure 7.14) conform to this format, despite Hunt's assertion that the background was painted from nature (1, 236). Similarly, the initial linear sketches for *The Scapegoat* (1854, Walker Art Gallery, figure 7.15) include brief references to an orthogonal crack in the salt which reappears in the final work. The right angle triangle created by the upright figure and the shadow along the ground and up the wall, in the sketch of *The Shadow*, is also exactly reproduced in the painting.

The characteristics of the designs dominate the organisation and the detail of finished oil paintings, therefore. Compare *The Lady of Shalott* (1886–1905, Wadsworth Athenaeum, Hartford, Connecticut,

7.13
[*Right*]
Hans Memlinc,
The Donne Triptych,
c. 1470

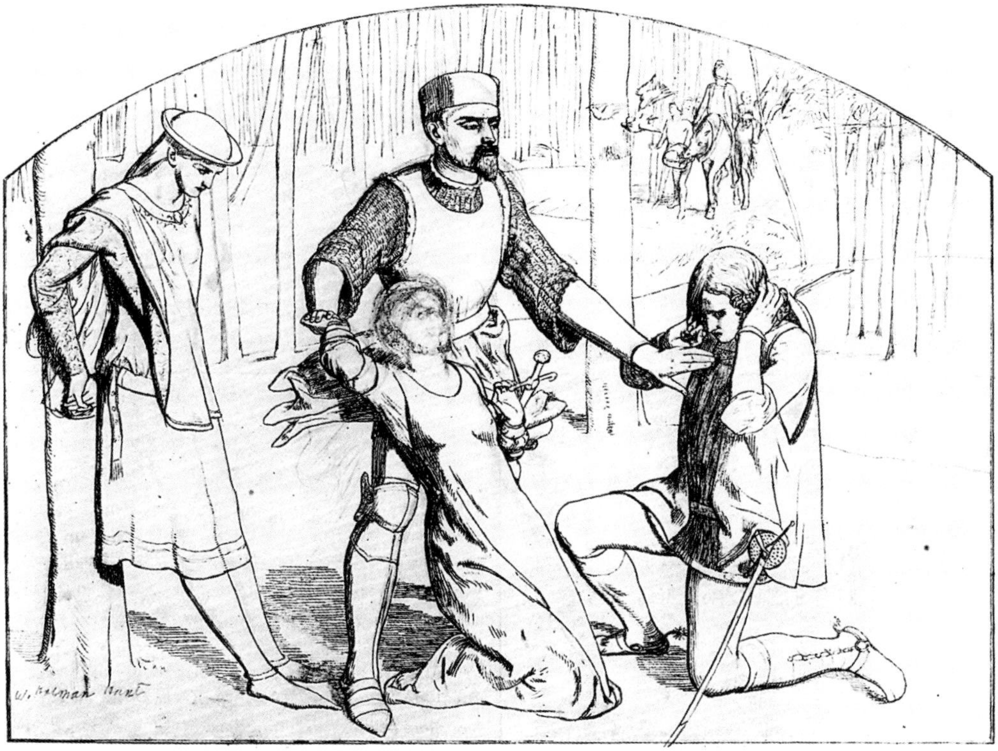

7.12
William Holman Hunt,
Valentine Rescuing Sylvia from Proteus, 1850

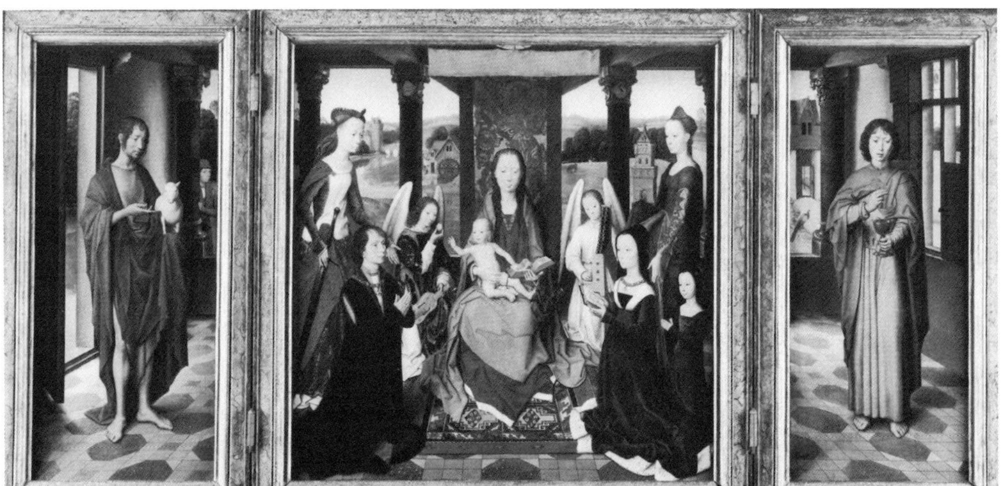

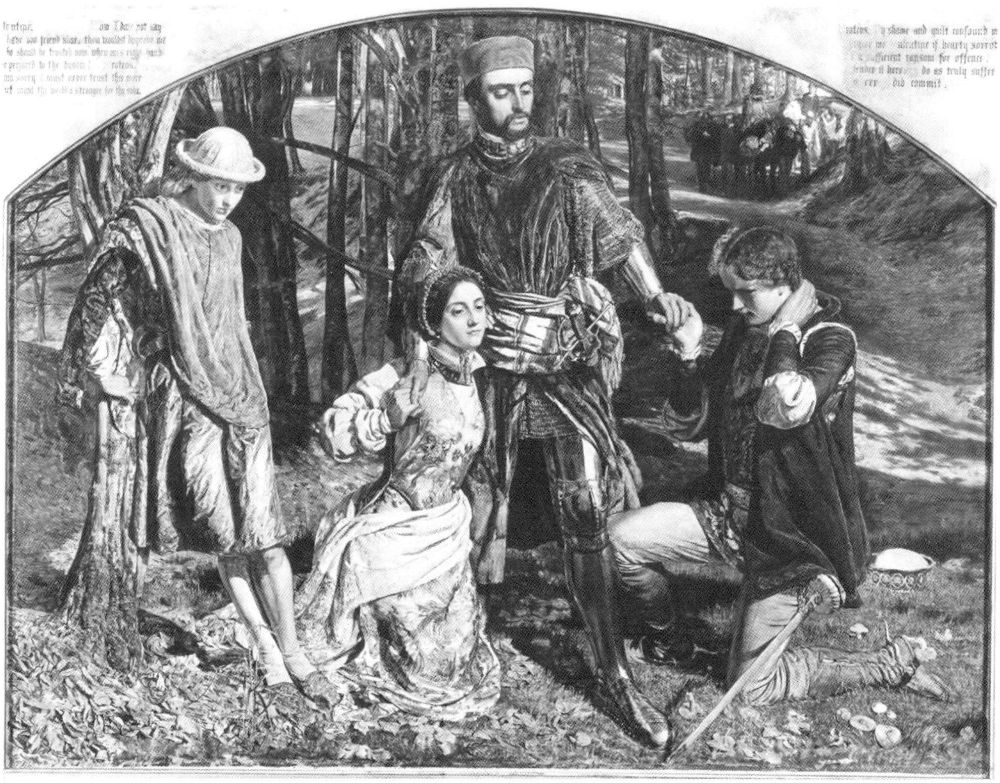

plate 18) with the version made for Moxon thirty years before (1857, figure 7.17). The earlier work possesses the linear qualities that would be expected in an engraved illustration. Pattern is emphasised, as in the twisted columns of the tapestry frame. A repetition of circles and crescents dominates the composition in the three round frames, the colonnade above Lancelot, Christ's halo, the crescent moon, the Lady's cranium and the balls of thread. Modelling in light and shade is minimised, flesh is left entirely white. The background, darkened in order to contrast with the vision in the central mirror, is only single-hatched rather than shaded. Mass is also minimised and volume is, instead, characteristically created geometrically, through outline. Foreshortened circular shapes, the tapestry frame and the Lady's waistband, are emphasised as perspectival clues to depth by their contrast with unforeshortened circles. Line is, finally, given a spectacular and expansive life of its own in the form of the hair and the skein of thread snaking about the room. In the oil version of this subject, each form is modelled and coloured-in, but the geometric arrangements are preserved in the sharp contours that still dictate the composition.

7.14
William Holman Hunt,
Valentine Rescuing Sylvia from Proteus,
1850–51

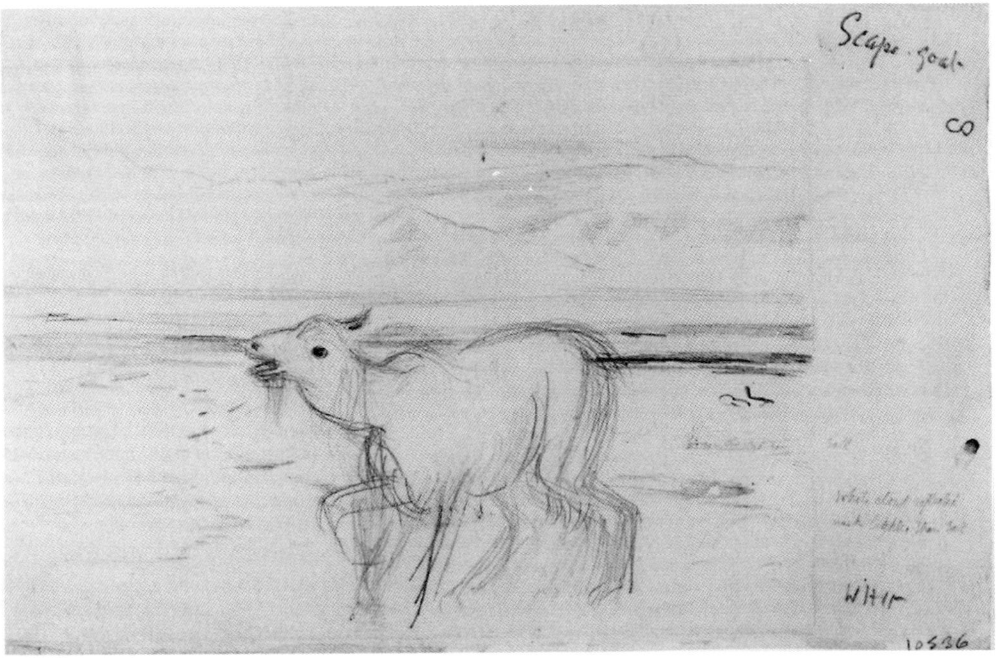

7.15
William Holman Hunt,
Study for the goat in 'The Scapegoat',
1854

Pattern can be even more elaborate in the oil paintings, recalling quattrocento painting. *The Lady of Shalott* exhibits an inlaid marble floor, decorated with relief, and intricate decoration on the wall, tapestry frame and lamp. *The Shadow* contains pattern in the belt of Christ, Mary's dress and the decorated box and shawl, and *Isabella* features marquetry, tapestry, patterned tiles and fabrics. *The Triumph* presents a string of circular shapes – halos, bubbles and pots – similar to those in *The Lady of Shallot*. The threads and threadlike hair of *The Lady of Shallot* also reappears in the *The Shadow* in the fringes of the Virgin's draperies and the convolutions of the shavings.[17] Hunt's frames exhibit further evidence of his interest in linear, two-dimensional design.

It can be concluded that the conception, composition, accessories and decoration, as well as the pose, gesture and grouping of the figures in Hunt's pictures are worked out before painting from nature and in linear terms. This supports the argument, proposed in the previous chapter, that Hunt contrives conventions of depth and employs the lines and arrangement of the composition to suggest an elaborate *reading* of space which precedes and underpins mimetic effects. For example, in the landscape settings of *Valentine*, *The Hireling Shepherd*, *The Scapegoat*, and *The Triumph*, rows of trees, cracks in the salt and a stream act as artificial substitutes for real orthogonals. A landscape that is not inherently box-shaped is nonetheless constructed

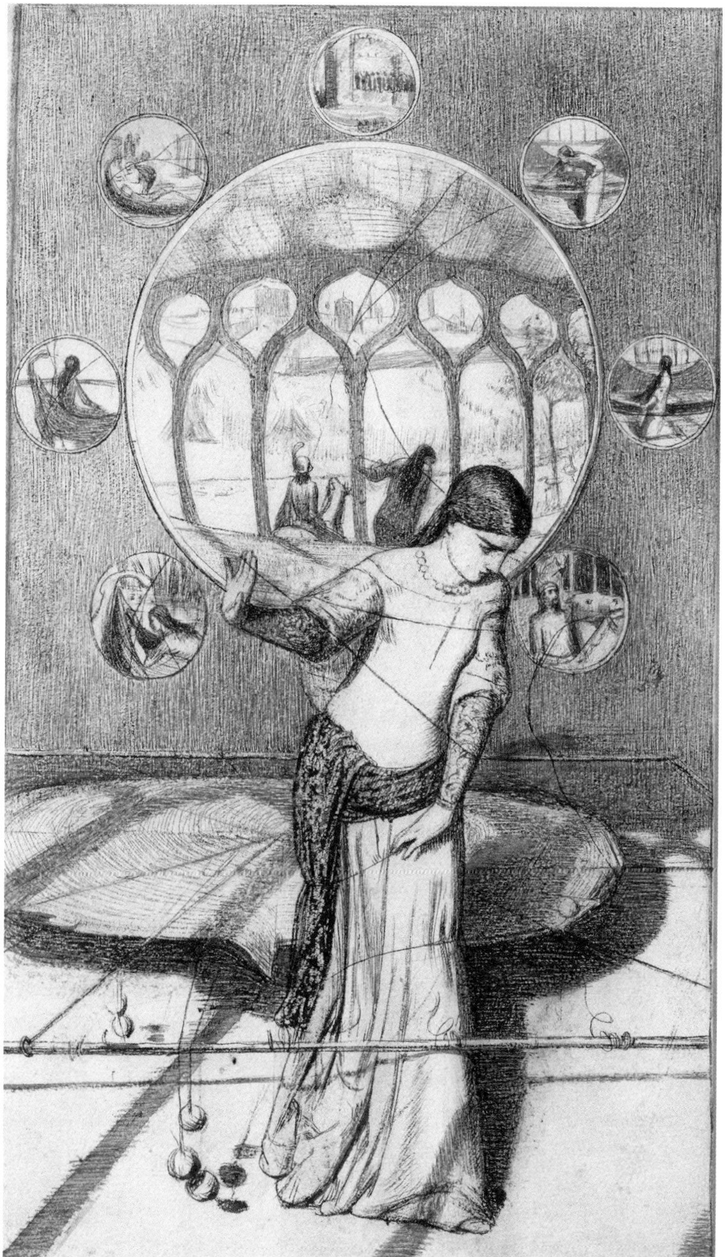

7.16
William Holman Hunt,
The Lady of Shalott,
1850

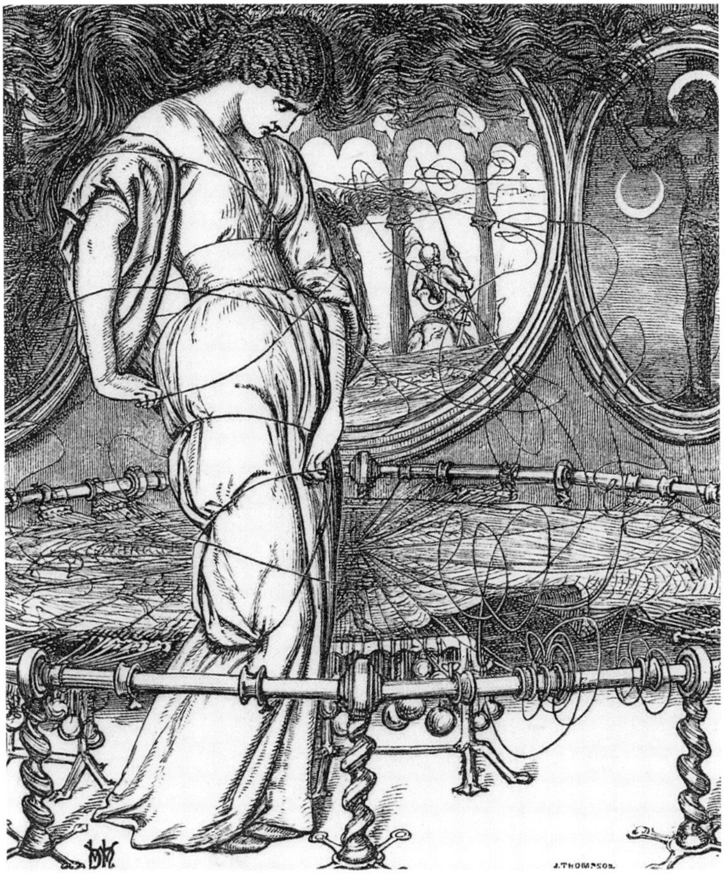

7.17
William Holman Hunt,
The Lady of Shalott,
headpiece,
engraved
J. Thompson

as a stage to contain the figures through the arrangement of its parts as geometrical signifiers.

The use of linear perspective also reinforces compositional hierarchy. In *The Shadow*, the artificial vanishing point, created by the edge of the chest, chair and saw, follows the convention of falling within the figure of Christ. This is also the case in *The Light of the World* and *The Finding*. The crack in *The Scapegoat* and the stream in *The Triumph* also intersect with the main figure. As Norman Bryson says, in *Word and Image*: 'Perspective, besides being a technique for recording a certain optical phenomenon, is also a technique for distributing information in a pattern.'[18]

Iconographical structure, the choice of subjects, types *and* their relations to each other are a product of intellectual decisions. Pictorial order and meaning are conceived through reference to the artist's imagination and to cultural, rather than natural, sources: other visual and literary texts that are themselves conventional and pre-arranged. The literary and pictorial references identified in *The Shadow* and *The Triumph* in Chapters 3 and 4 are examples of this. The fantasy of a divine pattern in nature is imposed before painting from it, through imaginative selection and a conceptual, patterned, linear construction.

The subsidiary role of direct observation is further demonstrated by the fact that, unlike many artists, Hunt has not left a large body of incidental notes from life.[19] In an early letter to Stephens, he states his opinion that 'all study, apart from that of the figure, unless required for a picture is thrown away', and chides him for sketching in Westminster Abbey unless it is for the background of a planned composition: 'drawing designing and painting . . . should not be practised unless for a purpose. No great painter, good or bad, ever wasted his time and energies upon preparatory work longer than was necessary to give him a rude power of expressing his thoughts.'[20] Copying is clearly harnessed to the usefulness of the view or object to 'thoughts', the intellectually conceived design, and a pronounced economy is evident in Hunt's surviving preparatory work.

Although *Pre-Raphaelitism* reprises Ruskin's argument for a selective, moral way of looking at nature[21] (specifically employing the critic's description of 'God's sky' as the first 'type' of divinity, 1, 150),[22] Hunt's advice to Stephens signals a departure from the model proposed in *Modern Painters*. Ruskin stresses that a long and painstaking observation of nature is first necessary to learn to distinguish that which is beautiful and divine,[23] and exemplifies this process by executing a profusion of careful drawings from landscape. Hunt's output does not exhibit this humility, it enacts a more didactic, prophetic role. Scrutiny is restricted to parts of nature that have already been selected to fit iconographical schemes which, as has been demonstrated in Chapters 3 and 4, are the product of highly subjective fantasies.

Elements of reality are quite consciously chosen to fit a design. *Pre-Raphaelitism* recounts many searches for suitable models and backgrounds. It describes arrival in Damascus: 'As an artist, I was disappointed. No mass of buildings showed above the line of the city wall, having the designs for Tennyson's poems already in consideration, I had counted upon finding some delightful external views of the city appropriate' (2, 62–3). This approach sits oddly with Ruskin's plea to 'go to nature in all singleness of heart, . . . selecting nothing, rejecting nothing'.[24]

Tupper puts it differently in his inaugural article for *The Germ*, 'The Subject in Art': 'Objects they [artists] depict excite the beholder, just as those objects in nature would excite his [the artist's] interest, if by any associations of idea in the one case, by the same in the other.'[25] Nature is portrayed as an assemblage of individual 'objects', each causing a particular effect and suggesting an idea.[26] Hunt appears to have gone to nature with a preconceived notion of what part, what 'object', he wanted.

The memoir echoes Ruskin's exhortation in its description of *Rienzi*: 'painting the whole out of doors, direct on the canvas itself, with every detail I can see' (1, 91). However, by 'the whole' it means that every part of the picture is painted out of doors, not the entire scene. The fig tree and a section of foreground were done in the garden of Stephens's father, and later:

> I . . . gained the opportunity to paint a row of young saplings on a sloping hillside of grass . . . Beyond the line of the slanting field I introduced the top of a foliated tree; these latter features were painted at Hampstead . . .
>
> For the sake of getting the foreground and hillside completed while the summer lasted, I had deferred drawing some of the figures from the nude, and these I now set myself to do. The costumes, armour and distant architecture needed research . . . My good friend . . . supplied me with models for the horses. For the shields and spears I went with my canvas to the tower. (1, 111–12, 114–15)

The drawings for *Rienzi* are, correspondingly, specific to the subject. These focus on the figures and parts of figures: two of the dead boy, the consoling Adrian, Adrian's hand, Adrian's head, Rienzi's leg, Rienzi's head, horses, the kneeling soldier and a study for his head, the soldiers on horseback, and a standing figure whose feet are even left out as they will be obscured by the dead boy's body.[27]

Although this is an early work, the habit of making very particular drawings of disparate items which were then transposed into paintings, continued throughout Hunt's career. Very few sketches fall outside this category. Surviving studies for *The Shadow* depict the interior of a carpenter's shop, carpenter's tools, a fig tree, windows and the head of Christ.[28] Studies for *The Triumph* are confined to sketches of the Innocents, Mary and Jesus, Joseph, a dog, the donkey and foal, a waterwheel and the globes.[29] Hunt writes to Stephens from Florence in 1869 about collecting objects to put in his pictures, citing 'a quattrocento chess board – very dilapidated – but with a useful inlaid pattern'; he calls these 'properties'.[30] Nature too constitutes an array of properties to be chosen as appropriate to the artist's 'thoughts'. They fulfil the same authenticating role as the 'data' or 'evidence' presented in the memoir, but their choice and arrangement is, once more, highly artificial.

Hunt's final painting technique is based on filling in outlines in the way Hamerton attributes to quattrocento painters. *The Graphic Arts* draws a distinction between the 'Van Eyck system of painting' and 'the maturer principles of Rubens', and stresses that the former situates expression in the design rather than in the application of paint:

'Early varnish painting expressed nothing by handling; faces might be made expressive, though they were generally too placid for that, but the painting itself, the method of laying on the pigments, was absolutely neutral.'[31] Hunt describes using this method for *The Shadow*, *The Triumph*[32] and for *Bianca*: 'I commenced this picture in tempera, tracing out the design in light and shade, as many of the old masters did, in the end adding the finishing painting in oil varnish' (2, 256).

This containing of colour within a network of outline recalls stained-glass technique and complements Hunt's use of smooth, brilliant, semi-transparent paint. In *Word and Image*, Norman Bryson links the linear format of stained glass and a suppression of natural detail, such as modelling, to the pictorial communication of literary, particularly religious, messages, and a demand to be read. He sees this as a stress on 'the Word', or the 'discursive' rather than the 'figural'.[33] This parallel underlines the importance of the design as a vehicle for the spiritual content of Hunt's images, and the dependence of these ideas on textual models.

Textuality of the design

The subjective input of the artist goes beyond the obvious process of conceiving the subject matter. It is present within a complex system of linear orderings throughout the painting. The linear element represents the imaginative authority and control discussed in Chapter 6. This production of iconography and pictorial order is a graphic, language-like process. It is, in semiotic terms, a structuring of signifiers (self-sufficient icons) into a pattern (geometrical and narrative) of meanings. Hunt excludes 'every distracting accident',[34] or, as Bryson says, all that is not 'semantically useful'.[35]

Despite Hunt's reputation for 'copying' nature, therefore, his pictures are composites of parts of nature. The insistent use of discrete outlines or 'sharp' contours,[36] preserves the integrity of each selected element as a sign within a structure or system; a fixing of its signifying role within the syntax of the painting. *Pre-Raphaelitism* emphasises the mimetic appropriation of these parts, expressed as 'truth to nature', to authenticate the subject as a whole. Its veiling of the importance of the mechanism of selection and arrangement of these units of visual evidence echoes its denial of authorial subjectivity and rhetorical intervention.

Hunt's 1855 journal records moving a cloud from the side of *The Scapegoat* to the centre.[37] A letter to Tupper mentions a plan for 'The Visit of Nicodemus', which 'I keep in my mind as a picture to be painted . . . after I have knocked to pieces the old design and put it together again in a promising way'.[38] Do these 'pieces' of visual evidence, at least, constitute an element of naturalism, islands of the real within the design?

Charles Peirce's notion of the icon would seem to be a useful starting point to explore Hunt's mimetic depiction of isolated objects. In her essay, 'Saussure versus Peirce: Models for a Semiotics of Visual Art', Margaret Iverson usefully summarises his concept of three kinds of visual sign: icon, index and symbol:

> The icon signifies by virtue of a similarity of qualities or resemblance to its object . . . The index signifies by virtue of an existential bond, in many cases a causal connection, between itself and the object . . . for example a footprint indicating that someone has been on the beach . . . The symbol signifies by virtue of a contract or rule.[39]

The visual symbol is considered to be the closest to the written word because it requires the observer to acknowledge a 'contract' that connects it with what is being signified. The apple between the lamb's feet in *The Hireling Shepherd* (plate 5) is a convenient example; it can signify 'the fall'. In this respect its role is not visual, but intellectual, dependent on a cultural convention.

The index has the potential to introduce action, or narrative. The proximity of the lamb's mouth to the apple and the parallel furrows on its surface, imply that the lamb has bitten the apple. Iverson remarks that the index, unlike the symbol, does not require interpretation. However, some degree of intellectual contribution would seem to be demanded to construct an event from the mere positioning of the two elements within the design. A contract, or prior understanding, is certainly necessary to perceive the full indexical function of this configuration, that the green apple will make the lamb sicken and die. This augmented indexical meaning slides into the purely conventional, symbolic idea of the fall. The symbol, index and icon are, in practice, blurred categories requiring degrees of conventional input to signify.

An interrogation of the so-called 'independence', or natural status, of the icon can clarify Hunt's so called 'sacred naturalism'. Peirce suggests that the icon signifies in a direct visual sense: 'The icon is a representamen of what it represents and for the mind that interprets it as such, by virtue of characters which belong to it in itself as a sensible object, and which it would possess just the same were there no object in nature that it resembled, and though it were never interpreted as a sign.'[40] The first part of Peirce's statement: 'The icon is a representamen of what it represents . . . by virtue of characters which belong to it in itself as a sensible object' echoes Tupper's words in *The Germ*: 'the subject in a work of art affects the beholder in the same sort of way as the same subject, occurring as a fact or aspect of Nature, affects him'.[41] It would seem to imply a kind of 'realism' which is independent of reading, particularly applicable to the mimetic style of a painter like Hunt. It is therefore useful to interrogate it in this context. Peirce and Tupper's statements share an emphasis on sensual effects common to the object and its representation, recalling Ruskin's description of Hunt's work as creating the 'same impressions on the mind which were caused by the light itself'.[42] Ruskin and Tupper are expressing an idea of 'innocent' vision which was emerging in the nineteenth century. In *Techniques of the Observer: On Vision and Modernity in the Nineteenth Century*, Jonathan Crary defines this as 'primal opticality', a way of seeing nature which is independent of interpretation, 'uncluttered by the weight of historical codes and conventions of seeing'.[43]

Ruskin's idea of the innocent eye applies to looking at nature itself, but his description of the reproduction of this kind of optical experience in paint admits only a partial loss of certain sensual qualities, such as luminosity.[44] Peirce also suggests that a representation of an apple shares optical characteristics with an apple in nature. How true is this? What 'characters' does the apple in *The Hireling Shepherd*, for example, actually share with the 'sensible object' that it represents? It shares no non-visual characteristics except perhaps a smooth, shiny texture. It does not smell, or taste, like an apple. The sounds that might accompany the Royal Academy visitor are not consistent with those of the rural scene. Does it even share visual characteristics? It is flat, rather than rounded. It is one inch high, about a third less than one would expect. It is certainly not even vaguely circular, but cut off by the lamb's foot and chest. At a certain distance and from a single viewpoint it may look three-dimensional, but once the observer moves the illusion is lost. This may seem pedantic, but it does establish that Peirce's 'shared characteristics' are limited, and often exceeded by contradictory characteristics.

There is a more important point: in order to apply Peirce's definition, we must construct a notion of some original, real apple. In doing this, we are in danger of falling prey to the propaganda of 'truth to nature' that is promoted in Hunt's writings. They imply that his paintings are a transcription of something that has actually existed. In a general sense this conceit is clearly absurd, especially in the case of fictional subjects, but what of individual icons? The actual green apple that Hunt might have looked at when he needed visual information about 'characters which belong to it in itself as a sensible object', cannot be identified as any actual object. *The Hireling Shepherd* is no more proof of the nature or existence of this apple than *The Finding* is proof that Christ was a redhead.

Circumstantial knowledge about Hunt's painting technique leads us to imagine him looking intently at a model apple and transcribing what he could of its appearance. However, as I shall show in Chapter 8, there were probably several apples. Differences between them would have been suppressed and imperfections eliminated. Peirce alludes to this when he notes that the visual 'characters' of an icon 'belong to it in itself as a sensible object', and that it would possess them 'just the same were there no object in nature that it resembled'. His definition is ambiguous, but it implies a modification of the myth that mimetic art involves the reproduction of an actual prior object, suggested by Ruskin and Tupper; 'what it represents . . . by virtue of characters which belong to it in itself as a sensible object' exists only in 'the mind that interprets it as such'.[45]

Hunt's writings promote the myth that his images have a prior existence in nature as a means of constructing them as true: 'my first object as an artist was to paint, not Dresden china Bergers, but a real shepherd, and a real shepherdess, and a landscape in full sunlight, with all the colour of luscious summer, without the faintest fear of the precedent of any landscape painters who had rendered Nature before'.[46] The mention of Dresden china echoes the dispute with Gladstone about spatial illusion set out in Chapter 6. The conventions of artistic language are constructed as other to the transcribing of 'real' figures and sensual effects of sunlight and colour. *Pre-Raphaelitism* promotes the 'found' nature of the landscape background with a description of a journey through the countryside around Ewell (1, 263–4): 'I soon found all the *material* I wanted for my landscape' (emphasis added). It even provides a witness, mentioning Millais, painting nearby, 'eager to see how I had placed upon the canvas the features of the landscape I had chosen'. The importing of the real, noted in Hunt's public writing style itself, is here constructed as an unproblematic process of painting as well: 'features' are simply 'placed upon the canvas'. The accurate transcription of the colours of nature, the 'fastidious hue', is also promoted by an account of the use of white palettes which facilitate accuracy. However, this 'record' of painting is no less a construction than the image itself.

It is important not to interpret Peirce's model of the icon as implying the notion that a prior, 'found', reality has necessarily existed because we now see it represented in a painting through a few of its 'shared characteristics'. Peirce's relationship of 'shared characteristics' exists not between a specific apple and the apple icon, but between the artist's or the viewer's consensual, or shared, conception of an apple and the apple icon. This constitutes a convention, although it may be a different kind of convention from that which pertains to the pictorial symbol.

There are various other explorations of this question. Both Ernst Gombrich[47] and Meyer Schapiro[48] survey the way that pictorial signs frequently signify through a conventional rather than a representational link. In particular, Wittgenstein identifies the difference between 'seeing' and 'seeing as';[49] the difference between seeing a thing and seeing similarities between two things. He discriminates between the 'object' of these two kinds of seeing, stressing the subjective nature of the object of 'seeing as'. Wittgenstein's description of 'noticing an aspect' of similarity relates to Peirce's 'shared characteristics', but he clarifies the intellectual rather than the sensual nature of the process. N.R. Hanson adds the concept of 'seeing that', which extends the idea to its indexical functions.[50]

The recognition of a sign is also dependent on its place within a signifying system. In 'Some Aspects of the Pictorial Sign', Jîrí Veltrusky reviews the work of Schapiro, Gombrich and Peirce and asserts the considerable role of convention in the way that a pictorial sign creates meaning.[51] In particular, he draws attention to the importance of the position of an icon within a scheme of other icons, noting Panofsky's analysis of the way a charger held by a woman came to connote the beheading of a man, but that if the female figure had a sword, then Judith, rather than Salome, was signified.[52] He concludes that icons function as part of a system and that the way pictures signify is generally language-like: 'The question arises whether to connect significant and signifie [*sic*] some sort of contiguity is not necessary to connect any kind of sign.'[53] The role of pictorial signs within the painting is at least partly a language-type structuring. The signs themselves, even Pierce's index and icon, derive signification from a range of conventions, and their overall *arrangement*, the design, is, itself, a process of definition.

The intellectual nature of the design, and Hunt's close adherence to it in the form of the guiding outlines he uses while he paints, demonstrate the mechanism of imaginative control and inscription of Christian fantasy within the image. Hunt's method can be thought of as a fragmenting of nature into signs to facilitate and strengthen their role within a language-like pattern.

The highly contrived character of this procedure perhaps clarifies the emphasis on reading noted in criticism on Hunt. Most critical texts reproduce his work in black and white (or not at all) and, thus, present the image in a form which is closer to its preliminary state before colour is added, emphasising design and iconography. Commentators tend to approach Hunt's work in a fragmented way, listing objects and their symbolic significance one by one.[54] Landow's *Typological Symbolism* painstakingly unpacks and interprets each type, as does Errington's study. She notes that, in turn, *Rienzi* 'was taken, in a careful, item by item, manner, from Bulwer Lytton's novel'.[55] As Robert Hughes puts it: 'nature presents itself as a web of moral symbols . . . Every detail tells a story and wants to be decoded. It can be quite tiring "reading" . . . [paintings] such as The Hireling Shepherd'.[56]

Hughes's sense of laboriousness is echoed in the painstaking quantity of attention that has been apportioned to just this process by Ruskin, Farrar, Sussman, Landow, Errington and others. This critical phenomenon is a measure of both the elaboration and the idiosyncratic quality of Hunt's iconographical schemes. It supports the argument in Chapters 3 and 4, that his iconography represents a modification of nineteenth-century Christian ideologies which express personal, complex and ambiguous ideas about evidence, authority and identity. The *Illustrated London News* reviewer remarks on the singular and eccentric design of *The Shadow* and comments: 'it is something like erasing from his memory his mother tongue and inventing for himself a new language'.[57]

Landow suggests that typological symbolism might strike 'the informed spectator as a natural language inherent in the visual details themselves – and not as something laid upon the objects in some artificial manner';[58] *Pre-Raphaelitism* says, 'There is no more reason why the features belonging to a picture should be distorted for the purpose of such imaginative suggestion than that the poet's metaphors should spoil his words for the ordinary uses of man' (2, 260–1). However, Hunt's pictorial language is no more natural than any language. It depends on a discursive composition, or structure, parallel texts, a variety of conventions and an 'informed observer'.

The restless sign

The writings of critics such as Landow continue the explanatory work of the memoir and Hunt's exhibition pamphlets. They 'decode' and 'inform' us about historical and literary background in order to provide us with contracts that might make sense of his images. However, the very complexity of this enterprise calls into question the efficacy of Hunt's inscription of meaning. Sussman maintains that the identification of contradictions in Hunt's application of symbolism to natural appearances by certain critics is merely a result of their failure to accept the philosophy of a sacred naturalism. Such contradictions go deeper than philosophy. The iconographical tension between the literal and the symbolic aspects of Hunt's paintings, identified in Chapter 3, manifests itself as a dislocation within their pictorial language itself.

Pre-Raphaelitsm distances Hunt's style from that of Rossetti: 'Dantesque shapes of imagery became Rossetti's alphabet of art, and in his designs, as in his poems, his mind expressed itself in a form independent of new life and the joy of nature . . . ; it was the finished phraseology, the mode of delineation, that dominated him' (1, 148–9). Rossetti's approach is explicitly associated with that familiar equation of lack of life and eloquent artifice. It is therefore ironic that this passage almost perfectly describes Hunt's own method of design: a language-like 'delineation' of literary ideas at a distance from nature. The memoir goes on, however, to contrast Rossetti's 'indifference to the actuality of a poetic subject' by stressing the second stage of its protagonist's practice: his 'rough experience' and mimetic attention to 'actuality'. Indeed, although Hunt's drawings for the Cyclographic Society look almost identical to those of Rossetti, his intensely detailed paintings are obviously very different. Hunt's typological realism is a two-stage process: design followed by mimesis. During painting, each icon is endowed with vivid modelling, colour and texture, importing as many 'characteristics' of the real as possible. The second step of manufacture represents a second form of authority of the eye: it augments the imaginative control of the outlines with the optical control of pure vision. The synthesis of the spiritual and the literal gaze, discussed in the previous chapter, is enacted in practical terms by the filling in of the imaginative design with illusionistic detail.

Peirce's idea of the icon is a useful tool in analysing this mimetic component. It draws attention to a variation in types of visual sign, where some possess more visual 'characters' based on sensual appearance than do others. His idea of a symbol draws our attention to the fact that other visual signs are less dependent on detail and draw their meaning from a particular cultural or literary code. Even if we have established that both kinds of sign might communicate in a conventional way, the important fact remains that they are different from each other and communicate different kinds of things. Peirce's icon suggests aspects of the physical world, whereas his symbol can suggest literary or abstract ideas. This can be demonstrated by considering one of Schapiro's examples of visual convention, the association of the cross with a range of open-armed figures.[59] This motif is used in *The Shadow*, *The Triumph* and *Christ and the Two Marys* (1847–*c.* 1900, Art Gallery of South Australia, Adelaide). In *The Druids* (1849–50, Ashmolean Museum, Oxford), Hunt signifies the cross in a purely conventional way, by means of the cross symbol painted on the door. *The Light of the World* alludes to the physical characteristics of a wooden upright and crosspiece in the background branches and Christ's raised right arm. In *The Finding* (figure 7.18) two pieces of wood are arranged at an angle in the temple courtyard. 'Cross' is therefore signified through a wide range of 'characters'. Moreover, the same characters can suggest a variety of aspects of the term, ranging from symbol through index to icon: the Christian symbol, the crucified man, the bare physical structure of the object. The visual sign is restless, shifting between literal and symbolic meanings.

Having dispelled the idea that an icon necessarily refers to a real object outside the painting,[60] Peirce's model provides a way of talking about a continuum of differing types of signification within the painting. The two pieces of wood in *The Finding*, for example, function as a symbol *and* as an icon, merely two pieces of wood. Moreover, an indexical reading of the motif can suggest construction

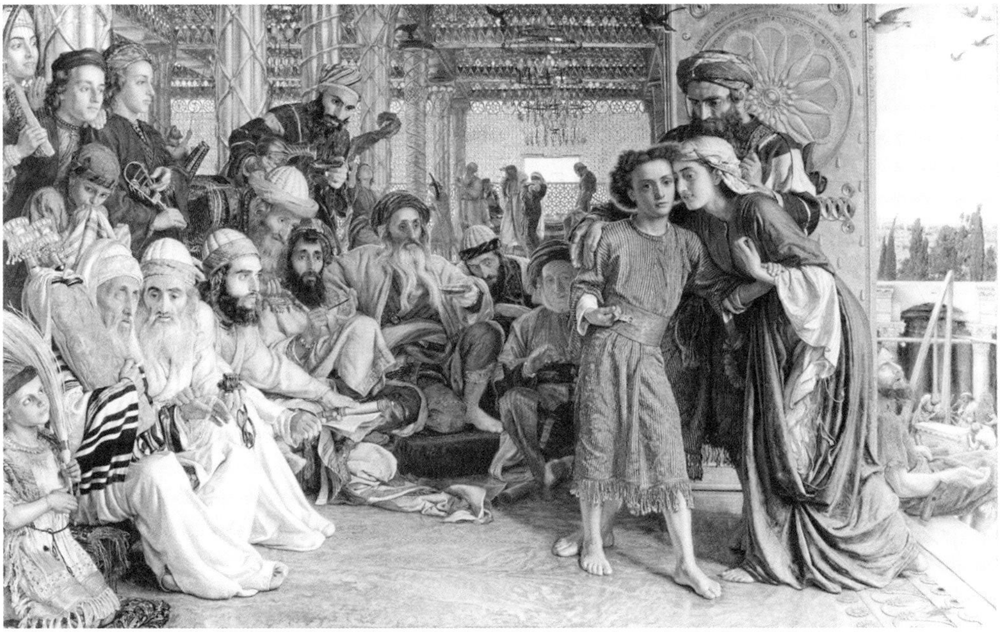

7.18
William Holman Hunt,
The Finding of the Saviour in the Temple,
1854–60

work, or construction work pertaining to the building of the church, or the construction of the cross, or simply Christ's future crucifixion, or all of these, depending on the amount of scriptural convention that is bought to bear on it. Like the apple and the lamb, the indexical significance of this object becomes less literal as it becomes more informed by its symbolic and cultural associations. The same sign placed within a related but different design, *Lorenzo in the Warehouse* (1848–50, Musée du Louvre, figure 7.19), has a different set of meanings again. The object is multivalent, producing an array of meanings which slide between literal and symbolic aspects of *itself*; icon, index and symbol are simply useful, but artificial, calibrations.[61]

This capacity to produce multiple meanings is typical of motifs within Hunt's work. Sensitivity to these different operations, 'the varying natures of each object in the picture',[62] is manifested by a simultaneous promotion of and vigorous exercise of control over every function. The role of each item as icon is powerfully strengthened by both the intense detail with which it is painted and by its position within 'natural' surroundings. Indexical and symbolic significance are enhanced through the discrete and careful situation of each object within precise designs crowded with other objects which reinforce the desired meaning. The rack of tools in *The Shadow*, for instance, functions iconically as a highly illusionistic rendering of a wooden rack of carpenter's tools in a workshop. It functions indexically on several levels, implying both the present occupation of Christ and the

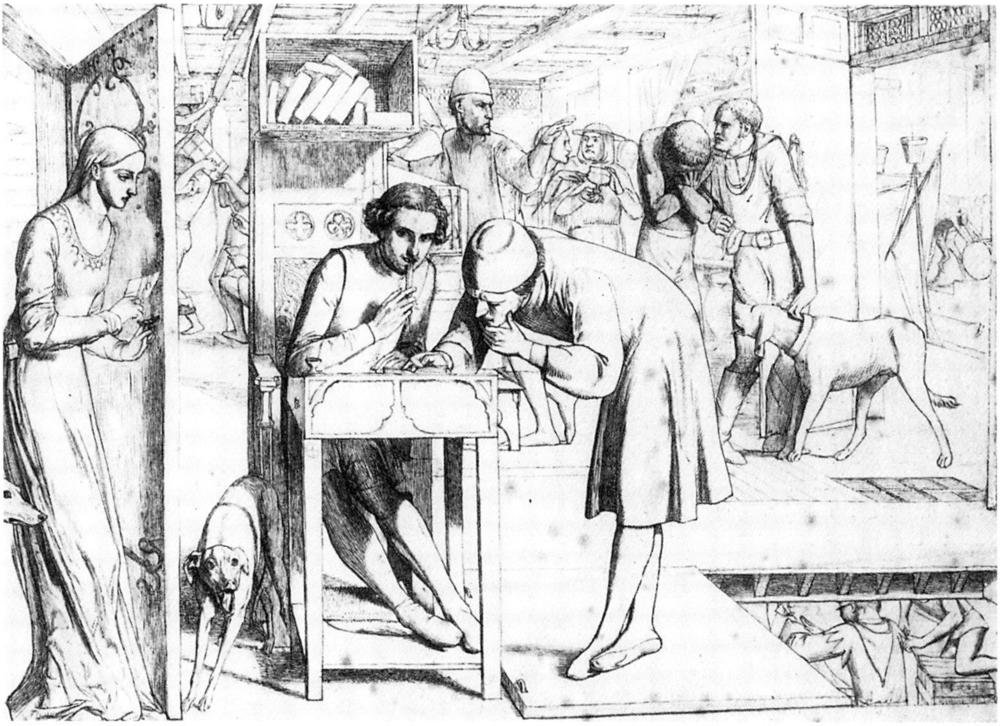

7.19
William Holman Hunt,
Lorenzo at his Desk in the Warehouse,
1848–50

future narrative of crucifixion, the torture, nailing, piercing, and the removal of the nails. The shape of the tools and the rack create the form of a cross in a way which can be narrative and symbolic. The more sacred references are enhanced by the position of the motif within an arrangement containing other elements which strengthen themes of crucifixion. The saw buried in the wood, the fruit, the red bandana, the crucified stance of Christ and his shadow contribute equivalent symbolic and indexical meanings. The juxtaposition of Joseph and the tools on the workbench in *St Joseph Mending Mousetraps* (*c.* 1420's, *Merode Alterpiece*, Master of Flemalle, Metropolitan Museum of Art) produces a richer set of associations than are likely to be prompted by an alternative scheme such as an illustration in a DIY manual. The addition of an excess of mimetic detail to carefully arranged and potently language-like signs, heightens both icon-like and indexical/symbolic identities.

This exercise of control over each function of every motif extends beyond the picture space through the title, frame and accompanying pamphlets. As Landow says:

> From Hogarth, Hunt . . . learned to employ documents, labels, and inscriptions within and without the picture to intensify the effect of visual . . . language.

> His later practice of appending texts directly to his pictures arose in the annoying lack of comprehension encountered by *Our English Coasts* . . . and when The Light of the World, The Awakening Conscience, and The Scapegoat showed that even such appended texts were insufficient to inform the spectator, he began to accompany his pictures with key-plates, commentaries, and manifestos.[63]

The pamphlet for *The Shadow* is typical in that it identifies the real sources of each item as icon and its role in the narrative.[64] The gilded frames, on the other hand, reinforce sacred connotations and include motifs which point up the symbolism within the picture.[65] As the *Manchester Guardian* review of *The Finding* exclaims: 'Nay the symbols have overflowed the picture and expanded themselves all over the frame.'[66] The frame of *The Scapegoat* bears seven stars, a seven-branched candlestick, a dove, olive branch, cross and heartsease.[67] *The Shadow* and *The Triumph* have relatively plain frames but their pattern recalls the embossing and gilding of mediaeval halos and presents the image within its own nimbus, or glory. Biblical quotations on the frames or in catalogue notes also highlight the symbolic and textual aspects of the design.

The display of Hunt's work after 1860, on its own, in controlled lighting conditions[68] also emphasises the sacred, having far more in common with the experience of an alterpiece in a church than exposure on the cluttered walls of a crowded exhibition. This precaution also emphasises illusionism, minimising any contradictory sense impressions that might distract from the scene; a device which is used today in cinemas. Edmund Gosse describes viewing *The Finding*:

> We paid our shillings and ascended with others to an upper room, bare of every disturbing object, in which a strong toplight raked the large and *uncompromising* picture.
>
> We looked at it for some time in silence. (emphasis added)[69]

Almost all, if not every item in a painting by Hunt works as a symbol, index and icon. He rejects the purely symbolic, like the flag of the resurrection which he associates with pure language, an 'alphabet' of faith (1, 84–5), but it is equally difficult to find any object which is only an icon. Even peripheral accessories in *The Shadow*, such as the stool and the vice, have a potent indexical motivation in that they establish the time, place and the humble, laborious nature of Christ's lifestyle, and recall the sacred associations of these objects in quattrocento painting. Both also have important compositional roles in that they direct the eye and define space. This persistent wedding of the iconic to the indexical and the symbolic represents, at the most basic semiotic level, Hunt's need for a simultaneous optical and imaginative control and a simultaneously material and spiritual manifestation of the divine.

Hunt's verisimilitude is only one of an array of pictorial strategies, all orientated towards the promotion of signification. The extremes to which each of these strategies are taken, be it through the vehicle of painting or design, represent a search for certitude. In pursuing these extremes, however, the limits of the pictorial language are revealed.

The fragmented sign

Hunt's explanation of the 'river of life' and other elements in *The Triumph* expresses for itself the dynamic exchange between icon, index and symbol produced by individual motifs and the breakdown in signification that occurs when this is pushed too far. It is necessary to quote the description at length to illustrate how the literal, or realistic/historical nature, of the imagery is established, and how the indexical and symbolic associations flow from the indexical narratives that this constructs. The beginning is documentary, emphasising the role of each element in the picture as icon. The weather, topography and even the breed of the ass are specified, and the use of the present tense creates a sense of naturalism and immediacy:

> The flight into Egypt I have assumed to have occurred about sixteen months after the birth of Jesus. Guided by Christian tradition, and holding the birth of our Lord to have taken place in December, it follows that the period which I have assigned to the Flight into Egypt is the second April of his life.
>
> During the spring-time, rich in flowers and first fruits, the HOLY TRAVELLERS are represented as passing the Philistine plain on the road to Gaza at a distance of about thirty miles from the point of departure. The night is far spent. While the declining moon sheds its last rays on the natural objects in the picture, unearthly light reveals the embodied spirits of martyred Innocents advancing in procession.
>
> The virgin is seated on a she-ass of the breed now known as the Mecca race, and the foal follows its mother, as is seen to this day in the East. Signal fires – still lit in Syria in time of trouble – are burning on the slope looking down from the tableland. St Joseph is watching these fires intent on discovering any signs that may present themselves of a movement of soldiery upon the road. Of the trees that enrich the landscape, the nearest ones shelter a waterwheel used for the irrigation of the land. The more remote group clusters round a village, with its few huts visible by the lights that burn within. Having left the colder climate of the high country, then thickly populated and well cultivated, the fugitives have descended into the rich and more balmy atmosphere of the plain. As they advance nearer to a place of safety they feel the blessed relief of a sense of peace after disturbance and terror.
>
> Conscious of divine mercy, the heart of Mary, rejoicing over her rescued son, feels compassion for the murdered Innocents, and for the childless mothers less happy and less honoured than herself. It is at this

moment, when the Virgin has been replacing the garments in which the infant has been hurriedly wrapped at the time of escape from Bethlehem, that Jesus recognises the spirits of the slain Innocents, His little neighbours of Bethlehem, children like Himself. They reveal the signs of their martyrdom. Garlanded for the sacrifice, bearing branches and blossoms of trees, they progressively mark their understanding of the glory of their service. An infant spirit isolated in wonder, finds no mark of harm where the sword wounded him, permitted to appear on his glorified body . . . The shallow stream over which the procession passes, reflecting the quiet beauty of the night sky, is unruffled except by the steps of Joseph. The flood upon which the spiritual children advance forms a contrast to this, by being in motion. The living fountains of water – the streams of eternal life – furnish this, mystically portrayed as ever rolling onward. Instead of being dissipated in natural vapour, the play of its wavelets takes the form of airy globes which image the Jewish belief in the millennium that is to follow the advent of the Messiah.[70]

Hunt's ekphrasis clearly demonstrates the way that the symbolic contract arises from a series of indexical connections, all ultimately dependent on the success of icons. The conventional symbolic link between the image of the stream and 'life' is mediated by indexical associations: 'Of the trees that enrich the landscape, the nearest ones shelter a waterwheel used for the irrigation of the land'; it is 'springtime, rich in flowers and first fruits'. The first-born children also connote 'first fruits' and their movement parallels and echoes that of the water, 'ever rolling 'onward', accompanied by branches, flowers, wavelets and bubbles. Jesus holds out a sprig of wheat that just touches (visually) the cultivated plain behind, and so completes a mutually reinforcing system of nurture – birth, fruit and water – rebirth, first fruits and baptism.

However, in order to express the mystical aspect of the image, the signifying power of the icons is promoted further. The globes caused some controversy, and the pamphlet explains:

The stream is ever rolling onward and breaking – where it might if real water be dissipated in vapour – into magnified globes which image the thoughts rife in that age in the minds of pious Jews, particularly in those in great tribulation, of the Millennium which was to be the mature outcome of the advent of the Messiah . . . The dream at Bethel first clearly speaks of the union of Earth and Heaven . . . and accordingly the large orb reflects dimly the Patriarch asleep with a twofold ladder or pathway up and down, which is traversed by the servants of God. The intention is to combine with the first beautiful dream of the Patriarch other ideas of the Messiah's reign which harmonise with this, and which were developed later. Heaven is indicated by the elders of the spotless lamb, and the broken heartedness of those who turn towards heaven is illustrated by the fallen penitent, by the young child, while the tree of life in the midst bears the fruit for the healing of the nations.

The depiction of the globes involves a neglect of the icon- and index-type functions which is exceptional in Hunt's work. Unlike the wheat and the signal fires, these signs lack strong supporting literal or narrative identities. They are not an expected or natural part of the landscape, being too big to have been produced by the stream. Their contents are small and unclear and do not fit into any coherent sequence of events. An attentive cognitive, indexical understanding of the signs in the bubbles could allow some of them to function. The tree of life reprises the real trees, as the pathway suggests the happy path of the main figures. However, the 'spotless lamb', and the 'penitent' signify only symbolically. Bethel's dream, the elders and the millennium, rely entirely on Hunt's accompanying text, which is, itself, far from clear.

We see that as the function of icon and index diminishes, so does 'symbolic' signification. A symbol which signifies in total absence of other properties is, in effect, working exclusively within a literary system rather than a visual system. In order to make these symbols visible, Hunt needs to label them like a diagram in his catalogue notes. Stephens's contemporary criticism of the painting concentrates on this collapse of meaning: 'The reader will guess that here are mysteries indeed, such as art seldom ventures to deal with, and less often succeeds with.'[71] He rationalises his dissatisfaction by attacking 'an attempt to represent the unseen by substantial means'.[72] This is contradictory in the light of the moral/spiritual/Christian thrust frequently attributed to the art of the period. It does, however, point to a sense of the limits of a visual semiotic that is trying to accommodate both materialist and religious ideas. Stephens's failure to read the design enacts the failure of consensus that Hunt attributes to his audiences.

The fact that Stephens's sense of artificiality and a dislocation between the real and the symbolic is so common in other responses to Hunt's work suggests that this failure to integrate the design and the mimetic detail in *The Triumph* is symptomatic of a more general problem. Bryson suggests that the realism of an image is less dependent on its natural, mimetic, or 'figural' appearance than upon a hiding of the 'discursive' within the 'figural'. Meaning that is discovered by the viewer in the 'figural' is perceived to have originated within the natural subject matter of the image rather than being artificially imposed upon it by the artist.[73] This presentation of meaning as found within the actual world would seem to be a good description of Hunt's use of signs which are both icon and symbol. However, Bryson goes on to assert that the integration of the figural and the discursive must be subtle in order for the image to appear natural, or transparent, and that a picture needs areas of 'non semantic' or 'peripheral' detail to achieve this.[74] Because *every* icon in Hunt's pictures originates in the discursive design, and therefore also has a highly intellectual/contractual role, all non-semantic elements are excluded. The strict complexity of the design, its potent literary arrangements, constitutes, as Robert Hughes says, a demand to be read. In so doing, the viewer recognises the symbolic, or discursive, as contrived.

Hunt's inscription of sacred significance is not integrated. It resides exclusively within a design which is executed at a distance from nature. His images therefore split; Errington describes Hunt's work as having two 'layers'.[75] As we identify and, therefore, separate out the exterior, organising programme, we empty the figural of meaning. We are thus left with a dying goat, a shadow, a bubble, something 'finite' and merely material, like the 'March sky'. As Landow says of *The Scapegoat*: 'all the drama (as well as all the symbolic details) exists in the language of the glosses, and the canvas contains none of them'.[76] The *Illustrated London News* complains similarly that 'the realistic details' in *The Shadow*, 'divide or usurp the attention which should be concentrated on the principle truth'.[77] Stephens's sense of the absurd, or artificial, in *The Triumph*, results from an awareness of the same disparity between the role of the children as sacred symbols and as highly physical icons.[78]

This splitting of the symbol from the icon, the 'discursive' from the 'figural', is reflected more generally in the polarisation of critical approaches noted in my introduction and Chapter 3. Reviewers are frequently dissatisfied with the combination of 'real and imaginary elements'[79] and, as Sussman notes, discuss the symbolic and the realistic aspects of Hunt's images separately, often mocking the 'droll' discrepancy between the two, as Stephens does. Other critics concentrate solely on interpretation. Critical neglect of aesthetic appearance in favour of the twin preoccupations with the artist's persona and with readings of his work represents, in part, this separating out of a discursive arrangement and the pronounced awareness of the role of the artist which it implies. The *Illustrated London News* finds the lesson in *The Shadow* 'obvious' and concludes from this that 'this picture (like the others before it, in a less degree) has an autobiographical – we might almost say psychological interest'.[80]

Hunt's promotion of the symbolic and his neglect of more direct visual signification in the case of the globes, recalls his exceptional promotion of the artist's imaginative (or prophetic) vision involved in the fantastical imaging of the Innocents themselves. A pictorial representation of scriptural dogma and an event beyond death, an intellectual or abstract concept, can be expressed only linguistically and must dispense with all but symbolic signification. Without the invented globes, Hunt's scene would depict babies, perhaps cherubs, in unusual combination with the Holy Family, but would not signify the resurrection of the Innocents clearly unless a new contract had been asserted by means of a parallel text, an alternative method of signification which Hunt uses in the title and in the pamphlet.

Wheeler notes how the subjects of 'death and future life' challenge the language of religious literature and painting in the nineteenth century.[81] The highly conceptual nature of Hunt's designs is a function of their role as expressions of abstract faith. Their precise elaboration is, correspondingly, an attempted expression of prophetic authority, an enactment of imaginative control which binds every icon into an order which equates to 'God's order'. Hunt pushes the visual language to extremes so that it might perfectly embody divinity, but, in so doing, he exposes its limits. As Wheeler says: 'it is at the very point of stress or fracture in the language of consolation that both the provisional nature of language and communication and the very grounds of Christian faith are laid bare'.[82]

The dislocated senses of subjective artificiality and prosaic literality experienced by observers of Hunt's work offer a clue to his own twin preoccupation with the false and the merely material. Wheeler quotes Austin Farrer's observation about the limits of the religious analogy, 'faith discerns not the images, but what the images signify'.[83] The contract which ratifies symbolic meaning depends on an acceptance of scripture, or faith. Hunt's textual expressions of faith are, as we've seen, inconsistent, anxious, reliant on delusions of prophetic authority or reasoned evidence as a precondition of belief. Analogies, or natural symbols, do not, therefore, signify fully. When faith falters, the symbol pulls apart from the icon and the image becomes a spectacle of dandaical artifice or meaningless materiality.

Writing to Scott while working on *The Shadow*, Hunt identifies 'two views on life': 'What is the reason for the dead-alive poetry and art of the day, if not in the totally material nature of the views cultivated in the modern schools? Trying to limit speculation within the bounds of sense only must produce poor sculpture, feeble painting, dilettante poetry.'[84] An icon which signifies in a merely sensual manner, without symbolic augmentation, fails to represent salvation. It is no less redolent of sickness and death than purely symbolic, subjective art such as that of Rossetti. This problematic relationship between the designed and the natural is dramatised by Hunt's technique of painting, discussed in the next chapter.

Notes

1 Prettejohn, *Pre-Raphaelites*, p 111
2 Letter to Tupper, 20 June 1878, *Correspondence*, p 246
3 Landow, *Typological Symbolism*, p 20
4 Landow, G.P., '"Christ the Pilot": A Panel from William Holman Hunt's Unfinished Triptych', *Journal of Pre-Raphaelite Studies*, 5 (1980), p 81

5 Letter to Tupper, 20 June 1878, *Correspondence*, p 246
6 Forsyth, P.T., *Religion in Recent Art: Expository Lectures on Rossetti, Burne-Jones, Watts, Holman Hunt and Wagner* (1889) (London: Hodder and Stoughton, 1901), p 178
7 Sussman, 'Hunt, Ruskin', p 90
8 Errington, *Themes*, pp 276–87
9 Letter to Stephens, 3 February 1869, BL, MS Don. e 67, 32
10 Letter to Bunney, 11 July 1876, quoted Bennett, 'Footnotes', p 46; letter to Combe, 20 May 1870, JRL, MS 1213, 23
11 Townsend, Ridge and Hackney, *Pre-Raphaelite Painting Techniques*, pp 51–3
12 Hackney, Jones and Townsend, *Paint and Purpose*, p 82
13 An oil study for *The Eve of St Agnes* (1847, private collection) builds up form in blocks of vivid paint, as do copies from painters whom Hunt admired as colourists, such as *Bacchus and Ariadne* (1846, private collection). However, these are rare, early examples.
14 Bronkhurst, 'Holman Hunt', p 352
15 Ibid., p 319
16 Ibid., p 330
17 These threads, also seen on the floor of *The Awakening Conscience*, connote disorder; Hunt complains about the 'tangled knotted thread of racking work', letter to Lear, 14 June 1857, JRL, MS 1214, 24
18 Bryson, N., *Word and Image:French Painting of the Ancien Regime* (Cambridge: Cambridge University Press, 1989), p 42
19 The only reference to an actual sketchbook is to one produced during his student days (1846–47) featuring anatomical studies. Bronkhurst identifies the most likely source for these drawings as a book, James Scratchley's *The London Dissector*, published in several editions around this time, 'Holman Hunt', pp 305–6
20 Letter to Stephens, October 1852, BL, MS Don. e 66, 16
21 Ruskin, *Modern Painters*, 2, in *Works*, 4, pp 51–9
22 Ibid., p 91
23 Ruskin, *Modern Painters*, 1, in *Works*, 3, pp 624–7
24 Ibid., p 624
25 Tupper, J.L., 'The Subject in Art', *The Germ: Thoughts towards Nature In Poetry, Literature and Art*, 1 (January 1850), p 11
26 Landow suggest that the word 'idea' encompasses objects and effects for contemporaries of Hunt, *Typological Symbolism*, p 17
27 Bronkhurst, 'Holman Hunt', pp 349–58
28 Bronkhurst, 'The Shadow of Death', in *The Pre-Raphaelites* (Tate Gallery, 1984), p 223
29 Bennett, *Hunt*, p 53
30 Letter to Stephens, 22 June 1869, BL, MS Don. e 67, 30v
31 Hamerton, *Graphic Arts*, pp 196–7
32 Letter to Combe, 20 May 1870, JRL, MS 1213, 23; letter to Bunney, 11 July 1876, quoted Bennett, 'Footnotes', p 46
33 Bryson, *Word and Image*, pp 3–5
34 Letter to Tupper, 20 June 1878, *Correspondence*, p 246
35 Bryson, *Word and Image*, p 13

36 'The Shadow of Death', *Spectator*, 46 (6 December 1873), p 1538
37 Journal, 13 March 1855, JRL, MS 1211, 7
38 A proposed design showing Nicodemus meeting Christ at night, never completed, letter to Tupper, 28 December 1876, *Correspondence*, p 214
39 Iverson, M., 'Saussure v. Peirce: Models for a Semiotics of Visual Art', in *The New Art History*, eds A.L. Rees and F. Borzello (London: Camden Press, 1986), p 89
40 Peirce, C., 'Logic as Semiotic: The Theory of Signs', quoted ibid., pp 89–90
41 Tupper, 'The Subject in Art', p 16
42 Ruskin, *The Art of England*, p 11
43 Crary, J., *Techniques of the Observer: On Vision and Modernity in the Nineteenth Century* (1990) (London: MIT Press, 1995), pp 95–6
44 Ruskin, *Modern Painters*, 1, in *Works*, 3, p 164; 'every picture must be false which endeavours to represent living sunlight with dead pigments', *The Times* (30 May, 1851), p 8
45 Douglas Greenlee notes that Peirce's theory of the 'surrogate' nature of the visual representation is ambiguous and does admit to an intellectual aspect of recognition, Greenlee, D., *Peirce's Concept of the Sign* (The Hague: Mouton, 1973), pp 57–61
46 Letter to J.E. Pythian, 21 January 1897, quoted Bennett, *Hunt*, p 29
47 Gombrich, E., *Art and Illusion: A Study in the Psychology of Pictorial Representation* (1959) (London: Phaidon, 1993)
48 Schapiro, M. 'On Some Problems in the Semiotics of Visual Art: Field and Vehicle in Image-Signs', *Semiotica*, ed. T. Sebeok, 1 (1969), pp 223–42; also, *Words and Pictures, On the Literal and Symbolic Meaning in the Illustration of the Text* (The Hague: Mouton, 1973), p 37
49 Wittgenstein, L., *Philosophical Investigations* (Oxford: Blackwell, 1968), pp 193–4
50 Hanson, N.R., *Patterns of Discovery, An Inquiry into the Conceptual Foundations of Science* (London: Cambridge University Press, 1972), chapter 1
51 Veltrusky, J., 'Some Aspects of the Pictorial Sign', in *Semiotics of Art*, eds L. Matejka and K. Titunik (1976) (Cambridge, Mass.: MIT Press, 1989), pp 245–64
52 Panofsky, E., *Studies in Iconology, Humanistic Themes in the Art of the Renaissance* (1939) (New York: Harper and Row, 1972), p 12
53 Veltrusky, 'Pictorial Sign', p 261
54 *Saturday Review*, 26 (6 December 1873), p 728; *Illustrated London News* (6 December 1873), p 543
55 Errington, *Themes*, p 211
56 Hughes, *Nothing If Not Critical*, pp 115–16
57 *Illustrated London News* (6 December 1873), p 542
58 Landow, *Typological Symbolism*, p 4
59 Schapiro, M. 'Semiotics of Visual Art', pp 223–42
60 Gombrich notes this variety in the way visual images signify and rejects the 'conventionalist' stance to reassert the significance of 'imitation', characteristics shared by the image and real appearance, in the case of some kinds of sign. Gombrich, E.H., 'Image and Code: Scope and Limits of Conventionalism in Pictorial Representation' (1978) *The Image and the*

Eye: Further Studies in the Psychology of Pictorial Representation (London: Phaidon, 1982), p 278

61 Thomas Mitchell's *Iconology: Image, Text, Ideology* (1986) (London: University of Chicago Press, 1987) criticises the nature/convention debate and draws attention to Nelson Goodman's *The Language of Art* (1976). Although Goodman suggests that the image signifies through a range of conventions, he rejects the idea that it is like language and proposes instead that it is distinctive in that, unlike language, it lacks differentiation. Every part signifies in relation to every other part, like an uncalibrated thermometer, pp 63–8

62 Letter to Tupper, 20 June 1878, *Correspondence*, p 246

63 Landow, *Typological Symbolism*, pp 38, 44

64 *The Shadow of Death*, quoted Bennett, *Hunt*, pp 49–50

65 I designed a frame for it which . . . made the picture look quite precious', undated fragment Holman Hunt papers, quoted Maas, *Hunt*, p 71

66 *Manchester Guardian* (24 April 1863), quoted, Bennett, *Pre-Raphaelite Circle*, p 80

67 Ibid., p 70

68 Maas, J., *Gambart: Prince of the Victorian Art World* (London: Barry and Jenkins, 1975), p 127

69 Gosse, *Father and Son*, p 192

70 *The Triumph of the Innocents*, quoted Bennett, *Hunt*, pp 53–4

71 Stephens, F.G., 'The Triumph of the Innocents', *Portfolio*, 16 (April 1885), p 81

72 Ibid., p 83

73 Bryson, *Word and Image*, pp 9–16

74 Ibid., pp 19–20

75 Errington, *Themes*, p 278

76 Landow, *Typological Symbolism*, p 111

77 *Illustrated London News* (6 December 1873), p 542

78 Landow, *Typological Symbolism*, p 80

79 *Illustrated London News* (14 March 1885), p 288

80 Ibid. (6 December 1873), p 542

81 Wheeler, *Heaven, Hell*, p 3

82 Ibid.

83 Farrer, A., 'The Glass of Vision', *Bamton Lectures* (1948), quoted Wheeler, *Heaven, Hell*, p 19

84 Letter to Scott, 10 August 1870, *Notes*, 2, p 95

8

Painting: mimesis and design

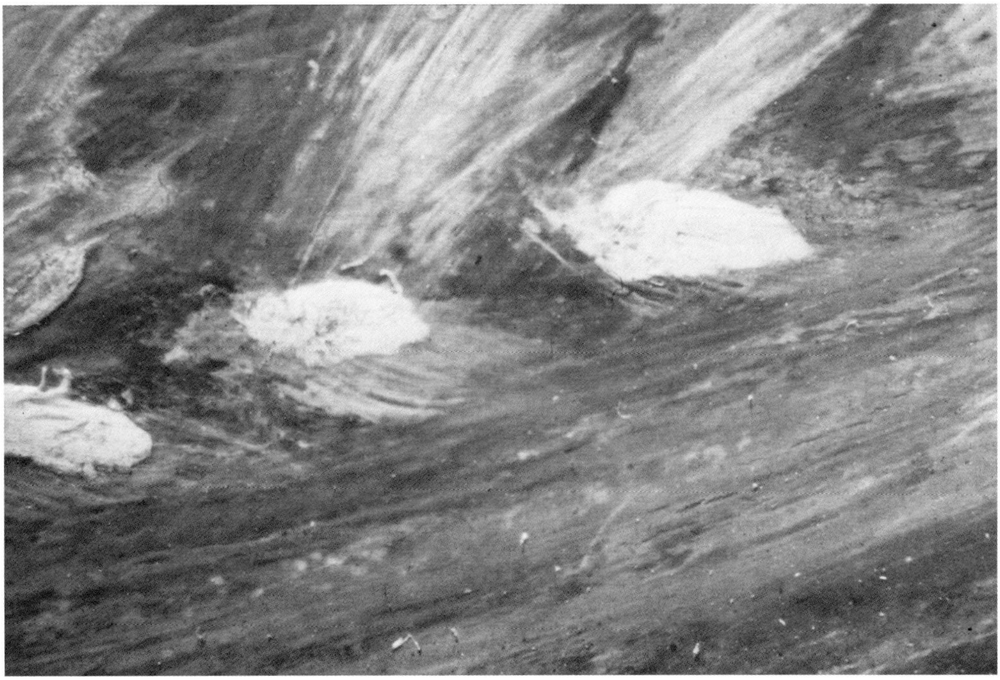

8.1
William Holman Hunt, *The Afterglow in Egypt*, magnified detail, sheaf of wheat, upper left-hand side

Hunt's technique of completing his canvases in front of real figures, objects and landscapes requires the closest work from nature at the painting stage. Colour, detail and three-dimensional light effects are introduced quite suddenly. This mimetic process is central to Hunt's religious understanding of art as an act of witness, as I have shown, but it tends to enhance the literal quality of his imagery and subvert the sacred meaning of the design.

Hunt, himself, makes no distinction between mimesis and meaning-making, and elides the difference between seeing and the interpretation and reproduction of what he sees, claiming to transfer nature's beauty directly on to the canvas (2, 452). He selects the landscape and accessories of the Holy Land as aspects of nature which are inherently sacred, but his attitude to the appearance of the figures in his paintings reveals difficulties.

Ordinary, contemporary models have to be used as substitutes for long-dead and sometimes exceptional or holy persons. Hunt therefore insists on the exceptional character of his models, conflating inner and outer beauty. The inscription for *Bianca – 'The Patroness of Heavenly Harmony'* (1868–69, Worthing Museum and Art Gallery, figure 8.2), indicates that the figure is supposed to be more than a portrait. When the sitter's beauty is criticised by Stephens, Hunt defends her good character. Her American nationality causes him embarrassment and he fiercely repudiates Stephens's term 'Yankee'.[1]

The act of painting Christ condenses this difficulty. In his chapter on Hunt in *Five Great Painters of the Victorian Era* (1902), Wyke Bayliss offers a somewhat far-fetched justification of the possibility of representing Jesus. He asserts that portraiture was the only achievement of Roman art and that this enabled the likeness of Christ to be passed down through the centuries. He places Hunt at the end of a historical tradition of authentic representations that has its origin in the catacombs: 'living so far away from the place and time when men could see him face to face – [Hunt] can yet paint Him, knowing that he is painting a reality, not a myth'.[2]

This historical authentication does not help with the concrete problem of painting a likeness of an absent person. In actuality, Hunt derives his images of Christ from a variety of people. In the above letter to Stephens, he links the issue of his model for *Bianca* to that of the models for the Christ in *The Shadow*: 'What you say about "Bianca" is like what the people of Bethlehem say of my work there – that it is a collection of portraits of the particular fellahin who sat to me altho' as it happens the models for one figure alone have been three or four.'[3] In practical terms, the problem of finding divine appearance in real persons is partially solved, not by an exact matching of model to subject, or by simple idealisation, but by selecting features from a 'collection' of models. Like nature, the figures are not copied

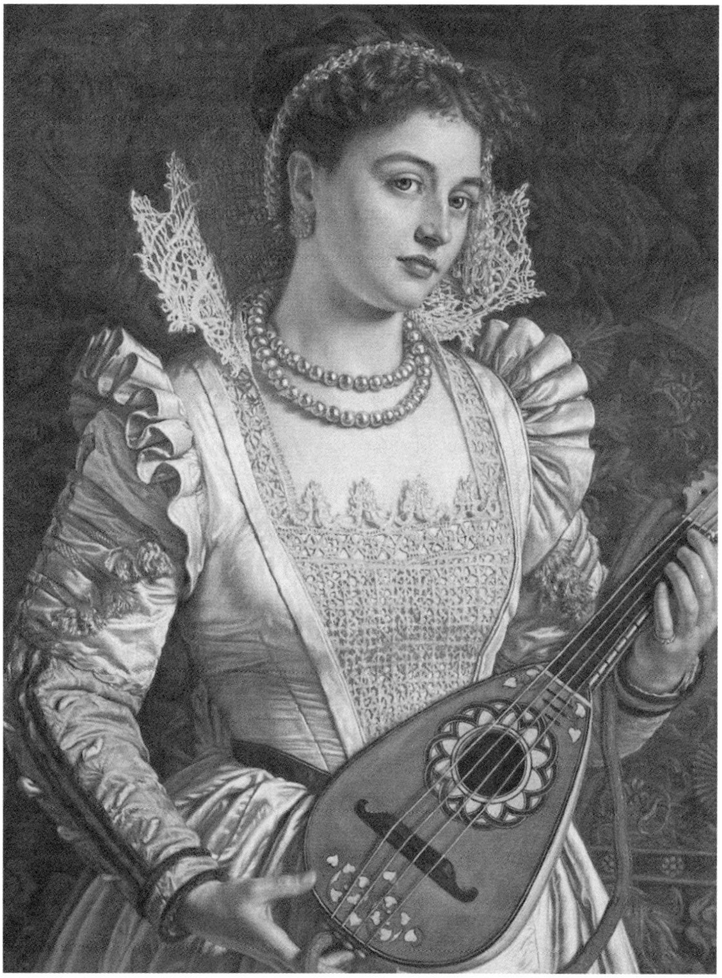

8.2
William Holman Hunt, *Bianca – The Patroness of Heavenly Harmony*, 1868–69

wholesale; they are divided up and the beautiful parts are chosen and ugly, or inappropriate, parts are omitted.

Maas suggests that in the case of *The Light of the World*, this idea of a composite is in part an invention devised by Hunt to get around the tricky problem of distancing his image of Christ from any one mortal character, while preserving the legend of his realism.[4] However, Hunt's journals and letters reveal that he continues to use this technique. While completing *The Finding*, he sends to Tupper for a 'young lady . . . to finish the Virgin's face from – not to copy except for what of softness and refinement of modelling and colour *I may find* in my model' (emphasis added).[5] During 1872 alone, Hunt hires several models for *The Shadow*, paints from himself and gleans 'one or two points' from visitors.[6] The children in The *Triumph* are also made up of a 'digest' of small sections of many models.[7]

Hunt's authority for this complex process of selection is the artistic ability to 'find' the beautiful and the sacred which is promoted in *Pre-Raphaelitism*. Bayliss implies that Hunt is a special kind of 'witness' and possesses spiritual qualities which allow him to recognise and choose appropriate features.[8] When Stephens, on the other hand, finds *Bianca* ugly, he is, at the same time, questioning Hunt's eye and persona. Hunt retaliates by implying that Stephens's opinion is both falsely influenced by social convention, and as primitive as that of the local heathens, neither objective nor spiritual.

Tupper obviously understands Hunt's consternation about Stephens's criticism. His reply to Hunt's letter about it contains a consoling discussion of the difficulty of portraying 'sight of God in nature'. He puts his finger on Hunt's precise practical predicament. He identifies the moral element as given, prescribed – 'abstract principles . . . action, love, honour, justice &c.' – but asks how it can be seen: 'what things will represent these principles, and what not?', noting that 'principles are not to be confounded with things'. He goes on to answer this question, but only in abstract terms; like Bayliss, he stresses Hunt's 'higher natural gifts', an innate, but vague, capacity to effect such a selection.[9]

This inspirational aspect of the act of painting has a long pedigree, and has often been used to justify idealisation in art, especially of holy figures. However, the prioritisation of factual truth in Hunt's system of belief, and his rejection of conventional idealisations, undermines this principle. His use of multiple models represents an attempt to fulfil a paradoxical specification, to paint a subjective concept as though it were 'tangible' evidence.

Thus, for Hunt, the painting of Christ involves more than importing likenesses of a Galilean, a view of Nazareth and sundry accessories into the preconceived design discussed in the last chapter. Hunt's subjective input extends to the process of making these likenesses, the sifting of appearances for what is divine and what is not. The validation of his religious and artistic beliefs and, with it, his security in this world and the next, are dependent on the judgement of God and critics, of which he so often speaks (Chapter 4). However, at the point of painting, Hunt's self-identification as prophet/artist hinges on small judgements of his eye. This simultaneity of judgement reinforces the importance of Hunt's prophetic self-image and the *practical* role of the 'special' vision of the artist to this fantasy. My point is that the act of painting, the touch of the brush, both depends on, and bears the weight of, belief and self-image.

The reciprocal verification of image and artist is dependent on a notion of painting as an act of inspired reflection, rather than a process of construction. Hunt's published writings obscure the constructive painting process: 'a man's work must be the reflex of a living image in his own mind' (1, 150), but how is this actually effected? 'Reflex' inspiration must take place in front of a paradoxically banal, changeable, material reality. Some sifting out of the divine has been achieved through the subjective choice of subject, design, model, accessories and setting, and parts of these. Can the close mimetic act of copying these parts include both imitation *and* invention, more than 'speculation within the bounds of sense',[10] as Hunt suggests?

The mimetic technique

Although we have ascertained that the orthodoxy concerning Hunt's truth to nature represents an incomplete concept of his procedure, accounts of Hunt's mimetic method suggest that at the painting stage each mark is dictated directly by sensual experience, what Tupper calls excitation of the eye. This practice would tend to place an extreme stress upon surface effect, light and colour, rather than outline. A close examination of Hunt's style bears this out.

Pre-Raphaelite technique has, until recently, been discussed as a uniform practice, but the relative singularity of Hunt's approach can be demonstrated by comparing it to that of close contemporaries who are producing similar subjects on a similar scale. Both Millais' *Autumn Leaves* (1856, plate 15) and Hunt's *The Afterglow in Egypt* (1854, 1860–63, plate 14) suggest ideas of transience by situating female figures against a receding landscape at around dusk. Millais' canvas bears a less uniform layer of paint, however, and umber underpainting shows through in areas of shadow. Hunt uses this technique in very early works, such as his *Self-Portrait* (1845, plate 10), but in *The Afterglow*, every part of the surface is evenly covered. Even transparent passages have a firm enamel quality. When viewed from close quarters, the surface of Millais' image dissolves into its component materials in a way that Hunt's does not. The white ground of *The Afterglow* is completely concealed beneath an unbroken 'skin' of paint that systematically records the colour and texture of each depicted surface.[11] Only some of Millais' leaves on the bonfire are defined, but Hunt depicts each kernel of the sheaf of wheat carried by the girl (figure 8.1). The foliage behind Millais' children is generalised, but Hunt picks out the irregular branches of his distant palm tree, the bits of grass growing in the wheat field and the patterns on the feathers of the birds over the pool.

The Afterglow presents an array of full, curved volumes in contrast to the slightly flattened appearance of *Autumn Leaves*. The madder headdress of the Egyptian girl is much more meticulously modelled than the red scarf in Millais' painting. Hunt enhances three-dimensionality through a generous dispersal of highlights, whereas Millais expresses recession mainly through chiaroscuro. He uses highlights less freely and for a different purpose, to heighten theatrical effect. The scarf, the apple, the yellow leaf and the children's faces emerge tellingly from the gloom. Whereas Millais is prepared to sacrifice the representation of all three, visible sides of objects to overall design, Hunt never allows shadow to replace local colour or detail. Each form is rounded in modified hues. The boots of Millais' little girl are half obscured in darkness, but the feet of Hunt's Bedouin and the shaded area around them are just executed in darker tints. Although *The Afterglow* is supposed to occur at the approach of evening, in keeping with its title,[12] its clarity creates the odd impression of it being both dusk and noon.

It might be suggested that discrepancies between Millais' scene and that of Hunt result from Millais' initial choice of a darker, smoky setting. However, Hunt's night pieces exhibit the same integrity of form and hue. *The Light of the World* (plate 4) suggests darkness through deep greens, blues and browns. No contour is blurred and local colour is still recognisable; every one of Christ's toes is fully rounded. Even the branches in the background do not flatten into silhouette. Hunt says that he abandoned working by oil lamp because it blinded him to 'subtleties of hue of the moonlit scene'; he worked by candlelight instead (1, 299). The same intense clarity of colour and modelling distinguishes the nocturnal setting of *The Triumph* (plate 3).

Reviews of Hunt's work comment on this precise, modelled quality and identify it as an idiosyncrasy. Edmund Gosse describes *The Finding*:

> The exact, minute and hard execution of Mr Hunt was in sympathy with the method we ourselves were in the habit of using when we painted butterflies and seaweeds, placing perfectly pure pigments side by side, without any nonsense about chiaroscuro. This large, bright, comprehensive picture made a very deep impression on me, not exactly as a work of art, but as a brilliant natural specimen.[13]

Hunt's painting style clearly privileges detail, form, surface and local colour over any other pictorial concern, no matter how peripheral the object. This suggests that he simply reproduces hue as he sees it at each point of each lit form.

Microscopic examination of *The Afterglow* reveals the sequence of tiny, prismatic strokes spoken of by Gosse. The brown wing of the bird perched on the wheat sheaf, for example, contains umber, madder pink and Prussian blue dabs which transcribe every incident of light across the opalescent feathers.[14] A microphotograph of a ruffle in the brown pigeon in the shadows, in the lower left-hand corner of the painting, reveals wispy marks of yellow, vermilion and blue (plate 20). The eye of the first bird is more blended in yellow and vermilion with a touch of emerald green (plate 21). Both these areas are carefully modelled in colour rather than line or light and shade, and three-dimensionality is enhanced by small, carefully aligned and shaped highlights in white. A similar technique has recently been observed during scientific analysis of earlier works carried out at the Tate Department of Conservation.[15]

The painstaking observation and transposition of effect seen in *The Afterglow*, even in relatively insignificant and drably coloured parts such as the brown birds, is the cause of Hunt's famously protracted painting technique. Millais is reported to have been 'in high spirits and much delighted with the rapidity of his execution' of *Autumn Leaves*,[16] but Hunt is incessantly depressed by delays. He tells Lear that the pigeons alone 'threaten to occupy me for the remainder of my life'.[17] Scott remarks that Hunt was generally in the habit of being seduced into endless 'little scrapings and stipplings up of odd corners'.[18]

The absence of any 'false touch' (1, 53) seen in Hunt's precise, uncorrected strokes, is a result of his uncompromising practice of obliterating errors and painting afresh on a renewed ground. This is vividly dramatised in the 1872 journal where he constantly scrapes off imperfect areas of *The Shadow*: 'erase, not retouch but repaint my yesterdays work'.[19] This method further privileges immediate optical sensation over an approximation of appearances over time. Hunt's time-consuming blending of different hues to depict smooth surfaces, such as flesh, therefore causes particular difficulty, and he writes to Combe of problems in completing parts of *The Afterglow* and his constant fear that 'the paint will dry ere it is finished'.[20] He voices a similar concern during work on *The Shadow*,[21] often regretting his susceptibility to detail: 'when I am sitting down at a thing I keep seeing more and more of the beauty of delicate intonations and modellings in nature so that the work never seems to be finished'.[22]

Changes of light also cause him to paint anew: 'there is an alteration of effect and form and every time nature looks better – and so exclusively indeed the only right thing that I can't resist changing my picture more or less'.[23] Sizeranne notes this optical fidelity to lit surfaces in 'the blood red sheep in indigo bushes, on rocks chiselled like sugar candy', in *Our English Coasts*.[24] This attention to brilliant light effects can be seen in a microphotograph of the far margin of the water of *The Afterglow* (plate 22).

As Staley and Prettejohn have noted, Hunt's fidelity to transient effect recalls that being explored by the Impressionist painters during the same period. In the 1870s, they too painted from nature in natural light and observed unconventional colours and shadows rather than traditional chiaroscuro.[25] Like Hunt, they kept in close touch with advances in artists' materials and employed light grounds and new prismatic pigments to maximise luminosity.[26] Magnified views of Hunt's work present a sequence of bright, direct marks similar to those in Impressionist paintings (plates 22 and 23). He practices on a different scale to the Impressionists, however, rejecting the geneal-isations and display of large brushstrokes needed to capture a fleeting impression of a whole scene. As Prettejohn notes, 'sunlight does not dissolve forms or blend objects into an overall effect, as it often does in French Impressionist painting. Instead it creates conditions where each form and each colour are seen more intensely.'[27] The Impressionists exhibit their paint, preferring a thick consistency straight from the tube, but Hunt seals optical effects within a uniform, mirror-like surface. He shares the materialism of a modern way of looking, but responds to it in a different way, seeking to adapt it to his pre-modern idea of art as an illusionistic 'reflection' of nature.

Moreover, Hunt's conception of art as a manifestation of divine meaning and order requires him to accommodate sensual characteristics within his sacred designs. Each of Hunt's icons retains the integrity of its outline and anomalies of vision or atmospheric effect are never allowed to obscure the boundaries of an object. In *The Body in Pieces*, Linda Nochlin explores Manet's use of fragmented figures and comments on his ability to 'play with habitual boundaries of all sorts, an oscillation between contingency and determination'. Manet's cropping is both an acceptance of the casual realism of photography and 'a laying bare of the device'.[28] Hunt's work, by contrast, exhibits no sense of play. He seeks total control over the device, the icon with its predetermined signifying role within the design, and disguises it by dressing it up in the contingent, immediate optical appearance.

The accidental, variable or 'disordered' aspects of the contingent are controlled. Only tiny areas are transcribed in order to enhance accuracy and minimise the effects of movement or of changing light. Hunt waits for nature to repeat a certain atmospheric effect before continuing on to another area. On the 3 May 1872, his journal records: 'A fine morning go out and paint the ear in shadow'.[29] Hunt's images are the sum of minutely scrutinised selected parts rather than the outcome of a total, momentary glance.

Mimesis and design

Hunt's method of painting requires a highly localised, sensual focus which is the opposite of the overall, imaginative, organising gaze that assembles the design. Two techniques coexist on one canvas. Raymond Watkinson inspects the execution of *Valentine* and concludes: 'a mosaic of local colour is accurately mapped on a scaffolding of no less accurate drawing'.[30]

The individual objects in Hunt's images are, as I've shown, connected by the spatial relations dictated by the design, a two dimensional web which operates in terms of narrative and symbol, conventions of depth and geometrical line and pattern. However, the mimetic method involves executing small parts of the painting without reference to other objects. This entails a privileging of local surface over overall space which is reminiscent of pre-Albertian approaches to perspective. In *The Birth and Rebirth of Pictorial Space*, John White comments on the emergence of objects set at oblique viewpoints which coincided with artists 'inquiring most acutely into what it was they could actually see, who were looking most intensely at the individual objects in the world about them'.[31] This throws light on Hunt's habitual use of three-quarter profiles, and items set at an angle to the picture plane, noted in Chapter 6.

The local gaze, described by White, also explains the lack of clean diagonals to offer the eye a smooth perspectival sweep, in Hunt's work.[32] White notes that concentrating on individual forms rather than on overall space creates a heterogeneous build-up of multiple spaces, each defined by the object inhabiting it. Hunt's two-stage method, therefore, produces space in two ways: the design constructs a generalised space, through an arrangement of depth clues and geometric perspective, according to a single viewpoint. The mimetic method creates a multiple array of spaces defined by individually modelled and foreshortened objects, each the subject of its own localised viewpoint.

The effect of this can be most clearly seen in *The Scapegoat* (plate 1) because it is an unusually uncluttered design, dominated by a single figure. The goat seems oddly separate from the landscape, despite the fact that its hooves are embedded in the salt. The surrounding plain is carefully designed to recede to a single vanishing point along artificial orthogonals provided by leaves and cracks (which converge on the mountain peak), but the animal seems to lean outwards. The distant hills also appear to stand up and step forward, as though they are hovering directly over the goat. Hunt's restricted and equally focused painting of animal and hills brings both towards the viewer and disrupts the spatial arrangements of the design.

The parts of the goat also generate a sense of spatial confusion. The nearest hind leg and foreleg penetrate the ground at the same distance from the painting's edge, yet the body as a whole is not parallel to the picture plane. It appears to be shown in a three-quarter view; the head comes towards the observer even though it does not seem to be bending away from the body. The head also seems somehow detached from the body. This peculiarity reoccurs in the children in *The Triumph* (plate 3), especially the foremost child who again combines a side and three-quarter view. Their heads appear similarly detached, and even individual curves of flesh bulge independently towards the viewer. The reviewer for the *Illustrated London News* also experiences 'an embarrassing difficulty in realising the relative position of the objects' in *The Shadow*.[33]

This phenomenon results from Hunt's method of painting part by part. He states in the *Contemporary Review* that he worked methodically from the top of the picture downwards,[34] but Bennett notes that the view of the Dead Sea seems to have been executed from more than one point, and that other parts of the scene, and the goat itself, were painted from several locations and models back in Jerusalem.[35] Hunt's journal records executing the scapegoat's hind leg, foreleg, head and body separately, interspersed with attention to items in the background.[36] Hunt describes painting the Innocents in 'fragments'[37] and the execution of *The Shadow* follows a similar pattern. Christ's 'beard', 'neck', 'left leg', and the 'sky' and 'leaves' are all worked on during two days in January 1872, and Hunt continues to paint the figure in isolated sections: 'touch on legs which makes me late returning to /the/ neck'.[38] He concentrates particularly on the head and therefore has trouble making it sit properly on the body.[39]

Hunt eventually alters the head's angle and the distribution of the beard to solve the problem. He has to step back from mimetic painting to find this solution. His expedient for joining head and body is arrived at away from the model, through a dream of a painting of Christ in the style of Van Dyck.[40] An artificial transition is again utilised in *The Triumph*, where the children wear beads and garlands around their throats.

Hunt uses traditional perspective in his designs, but relies on what looks right to the eye in the case of specific objects. This twofold approach to the general (design) and the local (imitation) is clearly expressed: 'I was dissatisfied with the proportions of the columns and not seeing the opportunity for getting the result better by rule I added to the bulk until this satisfied my eye.'[41] Hunt notes that the general, single viewpoint, 'one point of sight', is inadequate, causing distortion in peripheral objects. He replaces it with a more local viewpoint during painting.

Two ways of looking emerge: the mimetic gaze, a sensual scrutiny of each part in terms of 'bulk', form and surface, and the general gaze, an intellectual assessment of the whole design. The multiple viewpoint and 'problematic depth of field',[42] which both Smith and Prettejohn detect in Pre-Raphaelite painting, relates to the multiple foci of the highly mimetic technique. Each area is, in effect, a small composition in itself, in perfect focus. Hunt describes looking at *Valentine*, 'one sunny morning, when after a sleepless night, I was staring at my canvas, which looked like a half arranged puzzle for which the further pieces could not be found' (1, 243). A better photographic analogy than the stereoscope would be the combination printing of Oscar Rejlander, or even the multiple Polaroids of David Hockney.

Hunt's attempt to combine interpretation with experience is impeded by the separation of each into two stages of production and by the seeking of extreme control over both of them. He binds highly accurate sense impressions into a highly defined imaginative design. The design positions the viewer (initially, Hunt) at a point of universal focus, but the copied parts position him at multiple points of local foci. Hunt seeks total control of all parts of the painting. At the same time, in my view, he relinquishes control of the painting as a whole, as it has no single, coherent focus.

This accounts for the impression that Hunt's paintings are too real, or for Ironside's sense that they have been painted with the eyes pinned open.[43] This surreal effect dissolves when particular parts are focused upon. It is, therefore, difficult to deny the urge to reject the overall view and inspect the details of an image by Hunt. The kind of look that produced each icon, one by one, dictates the kind of look that they demand of the observer. A picture which is dominated by traditional perspective constructs the eye of the observer as stationary and central, but the individual elements of a picture by Hunt construct the eye of the observer in several places. The means of consumption retraces the means of production. The compositional whole is fragmented; the initial gaze breaks into a restless pattern of subsidiary gazes, dictated by the hierarchical arrangement of the icons.

This phenomenon is evident in descriptions of Hunt's images. Gosse's is typical: 'We looked at it [*The Finding*] for some time in silence and then my Father pointed out to me various details, such as the phylacteries and the mitres, and the robes which distinguished the high priest'.[44] The pointing finger, directing the eye in different directions, seems to express the localised viewpoint of each motif. This way of looking is imaged by the key plates which are used to identify the different objects in Hunt's work (figure 8.3).

Gosse's observation of individual brushstrokes, later in this passage, implies that he has rejected the overall viewpoint altogether and moved close to the picture to inspect its details. Ruskin's comments on *Valentine* also commend the 'perfect truth, power and finish' of 'the black sleeve of Julia' or 'the velvet on the breast . . . of Valentine', foregrounding the completeness of individual parts of the composition and seeming to allude to their power to draw the gaze.[45] Reviewers of Hunt's work commonly list objects one by one, as though they were self-sufficient; the *Illustrated London News* description of *The Shadow* quoted above is a typical example.[46] Another example is Ruskin's explanation of *The Awakening Conscience*, in which he concludes: 'a strange interest exalts the accessories of the scene'.[47]

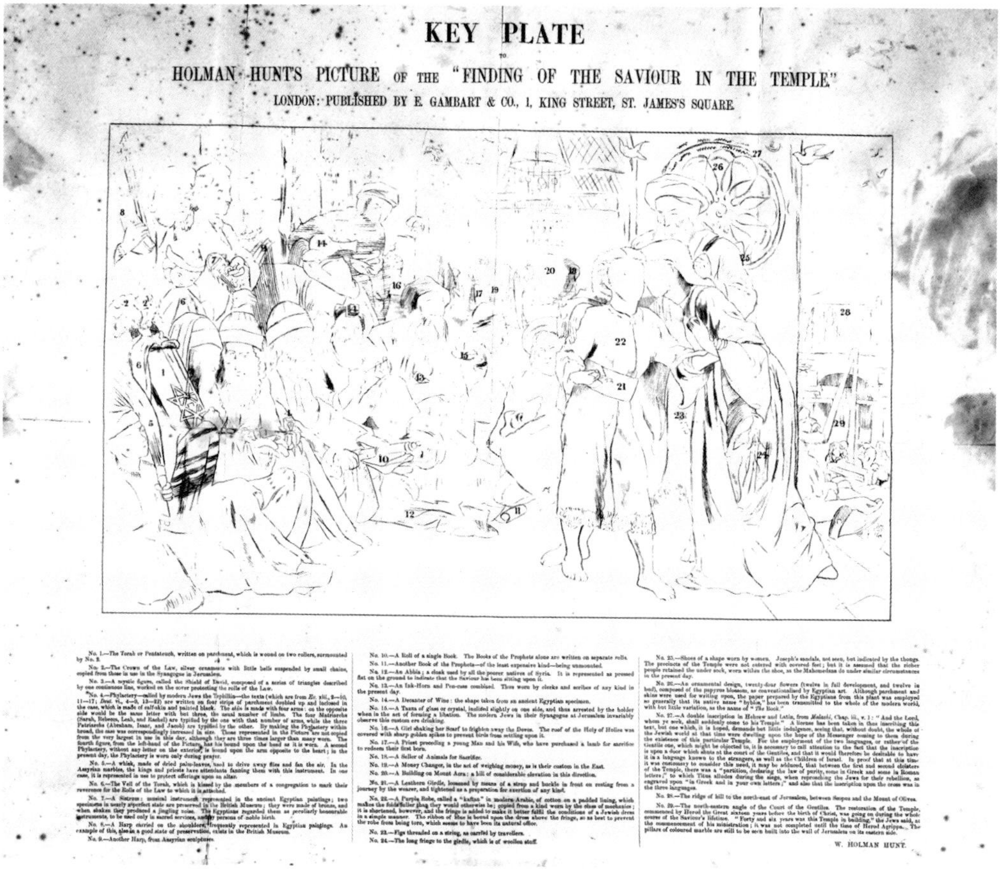

8.3
William Holman Hunt, *Key to 'The Finding of the Saviour in the Temple'*, reconstructed from that published by E. Gambart and Co., 1860

Ruskin's phrase again reveals a sense of a lack of conventional visual hierarchy, an odd prominence of individual objects. The *Spectator*'s reviewer describes being forced to restrict his/her focus in front of *The Shadow*: 'we felt disposed to hold up a hand so as to shade the eye from the distracting influence of the fidgety mass of shavings'.[48] *The Times* critic says:

> Every detail . . . is painted with a determined and equal completeness . . . It is evident at once that the painter of this picture rejects all the accepted rules as to selection, compromise, and designed variation of pictorial emphasis according to the relative importance of the thing painted. For him a fact is a fact, great or small, and there is only one way of painting facts – that is as thoroughly as a painter can. The artist's imaginative art . . . is exhausted when he has thought out the picture. In executing it he has only one rule to follow: paint everything in the same way, with the same insistence and the same care.[49]

Many reviewers of this picture also experience 'many points of view', and blame it on Hunt's pursuit of detail, 'an unthinking camera' which concentrates on mere 'details', or 'fragments'.[50] The writer in *The Times* is, however, more accurate when he ascribes the stepping forward of individual objects to a separation of the painting of 'facts' (mimesis) from the 'thinking out' (design).

My experience of being forced to compartmentalise my gaze in front of paintings by Hunt is apparently a common one. This is a result of a multiple focus defined by Smith as stereoscopic and by Barlow as a hierarchical division of spaces (pp 146 and 142). These recent explanations share a common theme with nineteenth-century responses, an uncomfortable awareness of a spatial assertiveness of parts that is not in keeping with the whole. I concur with Smith when she suggests that this feature is a result of the artist's concentration on the act of looking. The conception of a design as a system of signs, and the subsequent close scrutiny of each icon individually in order to import visual characteristics into the painting, seems to me the most simple explanation. These fragmented viewings relate to Hunt's fragmented process of production.

Mimesis and the gazes it provokes distract from the coherence of the design. This clarifies the common complaint that the realism of Hunt's work is inimical to its spiritual scheme and subject. A reviewer of *May Morning at Magdalen Tower* feels that fullness of 'effect' tends to 'crack the drawing convention' and generally prefers Hunt's images in black and white. The subversion of the linear design by fullness and 'effect' simultaneously subverts the meaning which it carries, what the reviewer calls 'the principle truth'.[51] The *Art Journal* also complains that the 'fierce effect' of *The Shadow* renders it unintelligible.[52]

This fragmentation of the gaze that apprehends the signifying scheme of the design, and consequent subversion of meaning, is demonstrated by an account of the exhibition of *The Light of the World* in Sydney, quoted by Maas: 'An elderly captious-looking gentleman had brought a cutting from the paper and was practically ticking off the points of the picture with the aid of this microscope. I could imagine his mind working this item:- ' "Apples on the ground representing harvest season".'[53] The restless identity of Hunt's multivalent details (see Chapter 7) is being dramatised here. The journalist mocks the contract between 'apples on the ground' and 'harvest season', recalling Sussman's 'droll' juxtaposition of tablecloth and sacred robe. The problematic reading of Hunt's images is directly related to the singularity of isolated, over-material icons whose relationship to their signifying function within the design is stylistically dislocated and therefore *revealed*, appearing contrived and absurd. Far more earnest and artificial images, such as those by Raphael, do not strike viewers as droll.

When more than one observer is viewing Hunt's work, the fragmented gaze becomes an actual diversity of viewpoint, enacting the diverse and alternative gazes of critics which Hunt feared so much (Chapter 4). The same journalist stresses the variety of gaze in the crush, each with its own response. These responses are linked to different parts of the painting. One person is looking at the blackberry leaves, another at the fingernails, or apples, or halo. Where one sees a halo another sees a moon, where one sees the 'Man of Meekness', another 'the king', mistaking the figure for Victoria's consort. The fragmented gaze of the artist, oversusceptible to literal, visual effect, weakens the signifying scheme and encourages a failure of consensus. Hunt's juxtaposition and elaboration of two mechanisms of control, the precision of the design and his exacting mimesis, paradoxically undermine the universality of the singular truth which he intends to depict.

The different gazes exhibited by viewers in front of Hunt's images are reminiscent of the diverse gazes of the figures that accompany the enlightened protagonists within the paintings themselves. The inspired gaze is usually represented in the form of an upward, outward general stare, exhibited by Hunt's Christs, his *Early Christian Missionary*, and *Rienzi* (plate 19). This connotes enlightenment and the prophetic role and can be equated to the gaze that sees the divine pattern in the world, reminiscent of the overall glance of the design. The protagonist's view is always pointed up by figures orientated in alternative directions, often contemplating death or falsehood. Their worldly focus on the merely material, unaugmented by spiritual meaning, recalls the localised, objective gaze.

Valentine (plate 7) suggests four different responses to a worldly event (deceit and sexual transgression as moral death) by focusing each person's thoughtful stare at a different point, a trick used again to great psychological effect in *The Hireling Shepherd* and *The Awakening Conscience*. The 'fallen' woman looks up and into nature and salvation in the latter, but the earlier female figure remains poised between death and life, distracted by her sensual partner's musing on details of mortality and superstition. A complex selection of gazes, including one which is blind, expresses a divergence of reaction to the spectacle of enlightenment in *The Finding*. Twenty-five figures look in different directions! This array of points of view articulates Hunt's sense of the world's diverse and uncomprehending reception of his pictures.

The Shadow offers the most extreme example: the Virgin's opposing gaze traces a trajectory which is the absolute reverse of that of the visionary. In *The Triumph*, however, their gazes are aligned. As in *The Shadow*, Christ's gaze is focused on redemption, but this Virgin's gaze has altered from a contemplation of mortality and artifice to a contemplation of the resurrected child. The two modes of death as physical mutilation and spiritual salvation held in tension in the earlier picture reside simultaneously in the gaze of the Virgin. Her son has escaped the 'terror'[54] and will be resurrected like the innocent (Chapter 4).

However, the apparent triumph of this unusual picture is not a complete one. Its production is accompanied by doubts and distress which subvert Hunt's assertion of the non-relative status of his prophetic vision. This ambivalence is betrayed by the opposing gaze of Joseph. He does not see the revelation, but looks away, 'intent on discovering any signs . . . of soldiery upon the road'. Like the Virgin in the previous picture, he focuses only on shadows of death, imaged by the wild dogs and the saw he carries. Stephens dissects this unsatisfactory configuration. Joseph's inability to perceive the Innocents causes him to deduce that 'Mary does not see these marvels; they are visible to Christ alone and to ourselves, who, nevertheless, cannot be supposed to be alike inspired. On the other hand, as we are on a parity with Joseph and Mary, it is hard to guess why we see more than they have the power to do.'[55] Hunt's conceit disintegrates under Stephens's ruthless logic. The alternative gaze of Joseph confers mortal status on all non-holy participants, including the observer and, by extension, Hunt himself. Characteristically, Hunt has included two different kinds of perception. His defensive representation of an incomplete, fearful and merely sensual point of view deconstructs his promotion of his own mortal gaze to a prophetic apprehension of the supernatural.

Stephens's tone is, like that of the Australian journalist, ironic; but he ridicules the strenuously elaborate depiction of the Innocents by means of a diversity of views within the painting, rather than without. He mocks Joseph's blindness to the Innocents: 'Even the splendid lustre which magically displays . . . the forms of his companions claims no more attention than the ass bestows on it.' In particular, he uses Hunt's extreme attention to detail, especially surface, to undermine the notion that the highly material children are a spiritual vision, 'they shine with inner beams, and are self-radiant, though massive'. Joseph's comic refusal to recognise their 'display' stands in for Stephens's sceptical refusal to acknowledge any more than a literal understanding of the mimetic elements of the picture.

Hunt's fears of relativity, of the alternative readings of the audience, are realised. Like other reviewers, Stephens unmasks the unilateral, subjective, artificial nature of the sacred design. However, it is Hunt's own anxious awareness of the relative nature of vision, his inclusion of the merely sensual focus, that of Joseph, that fragments the illusion, just as Issa does at Mount Hermon (Chapter 2). The tensions detected within Hunt's paintings by commentators only reflect tensions conceived by the artist himself, his own paradoxical, but failed, desire to reconcile 'the two views of life'. The artificiality identified by Stephens and others reflects the inherent tendency of the mimetic, materialist gaze to betray the artificial, constructed nature of the design, articulated by a dislocation of focus.

The different points of view included in Hunt's compositions echo those found so frequently in *Pre-Raphaelitism*. 'Evidence' in the form of description and quotation undermines the scheme of belief in the memoir (Chapter 1). Similarly, the sensual focus, in the form of the gazes of his figures and the mimetic exactitude of the artist, undermines the scheme of belief in the paintings. Hunt's anxious inability to reconcile his 'double awareness', his faith and his experience, demonstrated in the fluctuating doubt and conviction of his journals, inscribes itself into the art object via technique, as well as iconography, therefore, depicting and producing multiple viewpoints, and fragmenting authoritative, religious meaning. I shall now explore this conflict between the optical and the imaginative with reference to Hunt's records of the actual experience of colour painting from nature.

Mimesis and absence of meaning

Ruskin describes nature in *The Elements of Drawing* (1857) in a way that corresponds to Hunt's mimetic practice of replacing generalised impressions with defined forms: 'In the darkness of ground there is the light of the little pebbles or dust; in the darkness of foliage, the glitter of leaves, in the darkness of flesh, transparency; in that of a stone, granulation.'[56] He urges the artist to cultivate 'the innocence of the eye'; that is to say 'the sort of childish perception of these flat stains of colour, merely as such, without consciousness of what they signify'.[57]

Ruskin's description of a 'primal opticality'[58] evokes the incomplete, experiential state of the child, discussed in Chapter 3. There, I noted that the distant, subjective viewings of the tourist reinforce prophetic fantasies, but that when Hunt is painting close to, confidence is undermined and a childish self-image often prevails. A sense of meaning and order is disrupted. The distant, subjective way of looking relates to the design process, but the 'childish', mimetic procedure contradicts the design and undermines authority: 'quite bewildered about the head which looks right close but at a distance looks wrong I am quite in despair'.[59]

During painting, the signifying status of the complete object within the design, represented by its outline, is superseded by its status as a producer of local sensual effect. The initial imaginative process which prescribes objects in terms of their iconographical role and arrangement, alternates with the mimetic process which deduces them in terms of colour, 'without consciousness of what they signify', temporarily dissolving their identity as sign. Prettejohn comments on Hunt's execution of the fur in *Claudio and Isabella*:

> Landseer makes his fur brown – the colour we know fur ought to be. But Hunt gives us a kaleidoscopic mixture that seems to represent, not the colour the brain associates with fur, but the myriad hues the eye might perceive, at close range, in bright light – without trying to interpret the perceptions as representing fur'.[60]

Conversely, intellectual recognition of signifying potential will, as Ruskin notes, undermine the 'innocence' or mimetic sensitivity of the eye. Hunt, however, seeks to synthesise these two types of looking. Ruskin asserts that there are no outlines in nature and his own drawings dwindle at the edges, but Hunt, by contrast, has the contours of his design as artificial containers. He worries that he will not complete the children in *The Triumph* before they 'grow out of their outlines'.[61] Ruskin's studies stand alone, but Hunt's attempt to be parts contained within a linear map of meaning.

Executing *The Shadow* confronts Hunt's fear that he cannot reconcile reality with divine design. It is therefore not surprising that this Christ is even more 'firmly and substantially there'[62] than those in *The Light of the World* and *The Finding*. The only other figure faces away from the viewer. Christ is practically naked, near the observer and in a space which equates to real space. He is open-armed, fully exposed, no other object overlaps him. The slightly raking, evening light illuminates brightly and clearly. He is an adult, a man who works, who interacts with the real world of wood and metal in the room. His fingers curl, his biceps tense, his eyes roll, his mouth moves, he has teeth. His muscles are not the idealised or expressive contours of Raphael, but anatomical working parts. He is an extraordinarily physical Christ.

Just as the fact authenticates the image in the case of the landscape of the Holy Land, for Hunt, this image authenticates a desired fact at a time when his faith has been shaken by bereavement, as I have suggested in Chapter 4. The logic is a photographic one, as David Clarke has noted: 'mimetic art is produced as if it were something (some thing) having a reality prior to, or independent from the image.'[63] The problem that no mechanical device, no physical eye, could have actually witnessed this scene is explained away in Hunt's writings by the added factor of the metaphysical inner eye, or imagination. As I have established, the successful execution of this image verifies Hunt's imaginative capacity to witness the divine. The realisation of Christ is a realisation of his own artistic self-image. The actual act of mimesis is emotionally and intellectually loaded.

However, the close concentration necessary during mimetic painting biases Hunt's evaluation of the work away from his imagined ideal of Christ and towards form and paint. This is demonstrated by his frequent references to pigment and medium in the journal (noted in Chapter 5), and in a letter to Tupper: ''tho I trouble myself very much to make the form fine I fear sometimes my eye can scarcely be trusted having dwelt on it so long . . . it is a delicious canvas taking the paint like a hungry thing'.[64]

The reduction of the icon to a set of 'stains of colour' during close observation of nature necessarily interferes with imaginative judgement, or selection of what is beautiful or divine and what is not: 'I fear sometimes my eye can scarcely be trusted.' This diversion of focus from the whole, the significant and the sacred, to the meaningless, the sensual and the incomplete, perhaps augments Hunt's frequent failures of confidence in himself and his faith, during this period. The journal and the extensive discussions about belief in his letters reveal intense anxiety about his vision of the divine (Chapter 4). He fears critical scrutiny, yet longs for the consensus of another viewer, proof that his picture signifies successfully.

The crucial act of putting flesh on the textual skeleton of the design, of providing a physical image equivalent to a real, sensual experience of Christ, is described by Hunt at length in his journal. The reconciliation of the imagined and the optical is revealed to be deeply problematic. The importance of the head has been established and I shall confine my extracts to this particular task. In January, Hunt is already working from three models, and attempting to find a combination of features which matches his conception.[65] He goes on to study from himself and two sisters for the hair[66] and eventually employs a fourth model for the head.[67] He is indecisive, cannot settle on the best arrangement, sketches from guests, and often has three models waiting.[68]

This description of the actual painting method is typical of others in the diary:

> I am bewildered further with the difficulty of getting the head placed rightly on the neck I draw it rightly from Isaac but then his face is a very irregular one with jaws that spread out under the ears and with cheek bones that bulge out awkwardly, when I begin to refine upon this and succeed in getting the proportion of the face to suit the character, lo! the head has got out of place again.[69]

As with *The Scapegoat*, focusing on the head disrupts its relationship to the neck. More importantly, at the beginning of this passage, Hunt's gaze is scrutinising the anatomy of Isaac. It then transfers to an internal idea of the 'character' of Christ. He 'refines' the image towards this, but when he assesses it again, it has become anatomically incorrect. The non-signifying mimetic gaze and the signifying imaginative gaze do not coincide.

This tension between mimesis and meaning, real and imaginary appearance, is demonstrated throughout the diary in the pattern of Hunt's day. He tends to work from the model in the morning and evening, when the light is right, and refine the picture from imagination in the day or the late evening. He is almost always shocked at the aspect of his previous painting. In the morning, he often scrapes back a part, renews the ground, and starts again. The image seems able to satisfy only one set of criteria at once and disappoints when viewed afresh. It is interesting to note that this discrepancy might have been exacerbated by the fact that the ultraviolet component of direct sunlight may well have caused the zinc white that Hunt tended to use in underpainting to fluoresce. As a result, during *plein-air* viewing unpainted areas would have appeared brighter, and adjacent painted areas duller that at other times.[70]

The two modes of looking undermine each other. When Hunt works from the model, 'everything looks bad and hopeless',[71] but when he works from 'feeling', or from a dream of a painting of Christ, which furnishes him with details which are 'beautiful in many points',[72] the image fails to look realistic.[73] This results in daily repainting. The pattern of work is so astonishing that I have itemised it below:

8 February – 'I am bothered much about the head.' A long and minutely detailed analysis of the expression and angle of the face follows, concentrating on the open mouth. 'I work on in a fever to get it right.'
3 March – 'correct my face'.
16 March – changes the head again, although he has shown it to friends who consider it already perfect.
30 March – redesigns the head again.
7 April – feels 'head is right for finishing'.
12 April – alters the head.
17 April – scrapes back and renews the white ground on the head.
22 April – repaints the head.
26 April – 'Touch a little . . . on the head bringing the line of the left cheek a little further out, also the forehead'.
2 May – 'To get it [the head] ready for my final days painting make several changes in drawing in little parts'.
3 May – 'shocked to find' this 'too extreme and too partial . . . quite bewildered about the head which looks right close but at a distance looks wrong I am quite in despair'.
6 May – renews the white ground and makes the head smaller.
7 May – decides that the head is too small, and makes it larger.
9 May – repaints most of the head.
11 May – repaints the face, ears and 'expression' which is 'too painful'.
18 May – feels he has almost finished.
21 May – repaints hair for a second time.
30 May – alters the head again.
1 June – finds that the ground has become sandy in texture and renews it.

6 and 7 June – repaints the head.
7 June – finds the cheek is still rough and redoes it.
9 June – finds 'the head done but wanting a few touches'.
11 June – amends 'the contour of the cranium'.[74]

These entries represent work on just one area over only five months of the five years spent on the picture. Hunt sends it back to England on 15 June 1872, but after it is gone he still dreams of the head, 'and how it can be redone'. The painting is not completed until February 1873.[75] Other parts of Christ's body cause similar trouble. The journal reveals an artist who is locked into a cycle of destroying and renewing, or resurrecting, his painting, imitating the cycle of fear and hope demonstrated in his writings during this period.

The double vision exhibited in front of *The Shadow* occurs in front of *The Scapegoat* seventeen years earlier. Again, Hunt is disappointed every time he surveys what he has done and is delayed by a continuous need to repaint. On 2 March: 'Find my work of yesterday [the leg of the goat] utterly worthless'.[76] On 7 March, still working from the model of the goat: 'My first view of yesterday's work produces a fit of dissatisfaction.'[77] When he has copied a part of the model he 'grows satisfied with the result',[78] but when he alters his frame of reference, often the following morning, the appearance of the image fails to satisfy an imagined ideal.

Hunt is aware of this, and often dares not survey his picture in this comparative way, limiting his gaze to the part he is copying to avoid despair and help him concentrate: 'I dare not look at yesterday's work [the hair of Christ] but eagerly take advantage of the opportunity to work from Isaac to finish arms and body, begin at the rt hand and proceed downwards where am confronted by the hair I grow very unhappy admitting that it will never do'.[79] This account vividly demonstrates the restriction of focus during the mimetic painting process. The creation of the image is not an homogeneous, selective compromise between observation and imagination, but two separate acts which imply two strictly divided ways of looking, the isolated mimetic gaze and the overall imaginative gaze.

Hunt's susceptibility to optical effect at the expense of meaning and pictorial and spiritual coherence reinforces the idea that he is contending with a modernist awareness of the material character of nature and visual sensation. The mimetic process focuses this awareness, distilling a cognisance of the relativity of vision and of differences between the real and the imagined, and prompting the deepest periods of anxiety about belief and alienation, and the most determined efforts to reconcile these tensions.

The refusal of optical evidence to accord with Hunt's vision of the sacred undermines his faith and his persona. It produces a sense of mortality and physical symptoms which recall his description in *Pre-Raphaelitism* of copying from nature without spiritual insight, cited at the beginning of the previous chapter: 'a mere imitator gradually comes to see nature as claylike and finite, as it seems when illness brings a cloud before the eyes . . . [and] makes us esteem the world as without design or finish, unbalanced, unfitting, and unlovely, not interpreted into beauty as true art makes it' (1, 150). The journal records frequent illness. Hunt's eyesight falters,[80] and the weather, too, seems permanently cloudy. He transcribes the curls of hair on the model's chest, but they 'seem ungraceful'.[81] This lack of grace, or 'design', implies an absence of holy design in the world. The act of painting catalyses the concerns about sanity, health, critical and divine judgement and religious despair, described in Chapter 4.

This subversion of faith and meaning by physical effects echoes the subversion of the hopeful, abstract elements of Hunt's iconography by his depiction of references to physical death and suffering (Chapter 4). It also echoes the tendency of each individual icon to shift away from its symbolic role (Chapter 7). This breakdown of the visual language is accompanied by a breakdown of language itself. The structure of Hunt's letters and journals becomes disjointed, as it is in the painting notes from the Dead Sea. Hunt writes to Combe:

> I am in one of my stupid moods today and can ~~hardly~~ scarcely think of words to express my meaning in anything –. I wonder whether others ever get into the state in which even doubts come about the true value and even existence of the most simple word . . . I am in fact thinking about my picture.[82]

While painting *The Scapegoat* he says, 'I wish I could tell the tale as intelligibly as a stammering child to its mother.'[83] Direct confrontation with the material undermines imaginative coherence and a sense of childish weakness and confusion replaces authority.

The painting process described in the two diaries appears to be typical of projects throughout Hunt's life. There is no journal record of the production of *The Triumph*, but Hunt displays an even greater inability to finish. As I have shown, his letters during its execution again complain of doubts, illness, blindness and cloudy weather. Even in August, the days are 'short and dark'.[84] A letter to Tupper expresses the dislocation between the mimesis of small parts and overall signification, in language which is equally fragmented: The picture is:

> shewing itself forwarder . . . at spacious intervals of two weeks or more, /altho' not perceptively in shorter periods/. The work which tells being not so much that /done/ with the model before /me/ but that which I do as a sort of digest of my observations, which are /of isolated fragments of my model/ too ~~entangled~~ /confused/ to be helpful at the time.[85]

The alignment of the childish and prophetic vision depicted in this image seems to articulate Hunt's desire to achieve a reconciliation of experience and fantasy through a synthesis of the mimetic and imaginative gaze. Hunt describes his models as 'filthy, stupid, savage little urchins', however; the more fantastical the subject, the greater the disparity between it and reality. He is, as a result, forced to dissect the children into increasingly tiny, non-signifying 'fragments' in order to reconstruct them in a way that accords with his concept. More is demanded of the inner eye, requiring a promotion of artistic licence which parallels Hunt's new decision to image the supernatural in this image, and which perhaps contributes to his increasingly anxious need to claim prophetic sight during its execution (Chapter 4).

The failure of the material to conform to belief enacts itself in philosophy, iconography and the painting process, all of which interrelate. An inevitable dichotomy arises between the artistic, prophetic or imaginative, view and the sensual, childish, experiential or mimetic one; at a level even more fundamental than that discussed in previous sections. A heightened expression of this phenomenon occurs when Hunt is painting images of Christ and redemption, concepts which have been shown to be increasingly central to his self-image and his sense of security. *The Scapegoat*, *The Shadow* and *The Triumph*, are examples of this. The strenuous realism which commentators dismiss as inappropriate for ideal scriptural subjects is, in fact, an essential answer to questions about the truthfulness of the artist's vision in the face of fears about authority, propagating a circular, self-perpetuating attempt to synthesise reality and belief, expressed as repeated repainting.

Hunt bemoans the fact that each project is dragging on, but does not seem to be able to finish, despite the fact that he is continually claiming that a painting is complete. In August 1863, he plans a year-long visit to Jerusalem and expects to complete three or four paintings there.[86] He does not leave until 1866, and the death of Fanny delays his arrival until 1869. He stays in Jerusalem for over three years and only begins *The Shadow*. His letters are almost comically self-deceiving in their repeated claims that the work is almost ready. The 1872 journal reveals that he intends to send the painting off at the beginning of March. He revises his plan and hopes to send it by the end of the month.[87] On 13 April he expects to finish the head within four days, and on both the 2 May and 7 May, he thinks it will require only one more day's work.[88] He finally completes it in London in 1873. In 1877, Hunt writes from Jerusalem that he will finish *The Triumph* in the coming autumn.[89] It was in fact abandoned in 1880 and completed on a new canvas in 1884. He writes to Stephens of his slow progress and recent problems with materials, and adds: 'my work at the time was almost more than I could bear, there was scarcely a line in it that I could leave from one day to another'.[90]

The mimetic process undermines the arrangements of Hunt's life as well as the 'settled lines' of his designs (2, 295). The encounter between fixed plan and changeable experience, between fantasies about self-image, eternity, a divine order in nature, and fleeting nature itself, the limitations of eye, hand and paint, undermines the continuity between imagination and found experience, paint surface and vision, which Hunt asserts in *Pre-Raphaelitism*. It heightens fears that the image and the artist are not ready for judgement and not yet complete.

Notes

1 Letter to Stephens, 21 June 1870, BL, MS Don. e 67, 58v–59
2 Bayliss, W., *Five Great Painters of the Victorian Era* (London: Sampson, Low, Marston, 1902), p 110
3 Letter to Stephens, 21 June 1870, BL, MS Don. e 67, 52
4 Maas, *Hunt*, pp 38–42
5 Letter to Tupper, 21 November 1859, *Correspondence*, p 53
6 Journal, 31 March 1872, JRL, MS 1212, 17v; 28 January 1872, 5v; 3 March 1872, 13
7 Letter to Tupper, 28 December 1876, *Correspondence*, p 213
8 Bayliss, *Great Painters*, pp 122–3
9 Tupper, letter to Hunt, 24 May 1870, *Correspondence*, p 121
10 Letter to Scott, 10 August 1870, *Notes*, 2, p 95
11 A similarly 'democratic' approach is observed in earlier works by Hunt in Prettejohn, *Pre-Raphaelites*, pp 151–2; and Ridge, Hackney and Townsend, 'Pre-Raphaelite Technique'
12 Letter to Ernest Chesneau, 3 December 1882, 'Letters from John Everett Millais and William Holman Hunt in the Henry E. Huntingdon Library', ed. M. Lutyens, *Walpole Society*, 44 (1974), p 87
13 Gosse, *Father and Son*, p 192
14 Examined by the author, 15 February 1996, Southampton City Art Gallery
15 Ridge, Hackney and Townsend, 'Pre-Raphaelite Technique'; see also Hackney, Jones and Townsend, *Paint and Purpose*, p 83
16 Millais, E., diary, private collection, quoted Warner, M., 'Autumn Leaves', in *The Pre-Raphaelites* (Tate Gallery, 1984), p 141
17 Letter to Lear, 10 September 1862, JRL, MS 1214, 35
18 Scott, *Notes*, 2, p 50
19 Journal, 30 January 1872, JRL, MS 1212, 6
20 Letter to Combe, 11 May 1862, BL, MS, quoted Bronkhurst, J.E., 'The Afterglow in Egypt', in *The Pre-Raphaelites* (Tate Gallery, 1984), p 162
21 Journal, 1 March 1872, JRL, MS 1212, 12v
22 Journal, 29 February 1872, JRL, MS 1212, 12
23 Letter to Stephens, 3 February 1869, BL, MS Don. e 67, 33
24 Sizeranne, R. de la, *La Pienture anglaise contemporaine* (1895), quoted Rose, A., *The Pre-Raphaelites* (1977) (London: Phaidon, 1981), p 16
25 Bomford, D., et al., *Art in the Making: Impressionism* (London: National Gallery/ Yale University Press, 1990), pp 23–5

26 Ibid., p 43; also pp 27, 52
27 Prettejohn, *Pre-Raphaelites*, p 158, also p 178
28 Nochlin, L., *The Body in Pieces: The Fragment as a Metaphor of Modernity* (London: Thames and Hudson, 1994), p 37
29 Journal, 3 May 1872, JRL, MS 1212, 18
30 Watkinson, R., *Pre-Raphaelite Art and Design* (London: Studio Vista, 1970), p 72
31 White, J., *The Birth and Rebirth of Pictorial Space* (1957) (London: Faber and Faber, 1987), p 34
32 Barlow, 'Pre-Raphaelitism', p 74
33 *Illustrated London News* (6 December 1873), p 543
34 'A Fight for Art', p 477
35 Bennett, *Pre-Raphaelite Circle*, p 71
36 Journal, February–March 1855, JRL, MS 1211, 2–7
37 Letter to Tupper, 28 December 1876, *Correspondence*, p 213
38 Journal, 14–16 January 1872, JRL, MS 1212, 2; 13 February 1872, 9
39 Ibid., 8 February 1872, 7v
40 Ibid., 3 March 1872, 13
41 Letter to Tupper, 23 September 1876, *Correspondence*, p 208
42 Prettejohn, *Pre-Raphaelites*, p 136; Smith, 'Elusive Depth of Field', p 95
43 Ironside, R. and J.A. Gere, *Pre-Raphaelite Painters* (London: Phaidon, 1948), p 13
44 Gosse, *Father and Son*, p 192
45 Ruskin, J., 'The Pre-Raphaelite Artists', letter to the Editor, *The Times* (30 May 1851), p 8
46 *Illustrated London News* (6 December 1873), p 543
47 Ruskin, J., 'The Pre-Raphaelites', letter to the Editor, *The Times* (25 May 1854), p 7
48 *Spectator* (6 December 1873), p 1538
49 'Mr Holman Hunt's "Shadow of Death" ', *The Times* (2 December 1873), p 4
50 *Illustrated London News* (6 December 1873), pp 542–3, see also Prettejohn, *Pre-Raphaelites*, p 136
51 *Illustrated London News* (23 May 1891), p 275
52 *Art Journal* (1873), p 87
53 Maas, *Hunt*, pp 157–9
54 *The Triumph of the Innocents*, quoted Bennett, *Hunt*, p 53
55 Stephens, 'The Triumph of the Innocents', p 82
56 Ruskin, J., *The Elements of Drawing* (1857), ed. B. Dunstan (London: Herbert Press, 1991), p 27
57 Ibid., p 18
58 Crary, J., *Techniques of the Observer*, pp 95–6. Prettejohn parallels Pre-Raphaelite use of colour with a childlike perception in *Pre-Raphaelites*, p 151
59 Journal, 3 May 1872, JRL, MS 1212, 22
60 Prettejohn, *Pre-Raphaelites*, pp 144–5
61 Letter to Tupper, 28 December 1876, *Correspondence*, p 213
62 Ibid., 20 June 1878, p 247
63 Clarke, D. 'Gaze and the Glance', p 81

64 Letter to Tupper, 20 June 1878, *Correspondence*, p 247
65 Journal, January 1872, JRL, MS 1212, 2–4
66 Ibid., 30 January 1872, 6
67 Ibid., 6 February 1872, 7
68 Ibid., 2 March 1872, 12v
69 Ibid., 8 February 1872, 7v
70 Ridge, Hackney and Townsend, 'Pre-Raphaelite Technique'
71 Journal, 12 March 1872, JRL, MS 1212, 14v
72 Ibid., 3 March 1872, 13; Hunt's 'vision' of a painting of Christ in the style of Van Dyck is perhaps a memory of his *The Resurrection* (*c.* 1630–32, Wadsworth Athenaeum, Hartford), which seems to relate to the rather structured, idealised, linear sketch for the head reproduced in *Pre-Raphaelitism* (2, 297, figure 7.7). Hunt also owned a Van Dyck *Lamentation over the Dead Christ*, Holman-Hunt, D., 'The Holman Hunt Collection: A Personal Recollection', in *Pre-Raphaelite Papers*, ed. L. Parris (London: Tate Gallery/Allen Lane, 1984), p 218
73 Journal, 8 February 1872, JRL, MS 1212, 7v
74 Ibid., 1872
75 Letter to Lear, 11 February 1873, JRL, MS 1214, 45
76 Journal, 2 March 1855, JRL, MS 1211, 5v
77 Ibid., 7 March 1855, 6v
78 Ibid., 2 March 1855, 5v
79 Journal, 30 February 1872, JRL, MS 1212, 6
80 Ibid., 2 March 1872, 12v
81 Ibid., 2 February 1872, 6v
82 Letter to Combe, 10 October 1870, JRL, MS 1213, 25
83 Journal, 7 April 1855, JRL, MS 1211, 11
84 Letter to Stephens, 16 August 1879, BL, MS Don. e 68, 51
85 Letter to Tupper, 28 December 1876, *Correspondence*, p 213
86 Letter to Stephens, 25 August 1863, BL, MS Don. e 66, 79
87 Journal, 26 February 1872, JRL, MS 1212, 11v; 3 March 1872, 13; 15 March 1872, 15
88 Ibid., 13 April 1872, 20; 2 May 1872, 22; 7 May 1872, 22v
89 Letter to Tupper, 15 July 1877, *Correspondence*, p 222
90 Letter to Stephens, 21 June 1870, BL, MS Don. e 67, 58

9

Body: painter, painting and paint

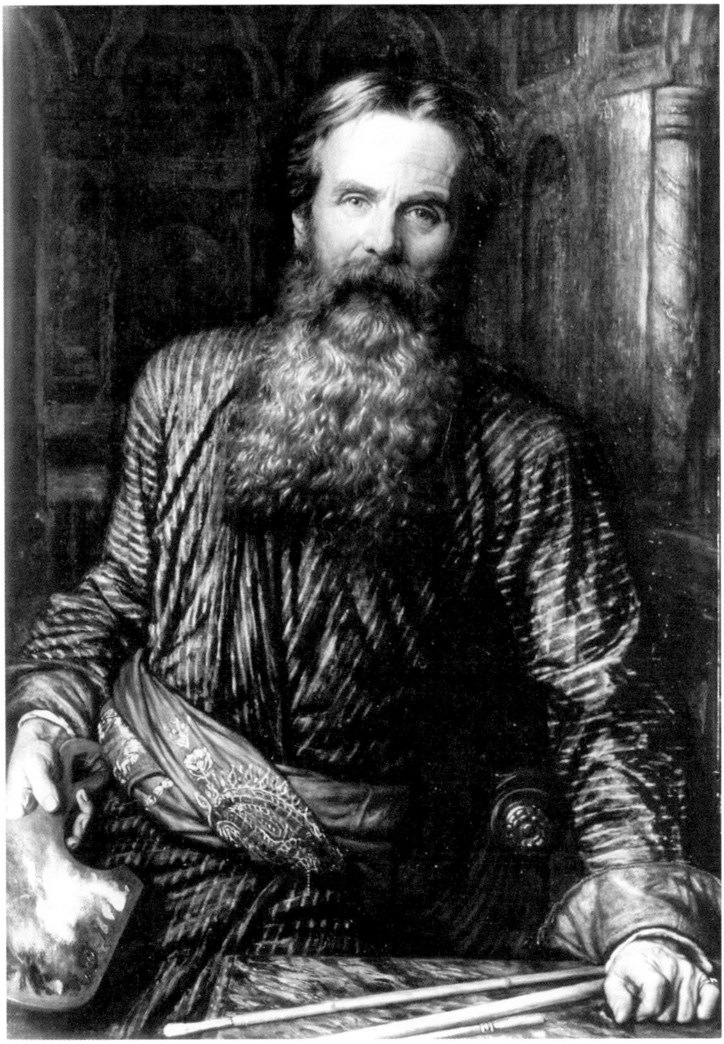

9.1
William Holman Hunt,
Self-Portrait,
1868

The previous two chapters demonstrate how the exploration and elaboration of imaginative and optical control over the image tend to expose the limits of this control. Moreover, an uncompromising pursuit of each form of visual authority hinders a synthesis of the two. Hunt's public writings present his optical mastery in terms of a scientific perception of the materials of the art object as well as an objective perception of nature. In the work of art, the latter, the perception of nature, is represented alongside moral and imaginative perceptions, by the image, but the perception of the material constituents of the object must be disguised in order to avoid the deconstruction of this image. Scientific acknowledgement of the material identity of the painting is redirected against itself, to serve the reproduction of the artist's vision.

This contradiction is distilled at the point of laying the brush on the canvas. Considerations of hue, viscosity and drying time interface with considerations of verisimilitude and meaning. The paint is simultaneously itself and that which it is depicting. Hunt's journals and letters reveal a practice of painting which is not an easy or empirical transformation from materials to image, but fraught with doubts about artistic skill, vision and authority. In the case of Hunt, these are addressed through an attempt to validate and reconcile the imaginative with the mimetic and the material, but when the latter – canvas, medium and paint – reasserts itself as such, artistic authority is undermined.

The immortal object

The thrust of Hunt's argument to the Society of Arts is towards an empowering of the artist to master technique through research and education. Hunt seeks an unusual degree of control over his materials in order to minimise their potential to deconstruct the image. He also worries about future degradation of the finished art object. The address exhibits a concern for material longevity and catalogues examples of deterioration to paintings by other artists. These represent a reversal of Hunt's proposed hierarchy of mastery: the materials attacking the image. Hunt's preoccupation with conservation equates to his search for immortality. However, the sealed perfection that he seeks implies an awareness of the potential of the paint surface to fracture and fall apart.

Hunt is well informed about conservation issues and, by the 1870s, he is paying close attention to the reliability of his supports, pigments, media and technique. He also takes pains to monitor and restore his paintings after they leave his studio (2, 343). He describes pictures by Hogarth cracking badly from being 'treated like dishes rather than pictures' and hung over hot pipes (2, 230). *The Light of the World* suffered a similar fate in Keble College, despite Hunt's advice (2, 411). He comments disparagingly on the inadequacies of transport and gallery staff (2, 457),[1] and records his own precautions in packing *The Triumph* on 'a bed of wedges in the case . . . face downwards with especial care to keep the surface from being touched'.[2]

Hunt's practice of having his paintings lined (usually a conservation measure reserved for aged works) before, or during, their execution doubled their strength as well as their rigidity. He also exhibits a sophisticated understanding of the way an extra canvas or wooden barrier can act as a buffer against humidity change to reduce 'expanding and contracting and so disturbing the preparation'.[3] Laurie explains this:

> Canvas has two great defects. In the first place it does not protect the back of the paint film from the attack of air and moisture. In the second place it is always changing, owing to the fibres readily absorbing moisture from the air . . . This . . . tends to crack the paint and loosen the priming from the canvas, and is probably the reason why relining is so often necessary.[4]

The use of loose linings and blind stretchers, for example on *The Triumph*, are a common feature of Hunt's paintings. They were understood to protect the rear of the canvas from dirt and pollution or 'foul air', as well as from humidity change.[5] The exposed side of the lining canvas was often further sealed with a layer of size and ground, as is the case with *The Scapegoat*. Glassed-in frames performed a similar protective function for the front of a picture. In addition, these barriers shielded the work from mechanical damage. The Society of Arts address recalls that Turner's *Childe Harold's Pilgrimage* (1832, Tate Britain) had been staved in from the back due to the absence of such protection.[6]

The strong, stiff canvas was intended to help protect the paint layer from mechanical movement which might cause cracks, as well as to present a firm surface. Hunt researched 'the difference of durability of good or bad cloth', and the address recommends sailcloth as 'the best preserved linen fibre, of the longest and finest character, chosen in order to make canvas of the greatest strength and lightness combined, suitable for lifeboats'.[7] Without a flicker of irony, it cites Turner's *Shipwreck* (1805, Tate Britain) as a work whose good condition illustrates the benefit of using this support.[8] Most other commonly available supports are berated as too flimsy or susceptible to atmosphere.[9]

The address catalogues unsuccessful grounds and the eventual disruption to the image that results from them.[10] It reports a restorer's discovery that 'Van Dyck's grounds were often very carelessly laid and . . . the characteristic slovenliness had . . . led to rapid deterioration'.[11] This is contrasted with well-preserved samples of Hunt's own painstakingly applied, multiple ground layers, manufactured after the manner of quattrocento artists.[12] Hunt's belief in the permanence of this firm ground is, however, misplaced, as it is designed for use on panels and tends to peel, crack or flake when supported on cloth. His use of strong, rigid canvas, linings and backboards are attempts to limit this effect, to give the canvas the invincible nature of the panel, but it is generally accepted that a thin, flexible ground is the safest way to accommodate the natural movements of a canvas support and reduce serious cracking.[13]

Hunt's precautions have, therefore, only been partially effective. The National Museums and Galleries on Merseyside conservation records for *The Scapegoat* and *The Triumph* report an absence of overall age craquelure, but they remark that a second kind of cracking has resulted from the inflexibility of the thick grounds. Conservation scientists at the Tate have noted a similar pattern.[14] Hunt's habit of including copal varnish in his priming mixture gives the surface a hard feel and look, but actually also renders it more brittle and likely to fracture. This is exacerbated by the addition of zinc white, which according to Laurie, 'does not form so flexible a coating in oil as white lead, and is considered by some to be more apt to crack'.[15] Hunt's use of copal and zinc to make the ground smoother also undermines the adhesion between it and the paint above. Manchester Art Gallery conservation records state that *The Shadow* exhibits delamination and lifting of the paint. Hunt takes the odd step of allowing aesthetic connotations of strength – the thick, rigid and impermeable glassy surface – to supersede actual material safety.

A similar bias is evident in Hunt's attitude to the medium. The address sensibly notes the ravages caused by the use of additives such as bitumen, wax and megilp and surveys painters, such as Reynolds, who have been 'seduced into its use'.[16] The addition of varnish is, however, defended. A pure oil medium is admitted to reduce cracking, but it is noted that, without varnish, it fails to produce 'a shining effect' or, more importantly, to preserve brilliance: 'colours made from lead are quickly oxidised by impure air, and colours of the slightest flightiness of disposition, if unprotected by varnish, soon fade or change'.[17] The smooth 'shining' oil/varnish surface is advocated as a necessary sealant, reminiscent of the glass of Hunt's frames.

Despite the acknowledgement that a pure oil medium is flexible, Hunt's address takes pains to promote the thin, uniform oil/varnish layer as equally resistant to fracture, blaming cracking on loose, thick handling. Reynolds's ruined works are linked to his experiments with texture, and it is noted that Turner's *Richmond Hill* (1819, Tate Britain) had cracked where there had been an extensive use of impasto, but not in the glazed areas.[18] *Pre-Raphaelitism* praises the smooth surface of Mulready's *The Wedding Gown* (1846, Victoria & Albert Museum):

> This painting had evidently been executed with care, no coat of paint being plastered over another, and the layers being limited, for the sake of purity of hue, to as few as could produce the desired tint. Pictures thus conducted are of admirable permanence, as quattrocento paintings testify. (2, 457)

The address describes an unnamed work by Reynolds as, conversely, weak, uncoloured, and incomplete: 'with its gaping fissures, its lost colour, and its avalanche of background, descending on to the very core of the picture, a cause of serious pain'.[19] In fact, the addition of copal varnish to an oil medium renders the paint layer very fragile and will have contributed to the cracking noted above. It is only careful handling of Hunt's work and their rigid supports that have prevented more serious deterioration.[20] The belief in the strengthening effect of varnish additives is only partially rational. Hunt's arguments for its use are based on a construction of the method as traditional. Again, it seems that the hard, smooth, saturated look connotes strength and a sense of 'complete' intactness in aesthetic terms, which override scientific objectivity.

The concept of aesthetic strength that characterises Hunt's choice of surface and support can be extended to his attitude to colour. The address repeatedly refers to pigments in exchangeable terms of strength and brightness: Field's 'madders were of far superior strength';[21] 'the earliest works are still the brightest and the strongest in colour'.[22] Van Eyck's paintings are eulogised as examples of the 'brightest' and 'strongest' pigment, exhibiting the same 'pure character, as the day they left the artist's studio'. Hunt regrets that for subsequent artists: 'the aim was gradually becoming less to obtain unsullied purity and brightness, but to develop all the lower harmonies of light and colour; but in the fewer points where brightness was sought, the power to produce and retain fullness is only less remarkable'. A series of his own pigments on 'trial canvases' are displayed to the Society of Arts audience and each is assessed in similar terms.[23] Little attention is paid to earth pigments, despite their extreme stability, and emphasis is given to bright blues, greens, reds and yellows, suggesting that, within this context, 'brightness' or 'fullness' is an aesthetic measure of strength and durability.

One cause of pigment instability is injudicious mixing, as some pigments can react with each other. The address cites the 'well-known misalliance, cadmium and emerald green . . . it was within two weeks of its first application – nearly black'.[24] The blackening properties of the red lead in Roberson's Vermilion contributed to the difficulties seen in the 1872 journal.[25] Hunt's habit of minimal colour mixing is a precaution against contamination and degradation as well as a means of maximising brightness. The sealing of pigments in varnish also keeps them pure.[26] The 'purity' of unmixed colour therefore connotes aesthetic strength and strength in the sense of resistance to contamination and degradation. 'Impure' oil is also blamed for darkening and subduing some pigments.[27]

Hunt's aesthetic preferences are based on a profound sense of the painting as whole and inviolable. The split gaze which constructs the art object in both aesthetic and material terms, surveyed in Chapter 6, merges into a conflation of aesthetic and material strength. In addition to this, Hunt's particular choice of vocabulary suggests that the tendency to conflate aesthetic strength and physical strength with moral strength, noted in Chapter 4, is also applied to his materials. The frequently used word 'power', for example, is multivalent. Copal varnish has 'much greater power'[28] than mastic. *Pre-Raphaelitism* cites post-Raphaelite art as ceasing to be 'a living power' and parallels this with the 'corruption' and 'disintegration' of that society (2, 488). When these usages are viewed alongside the repeated description of pigment in related terms of power, meaning brightness, strength and 'unsullied purity', the word seems to construct a blurred notion that is aesthetic, physical and moral.

Hunt's hierarchy of art materials is expressed in terms of moral strength. Spirituality, or divine beauty, is, in turn, expressed in terms of art, precious stones and colour. The address's emphasis on the jewel-like brightness and glassy surface of the painting recalls the revelatory language of glass and jewels employed in his visionary descriptions of landscape: 'the purity of the azure sky, the prismatic sweetness of the distant hills, the gaiety of hue in the spreading landscape, and the infinite richness of vegetation' (2, 492). Hunt's images are intended to be an actual reflection of the creation of the 'Master Artist', and it would seem that the constituents of the art object also enact this fantasy. The painting is both visually and materially spiritual. The promise of eternal life that Hunt finds in his augmented, symbolic perception of the world is literalised in the form of powerful, luminous, uncorrupted colours sealed into a glassy, invulnerable layer of paint.

The weak object

The issue of conservation, of the health or immortality of the art object, expresses related notions of health, virtue and spiritual immortality. Dull or textured paint and pigment are, correspondingly, spoken of as impermanent, low, cracked, ruined, polluted; as irresponsible, slovenliness, misalliance, flightiness of disposition, and that which is foreign, connoting disease, mortality and immorality. A letter to Tupper describes Roberson's orange vermilion as 'adulterated with 10 per cent of villainy'.[29] Orpiment, a chemically unstable pigment, is 'treacherous', and 'purple lake – now distrusted'.[30] Others are 'dangerous', and 'fickle', and need to be 'shut up in amber'.[31] Oil must be 'perfectly purified'.[32] Earth pigments, such as umber, are very stable, but Hunt calls them 'clays' and associates them with the 'claylike and finite' (1, 150), perceiving them as both dull and weak (2, 457). The most extreme language is reserved for 'the treacherousness of the rich brown' of seductive bitumen. Its use has caused pictures to be 'doomed to complete destruction' from it 'tearing the paintings to pieces'. The memoir reminds us that it is also called 'Mummy . . . for this is a preparation of Egyptian corpses' (1, 454–5).

The last chapters of *Pre-Raphaelitism* dwell on both the moral and material health of English painting: 'It is a history of a movement which strove to bring greater healthiness and integrity to every branch of formative art . . . which are all dependent on the use of materials for expression' (2, 466). These pages are cluttered with references to 'healthy work' (2, 485), contrasted with 'impurity' (2, 464). This polarity positions Hunt's own paintings as other to the sickly, flaunting and meretricious work of artist's such as Rossetti, 'surrounded by a host of flatterers that he is persuaded that his hand works miracles and so leaves the most mucky mess of opaque dirt to represent beautiful Flesh'.[33]

The penultimate chapter focuses on craft and contains a plea for conservation (2, 456–61). A single paragraph extends over five-and-a-half pages embracing materials, conservation and morality. It starts by reviewing instances of paintings being spoiled by rough treatment, dirt, and even the contaminating breath of onlookers. Cracked or porous paint layers, lacking medium, are identified as particularly susceptible (2, 458). The solution is to fill in cracks and re-saturate the surface with the original varnish medium. Only when it is sealed, and 'years have dried and hardened this coating', may an overall varnish (usually mastic) 'be employed with impunity, because it will not be sucked in by the original pigment'. The passage goes on to add, moreover, that 'Even thus protected, it should be remembered that pictures are not made to handle or touch, for the purity of the paint will be sullied by such treatment, and particles of dirt will be driven into the interstices.' This is a clear valorisation of the smooth, perfect surface as both integral to the art object and to its resistance to contamination or deterioration.

The paragraph goes further, however, claiming that the integrity of materials is fundamental to the moral pursuit of art itself, and to the identity of the artist: 'any indications in paintings, of want of loving thought and attention, to have the material employed well cared for, beautiful, and precious, is a sure sign that the fabricator is not an artist by nature' (2, 458). The address describes Hogarth taking similar pains in painting and varnishing and commends 'the simple, honest character' of his method.[34] To ignore this traditional care is to risk 'fatality', and will produce 'sottish barbarism'; even the 'nation is doomed' (2, 459). The tendency to do so is like a poisonous seed blown from abroad, producing 'noxious or benign growth'. The physical purity and safety of the painting is left behind as the text expands into a commentary on purity itself (2, 461–2). Art must be technically pure *and* free of 'degrading inclinations', such as 'the evil contagion of false sentiment' which might cause 'temporary disaster', or 'final catastrophe', to the nation. It blames copyright law, fashion and journalism for the 'breeding' of 'works done without a trace of patient study and bearing evidence of ignorant handling of materials'.

The structure of this extraordinary paragraph enacts the merging of physical and aesthetic strength and purity that I have identified in Hunt's painting practice, and also proposes more general connections with the moral corruption of the art object, the artist, and the nation as a whole. The Society of Arts address exhibits a similar pattern. Again, the durability of artists' materials is linked to national salvation: 'a painter's work is not worth the doing – to anyone but his humble self – if it will not last for generations of eyes'. The accumulating effects of a badly joined canvas are likened to a spreading cancer, 'a terrible growth requiring the surgeon's knife', but it is not clear whether the 'growth' represents the faulty canvas or the alleged national habit of their use and supply.[35] The metaphor returns at the conclusion of the address: 'It is my duty here to insist upon it that there is a sore, and to track the evidence of this, passing by all that betokens independent health . . . it is high time that the wound should be probed and that a remedy should be found'.[36]

This language makes use of a vocabulary of health and infection common in other nineteenth-century debates. The motif of a poisonous seed was in common usage. George Moore, for example, had described the New English art as 'a seed blown over-sea from a ruined garden', ten years before.[37] Anthea Callen has also found associations between both dark pigmentation and the broken surface and dirt and immorality in contemporary French discussions of Degas's pastels.[38] In *Illness as Metaphor*, Susan Sontag notes that cancer and TB, both associated with growths, were loaded with moral overtones, and concludes that 'In the nineteenth century, the notion that the disease fits the patient's character . . . was replaced by the notion that it expresses character'.[39]

In *Dangerous Sexualities: Medico-moral politics in England since 1830*, Frank Mort surveys the way that mid-nineteenth-century discourse presents epidemics in both physical and moral terms. He discusses reformers of public health who extended the significance of their influence to the moral safety of the country. He defines binary oppositions between 'physical health/non-health, virtue/vice, cleanliness/filth, morality/depravity' which are reminiscent of those displayed in Hunt's practice and writing.[40] Mort quotes one reformer, Charles Kay, in his autobiography of 1877, speaking of 'the inseparable connection between the mental and moral condition of people and their physical well-being' as a relevant factor in 'contending with the consequences of formidable social evil'.[41] It is necessary only to replace 'people' with 'painting' to provide a direct echo of Hunt's language of artistic 'moral contagion'.[42] The memoir constructs its protagonist as a comparable reformer of art and the morality of the nation as a whole. 'Hogarth, Reynolds, Raeburn, Gainsborough, and Romney' are characterised similarly: 'too strong to be repressed . . . they produced an art which was . . . healthy, robust, and superior to maudlin sentimentality and vice glamoured over with *fevered* tears' (emphasis added) (2, 477). The address employs equivalent terms, claiming that painting was 'resuscitated' in George II's reign.[43] Where Kay investigates the role of the state in public health, Hunt repeatedly returns to the responsibility of government to ensure that 'the true British distinction of art must not be impaired, and the energy of its leaders to keep it pure must not be frustrated' (2, 477).

This discussion is supplemented by two instances where a direct parallel is made between the professions of medicine and art. Both artists and doctors in the nineteenth century campaigned to elevate themselves to the status of expert, enfranchised in the running of the country.[44] The practical use of the painter to the nation was, however, more nebulous.[45] The memoir appeals for respect for the expertise of the artist and education in master technique by putting it in medical terms: 'He is only a quack who commences ministering to the sick in ignorance of those carefully tested experiments which have led to modern methods of healing.' It singles out the 'caretaking of materials' as one example of this learning (2, 486). The metaphor continues throughout the subsequent analysis of the role of morality in art, and that of the nation, claiming that 'Every age has its special trial. Ours today arises from an unprecedented blight, which ignores the reflection of heaven's beauty in Nature . . . The degradation of art is nothing less than a sign of disease in Society' (2, 488). A few pages before this, a conservation is recorded between Hunt' and his physician and friend, Dr Gull:

> Once talking with Sir William Gull of the force of heredity in disease, he reasoned that however strong this might be, there is a counterbalancing action in nature which throws off the taint and works for perfection; otherwise the transmission of disease would have destroyed the human race, and all creation, ages ago. I commend this scientific teaching to authors inclined to inculcate pessimism and revolt against moral law. (2, 470–2)

The memoir casts Pre-Raphaelitism as the redemptive, 'counterbalancing action in nature', citing its 'searching for the truth before nature herself', its 'prismatic hues' and purity of materials, as evidence of its healthy, *natural* role.

In contrast to this, Impressionism is singled out as an instance of 'a poisonous influence', recalling the poisonous seed. An anonymous, but vivid account of the violent and debauched life of the Beaux-Arts student is quoted at length (probably drawn from Du Maurier's *Trilby*, 2, 472–5).[46] It is interesting that the fate allocated to these delinquent artists, cast out by their families, living off prostitutes, 'leads nearer and nearer to the rat holes under the bridges of the Seine' (2, 474), paralleling the fate of the immoral woman in nineteenth-century myth. Lynda Nead's investigation of nineteenth-century notions of the 'fallen woman', *Myths of Sexuality*, explores a conflation of disease and immorality similar to that noted here and by Mort.[47] Foreign influence is associated with these ideas in Augustus Egg's *Past and Present III* (1858, Tate Britain), which depicts an outcast at the margins of the Thames under a bridge bearing advertisements for trips to Paris.[48]

Nead quotes a review in the *Art Journal*, which echoes this concern in its condemnation of European art in contrast to the English school where 'generally in short is found the "awakened conscience" somewhere, which in the end sufficiently well reconciles aesthetic effects to ethical laws . . . nothing . . . can be more healthful, honest, and heartfelt than many of our English pictures'.[49] Hunt speaks in a similar tone as early as 1855, when he writes to Tupper from Jerusalem of his determination to find 'some means of doing my part towards purifying London of some of the impurities therein'.[50]

The wide-ranging application of the pure–corrupt polarity in the last two chapters of *Pre-Raphaelitsm* reflects contemporary ideology in its declaration of the importance of the purity of art as a reflection of the health and morality of the artist and his influence on English society in general. This system of moral connections is, however, extended. Social, cultural and aesthetic ideas, couched in the vocabulary of health and disease, are related right back to the material purity and intactness of the art object. This intense concern for care over materials and conservation measures is, moreover, as we've seen, closely bound to the spiritual persona of the prophet. A similar, but negative, moral connection between paint and painter is expressed in Hunt's account of the Impressionist, who 'degraded in mind and crippled in all his powers of representation and expression, has produced on his canvas or in his clay the inevitable result of idleness, dissipation and corrupted taste' (2, 475). These 'hideous canvases . . . chaotic in form, of sullied pigment plastered on offensively, both as to tint and texture' recall Rossetti's 'mucky mess of opaque dirt to represent beautiful Flesh'.[51] Both styles are presented as the antithesis of Hunt's own. French sculptures 'of evil proportioned humanity displaying a series of monstrous developments in lieu of heavenly designed muscles' (2, 471), pointedly differ from the ideal body of his Christ. Impressionist immorality connotes the sickness and deformity of the artist, his art and the art object.

Poor materials are also personified in the Royal Society address, and again conflated with both image and artist. It details, for example, the degradation of Thomas Lawrence's portrait of *Mrs Siddons* (1789, Dulwich Picture Gallery) resulting from a bad canvas support: 'the whole canvas is mapped with seams, dividing all the work as though it were in preparation to turn it into a dissecting puzzle'.[52] Lawrence's portrait of *Benjamin West* (1821, Tate Galley), on the other hand, is on 'good . . . sturdy firm cloth' and 'well preserved'.[53] In *London, A Social History*, the late Roy Porter quotes a nineteenth-century account of lower-class prostitutes: 'bare-headed, in *dirty-white muslin* . . . with originally ugly faces horribly *seamed* with small-pox, and disfigured by vice' (emphasis added).[54] The material aspects of the paintings re-enact a valorisation of the artist and a condemnation of the artifice of the actress, in keeping with Hunt's distinction between artistic truth and theatrical fantasy, especially that of the acrobat/performer, as discussed in Chapter 4 (p 94). The dark and 'pernicious Dead Sea Pitch' is, similarly, associated with the role of the Dead Sea landscape as a 'figure of sin'.[55] The madness and violence of the subject matter of Géricault's 'Wreck' is conflated with the fate of the painting itself, 'doomed . . . to perdition by the use of the Dead Sea Pitch'.[56]

The process of selection and arrangement which constitutes the true artist's visual recognition of divinity in the world, is also applied to Hunt's choice and manipulation of materials. A moral hierarchy obtains concrete reality in the form of the art object, constructing a continuity between belief and tangible actuality.

The artist and the art object

Hunt's insistent valorisation of the painting in exchangeable terms of corporeal and moral health suggests that the intimate relationship between his work and his self-image, proposed in Chapter 4, may operate at the most fundamental physical level.

The preoccupation with technique and materials which culminates in Hunt applying to address the Society of Arts, coincides with his struggle to finish *The Triumph*, when, as we've seen, his writings set up complex parallels between artist and art. In October 1878, he takes precious time out for a trip to Paris to survey suppliers.[57] A letter to Stephens of the following January expresses heartfelt concern for the safety of the nation's paintings.[58] Hunt borrows books on technique in December,[59] and reads Eastlake, Vitruvius and Cennini in April 1880.[60] In the same month he writes to *The Times* on the subject, places an advert for aged pigment samples in the *Athenaeum* and delivers the address and publishes 'Materials in use by Artist Painters' in *The Architect*. This period is also characterised by profound doubts about God and the prophetic role associated with fears about skill and sanity and the success of the painting, and about the health of Hunt and his family. Hunt's campaigning for the immortality of the art object coincides with anxieties about the immortality of the artist.

Pre-Raphaelitism dates the beginning of an interest in conservation from the detection of the unreliable pigments used in *The Shadow*,[61] but private correspondence suggests a more intriguing origin. The concern arises before beginning this painting and before specific problems with pigment have arisen in any serious form. The first reference comes in 1868, in the period following Fanny's death and leaving Cyril in England. Hunt returned to Florence, partly to finish his wife's tomb. Letters from this time contain discussions of conservation measures in Florence, and plans for an article for the *Athenaeum* about crowds of careless visitors and consequent 'damage to works of art in Italian galleries'.[62] Hunt sends a draft to Stephens and also mentions a proposed pamphlet on 'the reputed discovery of oil painting by the Van Eycks'.[63] Concern about the care and durability of art can be seen to have emerged immediately after an experience of death, a failure of eschatological hope and the onset of anxieties about the care of the child.

These doubts coincide with a construction of the artist as vulnerable, neglected child which, as I have shown in Chapter 3, becomes particularly predominant in writings after 1867. This issue manifests itself in letters and published writings in the form of complaints that English art is inadequately nurtured or cared for. In the final chapters of *Pre-Raphaelitism*, the grievance is closely linked to themes of conservation: the inherent vulnerability of art objects, their inability to serve successive generations and a fear that successive generations will not, for their part, care for them. The 1877 letter to Tupper links the neglected artist directly to a failure to conserve his art, 'marbles broken . . . colours that have changed while the varnish is drying'.[64]

The 'loving thought and attention' (2, 458) required by the painting is related to personal issues of health and nurture in the letters written to Stephens shortly after Hunt's bereavement. There is great pressure to return immediately to England to facilitate the care of Cyril, 'Fanny's dying wish',[65] but Hunt attempts to look after the baby himself and to complete *Isabella*. Neither go well, and departure is postponed in the hope that Cyril can be returned to health and the picture can be completed. The discussions of conservation outlined above are accompanied by an odd layering of accounts of the child's plumpness with accounts of the progress of the painting.

In June 1867, Hunt describes typical 'difficulties' and delays in getting *Isabella* up to a point of 'finish' where he can take it to London and immediately speaks of Cyril in parallel terms, reminding us of the 'fat full firmness'[66] of his preferred paint surface: 'I shall rejoice beyond measure at taking my poor little baby away from here for England . . . I am continually persuading myself that he has got past all his difficulties and that he is on the point of becoming a proper fat little cherub, when suddenly he takes cold and loses all his infant plumpness.'[67] Further alternations of comments on the state of painting and of the child follow. Letters written between April and September of 1867 continually interchange frustrations with work and with the search for a suitable nurse to provide milk for the baby. They convey a powerful sense that Hunt cannot return to England until both the son and the picture are in a presentable state of fatness/finish. Problems in completing his picture become related to the wholeness of the child, both of which have been shown to be fundamental to the artist's sense of self. It is as though the habitual reluctance to reveal a work for judgement until it is faultless and invulnerable has been extended to Cyril. The perfection of the child represents, like the painting, a means of repairing self-image and reinstating the prophetic, 'adult' artist.

A sequence of unrealised claims that both baby and painting will soon be ready, foreshadow the language and the pattern of hope and delay exhibited while executing *The Shadow*. Fanny dies in December. On the 5 April Hunt says he will be ready to leave in 'a few days'.[68] On the 17 June, 'three or four weeks' are needed for 'touching'.[69] He finally returns in September. The painting is not complete and Cyril is very ill, as Hunt has accidentally employed a fake wet-nurse with no milk.

The anxieties about feeding the child have an odd affinity with anxieties about saturating the paint surface with medium. As we have seen, *Pre-Raphaelitism* states that premature varnishing (with mastic) of a paint surface that has not already been thoroughly saturated with a second application of oil/copal medium will cause the paint to be invaded by the varnish and cause cracking, which will in turn allow contamination by dirt or saliva (2, 457–8). This is not true. The pigment is personified, wrongly described as having 'sucked up' oil and dried out, therefore needing another application of medium to return its 'lustrous' character and its strength. This idea has no scientific basis because the 'drying' of a paint layer is misnamed. Paint in fact undergoes a slow chemical change which renders it progressively harder: 'Linseed oil is a "plastic", not a solution that dries by evaporation that can be reconditioned by adding more solvent.'[70]

The illusion that a paint layer 'drinks' medium does not occur in Hunt's detailed letters about the use of medium to Scott in the

1860s. Neither is it proposed to the Society of Arts. This is perhaps due to the fact that this particular interpretation of the behaviour of the paint surface has no scientific grounds. Its expression in *Pre-Raphaelitism*, in a paragraph dealing with wider notions of the care of the painting, of painters and with moral fitness, is perhaps conditioned by anxieties about artistic authority, which, as we have seen, are often expressed as concerns about nurture and health. The idea is reiterated in a letter to J.D. Batten, in 1907. It advises: 'feeding' the paint layer with medium to create 'a solid mass . . . like a plate of glass, and afterwards mastic varnish would do no harm'.[71]

The metaphor of feeding reappears in the 1870 letter to Tupper which discusses worries about the reliability of Hunt's eye: he consoles himself with the idea that the new canvas is 'delicious . . . taking the paint like a hungry thing'.[72] In the same year, the well-being of the painting is linked directly to that of his child: 'The Waughs of course being with him always cannot judge of his health, they take of course the view wh a painter does of the work under his eyes believing it to be what he intends it to be.'[73] Two months later he writes to Scott about convention in art: 'To measure and imitate the works of soul inspired workers of previous ages is not producing the bread of life. It is foolish as if it were to give a baby a lay figure for a wet nurse.'[74] Here, ideas about a failure of artistic vision become mixed up with ideas of starvation and neglect, and combine in the startlingly cruel and apt image of the lay figure as wet-nurse. Hunt's 1872 journal also reveals that he dreams alternately of his 'little boy' and 'defects' in the painting.[75] A clearly thought-out connection between the painting and the child cannot really be proposed from this evidence. However, the accumulation of anxieties around themes of artistic integrity, nurture and health does suggest that Hunt's habitual conflation of material and moral qualities extends to a more surprising conflation of two separate physical entities, the painting and the body, implying a literal application of the vocabulary surveyed in the previous section.

These corporeal associations are also evident during the execution of *The Triumph*. The wholeness, healing and nourishment represented by the iconography of the picture are undermined by metaphors of mutilation ascribed to battles with its materials detailed in Chapter 4. Struggles to 'cure' the weak support and repair 'serious sores' in the ground, recall the 'terrible growth requiring the surgeon's knife'[76] resulting from the faulty canvas mentioned in the Society of Arts address. Its subsequent recommendation of a sailcloth support, 'suitable for lifeboats',[77] relates these problems to a broader sense of vulnerability and neglect, so often expressed as a 'half made' boat negotiating a storm.

The split sense of self which is exhibited in the unresolved iconography of the images and in dislocations arising out of a split technique, is also expressed in Hunt's ambivalent personifications of the art object. Published texts valorise his technical expertise and ascribe a completeness, purity and durability to the objects he makes, in keeping with the prophetic persona. However, the actual process of manipulating the materials confronts the artist with the limits of mastery, and undermines fantasies of authority. Anxieties about mortality and a childish self-image become associated with the physical characteristics of the incomplete work of art, deepening the reciprocal relationship between the artist and the art object.

As I have shown, in private writings, concerns about health are closely juxtaposed with concerns about the practical difficulties of painting. The trials of *The Triumph* illustrate the idiosyncratically unremitting nature of this preoccupation. In December 1876, Hunt is already speaking of death and complaining of illness and headaches resulting from his work.[78] A letter of January 1877 speaks of exhaustion and an urgency to finish and concludes: 'I cannot get rid of a third alarm in the shape of the falling out of my teeth which frightens me with premature old age or imminent.'[79] In July, Hunt is beset by fevers and writes: 'There have been times "when I have been half in love with easeful death" '.[80] He returns to the subject of his draining strength later and adds: 'Perhaps one fact in my present experience makes me think more of troubles in battalions for the last few years I have been hindered in the most strange degree by difficulties caused by materials'. Subsequent correspondence continues to juxtapose these two themes. An account of 'hurt' to *The Triumph* during transit to London, in a letter to Stephens, is bracketed by complaints about the artist's own battered health.[81] After his return in April 1878, he repeatedly writes to Tupper of his conviction that both death and 'the renewal' are near.[82] In October, he is more hopeful after trying out a new ground: 'today I did what for a long time has been most rare, and that is made my picture forwarder instead of backwarder and so have eaten my dinner in better spirits'.[83] Frustrations persist throughout the year, however, as do complaints of illness.[84] The letter to Stephens in January 1879 containing a plea for conservation measures to protect the safety of the nation's paintings, infers that Hunt has been seriously ill.[85] By April, he is very weak; his handwriting is spidery and he requests the help of a boy to grind colours.[86] He goes partially blind for a period soon after.[87] In August 1879, he is still battling: 'Oh the darkness of the hour on which I first met with this canvas.' Tellingly, Hunt's preoccupation is still with the imperfect 'surface' of the painting.[88] Three weeks later, he continues to voice despair: 'My very life is bleeding away.'[89] In December, he considers abandoning the picture altogether: 'if I go on with it I am not sure that it will not kill me outright, as it nearly did a year ago'.[90] These are just a few references culled from many. The particular problems with the surface of this painting subvert Hunt's chosen image of resurrection, the sealed-up 'lustrous'[91] skin of the Innocents, and parallel the way that his failure to govern his materials subverts his own sense of safety.

The execution of *The Shadow* is also accompanied by a tendency to conflate the ills of the painting with those of the artist. The unreliable pigments cause a pictorial 'disorder'[92] which echoes a 'disordered state of body'.[93] Struggles to depict the flesh of Christ imitate the artist's own struggles of the flesh. He seeks 'richness and roundness' in his figure, but finds it 'rank and streaky',[94] and worries that 'the surface of the painting may be not be so unsullied as I should like'.[95] There are particular problems with saturation: 'all the paint sank in and dried while I was doing it and thus it wants that sweetness and freedom of truth which I wanted to give it'.[96] Hunt suffers stomach disorders, 'as is customary when I am working',[97] and undergoes periods of fasting.[98] The changeable pigment causes him to mistrust his vision: 'I nearly went crazy with the idea that my eye sight had accommodated itself to what could only be thought right by a fool when he was trying to delude himself',[99] and he again suffers fever, visions, nightmares and blindness.[100]

A failure to master materials is associated with mental disorder as well as physical vulnerability. Qualities of deceit, treachery, and even evil are attributed to them. A particularly paranoid note to Scott describes the faulty canvas of *The Triumph* as inhabited by a spirit, and describes seeing the devil jumping out of it on Christmas day.[101] Scott suggests that Hunt's problems are 'imaginary, not caused by the canvas, but in his own overworked or over-anxious brain'[102] and he dismissed this, displaying a literal conviction in a moral hostility in the inanimate.

The changeable pigments used for *The Shadow* are also a manifestation of 'villainy'. In 1871, Hunt writes to Scott of having dreams of 'paint drying before it could be blended, of wind blowing down my picture and breaking it', and concludes: 'I have too long left the dwelling place of comfort and now my paints, my brushes, my tools, my aids, the sun, morning, evening, working time and resting time, the wind, the clouds – all my helpers in proper place have risen with my peace of mind, long since unfaithful to me, to oppose resumption of my rights.'[103] The tools rising up of their own accord recall the knives in the letter to Lear (figure 4.1) and the tools in the painting, as well as the saw carried by Joseph in *The Triumph*. In all three instances, they represent threats posed by the diverse and unenlightened views of audience or society and 'the ravages of the outside scramble'.[104] 'Peace of mind', a fantasy of the work of art as an almost miraculous, reflexive manifestation of prophetic vision, falters during the actual process of painting. This lack of control is rationalised by casting the materials as aspects of the general hostility of a disordered, corrupt world.

The consoling notion that suffering and difficulties equate to sacrificial 'trial' is also extended to embrace the image. Painting and artist are constructed as the victims of persecution. Hunt describes *The Shadow* being repeatedly 'pulled to pieces' as the vicissitudes of unreliable models, weather and pigment force him to correct and re-correct his work.[105] The 'destructive process' of scraping areas of paint back to 'dead colour' is mentioned most often with respect to the figure of Christ. Hunt's own tools, condemned in the letter to Scott, enact the mutilation alluded to by the tools in the painting. The radiographs of *The Triumph* (figure 9.5) reveal a similar process. As lead-containing pigments, such as lead white, tend to appear as white in these photographs, the dark patches reveal parts which have been cut away. Hunt was usually in the habit of renewing with lead white, so these areas probably represent only some of his corrections.

This sense of reciprocal persecution is also manifested in Hunt's accounts of the display of his work. Anxieties about the 'lacerating' criticisms of an audience are echoed by a preoccupation with the hazards to the painting of 'rough treatment' (2, 457) and crowded exhibitions.[106] He warns Hamerton about 'accidental injuries, such as a push from the corner of a picture frame, which, if not visible at the time, may show years afterwards, in starred cracks in the hard paint'.[107] These depictions of the vulnerable object again correspond to the depictions of the artist threatened by knives, articulating fear of criticism and 'the ravages of the outside scramble'. Both critical and physical attacks against the picture constitute a deconstruction of the image which threatens the authoritative persona. The memoir's odd insistence that paintings be thoroughly saturated and sealed with varnish, and covered with glass, in order to protect them from the 'breath of spectators' and the saliva of people *speaking* nearby (2, 457–8), reinforces this connection between concerns about the actual and critical safety of the image.

A link now becomes apparent between the apparently arbitrary subjects that dominate chapter 15 of the memoir: the shrivelling of the surface of *The Light of the World* due to its neglect and exposure to heat (2, 411) and the discussion of Hunt's rivals and conflicting accounts of the brotherhood (Chapter 1). The integrity of the painter is intimately associated with the integrity of the painting and the paint layer. Its purity, smoothness and strength are revealed as a manifestation of authority and a defence against accusations of moral and artistic weakness, as well as physical harm. As I have shown in Chapter 4, anxieties over the vulnerability of both painter and painting are expressed in terms of corporeal danger. Pointon's reading of the 'obsessive depiction of the body's surface' in *The Shadow* as a response to Hunt's 'fear of death' or 'fear of mutilation'[108] can be extended to include his obsessive perfection and protection of the paint surface itself.

Specific references to fears about painting materials do not tend to occur in Hunt's earlier writing. However, a powerful sense of persecution, vulnerability and mortality are in evidence throughout correspondence dating from the beginning of his career. At the age of twenty-six he writes, 'I am tired. Oh so tired! I wish I could rest – sleep or die from this weary labour.'[109] The 1855 journal imagines the artist dead in twenty years, or, at least, a 'poor crippled weak old Holman'.[110] We see another example in 1864: 'I have no patience in my nature except for my slow art . . . My eyesight is not so good as before. My health is not so good as to make me see any long period of life before me . . . I look forward to the quiet sleep.'[111] This sense of imminent demise seems exaggerated, even pathological, in the light of the fact that Hunt lived another forty-seven years, dying in 1910 at the age of eighty-three. In June 1868, he sends Tupper a two-page letter attempting to clarify the chance remark of a chemist about the weather. He has been collecting a prescription and the assistant had commented on the heavy rain. Hunt interrogates Tupper about whether there is 'any real necessity to avoid such weather? . . . sudden changes in temperature, as, in leaving this Life at R.A. at 80° Far – to walk into Trafalgar Square at 35°. Also, I do not keep indoors in ~~dry~~ wet weather, only caring to keep in motion and not sit in wet garments'. He requests Tupper to ask his doctor, 'if he thinks these attentions sufficient, or if I must coddle myself a little'.[112] A preoccupation with avoiding any extreme of environment, particularly with respect to the weather, is a familiar nineteenth-century theme, and echoes Hunt's sense of the hostility of his environment, his sensitivity to environmental conditions when painting and to the environmental needs of his work.

Letters frequently muse about blindness. As early as 1860 Hunt complains to Combe: 'I have been working my poor eyes blind.'[113] In 1867 he writes to Tupper: 'To people like ourselves the loss of sight ~~cannot~~ never be thought of without shuddering.'[114] This fate does catch up with him at the height of problems with *The Shadow*, in 1872, and *The Triumph*, in 1879.[115] The disability becomes increasingly serious while painting *The Miracle of the Holy Fire*,[116] and the final version of *The Light of the World* is, ironically, conducted in a state of serious blindness. A conflation of fears for the safety of the sight of the artist and its brilliant representation on canvas seems the most inevitable of all the physical parallels between the artist and the art object. The prophetic power of perception that these paintings are meant to represent is undermined by a very real blindness, a poignant betrayal of the positive exchange between the physical and the spiritual proposed by Hunt's beliefs.

This physical connection between the artist and the art object is presented in a related form in the notion that the act of painting 'uses up', or spends, the life and strength of the artist. This is again a common attribute of disease.[117] References proliferate throughout Hunt's writings. In his autobiography, he mentions a 'daily fear that my means will be absorbed before my canvas has been turned into a picture' (2, 194). He writes that *The Triumph* will kill him: 'The canvas has certainly taken many years of my life away.'[118] This 'torment' has been 'wasting my life and health and powers'.[119] The theme of time and strength running out as they are invested in the act of painting emerges clearly.

Hunt asks: 'what is a person but his work which lives away from his body?'[120] These concerns feature with unusual frequency and gather momentum as he ages, particularly after the crisis of confidence which follows the loss of Fanny. The fact that worries about death and visual authority precede worries about the safety and purity of the pictures, suggests that an initial sense of the weak or deteriorating body and mind is displaced on to the paintings, producing a heightened set of fears about the hostility of disordered conditions and painting materials to the artist and the image. Ideas of deceit, delusion, damage and disease haunt painting and painter alike. Hunt's evangelical pursuit of mastery over his materials is an enactment of these anxieties.

Conception and making are far from separate. The way that the chemical minutiae of Hunt's paint contribute to a realisation of fantasy, reflects the way that minute observations are built up into a picture in his work. A tiny flaw in the paint surface is part of a continuum of signification which expands to the scale of universal philosophy:

> One stamp of great art in all ages was the artist's love and caretaking of the materials in which he expressed his meaning. In his hands common clay was impressed with sacred value as with the seal of divinity. Marble under his chisel sang itself into the holiness of the image of the Gods, and paint drawn from the earth, and the juices of perishing plants, by the artist's cunning became more entrancing than the precious stones that decorate a king's crown. (2, 486)

In locating spiritual value in the beauty, strength and health of the art object, the physical wholeness of that object becomes an issue. The close relationship between concerns for the intactness of paint and of body point to a conflation of painting and self which goes beyond iconography, linking physical aspects of the incomplete art object to the artist's fear of childish incompleteness, weakness and fantasy.

The invulnerable image

This section will bring together, and interrogate, several notions of smoothness and strength. In particular, it will relate the dialectical exchange between perfection and vulnerability, which characterises Hunt's iconography and his constructions of the art object and the artist, back to the appearance of his images.

As has been established in Chapters 6 and 8, Hunt's knowledge of materials is mobilised in order to facilitate his mimetic painting practice. This chapter has shown how materials take on a second kind of mimetic function, manifesting iconographical themes of purity, power and consequent safety in themselves, in the form of a strong, bright paint layer. This equivalence of form and content is further enhanced by a striking parity between the paint texture and the texture of the objects depicted. Hunt depicts an array of unusually firm, bright and reflective objects, reversing the descriptive relationship between paint and motif so that the image takes on the glossy qualities of the paint. The heightened similarity between picture surface and the surfaces pictured reinforces their reality, the sense that we could touch them. This 'strengthens' Hunt's presentation of his image as an equivalent to his understanding of the flawless, rich, prismatic qualities of 'healthful beauty and strength' (2, 452).

Reviews of Hunt's work exhibit a parallel tendency to conflate image and paint. Many link the brightness of the pigments and the shininess of the surface to the high illumination of the scene: 'the picture shines under the sun of Palestine'.[121] Similarly, ubiquitous references to 'perfection' and 'finish' tend to connote both the 'quality of the oil paint' and the texture of the objects it represents.[122] Maas reports that during the 1906 world tour, a reproduction of *The Light of the World* was used to advertise Solarine metal polish: 'Fancy having a Light of the World shine on your electroplate!'[123] Wood equates Hunt's style to the varnished surface when he finds 'the solidity of his modelling . . . somehow reminiscent of the heavy oppressiveness of the worst kind of Victorian furniture'.[124]

Hunt's magpie-like interest in hard, shiny textures, is exemplified by his personal taste in artefacts, gilded frames[125] and the accessories he introduces into his compositions. Meynell evocatively describes the drawing room of Draycott Lodge, Hunt's home after 1881, also illuminated by gleaming items, large windows and, 'here and there a Damascus lamp hanging, or Italian majolica deeply framed. Three doors tall, and bearing china jars . . . The beautiful chilly blue and white of a Luca della Robbia Madonna and Child stands over the needlework altarino, bearing goblets of old glass.'[126] Many of these pieces are used as 'properties'[127] in the paintings alongside other glistening textures such as silks, silken embroideries, brocades and metal and china artefacts, especially lustreware. The costumes of his eastern subjects and the golden interior of *The Finding*, are dramatic examples. *Isabella* and *The Lady of Shalott* are crowded with lustrous objects, and jewellery, tools and the ivory inlaid box of treasure also clutter *The Shadow*.

There are few opportunities for such artefacts in the rural scene of *The Triumph*, but even so, it is decorated with silky fabrics, glassy spheres, bubbles, pots, metallic jewellery and tools.

The particular valorisation of glass exhibited in Hunt's descriptions of revelatory landscapes and of the paint layer itself, is complemented by the inclusion of mirrors, glass or glassy bodies of water in many of his designs. The equivalence between painted surface and paint surface is, of course, most dramatic in the view through the window in *Master Hilary*. Hunt also paints water to appear highly reflective. Ruskin criticises its brightness in *The Scapegoat*,[128] and the stream in *The Triumph* is described by Stephens as 'gelid' and 'ice-like' (plate 3).[129]

This depiction of water is an example of the way that Hunt's treatment even hardens the appearance of surfaces which are not naturally solid. Hilton condemns the 'hard nastiness' of *The Scapegoat* (plate 1)[130] and its coat is typical of Hunt's approach to fur, wool or hair, in that it is painted in individual gleaming strands, each distinguished by a razor-sharp highlight. Hunt specifically rejects Landseer's treatment of animals, disliking the 'absence of firm bone beneath skins and the general melting away of every form into shapeless cloud'.[131] Hunt also gives a metallic look to the flesh of his figures. The skin of the girl in *The Afterglow* has an overall gloss and conspicuous highlights on the forehead, nose, elbows, palms, fingernails and eyes. Even shadows become discrete elements, as exemplified by the block of darkness cast on to the leg in *Study from a Mecca donkey* (figure 7.4). Reviewers often comment on this 'strong definition' of shading.[132]

Although it is said that Hunt's style became broader in later years,[133] this over-solid appearance does not diminish. Hair and softer fabrics retain their rigid definition. The gauzy robe of *Isabella* is so sharply painted with discrete white highlights that it appears brittle. The *Art Journal* remarks: 'the features are rather hard, and certainly the flesh in its metallic lustre is far from soft or winning'.[134] The *Athenaeum* notes a similarly 'crisp' quality to the 'strongly curled' hair of Jesus in *The Shadow*,[135] and the *Illustrated London News* criticises the flesh as too hard and 'metallic', disliking the unusual 'sharpness' of the painting as a whole.[136] Stephens finds the skin of the Innocents ridiculously solid, bright and 'lustrous', and, again, the shadows are too sharp,[137] while the flesh of *Master Hilary* is 'faultlessly solid' and 'needlessly hard and sharply defined'.[138] A visual hardness gives the painting a rigidity beyond that achieved through Hunt's particular choice of materials. The vitreous paint layer clearly relates to a personal aesthetic that privileges the strong, shiny surface in a way which is both actual, the paint itself, and illusion.

The consistency of the nineteenth-century complaints about Hunt's style underlines the singularity of his practice. In particular, his stubborn attribution of a metallic lustre to skin reinforces the idea that the strength or intactness of his paint layer relates to a sense of the intactness of the body. The 'bronze'[139] appearance of Christ, and the 'lustrous' flesh of the Innocents unite with the sealed paint surface to counter the implied penetration of the sharp implements which threaten them. The brightness and clarity of definition of their skin neutralises the metaphorical threat of the shadow and the darkness. The statement of immortality which is central to the iconography of these images, emerges in both their material and their stylistic execution.

Interestingly, the hardness of the image is furthered by Hunt's compositions. An illusion of depth tends to puncture the picture plane, and the careful construction of three-dimensionality, analysed in Chapter 6, would, therefore, seem to imply a departure from the promotion of the invulnerable surface. However, as I have noted in Chapter 8, Hunt's designs are a composite of icons removed from their found spatial relationships and inserted into an arrangement that is governed by narrative, symbolic and geometrical relations worked out in linear, two-dimensional terms. Moreover, Hunt's method of painting produces an emphasis on the 'bulk' of each object, its individual existence as solid form, rather than on a sense of the empty space between forms. His mimetic technique enhances the two-dimensional pattern of icons, dictated by the design, into firm modelled surfaces that still conform to an overall flatness. Each becomes three-dimensional in itself, but is arranged into the composition like boiled sweets filling up a glass jar. Contemporaries complain about this absence of an 'air medium',[140] and Wood describes a general, 'airless, artificial effect'.[141] This oddity represents an aesthetic which echoes the positive associations assigned to the 'fat full firmness'[142] of his paint: a hard material surface is packed with hard visual forms.

Hunt's characteristic use of a low viewpoint and/or architectural backgrounds enhances this sense of pictorial fullness. Almost without exception, landscape settings depart from convention in featuring a very high horizon which provides a wall of mass to enclose the figures. Stretches of sky are confined to apertures framed by trees, doors or windows, and prevent emptiness or recession. *Valentine* presents only a tiny glimpse of sky (plate 7). The receding forest floor climbs up the picture plane and is contained within a grid of branches. The landscape of *The Scapegoat* offers no opportunity for architecture or trees to enclose its panorama, but again the landscape confines the sky to a narrow strip, further framed at the top and left edge by banks of solidly painted cloud. A combination of interior and exterior setting, typical of quattrocento annunciations, is seen in *The Druids* and *The Finding*, while *The Shadow*, like *The Lady of Shalott*, occupies a confined area where the landscape is seen through a frame, as in northern paintings. In all these examples, therefore, the 'view' becomes literally this, an area of focus bounded by contours. Even space becomes a contained form. It is, like Hunt's discrete shadows, solid, another icon, the subject of the localised gaze.

This systematic denial of the emptiness of space is dramatically demonstrated by *The Triumph* (plates 3 and 24). Here, the landscape and trees leave only a blue rectangle of sky. Its colour and position behind Mary's head (encircled by a yellow and silver headdress), recalls the fields of blue employed in quattrocento and trecento frescoes, such as Giotto's *Flight into Egypt* (1300–5, Arena Chapel, Padua). The countryside in this part of the picture is rendered in similar hues to the sky's and both extend down behind a trio of floating children, strengthening the sense of it being a two-dimensional ground. Depth clues, such as the signal fires, *calibrate* depth, and allow us to 'read' this area of the painting as a receding plain, but visually, it tends towards flatness. The similarity between the distant stars and the Innocent's halos reinforces this effect.

Despite Hunt's location work, this landscape setting is not a depiction or an impression of space, but only a denotion of it. Its origin in the design ensures that it is a dense, interlocking structure of motifs each of which has a strong signifying function. Only one of these functions is to signify depth, connoting the location and the distance travelled by the family. The iconographical and narrative role of every sign is made clear by their specific mention in the accompanying pamphlet. The rising ground is 'the slope looking down on the tableland', bearing 'signal fires – still lit in Syria at times of trouble'. The blue colour indicates how 'the declining moon sheds its last light on *the objects* of the picture' (emphasis added).[143] The painting is, therefore as full of icons as it is of forms.

The density of this iconographical fullness, which includes substituting an effect of depth with an explanation of depth, clarifies the rather general notion of hardness assigned to Hunt's work by Hilton. He ascribes a contrastingly 'smudged' quality to Millais' *Autumn Leaves* (plate 15).[144] Unlike Millais, Hunt does not allow the eye to wander into the gloom. The potential of a distant recession to be ambiguous and inconclusive is curtailed visually by the flattening effect of the colour, by its confinement between the angle of the frame and the trees, by the clarity with which the landscape is painted and by the intrusion of the floating Innocents and the signal fires. It is also curtailed intellectually by the dogmatic specificity of its signifying role. The open-endedness of the space is belied by the confining of the gaze to a particular reading of it as a set of signs. As we know, Hunt's statements about mortality do not admit the acceptance of uncertainty or the transitory in nature which distinguishes *Autumn Leaves*. Millais' simple composition, soft, *sfumato* modelling and glimmering horizon express his comment to Hunt, 'Is there any sensation more delicious than the odour of burning leaves? To me nothing brings back sweeter memories of the days that *are gone*' (emphasis added, 1, 286). The physical, aesthetic and iconographical hardness of Hunt's work manifests the desired certitude of beliefs which repair, rather than accept, loss or death.

The Shadow (plate 2) exhibits a similar structure of motifs arranged into a dense pattern of signs that are both visually and iconographically firm. The small space between Jesus and Mary, for example, is filled by the stone wall, the shavings and the shadow of the spear. Even background shavings are carefully modelled cylinders. Hunt's habit of obscuring angles between vertical and horizontal surfaces, wall and floor, contributes to the eye's identification of mass rather than space. The base of the wall is covered, and so its position on a separate plane to that of the figures is suppressed. Like the landscape in *The Triumph*, it can be 'read' as behind, but comes forward to meet the gaze at the correspondingly hard surface of the picture. At an iconographical level, the gap between Jesus and Mary is filled by 'shadow' and 'spear', knitting into the tight web of signification created by the design.

This aesthetic and iconographic solidity results from and expresses the mechanisms of control that characterise Hunt's two-stage painting practice: his elaboration of designs and his particular way of 'looking most intensely at the individual objects in the world'[145] and prioritising mass over space. The eye is, consequently, presented with a surface which is firm in terms of the hard surfaces of the objects depicted, firm in terms of an absence of empty space, and firm in its dense, heavy iconographical definition, as well as firm in terms of its qualities as paint. These varieties of hardness are a defence against vulnerability and doubt, an expression of the authoritative persona.

The connection between art and artist which is endemic in accounts of Hunt's life and work is expressed in corresponding terms of personal and aesthetic rigidity. Gissing repeatedly describes Hunt as 'robust' and also says, 'Hunt's is a robust and manly art.'[146] Wood uses the same term and links Hunt's stern beliefs to his 'harsh' style.[147] The vocabulary of these accounts echoes Hunt's own language. In the memoir, themes of trial are frequently expressed as 'tempering', and metallic metaphors are used to valorise art and artist: 'our [convictions] were beaten upon the anvil of what experience we already had . . . the pure iron converted into tempered steel' (1, 100, also 1, 157). Hilton, too, equates Hunt's style, his didactic designs and his stubborn and undeviating character; opposing these to Millais' more versatile, 'winning' style and more allusive subjects.[148] Hardness and softness are thus associated with both art and artist and connote the paint itself and what is painted. In Hunt's case all of these are unyielding: 'Hunt, intent on being the great moral painter, came to deny himself the ravishments of paint.' That these ravishments are linked to a yielding softness is suggested by Hilton's feminine characterisation of the quality: 'that it charms us, bewitches, seduces . . . Sternly, dutifully, unswervingly, Hunt robbed paint of its power to please.'[149] Stephens comments on Hunt's 'solid, serious and religious character'. When he adds that 'the temper of the artistic metal . . . [is] rather inductile, although precious to the highest degree',[150] he could as well be describing the rigid iconographical definition or the vivid, inflexible surfaces (real and depicted) of Hunt's paintings.

The vulnerable image

Robin Ironside also links art and artist, but interprets them differently, reading Hunt's aesthetic and his iconography as manifestations of fragility. He astutely looks behind Hunt's public persona for an explanation of this, asserting a link between the appearance of his art and a 'private . . . inner disturbance':

> It is difficult to contemplate without real discomforture such works . . . as Holman Hunt's *Shadow of the Cross* . . . the distinct revelation of an inner disturbance and enthusiasm both in its themes and in its disquieting manner of execution, the awkward restraint of the gesture and attitude in the treatment of the figure, the feverish precision of drawing and occasional almost toxic virulence of colour.[151]

Ironside sees Hunt's aesthetic as expressing physical discomfort rather than strength, 'want of beautiful conditions of living',[152] and spiritual discomfort, a faltering of faith, 'its abyss was an ever more fearful aspect as scientific scepticism progressed'.[153] Both these have been shown to be central anxieties of the artist.

The phrases 'feverish precision of drawing', and 'toxic virulence of colour', are especially ironic in the light of Hunt's declarations of the purity and health of both his imagery and his pigment. They recall, rather, the negative characterisations of art and artist as sickly, in his private writings. They also recall the frequent allusions to the 'grotesque',[154] the insane, gloom and death in criticisms of Hunt's work. Hilton is typical when he links the artist to a 'shiny' aspect of his images when he describes Hunt as a '*gleaming-eyed*' variety of a man whose beliefs have become 'obsessive' (emphasis added).[155] It is clear that for many spectators, his images fail to connote either imaginative or physical integrity. We are brought, therefore, to our starting point: not simply the peculiarity of Hunt's aesthetic, but the consistency of its power to disturb in a certain manner and the continuity between the language it produces in viewers and that of the artist. Somehow, then, the images are revealing the ambivalent self-image of the letters and journals.

We have seen that Hunt's vulnerable persona is catalysed by practical frustrations with the creation of the work of art. The impressions of 'disturbance' experienced by observers of Hunt's paintings are, correspondingly, the result of inevitable contradictions arising out of practice. They are, in particular, the product of Hunt's multiple pursuit of authority, of material, optical and imaginative perfection.

Hilton's reference to 'gleaming-eyed' obsession draws our attention to one instance of this. Hunt's depiction of the eye is a good example of parity between the firm, shiny paint surface and the surface depicted discussed in the previous section. He elaborates his technique when painting them, adding varnish to achieve extra gloss.[156] Mimetic precision and close attention to form leads him, moreover, to represent the organ as a fully modelled specimen, a solid sphere, emphasising the shiny outer curve with a strong highlight. Despite studying Rembrandt's treatment of the eye,[157] Hunt does not permit the dissolving of the surface and the insubstantial, shadowy representation of the pupil which gives the sense of depth that creates Rembrandt's penetrating gazes. He approaches this in his early, Rembrandtesque self-portrait of 1845, but the eyes in his later work are 'glassy' in both senses of the word. This pursuit of optical and material completeness, or 'finish', contradicts iconographical clarity. It produces an unfocused effect. As a consequence, the visionary eyes of Christ in *The Shadow*, for example, give the disturbing impression that they belong to one who is tearful, mad or blind. The effect is exacerbated in *The Beloved* (1898, Royal Collection, figure 9.2).

As I have noted, Hunt has particular difficulties with the head of this Christ. His problems with the representation of the mouth also dramatise for us the practical processes that lead simulataneously to the promotion and to the breakdown of forms of firmness and control. The journal is very detailed on this point: Christ is praying aloud and therefore his mouth cannot be closed, but Hunt 'cannot bring my conscience under any circumstance to adopt the old master expedient of . . . the black patch'. The model is posed in various positions:

> if I have it only a little [open] so the teeth show as the only feature of the mouth for the sun being low down shines full upon them if I open it slightly more there is a line of white and below the parallel line of black of the shadowed cavity with the lips forming almost parallel boundaries above and below for at the point apart the lower lip has no curve in it and the upper one a poor one – when I open it further I get over the difficulty but I am afraid it makes the mouth a rather overpowering feature.[158]

This conundrum conveys a failed attempt to reconcile optical and iconographic authority, rigorous optical scrutiny and a spiritual ideal of 'conscience'. Hunt includes the teeth because he wants to avoid the 'black of the shadowed cavity'. He tries 'teeth closed with lips apart as tho' breathed through', but dismisses it as not Christlike enough

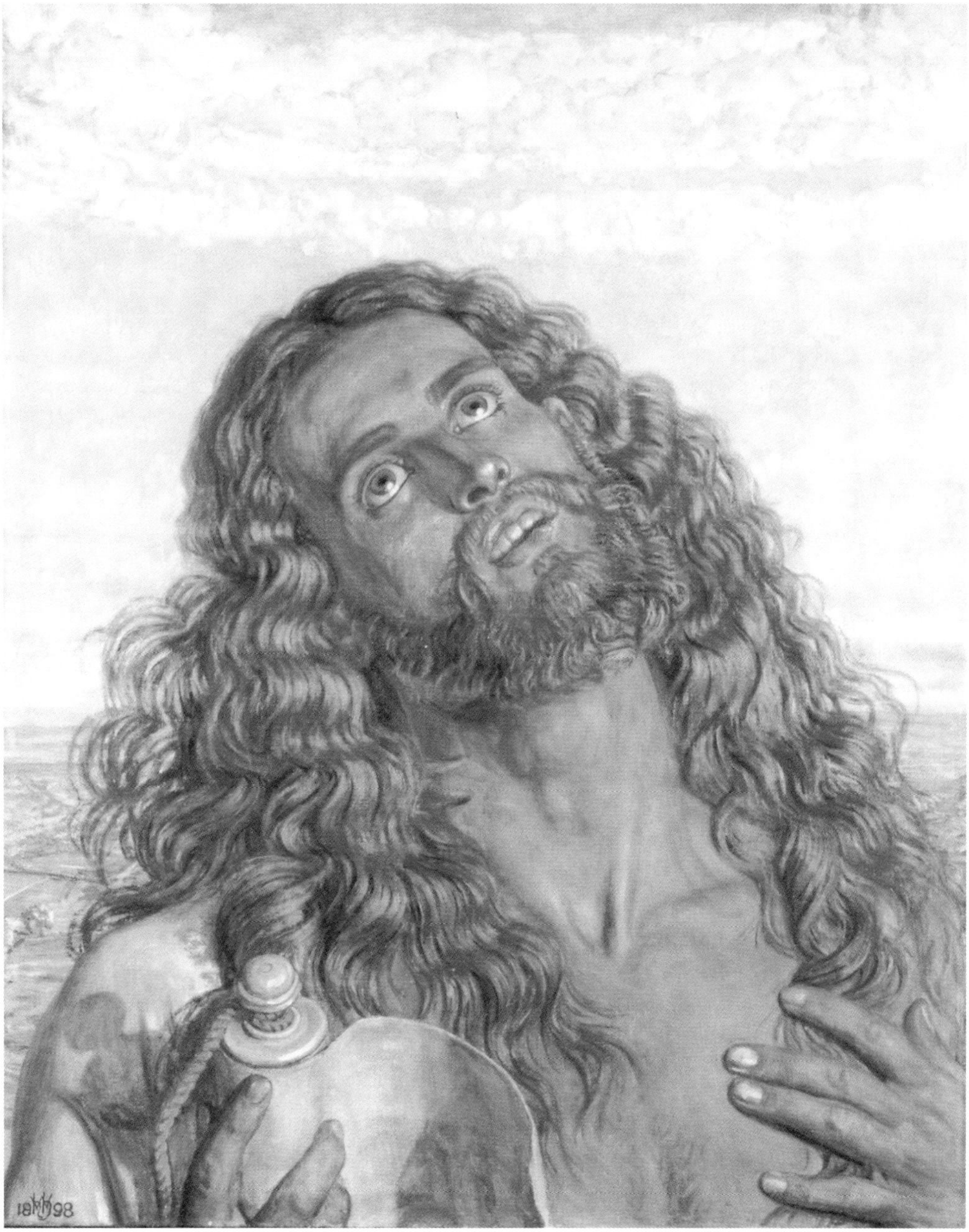

9.2
William Holman Hunt,
The Beloved,
1898

and attempts showing the teeth open with the mouth positioned in full sunlight. This precaution represents an effort to adapt a pictorial ideal, a Christlike Christ, to a material ideal, the firm, glossy surface. The shiny teeth are preferred to the obscure recess because it is important that a dull colour, a shadow or gap, does not invade the body at any point, but Hunt's mimetic fidelity prevents him from avoiding it altogether. The 'black patch' connotes weakness in material, visual and iconographical terms. It represents a pigment which Hunt considers to be feeble, 'claylike and finite', a breach in the invulnerable body of Christ, and an area of mystery which does not signify.

A breach of signification does, however, take place. Like the globes in *The Triumph*, Christ's expression is ambiguous unless viewed in conjunction with the pamphlet's explanation that he is praying.[159] Even so, the *Spectator* can see no 'moral' in the face,[160] and the *Art Journal* wonders if he is yawning.[161] Hunt's own letters of the time continue to worry that the figure's look is 'too painful'.[162] Christ's spoken announcement of his Father's rest is central to the message of resurrection which answers the crucifixion behind him, but like the millennial allusions in the later painting, it too is abstract and entirely imagined. It cannot be pictured and must be told. The unconventional, open mouth is an attempt to depict speech, but it produces an ironic silence in the signifying structure of the design, echoing the visual gap.

This iconographical failure privileges the more direct, or literal and indexical associations of the figure and its disordered surroundings, producing an uncertain reading of the Saviour. His divinity is undermined and he becomes a mere Galilean, the savage, 'clad in tatters, covered in vermin' seen by the *Art Journal*,[163] or worse, a grimacing madman. The figure's open mouth and oddly bared teeth, as well as his glazed eyes, expansive gesture and rolled-down tunic, give his overall pose an unfortunate and uncanny similarity not to the Christ in Raphael's *Transfiguration*, but to the convulsed child (figures 9.3, 9.4). Hunt's imaginative ideal of Christ is disrupted by his materialist focus. In the case of the mouth, the eyes, and the rippling skin, considerations of anatomical and material wholeness betray the intention to depict healthful beauty.

The fragmented image

As Pointon says, it is the intense detail of the 'sinews, body hair, sweat and dilated veins' of the body of the Christ in *The Shadow* which connotes masochism and disorder, creating a set of 'surfaces as disturbingly broken to the gaze as the chaotic fragmentation of the harshly lit room'.[164] The iconographical weaknesses caused by Hunt's pursuit of imaginative control (surveyed in Chapter 7), are compounded by a rupturing of aesthetic smoothness arising as a result of his pursuit of optical control (surveyed in Chapter 8). The multiple gaze which is demanded by the assertiveness of the individually copied parts of the picture creates a pictorial fragmentation. The 'sharp' boundaries

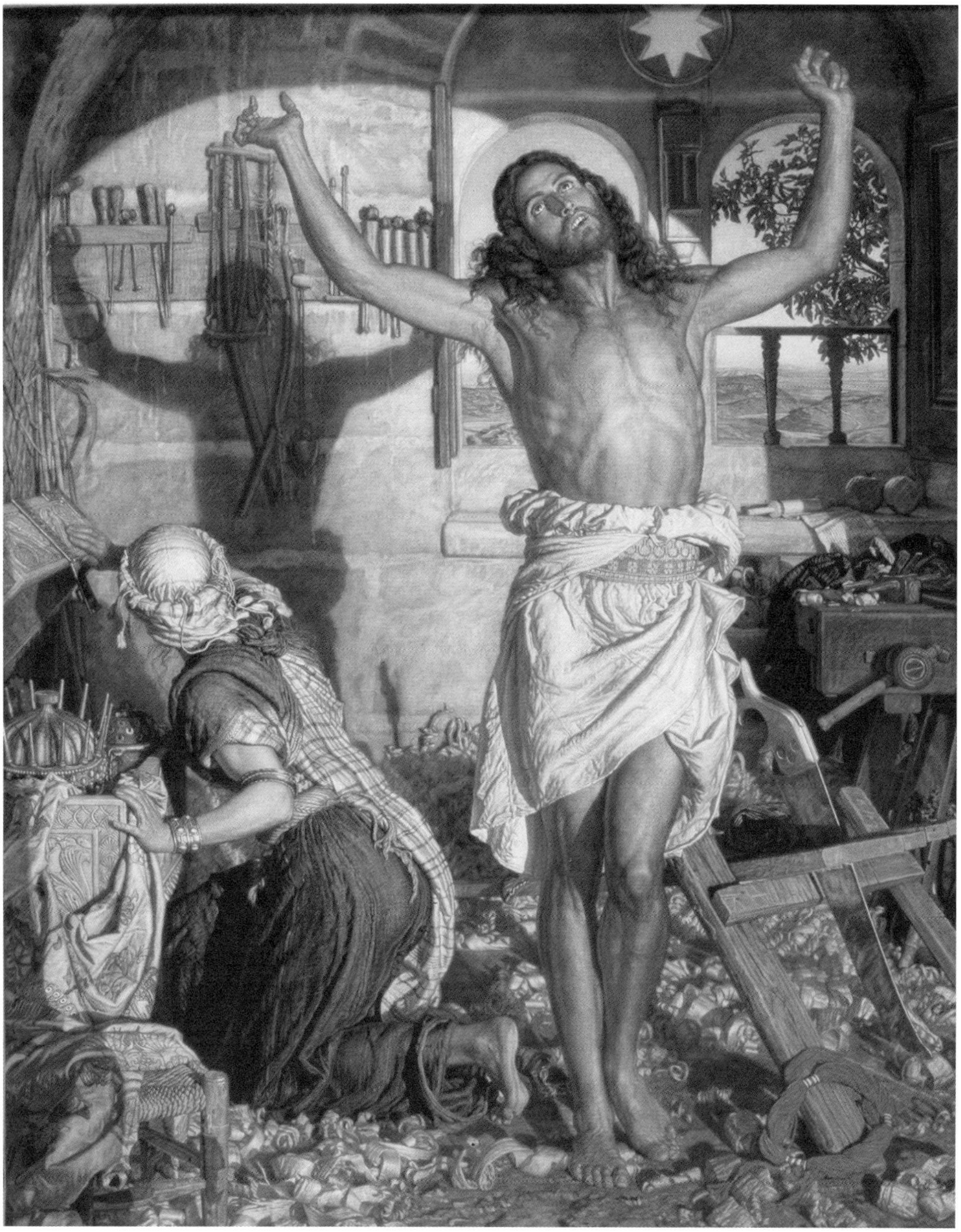

9.3
William Holman Hunt,
The Shadow of Death,
1869–73

which lock each object into the iconographic scheme become visual fissures. As contemporaries noted, the fullness of effect 'cracks the drawing convention'.[165] The 'multitudinous facts' fall apart to present a 'collection of conflicting elements'.[166]

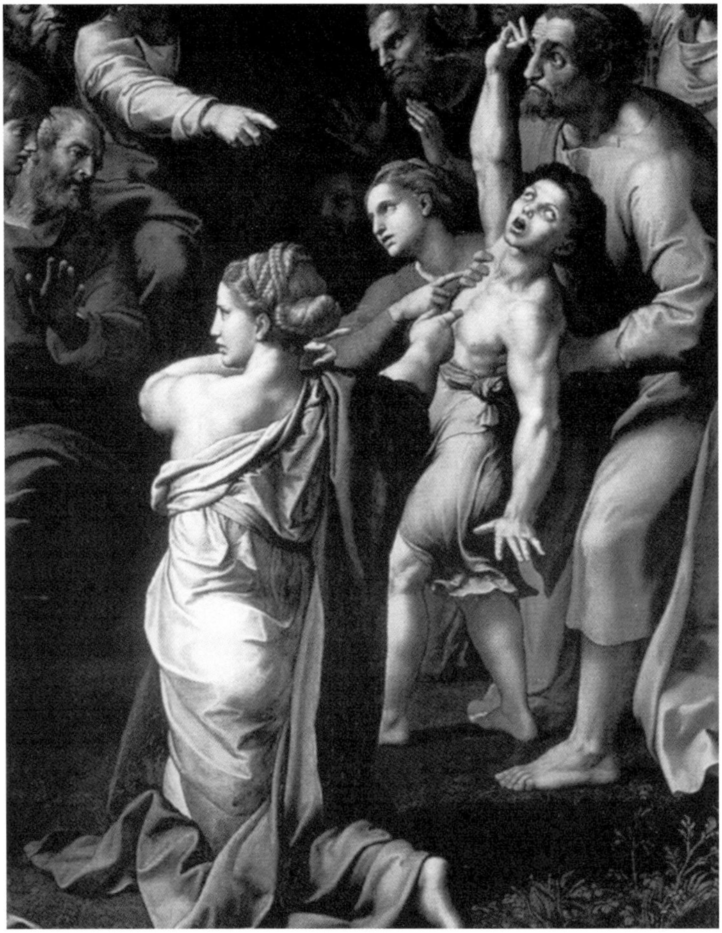

9.4
Raphael,
The Transfiguration of Christ, detail,
1517

Hunt is a tragic artistic Frankenstein. His mimetic practice of observing 'isolated fragments'[167] of his figures entails a visual dismembering which subverts both physical and metaphysical themes of completeness. The obsessive focus on Christ's head in *The Shadow* represents, for example, a kind of visual decapitation. An awareness of this optical disruption of corporeal wholeness is demonstrated by the long struggle to sit the head naturally on the neck. As I have noted, Hunt seems to have used the beard to obscure the join, but a line of darkness can be detected in the hair running from Christ's right ear to the left side of his chin. The use of wreaths and beads on the necks of the Innocents highlights the same difficulty. Despite, or perhaps because of this device, the heads of all the children, even that of Jesus, seem dislocated. The impression of them as a string of separate spheres is enhanced by their raised appearance and their similarity in shape and size to the over-solid, free-floating globes. These traces of the visual disruption enacted by the extreme focus of the painting stage represent a failure to hold together the imaginative design and a breakdown of the prophetic vision. They evoke the inability to see beyond the physical, imaged by Isabella's morbid fixation on the head of her lover, and the monstrous display of the beheaded and dismembered donkey in Titian's *Bacchus and Ariadne*.

Both the iconography and the aesthetic appearance of Hunt's work manifest the fragmentations inherent in its manufacture. Hunt's constant repainting of areas that are not considered to be perfect (in terms of pigment, surface or appearance, mimetic or imaginative), results in a literal 'pulling to pieces'[168] of the image. This process is pictured in the X-ray photograph of *The Triumph*, where dark shadows across Christ's neck and necklaces of marks on the Virgin and the Innocent reveal that these areas have been cut away particularly often (figure 9.5). Hunt's mutilation of his figures articulates the inevitable difficulty of reconciling material, optical and imaginative mastery, of accommodating specific materialist, modern perceptions of paint and appearances to an overarching concept of divinity.

The painting is not impenetrable or invulnerable. The sense of fragmentation, surrealism, madness and morbidity experienced by viewers of Hunt's work is a response to the way that the paintings themselves manifest the deranged, fearful and childish qualities which characterise Hunt's private constructions of self. The physical, visual and iconographical rigidity which Hunt seeks results, in practical terms, in a kind of visual and physical brittleness. The art object becomes an expression of weakness rather than strength.

Each of these forms of fragmentation arises as a direct result of Hunt's anxious confrontation with modernity, with nineteenth-century materialist philosophies, with the materials of the art object, with optical scrutiny of the material world and the nature of vision itself. They manifest, as Nochlin says in '*The Body in Pieces*', 'that sense of social, psychological, even metaphysical fragmentation that seems to mark modern experience – a loss of wholeness, a destruction or disintegration of the permanent'.[169] She concludes:

> it is by no means possible to assert that modernity may only be associated with, or suggested by, a metaphoric or actual fragmentation. On the contrary, paradoxically, or dialectically, modern artists have moved towards its opposite, . . . the struggle to overcome . . . disintegrative effects . . . by hypostatizing them into a higher unity. *One might, from this point of view, maintain that modernity is indeed marked by the will towards totalisation as much as it is metaphorized by the fragment.* (emphasis added)[170]

Hunt takes part in this struggle. It is, however, the *practical* processes of this battle to repair the 'loss of wholeness' inherent in modern experience with a synthesis, 'a higher unity', which undermines his aim.

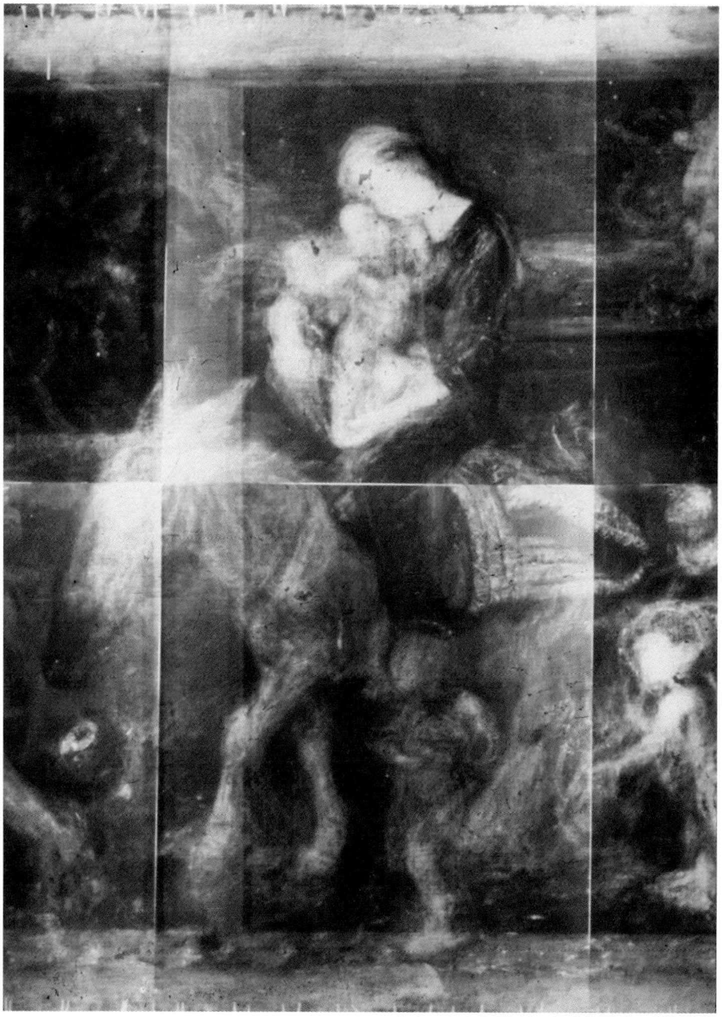

9.5
William Holman Hunt, x-ray photograph of detail of central group of *The Triumph of the Innocents*, finished sketch, 1870–1903

In Hunt's case, these processes constitute a kind of sacrificial, prophetic trial. The reactionary nature of his later art has always been pointed up by his seemingly anachronistic style and perceived hostility to European modernism; the decade that sees the completion of *The Triumph* coincides with the decade of Van Gogh's death. However, Nochlin's characterisation of the signs of mutilation in Van Gogh's work as an expression of 'deeply felt tensions – between art and nature, words and images, tradition and modernity'[171] recalls Hunt's work. She proposes a relationship between these and 'fragmentation . . . Decapitation – any self-mutilation',[172] and sees this sense of wounding and sacrifice as an integral element of modern art-making.

Hunt's career stages an array of collusions and collisions between fragmentation and totalisation, the relative and the universal, the experienced and the imagined, but it is the fastidious awareness with which these are pursued that sets his work apart from contemporaries on both sides of the Channel. It makes *visible*, in particular, a confrontation between intention and process which goes to the heart of that engagement with materialism that characterises the transition into what we call modernity. The art historian, no less than the artist, has tended to adhere to a myth of artistic authority in this respect; it lends an air of authenticity to the objects which give our practice meaning. Even those commentators preoccupied with work that acknowledges its material nature, discussed in Chapter 6, assume a certain accord between artistic direction and material manifestation, an equation which evades a whole drama of contested meanings emerging through the conflicts of process. Hunt's awful image of lay figure mistaken for a wet-nurse unmasks this fantasy: 'they take of course the view wh a painter does of the work under his eyes believing it to be what he intends it to be'.[173] The personal and painful nature of this metaphor expresses a tangled and troubled relationship between art and life, that extending well beyond the slippage between image and object.

Hunt should be repositioned as a reluctant, but vigorous, participant in the transition into modernism; one who, at the very least, tested the limits of art in his search for certainty, authority, control and something beyond the material. Analysis of his specific procedures of manufacture demonstrates the *practical* ways in which nineteenth-century paradoxes of belief and self-image are constituted within textual constructions of the artist, and within the art object through the materials, painting and design, creating a seamless cycle of exchanges between painter, painting and paint itself.

Notes

1 'Materials', p 497
2 Letter to Stephens, 24 April 1878, BL, MS Don. e 68, 10–11
3 'Materials', p 493
4 Laurie, *Painter's Methods*, p 66
5 Carlyle, 'Artist's Anticipation of Change', p 63
6 'Materials', p 493
7 Ibid., p 497
8 Ibid., p 494; Laurie, *Painter's Methods*, pp 65–6
9 'Materials', p 497
10 Ibid., pp 494, 497
11 Ibid., p 487
12 Ibid., p 497; Cennini, *Craftsman's Handbook*, p 74
13 Laurie, *Painter's Methods*, p 76
14 Ridge, Hackney and Townsend, 'Pre-Raphaelite Technique'

15 Laurie, *Painter's Methods*, p 83
16 'Materials', pp 490–1; Hunt admits using salad oil and megilp on an early picture in 1846 which cracked badly, p 494
17 Ibid., pp 490, 495; this was a common misconception in the nineteenth century, Carlyle, L. and J.H. Townsend, 'An Investigation of Lead Sulphide Darkening of Nineteenth-century Painting Materials', *Dirt and Pictures Separated* (London: United Kingdom Institute of Conservation, 1990), pp 40–3
18 'Materials', p 494
19 Ibid., p 490
20 Mayer, R., *The Artist's Handbook of Materials and Techniques* (1951) (London: Faber and Faber, 1987), p 200
21 'Materials', p 491
22 Ibid., p 487
23 Ibid., pp 494–5
24 Ibid., p 495
25 Letter to Tupper, 11 August 1875, *Correspondence*, p 201; *The Times* (4 May 1880), p 6
26 Katz, 'Hunt on Himself', pp 415–44
27 Carlyle, 'Artist's Anticipation of Change', p 62
28 'Materials', p 491
29 Letter to Tupper, 11 August 1875, *Correspondence*, p 201
30 'Materials', pp 488–9
31 Ibid., p 487
32 Ibid., p 490
33 Letter to Tupper, 28 December 1876, *Correspondence*, p 216
34 'Materials', p 493
35 Ibid., p 493
36 Ibid., p 498
37 Quoted Farr, D., *English Art 1870–1940* (Oxford: Oxford University Press, 1984), pp 44–5
38 Callen, A., *The Spectacular Body: Science, Method and Meaning in the Work of Degas* (London: Yale University Press, 1995), p 143
39 Sontag, S., *Illness as Metaphor* (1978) (Harmondsworth, Middlesex: Penguin, 1987), p 10
40 Mort, F., *Dangerous Sexualities: Medico-moral Politics in England since 1830* (London: Routledge and Kegan Paul, 1987), p 41
41 Ibid., pp 17–18
42 Sontag, *Illness as Metaphor*, p 10
43 'Materials', p 489
44 Mort, *Dangerous Sexualities*, p 66
45 This social transformation is surveyed by Paula Gillet in *The Victorian Painter's World* (London: Alan Sutton, 1990), p 12
46 This xenophobia towards the French is evident in 1852, when Hunt describes Napoleon III as 'a crawling reptile that sucks eggs such as would yield life enough to scare the loathsome creature into it's slimy hole! a liar! a thief! one with the heaviness of dissipation upon him, and enveloped in the cold sweat of hypocrisy' (terms of fever, again), letter to Stephens, 31 October, 1852, BL, MS Don. e 66, 19–19v

47 Nead, L., *Myths of Sexuality: Representations of Women in Victorian Britain* (1988) (Oxford: Basil Blackwell, 1990), pp 118–38
48 Ibid., p 75
49 *Art Journal* (1862), p 150, quoted ibid., p 57
50 Letter to Tupper, March 1855, *Correspondence*, p 47
51 Ibid., 28 December 1876, p 216
52 'Materials', p 493
53 Ibid., p 494
54 Porter, R., *London: A Social History* (London: Hamish Hamilton, 1994), p 199
55 Journal, November 1854, JRL, MS 1210, 4v
56 Letter to J.D. Batten, 11 November 1907, quoted 'Methods of the Pre-Raphaelite Brotherhood', *Papers of the Society of Mural Decorators and Painters in Tempera, Second Volume, 1907–24*, ed. J.D. Batten (Brighton: Dolphin Press, 1925), p 7
57 Letter to Tupper, 30 October 1878, *Correspondence*, p 260
58 Letter to Stephens, 28 January 1879, BL, MS Don. e 68, 40
59 Ibid., 27 October 1879, 54
60 Ibid., 10 April 1880, 82; 18 April 1880, 85
61 Letter to Tupper, 11 August 1875, *Correspondence*, p 200
62 Letter to Stephens, 25 July 1868, BL, MS Don. e 67, 22–3, this article was not published
63 Ibid., 14 September 1868, 24
64 Letter to Tupper, 15 July 1877, *Correspondence*, p 232
65 Letter to Stephens, 7 June 1867, BL, MS Don. e 67, 13
66 Letter to Scott, 11 February 1860, *Notes*, 1, p 49
67 Letter to Stephens, 7 June 1867, BL, MS Don. e 67, 12v–13
68 Ibid., 5 April 1867, 10v
69 Ibid., 17 June 1867, 12v
70 Mayer, *Artist's Handbook*, p 471. Spirit varnishes (resins dissolved in spirit such as turpentine) do dry by evaporation, but oil/varnish hardens by chemical reaction, Feller, R.L., N. Stoller and E.H. Jones, *On Picture Varnishes and Their Solvents* (London: The Press of Case Western Reserve University, 1971), p 3
71 Letter to J.D. Batten, 11 November 1907, quoted *Society of Mural Decorators*, pp 6–7
72 Letter to Tupper, July 1870, *Correspondence*, p 130
73 Letter to Stephens, 21 June 1870, BL, MS Don. e 68, 57
74 Letter to Scott, 10 August 1870, *Notes*, 2, p 95
75 Journal, 24 January 1872, JRL, MS 1212, 4v
76 'Materials', p 493
77 Ibid., p 497
78 Letter to Tupper, 28 December 1876, *Correspondence*, p 213
79 Ibid., 16 January 1877, pp 216–17
80 Ibid., 15 July 1877, pp 221–3
81 Letter to Stephens, 29 April 1878, BL, MS Don. e 68, 9; 2 May 1878, 12
82 Letter to Tupper, 26 April 1878, *Correspondence*, p 243. Hunt frequently speaks of 'renewing' his ground, when correcting
83 Ibid., 21 October 1878, p 259

84 Ibid., 23 January 1878, p 238. Letter to Stephens, 30 August 1878, BL, MS Don. e 68, 25; 5 November 1878, 25; 31 December 1878, 26
85 Letters to Stephens, 28 January 1879, BL, MS Don. e 68, 40; 31 December 1878, 40
86 Ibid., summer 1879, 45
87 Ibid., 26 August 1879, 52
88 Ibid., 5 August 1879, 50–50v
89 Ibid., 26 August 1879, 51v
90 Ibid., 4 December 1879, 62–62v
91 Stephens, 'The Triumph of the Innocents', p 80
92 Letter to Tupper, 11 August 1875, *Correspondence*, p 201
93 Journal, 9 April 1872, JRL, MS 1212, 19
94 Ibid., 22–24 March 1872, 16–16v
95 Letter to Tupper, 9 September 1872, *Correspondence*, p 162
96 Journal, 21 May 1872, JRL, MS 1212, 24v–25; also, 1 March 1872, 12v
97 Ibid., 22 April 1872, 20v. The frequency with which Hunt suffers from diarrhoea is hinted at by the fact that his wife seems to have deleted this indelicate word in many of his letters
98 Ibid., 14 January 1872, 2; 24 January 1872, 5; 22 April 1872, 20
99 Letter to Tupper, 11 August 1875, *Correspondence*, p 201
100 Journal, 20 April 1872, JRL, MS 1212, 20
101 Letter to Scott, 5 January 1880, *Notes*, 2, pp 229–31
102 Scott, *Notes*, 2, p 234
103 Ibid., 20 February 1871, pp 102–3. This is a reference to the tale of the Scythian warriors who were away fighting so long that their servants came to see themselves as masters and attacked them with their tools
104 Letter to Stephens, 3 May 1875, BL, MS Don. e 68, 147
105 Letter to Tupper, 9 September 1872, *Correspondence*, pp 162–3
106 Letter to Stephens, 25 July 1879, BL, MS Don. e 67, 22–3
107 Hamerton, 'Technical Notes', p 45
108 Pointon, 'Artist as Ethnographer', p 42
109 Letter to Stephens, 23 November 1853, BL, MS Don. e 66, 28v
110 Journal, 31 October 1855, JRL, MS 1211, 73v
111 Letter to Stephens, 29 July 1864, BL, MS Don. e 66, 99v–100
112 Letter to Tupper, 29 June 1868, *Correspondence*, pp 86–7
113 Letter to Combe, 19 October 1860, quoted Maas, *Hunt*, p 102
114 Letter to Tupper, 19 December 1867, *Correspondence*, p 81
115 Letter to Stephens, 16 August 1879, BL, MS Don. e 68, 52
116 Maas, *Hunt*, pp 101–3
117 Sontag, *Illness as Metaphor*, p 29
118 Letter to Stephens, 4 December 1879, BL, MS Don. e 68, 62
119 Letter to Scott, 5 January 1880, *Notes*, 2, p 258
120 Letter to Combe, 19 October 1876, JRL, MS 1213, 30
121 *Saturday Review* (6 December 1873), p 727
122 *Spectator* (23 May 1891), p 724
123 Maas, *Hunt*, pp 161–2
124 Wood, *Pre-Raphaelites*, p 106
125 Letter to Stephens, 22 June 1869, BL, MS Don. e 67, 30v

126 Farrar and Meynell, *Hunt*, p 26
127 Letter to Stephens, 22 June 1869, BL, MS Don. e 67, 30
128 Ruskin, letter to Hunt, 29 April 1858, quoted Landow, G.P., '"Your Good Influence on Me": The Correspondence of John Ruskin and William Holman Hunt', *Bulletin of the John Rylands University Library of Manchester*, 59, 1 (1976), p 123
129 Stephens, 'The Triumph of the Innocents', p 81
130 Hilton, *Pre-Raphaelites*, p 110
131 'Fight for Art', p 475
132 *Spectator* (6 December 1873), p 1539
133 Gissing, *Hunt*, p 218
134 'Isabella and the Pot of Basil', *Art Journal*, 30 (1868), p 97
135 'The Shadow of Death', *Athenaeum*, 2405 (29 November 1873), p 703, also *Saturday Review* (6 December 1873), p 727
136 *Illustrated London News* (6 December 1873), p 543
137 Stephens, 'The Triumph of the Innocents', pp 80–2
138 Stephens, F.G., 'Master Hilary the Tracer', *Athenaeum*, 3106 (7 May 1887), p 613
139 Gissing, *Hunt*, p 214
140 *Illustrated London News* (6 December 1873), pp 542–3
141 Wood, *Pre-Raphaelites*, p 81
142 Letter to Scott, 11 February 1860, *Notes*, 2, p 49
143 *The Triumph of the Innocents*, quoted Bennett, *Hunt*, p 53
144 Hilton, *Pre-Raphaelites*, p 78
145 White, *Birth and Rebirth of Pictorial Space*, p 34
146 Gissing, *Hunt*, p 217
147 Wood, *Pre-Raphaelites*, p 106
148 Hilton, *Pre-Raphaelites*, p 84
149 Ibid., pp 92–3
150 Stephens, 'English Painters of the Present Day, William Holman Hunt', *Portfolio*, 2 (March 1871), pp 33–4
151 Ironside, *Pre-Raphaelites*, p 18
152 Ibid., p 20
153 Ibid., p 14
154 *Illustrated London News* (14 March 1885), p 288
155 Hilton, *Pre-Raphaelites*, p 108
156 Letter to Blackburn, 17 November 1857, JRL, MS 1268
157 'Materials', p 488
158 Journal, 8 February 1872, JRL, MS 1212, 7v
159 *The Shadow of Death*, quoted Bennett, *Hunt*, p 49
160 *Spectator* (29 November 1873), p 1497
161 *Art Journal* (1873), p 86
162 Journal, 9 May 1872, JRL, MS 1212, 23
163 *Art Journal* (1873), p 87
164 Pointon, 'Artist as Ethnographer', p 41
165 *Spectator* (23 May 1891), p 275
166 *Spectator* (6 December 1873), p 1539
167 Letter to Tupper, 28 December 1876, *Correspondence*, p 213

168 Ibid., 9 September 1872, pp 162–3
169 Nochlin, *Body in Pieces*, pp 23–30
170 Ibid., p 53
171 Ibid., p 47
172 Ibid., p 49. Nochlin is here drawing on the opinion of the Surrealist writer, Georges Bataille, 'Sacrificial Mutilation and the Severed Ear of Vincent Van Gogh', *Visions of Excess: Selected Writings, 1927–39* (1993)
173 Letter to Stephens, 21 June 1870, BL, MS Don. e 68, 57

Conclusion

Critical commentaries on Hunt's work often concentrate on reading as a means of clarifying and valorising the images, but a painting is not an entirely literary text; its aesthetic and material nature must be addressed. In doing this, I have attempted to rationalise Hunt's problematic aesthetic. I have also redirected the privileging of biographical myth, endemic in texts about Hunt, towards a more intimate relation between painting and writing which embraces style as well as content, and which distinguishes between public and private. This has placed *The Shadow of Death* and *The Triumph of the Innocents* at a position of importance and crisis within Hunt's output, belying their relegation to a mere continuation of Pre-Raphaelitism and 'an unproductive late career'.[1] This neglect is perhaps, in part, due to the dogmatic and discomforting appearance of the images, a discomfort which in fact derives from the distress and contradiction arising from a clash between materialism and belief.

The painting of modern life does not have to entail the painting of modern subjects. These two works confront pivotal concerns of the time: the isolation of the individual, the collapse of faith and the status of art. The period after 1867 sees an acceleration of materialist concerns following a confrontation with death. Religious belief and technical mastery are vehicles for these:

> As to the question of a creative mind in the formation of the universe, it seems to me precisely equivalent to the enquiry whether in Tintoretto's pictures the flax of the canvas, the gesso, and the glue of the priming, the delightful forms and arrangement traceable on the surface came there by a happy chance, or whether all these materials were brought together by an intelligent mind, and the design was accomplished by wise direction and control. (2, 267)

Hunt's Christian ideas may seem anachronistic by the end of the century, but it is these which impel him to test the extremities of his art against modern circumstance.

The religious does not preclude the modern. A narrow understanding of modernity pertaining to the particular politics of a mid-nineteenth century France viewed from mid-twentieth century New York, has resulted in a perceived contradiction between the two which has helped to cast Hunt's biblical scenes as conservative and conventional. The fact that they are 'not good-looking', the rejection of the aesthetic manipulations of Rossetti and later contemporaries pursuing 'art for art's sake', has compounded this and added an air of misguidedness to his reputation. Yet these works are conspicuously idiosyncratic; visually arresting and thematically unique. The turned back of the Virgin is a motif of spiritual and emotional estrangement as revolutionary as the subverted Madonnas of Munch, Ernst or Offili. The garish angles and optical unease are a symptom of the existential concerns being explored in conception and execution. The paintings are not failed imagings of a comfortable middlebrow fantasy, but successful investigations of uncomfortable, not wholly controllable, individual actuality.

The association of troubling issues of materialism and the relative nature of vision, which characterise the modern outlook, with the clownish or childish state is an unfamiliar angle on a familiar avant-garde theme of the primitive. It is encapsulated in an account of a childhood event found early on in *Pre-Raphaelitism* (1, 5–6). Hunt describes his father lending him his paintbox for the first time. The text concentrates on the jewel-like brightness of the colour and the precision of the brush. The loss of the brush, Hunt's traumatic search and painstaking attempt to make another from his own hair are detailed at length. The possession of the brush, the organ of the father, implies an alignment with the authority figure, creative potency and mastery over the colours. Its loss is, characteristically, countered by an attempt to manufacture a 'double'. The failure to command or disguise the materials results, however, in the production of an absurd fantasy of a brush, provoking fear of derision and punishment.

This anecdote provides a striking model of the polarity between vulnerable child and authoritative prophet in Hunt's writings and articulates the physical vulnerability associated with Hunt's failure to control his materials, his own hair. The initial alignment with the father, imitating his artistic practice as the older Hunt felt he imitated the ~~God~~Father's creative act, shifts to the 'bungling', weak and deluded child, fearful of judgement. The fragility of the copy of the brush is specifically connected to it being recognised as a fake. A failure of realism, of strength and a lie or moral transgression all coincide:

> I went forward to him, *holding the trophy very tenderly lest it should fall to pieces.* He turned his eyes; they became bewildered; his usual loving look made a frown from him the more to be dreaded. I fortified my spirit saying, 'Thank you, father, for my brush.' He took it with, 'What's this?' and turned it over. Breathless, I sobbed; *he burst out laughing, and so brought a torrent of tears to my eyes.* He exclaimed, 'Oh, I see, it's my brush is it?' caught me up and tossed me aloft several times,

> ending with a scrubbing on my cheek with his close shaven chin. *This was the reception of my first work of art.* (emphasis added)

Hunt's first audience unmasks the incomplete, relative nature of his vision and his earnest endeavours are revealed to be no more than a fragile, childish fancy.

The memoir goes on to show the child developing into an accomplished and clear-sighted adult whose artistic vocation comes to fulfil the role of sage, or even Christ-like prophet. This persona is, in effect, a Christianised expression of a consoling Kleinian fantasy, which replaces weakness and fear of persecution with a sense of empowerment and wholeness. The imaging of prophetic perfection in the form of a corporeal being, such as Christ, constitutes an attempt to reconcile experience and imagination, the physical and the metaphysical. This synthesis is articulated in the paintings by the juxtaposition of elaborate design and mimetic precision, by the function of each element of the iconography as both symbol and icon, and by the allocation of spiritual qualities to the paint surface itself. Hunt attempts to bind materials and the material appearance of the world into a scheme which articulates his fantasies.

However, this imposition of a highly subjective sense of order produces a physical, visual and iconographical rigidity which, paradoxically, renders the painting physically, visually and iconographically brittle. Hunt's art exhibits the unstable characteristics of the artist's prophetic persona and is equally vulnerable to 'uncontrollable circumstance',[2] especially that of the emerging mass cultures of the nineteenth century. The inflexible paint layer is susceptible to the vicissitudes of travel and exhibition. The image, too, is vulnerable to public exposure. The gazes of a diverse audience deconstruct the artificial synthesis of 'materialism and mysticism'. They fragment pictorial coherence and create multiple, contradictory interpretations. Hunt's paintings are, like the paint brush, revealed as fragile and fanciful contrivances.

The themes of immortality and bodily perfection which characterise Hunt's iconography and his discussions of other aspects of the painting underline their significance as tokens of personal wholeness. Challenges to the physical and visual integrity of the painting therefore constitute a challenge to the integrity of the painter. The real conditions which threaten the authority of the art object or the artist are constructed as persecution. Imperfect materials, tools, weather, family, critics and the whole social order are all, at some time, associated with mutilation. The wounds that Hunt makes in his images represent reciprocal obliterations of aspects of the material world which do not accord with an imagined idea of divinity; passages which elude control and damage fantasies of safety.

Hunt's failure to complete *The Scapegoat* prompts him to admit to Combe: 'I must either put aside my task or my system. I have a good obedience to the law of order apart from painting – I think, but I cannot combine in service of the two'.[3] This statement acknowledges the fundamental paradox which bedevils the practical execution of his work: a collision between a concept of order, and practical experience of the real, the fleeting and the disordered. This tension between the prescriptive and the deductive is exemplified by the divided structure, and the divided narrator, of the memoir, the divided self of the letters and the divided procedure of painting.

Hunt demands a modern engagement with the material world, but also insists upon stamping it with the absolute eschatological certainty of eternity. The destabilisations of faith and self-image which characterise the modern experience are, in Hunt's case, obscured in published writings. They are, however, revealed in private texts and vividly in the paintings themselves. Once this paradox has been identified, it explains the ambiguity of both Hunt's iconographical and his literary language and justifies the range of interpretations which have been attached to his images. Discomfort with the aesthetic quality of his work becomes more meaningful when it is perceived as an expression of these tensions.

I am aware of the irony that, in my attempt to relate biographical and visual texts, meanings and the material construction of the work of art, I imitate the attempts of the artist to reconcile two poles of imaginative and sensual experience. However, the synthetic nature of this argument is, I hope, justified on two fronts. It proposes a continuity between constructions of the artist and the art object which goes beyond iconography and manifests itself in terms of the body of the artist and the physical nature of his art. In so doing, it offers a response to the relativities of time, taste and methodology which fragments art history itself, a possibility of constructive intercourse between a congregation of viewings, an art history of juxtaposition.

Notes

1 Bowness, 'Introduction', *The Pre-Raphaelites* (Tate Gallery, 1984) p 21; also Wood, *Pre-Raphaelites*, p 106, Prettejohn, *Pre-Raphaelites*, p 112; Hilton barely mentions Hunt's career after 1860, *Pre-Raphaelites*

2 Letter to Combe, 11 March 1855, JRL, MS 1213, 3

3 Ibid., 25 May 1855, 9

Bibliography

Hunt: letters and journals

Unpublished

John Rylands University Library of Manchester (JRL) manuscripts
MS 1210 (Dead Sea journal, November 1854)
MS 1211 (Jerusalem journal, 12 February–9 November 1855)
MS 1212 (Jerusalem journal, 14 January–July 1872)
MSS 1213 (Thomas Combe)
MSS 1214 (Lear etc.)
MSS 1215 (Edith Holman Hunt)
MS 1268 (Mrs Blackburn)

Bodleian Library, Oxford (BL) manuscripts
MS Eng. lett. c 32–51 (Sir Henry Acland)
MS Eng. lett. e 118
MSS Acland d 71 (Sarah Angelina Acland)
MSS Don. e 66–8 (F.G. Stephens)
MSS Don. c 78 (F.G. Stephens)
MSS Eng. lett. c 3 (Sir Henry Taylor)
MSS Eng. lett. c 32–5 (Sir Henry Taylor, Ruskin, Hunt)

Published

Letters to W.B. Scott, quoted, Scott, W.B., *Some Autobiographical Notes*, ed. W. Minto, 2 vols, London: Osgood, McIlvaine, 1892

Letter to J.D. Batten, quoted, 'Methods of the Pre-Raphaelite Brotherhood', *Papers of the Society of Mural Decorators and Painters in Tempera, Second Volume, 1907–24*, ed. J.D. Batten, Brighton: Dolphin Press, 1925, pp 6–7

Letters to John Wharlton Bunney, quoted, Bennett, M., 'Footnotes to the Holman Hunt Exhibition', *Liverpool Bulletin*, 13 (1969), pp 43–5

Lutyens, M., ed., 'Letters from John Everett Millais and William Holman Hunt in the Henry E. Huntingdon Library', *Walpole Society*, 44 (1974), pp 1–93

Landow, G.P., '"Your Good Influence on Me": The Correspondence of John Ruskin and William Holman Hunt', *Bulletin of the John Rylands University Library of Manchester*, 59 (1976–77), pp 95–126, 376–96

Landow, G.P., 'William Holman Hunt's Letters to Thomas Seddon', *Bulletin of the John Rylands University Library of Manchester*, 66 (1983), pp 139–72

Coombs, J.H., et al., eds, *A Pre-Raphaelite Friendship, The Correspondence of William Holman Hunt and John Lucas Tupper*, Ann Arbor, Michigan: University of Michigan Research Press, 1986

Hunt: publications

'Notes on the Life of Augustus Egg', *Reader*, 1 (1863), pp 462, 486–7, 557–8; 2 (1863), pp 42–3, 91, 516–17; 3 (1864), pp 56–7

An Apology for the Symbolism of 'The Light of the World', London: B.R. Rothschild, New Gallery, 1865, pamphlet, 3 pp

Mr Holman Hunt's Picture, 'The Shadow of Death', pamphlet, London: Thomas Agnew and Sons, 1873, 4 pp (other versions contain an extra 8 pages of press notices)

'Artistic Copyright', *Nineteenth Century*, 6 (1879), pp 418–24

'Pigments and Artists' Colours', *The Times* (28 April 1880), p 8, also (4 May 1880), p 6; (2 June 1880), p 12

'The Present System of Obtaining Materials in use by Artist Painters as Compared with that of the Old Masters', *Journal of the Society of Arts*, 28 (23 April 1880), pp 485–99

'Materials in use by Artist Painters', *Architect* (24 April 1880), pp 300–3; (1 May 1880), pp 327–9; (15 May 1880), pp 352–4

The Triumph of the Innocents, pamphlet, London: Fine Arts Society, 1885, 16 pp; also, Liverpool: Walker Art Gallery, 1891

'The Pre-Raphaelite Brotherhood: A Fight for Art', *Contemporary Review*, 49 (April 1886), pp 471–88; (May 1886), pp 737–50; (June 1886), pp 820–33

'Painting "The Scapegoat"', *Contemporary Review*, 52 (July 1887), pp 21–38; (August 1887), pp 206–20

'The Proper Mode of Study of Drawing', *Students' Magazine of Art* (1891), pp 80–5, 116–20

'The Capo Santo at Pisa', *The Times* (6 January 1892), p 2

'The Ideals of Art', *New Review*, 6 (May 1892), pp 420–31

'Keble College and "The Light of the World"', *The Times* (31 March 1894), p 6

The Obligations of the Universities towards Art, The Romanes Lecture, 1895: Delivered in the Sheldonian Theatre, May 30 1895, London: H. Frowde, 1895, 46 pp

'Religion and Art', *Contemporary Review*, 71 (1897), pp 41–52

Pre-Raphaelitism and the Pre-Raphaelite Brotherhood, 2 vols, London: Macmillan and Co., 1905–6; second revised edition, London: Chapman and Hall, 1913 (published after Hunt's death, some revisions may be therefore be the work of Edith Holman Hunt)

Oxford Union Society, The Story of the pictures on the Walls and the Decorations on the Ceilings of the Old Debating Hall (Now the Library) in the Years 1857–8–9, Oxford: Oxford University Press, 1906, 15 pp

'All Saints Margaret Street', *The Times* (4 January 1909), p 8

Other publications

Adams, J. Eli, *Dandies and Desert Saints: Styles of Victorian Masculinity*, London: Cornell University Press, 1995

Allentuck, M., 'William Holman Hunt, Monk and Ruskin: An Unpublished Letter', *Apollo*, 97 (1973), pp 156–7

Aranson, M., 'William Holman Hunt', unpublished, advanced level intern paper, Harvard, Mass.: Centre of Conservation and Technical Studies, The Straus Centre, 1986

Arscott, C., 'Employer, Husband, Spectator: Thomas Fairbairn's Commission of "The Awakening Conscience"', in *The Culture of Capital: Art, Power and the Nineteenth-century Middle Class*, eds J. Wolff and J. Seed, Manchester: Manchester University Press, 1988, pp 159–96

'The Scapegoat', *Art Journal*, 2 (1 June 1856), p 170

'The Finding of the Saviour in the Temple', *Art Journal*, 22 (1860), p 182

'Isabella and the Pot of Basil', *Art Journal*, 30 (1868), p 97

'Realistic Attempts at Sacred Art', *Art Journal*, 35 (1873), pp 86–7

'The Shadow of Death', *Art Journal*, 36 (1874), p 15

'The Scapegoat', *Athenaeum*, 1489 (10 May 1856), p 589

'The Shadow of Death', *Athenaeum*, 2405 (29 November 1873), pp 702–3

Barff, F., 'On Artists' Colours and Pigments', *Journal of the Society of Arts*, 19 (30 December 1871), pp 109–12; (6 January 1871), pp 120–4; (13 January 1871), pp 134–9; (20 January 1871), pp 156–62; (27 January 1871), pp 179–87

Barlow, P., 'Pre-Raphaelitism and Post-Raphaelitism: The Articulation of Fantasy and the Problem of Pictorial Space', in *The Pre-Raphaelites Re-viewed*, ed. M. Pointon, Manchester: Manchester University Press, 1989, pp 66–82

Barlow, P., 'Millais, Manet, Modernity', in *English Art 1860–1914: Modern Artists and Identity*, eds D. Peters Corbett and L. Perry, Manchester: Manchester University Press, 2000, pp 49–64

Barr, A., *Cubism and Abstract Art*, New York: Museum of Modern Art, 1936

Barringer, T., *The Pre-Raphaelites*, Everyman Art Library, London: Weidenfeld and Nicholson, 1998

Barringer, T. 'Rethinking Delaroche/Recovering Leighton', *Victorian Studies*, 44, 1, 2001, pp 9–24

Barringer T. and E. Prettejohn, *Frederic Leighton: Antiquity, Renaissance, Modernity*, London: Yale University Press, 1999

Barthes, R., *Image, Music Text*, trans. S. Heath, London: Fontana Press, 1977

Barthes, R., *Camera Lucida* (1980), trans. R. Howard, London: Vintage Press, 1983

Bartram, M., *The Pre-Raphaelite Camera: Aspects of Victorian Photography*, London: Weidenfeld and Nicolson, 1985

Bate, P., *The English Pre-Raphaelite Painters, Their Associates and Successors*, London: George Bell and Sons, 1901

Batten, J.D., 'Methods of the Pre-Raphaelite Brotherhood', in *Papers of the Society of Mural Decorators and Painters in Tempera, Second Volume, 1907–24*, ed. J.D. Batten, Brighton: Dolphin Press, 1925, pp 5–7

Bayliss, W., *Five Great Painters of the Victorian Era*, London: Sampson, Low, Marston, 1902

Belsey, C., *Critical Practice* (1980), London: Routledge, 1990

Bennett, M., *William Holman Hunt, An Exhibition arranged by the Walker Art Gallery*, Liverpool: Walker Art Gallery, 1969

Bennett, M., 'Footnotes to the Holman Hunt Exhibition', *Liverpool Bulletin*, 13 (1968–70), pp 26–64

Bennett, M., *Artists of the Pre-Raphaelite Circle, The First Generation, Catalogue of Works in the Walker Art Gallery, Lady Lever Art Gallery and Sudley Art Gallery*, London: National Museums and Galleries on Merseyside/Lund Humphries, 1988

Boime, A., 'William Holman Hunt's *The Scapegoat*: Rite of Forgiveness/ Transference of Blame', *Art Bulletin*, 84, 1 (March 2002), pp 94–114

Bomford, D., et al., *Art in the Making: Rembrandt*, London: National Gallery/Yale University Press, 1989

Bomford, D., et al., *Art in the Making: Impressionism*, London: National Gallery/Yale University Press, 1990

Bown, N., C. Burdett and P. Thurschwell, eds, *The Victorian Supernatural*, Cambridge: Cambridge University Press, 2004

Bowness, A., 'Interpreting Holman Hunt', *The Listener* (25 May 1978), pp 675–6

Bronfen, E., 'Risky Resemblances: On Repetition, Mourning and Representation', in *Death and Representation*, eds S.W. Goodwin and E. Bronfen, London: Johns Hopkins University Press, 1993, pp 103–9

Bronkhurst, J.E., ' "An Interesting Series of Adventures to Look Back Upon": William Holman Hunt's visit to the Dead Sea in November 1854', in *Pre-Raphaelite Papers*, ed. L. Parris, London: Tate Gallery/Allen Lane, 1984, pp 111–25

Bronkhurst, J.E., '*William Holman Hunt: A Catalogue Raisonné*, London: Yale University Press, forthcoming'

Bronkhurst, J.E., 'Holman Hunt's Picture Frames, Sculpture and Applied Art', in *Re-framing the Pre-Raphaelites: Historical and Theoretical Essays*, ed. E. Harding, Aldershot: Scolar Press, 1996, pp 231–51

Bryson, N., *Vision and Painting: The Logic of the Gaze*, London: Macmillan, 1983

Bryson, N., *Word and Image: French Painting of the Ancien Regime*, Cambridge: Cambridge University Press, 1989

Callen, A., *The Spectacular Body: Science, Method and Meaning in the Work of Degas*, London: Yale University Press, 1995

Carlyle, L., 'The Artist's Anticipation of Change as Discussed in British Nineteenth-century Instruction Books on Oil Painting', *Appearance, Opinion and Change*, London: United Kingdom Institute of Conservation, 1990, pp 62–7

Carlyle, L., 'A Critical Analysis of British Handbooks, Manuals and Treatises in Oil Paintings Published in Britain Between 1800–1900: With Reference to Selected Eighteenth-century Sources', Ph.D. thesis, Courtauld Institute of Art, University of London, 1991

Carlyle, L. and J.H. Townsend, 'An Investigation of Lead Sulphide Darkening of Nineteenth-century Painting Materials', *Dirt and Pictures Separated*, London: United Kingdom Institute of Conservation, 1990, pp 40–3

Carlyle, T., *Sartor Resartus* (1833–34), Oxford: Oxford University Press, 2000

Casteras, S., *Whisper of the Muse: The World of Julia Margaret Cameron*, catalogue, London: Colnaghi, 1990

Casteras, S., et al., *John Ruskin and the Victorian Eye*, essays, New York: Harry N. Abrams/Phoenix Art Museum, 1993

Cennini, C., *The Craftsman's Handbook* (1437), trans. D.V. Thompson, New York: Dover, 1960

Cherry, D. and G. Pollock, 'Patriarchal History and the Pre-Raphaelites', *Art History*, 7, 4 (December 1984), pp 480–95

Fine Victorian Pictures, Drawings and Watercolours, 3 June 1994, catalogue, London: Christies, 1994

Fine Victorian Pictures, Drawings and Watercolours, 9 June 1995, catalogue, London: Christies, 1995

Clark Amor, A., *William Holman Hunt: The True Pre-Raphaelite*, London: Constable, 1989

Clarke, D., 'The Gaze and the Glance: Competing Understandings of Visuality in the Theory and Practice of Late Modernist Art', *Art History*, 15, 1 (March 1992), pp 80–98

Codell, J.F., 'The Artist Colonised: Holman Hunt's "Bio-history", Masculinity, Nationalism and the English School', in *Re-framing the Pre-Raphaelites: Historical and Theoretical Essays*, ed. E. Harding, Aldershot: Scolar Press, 1996, pp 211–29

Cohn, N., *The Pursuit of the Millennium*, London: Paladin, 1972

Coleridge, M.E., *Holman Hunt*, London: T.C. and E.C. Jack, 1910

Colvin, S., 'The Shadow of Death', *Macmillan's Magazine*, 30 (1874), pp 215–24

Completing the Picture, Materials and Techniques of Twenty Six Paintings in the Tate Gallery, London: Tate Gallery, 1982

Coombs, J.H., et al., eds, *A Pre-Raphaelite Friendship, The Correspondence of William Holman Hunt and John Lucas Tupper*, Ann Arbor, Mich.: University of Michigan Research Press, 1986

Corbett, D. Peters and L. Perry, *English Art 1860–1914*, Manchester, Manchester University Press, 2000

Cowling, M.C., *The Artist as Anthropologist: The Representation of Type and Character in Victorian Art*, Cambridge: Cambridge University Press, 1989

Crary, J., *Techniques of the Observer: On Vision and Modernity in the Nineteenth Century* (1990), London: MIT Press, 1995

Dakers, C., *The Holland Park Circle: Artists and Victorian Society*, London: Yale University Press, 1999

Dali, S., 'Le Surrealisme spectral de l'eternel feminin pre-raphaelite' *Minotaure*, 8 (15 June 1936), p 49

Dearden, J., *John Ruskin and Victorian Art*, catalogue, Tokyo: British Council, 1993

Derrida, J., *Of Grammatology*, Baltimore: Johns Hopkins University Press, 1976

Derrida, J., 'Structure, Sign and Play in the Discourse of Human Sciences', *Writing and Difference* (1978), in *Modern Criticism and Theory: A Reader*, ed. D. Lodge, Harlow: Longman, 1997, pp 108–23

Dorment, R. et al., *Pre-Raphaelite and Other Masters: The Andrew Lloyd Webber Collection*, London: Royal Academy of Arts, 2003

Dormer, P., *The Art of the Maker*, London: Thames and Hudson, 1994

Ehrenzweig, A., *The Hidden Order of Art, A Study in the Psychology of Artistic Imagination* (1967), Berkeley: University of California Press, 1971

Elzea, R., *The Samuel and Mary R. Bancroft, Jr. and Related Pre-Raphaelite Collections at the Delaware Art Museum*, Wilmington, Del.: Delaware Art Museum, 1978

Errington, L., *Social and Religious Themes in English Art 1840–1860*, London: Garland, 1984

Farr, D., English Art 1870–1940, *Oxford: Oxford University Press, 1984*

Farrar, Archdeacon F.W. and Mrs A. Meynell, *The Life and Work of William Holman Hunt*, London: Art Journal Special Edition, November 1893

Feller, R.L., N. Stoller and E.H. Jones, *On Picture Varnishes and Their Solvents*, London: The Press of Case Western Reserve University, 1971

Field, G., *Chromatography, or a Treatise on Colours and Pigments, and of their Powers in Painting, &c.*, London: Charles Tilt, Fleet Street, 1835

Field, G., *Grammar of Colouring Rudiments of the Painter's Art*, London: John Weale, 1850

Flint, K., 'Reading "The Awakening Conscience" Rightly', in *The Pre-Raphaelites Re-viewed*, ed. M. Pointon, Manchester: Manchester University Press, 1989, pp 45–65

Flint, K., *The Victorians and the Visual Imagination*, Cambridge: Cambridge University Press, 2000

Forsyth, P.T., *Religion in Recent Art: Expository Lectures on Rossetti, Burne-Jones, Watts, Holman Hunt and Wagner* (1889), London: Hodder and Stoughton, 1901

Fredeman, W.E., *Pre-Raphaelitism: A Bibliocritical Study*, Cambridge, Mass.: Harvard University Press, 1965

Fredeman, W.E., *The P.R.B. Journal: William Michael Rossetti's Diary of the Pre-Raphaelite Brotherhood 1849–1853 Together with Other Pre-Raphaelite Documents*, Oxford, Clarendon Press, 1975

Fried, M., 'Three American Painters' (1965), in *Art in Theory 1900–1990*, eds C. Harrison and P. Wood, Oxford: Basil Blackwell, 1993, pp 769–75

Fuller, P., *Art and Psychoanalysis* (1980), London: Hogarth Press, 1988

Fuller, P., *Modern Painters: Reflections on British Art*, London: Methuen, 1993

Gaunt, W., *The Pre-Raphaelite Tragedy* (1942), London: Cardinal, 1975

Gere, J.A., *Pre-Raphaelite Drawings in the British Museum*, London: British Museum Press, 1994

Germ, The Literary Magazine of the Pre-Raphaelites (1849–50), Oxford: Ashmolean Museum, 1992

Gettens, R. and G. Stout, *Painting Materials: A Short Encyclopaedia*, New York: Dover, 1966

Gillet, P., *The Victorian Painter's World*, London: Alan Sutton, 1990

Gilman, S.L., *Health and Illness: Images of Difference*, London: Reaktion Books, 1995

Gissing, A.C., *William Holman Hunt: A Biography*, London: Duckworth, 1936

Gombrich, E., *The Image and the Eye: Further Studies in the Psychology of Pictorial Representation*, London: Phaidon, 1982

Gombrich, E., *Art and Illusion: A Study in the Psychology of Pictorial Representation* (1959), London: Phaidon, 1993

Gosse, E. *Father and Son, A Study of Two Temperaments* (1907), ed. P. Abbs, Harmondsworth, Middlesex: Penguin, 1986

Greenberg, C., *Art and Culture* (1959), Boston: Beacon Press, 1961

Greenberg, C., 'Modernist Painting,' (1961), in *Art in Theory 1900–1990*, eds C. Harrison and P. Wood, Oxford: Basil Blackwell, 1993, pp 754–60

Greenlee, D., *Peirce's Concept of the Sign*, The Hague: Mouton., 1973

Grosskurth, P., 'Where was Rousseau?', in *Approaches to Victorian Autobiography*, ed. G.P. Landow, Athens, Ohio: Ohio University Press, 1979, pp 26–38

Hackney, S., R. Jones and J. Townsend, *Paint and Purpose: A Study of Technique in British Art*, London: Tate Gallery, 1999

Hagen, M.A., *Varieties of Realism*, Cambridge: Cambridge University Press, 1986

Hamerton, P.G., 'Technical Notes – William Holman Hunt: An Interview with the Artist', *Portfolio*, 6, 1 (1875), pp 45–8

Hamerton, P.G., *The Graphic Arts*, London: Seeley, Jackson and Halliday, 1882

Hanson, N.R., *Patterns of Discovery: An Inquiry into the Conceptual Foundations of Science*, London: Cambridge University Press, 1972

Harding, E., ed., *Re-framing the Pre-Raphaelites: Historical and Theoretical Essays*, Aldershot: Scolar Press, 1996

Harding, J., *The Pre-Raphaelites*, London: Academy, 1977

Harley, R.D., *Artists' Pigments 1600–1835: A Study in English Documentary Sources*, London: Butterworth Scientific, 1970

Harrison, C. and F. Orton, eds, *Modernism, Criticism, Realism*, London: Harper and Row, 1984

Harrison, C. and P. Wood, eds, *Art in Theory 1900–1990*, Oxford: Basil Blackwell, 1993

Hartt, R., *History of Italian Renaissance Art: Painting, Sculpture, Architecture* (1987), London: Thames and Hudson, 1994

Helsinger, H., 'Credence and Credibility: The Concern for Honesty in Victorian Autobiography', in *Approaches to Victorian Autobiography*, ed. G.P. Landow, Athens, Ohio: Ohio University Press, 1979, pp 39–63

Hilton, T., *The Pre-Raphaelites*, London: Thames and Hudson, 1970

Holman-Hunt, D., *My Grandmothers and I*, London: Hamish Hamilton, 1960

Holman-Hunt, D., *My Grandfather, His Wives and Loves* (1969) London: Columbus, 1987

Holman-Hunt, D., 'The Holman Hunt Collection: A Personal Recollection', in *Pre-Raphaelite Papers*, ed. L. Parris, London: Tate Gallery/Allen Lane, 1984, pp 206–25

Hough, G., 'The Natural Theology of "In Memoriam" ', in *Tennyson: In Memoriam*, ed. J.D. Hunt, London: Macmillan, 1987, pp 138–54

Hughes, R., *Nothing If Not Critical*, London: Collins Harvill, 1990

'Holman Hunt's Picture of the "Finding of the Saviour in the Temple" ', *Illustrated London News*, 38 (28 April 1860), p 411

'The Shadow of Death', *Illustrated London News* (6 December 1873), pp 542–3

'Three Religious Pictures', *Illustrated London News* (14 March 1885), p 288

Ironside, R. and J.A. Gere, *Pre-Raphaelite Painters*, London: Phaidon, 1948

Irwin, L, 'The Painting Materials and Techniques of William Holman Hunt', diploma paper, Courtauld Institute of Art, University of London, 1977

Iverson, M., 'Saussure versus Peirce: Models for a Semiotics of Visual Art', in *The New Art History*, eds A.L. Rees and F. Borzello, London: Camden Press, 1986, pp 82–94

Iverson, M., 'What is a Photograph?', *Art History*, 17, 3 (September 1994), pp 450–63

Jacobi, C., 'William Holman Hunt: Revealing and Disguising the Object', *Visual Culture of Britain*, 14, 2 (2003), pp 1–20
Januszczak, W., 'Unhinged by Hunt's Scapegoat', *Sunday Times* (12 March 2004), pp 6–7
Jay, M., *Downcast Eyes: The Denigration of Vision in Twentieth-century French Thought* (1993), London: University of California Press, 1994
Jordanova, L., 'The Representation of the Human Body: Art and Medicine in the Works of Charles Bell', in *Towards a Modern Art World, Studies in British Art 1*, ed. B. Allen, London: Yale University Press, 1995, pp 79–94
Katz, M.R., 'William Holman Hunt, Artist's Materials and the "Pre-Raphaelite Technique"', *Historical Painting Techniques, Materials and Studio Practice*, Marina del Rey, Calif.: Getty Conservation Institute, 1995, pp 158–65
Katz, M.R., 'Holman Hunt on Himself: Textual Evidence in Aid of Technical Analysis', in *Looking Through Paintings: The Study of Paintings Techniques and Materials in Support of Art Historical Research: Leids Kunsthistorisch Jaarboek 11*, ed. E. Hermens, Leiden, Netherlands: Uitgeverij de Prom and Archetype Publications, 1998, pp 415–44
Keats, J., *John Keats Lyric Poems*, New York: Dover, 1991
Kern, S., *Eyes of Love: The Gaze in English and French Paintings and Novels 1840–1900*, London: Reaktion Books, 1996
Kestner, J.A., *Masculinities in Victorian Painting*, Cambridge: Cambridge University Press, 1995
Kingsley, C., *The Water-babies* (1863), London: Macmillan and Co., 1869
Kirby Tally Jr, M., '"All good pictures crack": Sir Joshua Reynolds's Practice and Studio', in *Reynolds*, ed. N. Penny, London: Royal Academy/ Weidenfeld and Nicolson, 1986, pp 55–70
Klein, M., *Contributions to Psychoanalysis*, London: Hogarth Press, 1950
Krauss, R.E., *The Optical Unconscious*, London: MIT Press, 1993
Landow, G.P., '"Your Good Influence on Me": The Correspondence of John Ruskin and William Holman Hunt', *Bulletin of the John Rylands University Library of Manchester*, 59, 1 (1976), pp 95–126
Landow, G.P., 'William Holman Hunt and the Missionaries', *Pre-Raphaelite Review*, 1 (1977), pp 27–33
Landow, G.P., ed., *Approaches to Victorian Autobiography*, Athens, Ohio: Ohio University Press, 1979
Landow, G.P., *William Holman Hunt and Typological Symbolism*, London: Yale University Press, 1979
Landow, G.P., '"Christ the Pilot": A Panel from William Holman Hunt's Unfinished Triptych', *Journal of Pre-Raphaelite Studies*, 5 (1980), pp 81–91; *Art Bulletin*, 65 (1983), 471–84
Landow, G.P., 'William Holman Hunt's Oriental Mania and His Uffizi Self-portrait', *Art Bulletin* 64, 4 (December 1982), pp 646–55
Landow, G.P., 'Shadows Cast by "*The Light of the World*": William Holman Hunt's Religious Paintings 1893–1905', *Art Bulletin*, 65, 3 (1983) pp 473–84
Landow, G.P., 'William Holman Hunt's Letters to Thomas Seddon', *Bulletin of the John Rylands University Library of Manchester*, 66 (1983), pp 139–72

Landow, G.P., 'How to Read Ruskin: The Art Critic as Victorian Sage', in *John Ruskin and the Victorian Eye*, essays by S. Casteras et al., New York: Harry N. Abrams/Phoenix Art Museum, 1993, pp 52–79

Landow, G.P. and R.M. Landow, 'William Holman Hunt's "The Shadow of Death"', *Bulletin of the John Rylands University Library of Manchester*, 55, 1 (Autumn 1972), pp 197–239

Laplanche, J. and J.-B. Pontalis, *The Language of Psychoanalysis*, London: The Institute of Psychoanalysis, Karnac Books, 1988

Laurie, A.P., 'The Late Mr Holman Hunt's Experiments in the Permanency of Artists' Oils and their Colours', *Journal of the Society of Arts*, 70 (5 May 1922), pp 432–8

Laurie, A.P., *The Technique of Rembrandt, Turner and the Pre-Raphaelites, and the French Impressionists: New Light on Old Masters*, London: Sheldon Press, 1935

Laurie, A.P., *The Painter's Methods and Materials* (1960), New York: Dover, 1967

Lutyens, M., ed., 'Letters from John Everett Millais and William Holman Hunt in the Henry E. Huntingdon Library', *Walpole Society*, 44 (1974), pp 1–93

Macmillan, J.D., 'Holman Hunt's Hireling Shepherd: Some Reflections on a Victorian Pastoral', *Art Bulletin*, 54 (1972), pp 187–97

Maas, J., *Gambart: Prince of the Victorian Art World*, London: Barry and Jenkins, 1975

Maas, J., *Holman Hunt and the Light of the World* (1984), Cambridge: Wildwood House, 1987

MacColl, D.S., *Confession of a Keeper: And other Papers*, London: Alexander Maclehose, 1931

Macleod, D. Sachko, *Art and the Victorian Middle Class: Money and the Making of Cultural Identity* (1996), Cambridge: Cambridge University Press, 1998

Marcus, L., 'Brothers in their Anecdotage: Holman Hunt's "Pre-Raphaelitism and the Pre-Raphaelite Brotherhood"', in *The Pre-Raphaelites Re-viewed*, ed. M. Pointon, Manchester: Manchester University Press, 1989, pp 11–21

Marcus, L., *Auto/biographical Discourses: Theory, Criticism, Practice*, Manchester: Manchester University Press, 1994

Marsden, G., *Victorian Values*, London: Longman, 1990

Matejka, L. and K. Titunik, eds, *Semiotics of Art* (1976), Cambridge, Mass.: MIT Press, 1989

Mayer, R., *The Artist's Handbook of Materials and Techniques* (1951), London: Faber and Faber, 1987

Mirzoeff, N., *Bodyscape: Art, Modernity and the Ideal Figure*, London: Routledge, 1995

Mitchell, J., ed., *The Selected Melanie Klein* (1986), Harmondsworth, Middlesex: Penguin, 1991

Mitchell, W.J.T., *Iconology: Image, Text, Ideology* (1986), London: University of Chicago Press, 1987

Morgan, H., *Burne-Jones, The Pre-Raphaelites and their Century*, catalogue, ed. P. Nahum, 2 vols, London: Peter Nahum, 1989

Mort, F., *Dangerous Sexualities: Medico-moral Politics in England since 1830*, London: Routledge and Kegan Paul, 1987

Nead, N., *Myths of Sexuality: Representations of Women in Victorian Britain* (1988), Oxford: Basil Blackwell, 1990
Nochlin, L., *Realism* (1971), Harmondsworth, Middlesex: Penguin, 1981
Nochlin, L., *The Body in Pieces: The Fragment as a Metaphor of Modernity*, London: Thames and Hudson, 1994
Panofsky, E., *Studies in Iconology, Humanistic Themes in the Art of the Renaissance* (1939), New York: Harper and Row, 1972
Parris, L., *The Pre-Raphaelites*, London: Tate Gallery, 1980
Parris, L., ed., *The Pre-Raphaelites*, London: Allan Lane/Tate Gallery, 1984
Parris, L., ed., *Pre-Raphaelite Papers*, London: Tate Gallery/Allen Lane, 1984
Perry, R., 'Pablo Picasso "The Three Dancers"', in *Completing the Picture, Materials and Techniques of Twenty Six Paintings in the Tate Gallery*, London: Tate Gallery, 1982, pp 82–6
Peterson, L.H., *Victorian Autobiography: The Tradition of Self-Interpretation*, London: Yale University Press, 1986
Pick, D., 'Stories of the Eye', in *Rewriting the Self: Histories from the Renaissance to the Present*, ed. R. Porter, London: Routledge, 1997, pp 186–99
Plesters, J., 'Tintoretto's Paintings in the National Gallery', *National Gallery Technical Bulletin* 4 (1980), pp 32–47
Pointon, M., 'The Artist as Ethnographer: Holman Hunt in the Holy Land', in *Pre-Raphaelites Re-viewed*, ed. M. Pointon, Manchester: Manchester University Press, 1989, pp 22–44
Pointon, M., *Naked Authority: The Body in Western Painting 1830–1908*, Cambridge: Cambridge University Press, 1990
Pointon, M., and K. Adler, eds, *The Body Imaged: The Human Form and Visual Culture since the Renaissance* (1993), Cambridge: Cambridge University Press, 1994
Porter, R., *London, A Social History*, London: Hamish Hamilton, 1994
Pre-Raphaelite Illustrations from Moxon's Tennyson (1857), London: Academy, 1978
Prettejohn, E., *The Art of the Pre-Raphaelites*, London: Princeton University Press, 2000
Rees, A.L. and F. Borzello, eds, *The New Art History*, London: Camden Press, 1986
Ribner, J.P., '"Our English Coasts", 1852: William Holman Hunt and Invasion Fear at Midcentury', *Art Journal*, (Summer 1996), pp 45–54
Ridge, J., S. Hackney and J. Townsend, 'Pre-Raphaelite Technique and its Consequence', Tate Gallery, 13 September 2002
Rose, A., *The Pre-Raphaelites*, London: Phaidon, 1981
Rose, A., *The Pre-Raphaelite Portrait*, London: Phaidon, 1981
Rosen C. and H. Zerner, *Romanticism and Realism, The Mythology of Nineteenth Century Art*, London: Faber and Faber, 1984
Rosenberg, J.G., 'The Two Kingdoms of "In Memoriam"', in *Tennyson: In Memoriam*, ed. J.D. Hunt, London: Macmillan, 1987, pp 200–15
Ruskin, J., 'The Pre-Raphaelites', letter to the Editor, *The Times* (13 May 1851), p 8
Ruskin, J., *The Art of England, Lectures Given in Oxford*, Orpington: George Allen, 1884

Ruskin, J., *Notes on Some of the Principle Pictures of the Holman Hunt Collection: Notes on the Pictures of Mr Holman Hunt Exhibited at the Rooms of the Fine Art Society, 1886. With Criticisms by John Ruskin*, London: Fine Arts Society, 1886, 40 pp

Ruskin, J., 'The Pre-Raphaelite Artists', letter to the Editor, *The Times* (30 May 1851), p 8

Ruskin, J., 'The Pre-Raphaelites', letter to the Editor, *The Times* (25 May 1854), p 7

Ruskin, J., *The Works of John Ruskin*, eds E.T. Cook and A. Wedderburn, 39 vols, London: George Allen, 1903–12

Ruskin, J., *Praeterita* (1885), Oxford: Oxford University Press, 1990

Ruskin, J., *The Elements of Drawing*, ed. B. Dunstan (1857), London: Herbert Press, 1991

Said, E., *Orientalism* (1978), Harmondsworth: Penguin, 1985

'Mr Holman Hunt's "Shadow of Death"', *Saturday Review*, 26 (6 December 1873), pp 727–8

Schapiro, M., 'On Some Problems in the Semiotics of Visual Art: Field and Vehicle in Image-Signs', *Semiotica*, ed. T Sebeok, 1 (1969), pp 223–42

Schapiro, M., *Words and Pictures, On the Literal and Symbolic Meaning in the Illustration of the Text*, The Hague: Mouton, 1973

Schapiro, M., *Theory and Philosophy of Art: Style, Artist and Society, Selected Papers*, New York: George Braziller, 1994

Simon, J., *The Art of the Picture Frame: Artist, Patron, and the Framing of Portraits in Britain*, London: National Portrait Gallery, 1996

Smith, K., 'The Post-Raphaelite Sources of Pre-Raphaelite Painting', *Journal of Pre-Raphaelite Studies*, 5 (1980), pp 41–53

Smith, L., 'The Elusive Depth of Field: Stereoscopy and the Pre-Raphaelites', in *Pre-Raphaelites Re-viewed*, ed. M. Pointon, Manchester: Manchester University Press, 1989, pp 83–99

Smith, L., *Victorian Photography, Painting and Poetry: The Enigma of Visibility in Ruskin, Morris and the Pre-Raphaelites*, Cambridge: Cambridge University Press, 1995

Sontag, S., *Illness as Metaphor* (1978), Harmondsworth, Middlesex: Penguin, 1987

Spitz, E.H., *Art and Psyche*, London: Yale University Press, 1985

'A Layman on Mr Holman Hunt's New Picture', *Spectator*, 46 (29 November 1873), pp 1497–8

'The Shadow of Death', *Spectator*, 46 (6 December 1873), pp 1538–9

'Mr Holman Hunt's New Picture', *Spectator*, 66 (23 May 1891), pp 724–5

Staley, A., *The Pre-Raphaelite Landscape*, Oxford: Clarendon Press, 1973

Staley, A., 'The Pre-Raphaelites in the 1860s: II, Holman Hunt', *British Art Journal*, 5, 1 (Spring/Summer 2004), pp 6–12

Staley, A., et al., *Pre-Raphaelite Vision: Truth to Nature*, London: Tate Publishing, 2004

Standage, H.C., *The Artist's Manual of Pigments showing their Composition, Conditions of Permanency, Non-Permanency, and Adulterations; Effects in Combination with Each other and with Vehicles; and the Most Reliable Tests of Purity*, London: Crosby, Lockwood and Co., 1886

Stanford, D., ed., *Pre-Raphaelite Writing*, London: Everyman, 1984

Steegman, J., *Victorian Taste*, London: Century/National Trust, 1987
Stephens, F.G., 'The Two Pre-Raphaelitisms: The Modern Pre-Raphaelites' (3), *Crayon*, 3, (November/December 1856), pp 289–92
Stephens, F.G., 'The Finding of the Saviour in the Temple', *Blackwood's Magazine*, July 1860
Stephens, F.G., *William Holman Hunt and His Works: A Memoir of the Artist's Life, with descriptions of his pictures*, London: Nisbet, 1860
Stephens, F.G., 'English Painters of the Present Day, William Holman Hunt', *Portfolio*, 2 (March 1871), pp 33–9
Stephens, F.G., 'The Triumph of the Innocents', *Portfolio*, 16 (April 1885), pp 80–3
Stephens, F.G., 'Master Hilary the Tracer', *Athenaeum*, 3106 (7 May 1887), p 613
Stokes, A., *Reflections on the Nude*, London: Tavistock Publications, 1967
Sweetman, J., *The Oriental Obsession: Islamic Inspiration in British and American Art and Architecture 1500–1920*, Cambridge: Cambridge University Press, 1987
Sussman, H.L., 'Hunt, Ruskin, and "The Scapegoat" ', *Victorian Studies*, 12 (September 1968), pp 83–90
Sussman, H.L., *Fact into Figure: Typology in Carlisle, Ruskin and the Pre-Raphaelite Brotherhood*, Columbus: Ohio State University Press, 1979
Sussman, H.L., 'Artistic Manhood: the Pre-Raphaelite Brotherhood', *Victorian Masculinities*, Cambridge, Cambridge University Press, 1995, pp 111–79
'Exhibition at the Royal Academy', *The Times* (7 May 1851), p 8
'Mr Holman Hunt's "Shadow of Death" ', *The Times* (2 December 1873), p 4
Tillyard, S., *The Impact of Modernism: The Visual Arts in Edwardian England*, London: Routledge, 1988
Townsend, J., J. Ridge and S. Hackney, *Pre-Raphaelite Painting Techniques*, London: Tate Gallery, 2004
Treuherz, J., *Pre-Raphaelite Paintings from Manchester City Art Galleries*, Manchester: Manchester City Art Gallery/Lund Humphries, 1993
Tupper, J.L., 'The Subject in Art', *The Germ: Thoughts towards Nature, In Poetry, Literature and Art*, 1 (January 1850), pp 11–18
Tytler, S., *Modern Painters and Their Paintings* (1873), London: Wm. Isbister Ltd, 1883
Vasari, G., *The Lives of the Artists* (1549), Oxford: Oxford University Press, 1991
Vaughan, W., 'Realism and Tradition in Religious Art', in *'Sind Briten hier?' Relations between British and Continental Art 1680–1880*, Munich: Wilhelm Fink Verlag, 1981, pp 207–23
Veltrusky, J., 'Some Aspects of the Pictorial Sign', in *Semiotics of Art*, eds L. Matejka and K. Titunik (1976), Cambridge Mass.: MIT Press, 1989, pp 245–64
Vidler, A., *The Church in an Age of Revolution* (1961), Harmondsworth, Middlesex: Penguin, 1990
Wather, L., 'The Invention of Childhood in Victorian Autobiography', in *Approaches to Victorian Autobiography*, ed. G.P. Landow, Athens, Ohio: Ohio University Press, 1979, pp 64–83

Watkinson, R., *Pre-Raphaelite Art and Design*, London: Studio Vista, 1970

Weber, M., *Max Weber: Essays in Sociology*, eds H. Gerth and C. Wright Mills, New York: Oxford University Press, 1958

Wheeler, M., *Heaven, Hell and the Victorians*, Cambridge: Cambridge University Press, 1994

Wheeler, M., '"The Light of the World" as "True and Sacred Art": Ruskin and William Holman Hunt', in *Ruskin's Artists: Studies in the Victorian Visual Economy, papers from the Ruskin Programme, Lancaster University*, ed. R. Hewison, Aldershot: Ashgate, 2000, pp 111–30

White, J., *The Birth and Rebirth of Pictorial Space* (1957), London: Faber and Faber, 1987

Whitely, J., *Pre-Raphaelite Paintings and Drawings*, Oxford: Phaidon/Christies/Ashmolean Museum, 1989

Wildman, S., *Visions of Life and Love: Pre-Raphaelite Art from Birmingham Museums and Art Gallery*, Alexandria, Va.: Art Services International, 1995

Williamson, G., *Holman Hunt*, London: George Bell and Sons, 1902

Wittgenstein, L., *Philosophical Investigations*, Oxford: Basil Blackwell, 1968

Wood, C., *The Pre-Raphaelites* (1981), London: Weidenfeld and Nicolson, 1994

Woodcock, S., 'The Roberson's Archive: Content and Significance', conference pre-prints, *Historical Painting Techniques, Materials and Studio Practice*, Amsterdam: University of Leiden Art History Department, Leiden, and The Centraal Laboratorium, 1995, pp 30–7

Wolff, J. and J. Seed, *The Culture of Capital: Art, Power and the Nineteenth-century Middle Class*, Manchester: Manchester University Press, 1988

Wright, E., *Psychoanalytic Criticism: Theory into Practice*, London: Methuen, 1984

Index

Note: 'n' after a page reference indicates a note number on that page